Id

Adobe
InDesign CC
2018 release

CLASSROOM IN A BOOK®
The official training workbook from Adobe

Kelly Kordes Anton & Tina DeJarld

Executive Editor: Nancy Davis
Senior Production Editor: Tracey Croom
Technical Reviewer: Chad Chelius
Production editor/Copyeditor: Dan Foster
Composition: Danielle Foster
Proofreader: Scout Festa
Indexer: Valerie Haynes Perry
Cover Illustration: Ruslan Khasanov (Russian Federation), behance.net/UnikFrik
 My Name is Wendy (France), behance.net/mynameiswendy
Cover Designer: Eddie Yuen
Interior Designer: Mimi Heft

Printed and bound in the United States of America

ISBN-13: 978-0-13-485250-8
ISBN-10: 0-13-485250-8

1 17

WHERE ARE THE LESSON FILES?

Purchase of this Classroom in a Book in any format gives you access to the lesson files you'll need to complete the exercises in the book.

You'll find the files you need on your **Account** page at peachpit.com on the **Registered Products** tab.

1 Go to www.peachpit.com/register.

2 Sign in or create a new account.

3 Enter the ISBN: 9780134852508.

4 Answer the questions as proof of purchase.

5 The lesson files can be accessed through the My Registered Products tab on your Account page.

6 Click the title of your product to proceed to the download page. Click the lesson file links to download them to your computer.

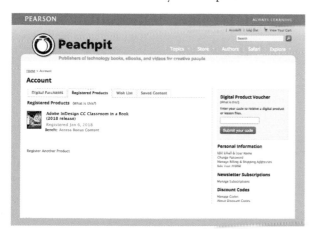

About the Authors

Kelly Kordes Anton has written and edited dozens of books and training resources on publishing technologies and InDesign, including six previous editions of *Adobe InDesign Classroom in a Book.* She is a Communications Specialist for MillerCoors, based at the Golden Brewery, home of the famed Coors Banquet. Kelly lives in Littleton, Colorado.

Tina DeJarld has worked on the front lines of taking designs from the computer screen to real-world production since before InDesign 1.0. As both a prepress master and production designer building files that will work correctly, she has handled thousands of large and complex projects, becoming an expert on InDesign best practices and techniques.

Acknowledgments

This book would not have been possible without the contributions of several invaluable collaborators. The authors would like to thank Nancy Davis for putting together a strong team; Chad Chelius, technical editor, for ensuring the accuracy of every word on every page; Candyce Mairs, keystroker, for testing every step in every lesson; Dan Foster and Scout Festa, for making sure every i was dotted and every t was crossed; Danielle Foster, production specialist, for polishing the layout of every page and preparing final files for print; and Tracey Croom, senior production editor at Pearson, for overseeing the entire production process and keeping everybody informed and on track. In addition, we appreciate the invaluable influence of John Cruise, whose contributions remain throughout this book. The authors would also like to thank the following photographers who provided many of the images used in the sample lesson files: John Anton, Shauneen Hutchinson, Sylvia Bacon, Diane Supple, and Eric Shropshire.

CONTENTS

GETTING STARTED

Welcome to Adobe® InDesign® CC (2018 release), a powerful page-design and production application that offers precision, control, and seamless integration with other Adobe professional graphics software. Using InDesign, you can produce professional-quality, full-color documents and print them using a variety of output devices, including desktop printers, high-resolution imaging devices, and high-volume color printing presses. You can also design publications for a broad range of electronic devices, such as tablets, smartphones, and e-readers, and export InDesign documents in several formats, including PDF, HTML, and EPUB.

Writers, artists, designers, and publishers can communicate to a broader audience than ever before through an unprecedented variety of media. InDesign supports this with its seamless integration with other Creative Cloud (CC) components.

About Classroom in a Book

Adobe InDesign CC Classroom in a Book® is part of the official training series for Adobe graphics and publishing software developed with the support of Adobe product experts. The lessons are designed so that you can learn at your own pace. If you're new to Adobe InDesign, you'll master the fundamentals and learn to put the software to work for you. If you've already been using Adobe InDesign, you'll find that this book teaches many advanced features and best practices, including tips and techniques for using the latest version of InDesign.

Each lesson provides step-by-step instructions for creating a specific project. You can follow the book from start to finish or do only the lessons that meet your interests and needs. Each lesson concludes with several optional tasks that let you further explore the features covered in the lesson, as well as a set of review questions and answers.

Prerequisites

Before beginning to use *Adobe InDesign CC Classroom in a Book*, you should have a working knowledge of your computer and its operating system. Make sure that you know how to use the mouse and standard menus and commands

Note: When instructions differ by platform, Windows commands appear first, followed by the macOS commands, with the platform noted in parentheses. For example, "Alt-click (Windows) or Option-click (macOS) the button."

and also how to open, save, and close files. If you need to review these techniques, see the help resources included with your operating system.

Installing the software

Before you begin using *Adobe InDesign CC Classroom in a Book*, make sure that your system is set up correctly and that you've installed the proper software and hardware.

The Adobe InDesign CC software is not included with this book; you must purchase the software separately (visit adobe.com/products/indesign). In addition to Adobe InDesign CC, some lessons in this book have steps that can be performed with Adobe Bridge and other Adobe applications. You must install these applications from Adobe Creative Cloud onto your computer. Follow the onscreen instructions.

Adobe Creative Cloud desktop app

In addition to Adobe InDesign CC, this training also requires the Adobe Creative Cloud desktop application, which provides a central location for managing the dozens of apps and services included in a Creative Cloud membership. You can use the Creative Cloud desktop application to sync and share files, manage fonts, access libraries of stock photography and design assets, and showcase and discover creative work in the design community.

The Creative Cloud desktop application is installed automatically when you download your first Creative Cloud product. If you have Adobe Application Manager installed, it auto-updates to the Creative Cloud desktop application.

If the Creative Cloud desktop application is not installed on your computer, you can download it from the Download Creative Cloud page on the Adobe website (creative.adobe.com/products/creative-cloud) or the Adobe Creative Cloud desktop apps page (adobe.com/creativecloud/catalog/desktop.html).

Classroom in a Book fonts

Note: For more information about Typekit, go to the Typekit home page at typekit.com/help. For information from the Creative Cloud Help file about adding fonts from Typekit, go to https://helpx.adobe.com/creative-cloud/help/add-fonts-typekit.html.

Some of the fonts used in the Classroom in a Book lesson files are installed with Adobe InDesign. Some fonts are not installed with InDesign but are instead available through Typekit, a font-subscription service from Adobe that offers access to a vast library of fonts for use in desktop applications and on websites. The Typekit service is integrated with InDesign's font selection features and the Creative Cloud Desktop application. Typekit is included with your Creative Cloud subscription.

By default, font syncing with Typekit is turned on for Creative Cloud applications, so when you open a lesson file that uses Typekit fonts that aren't installed on your computer, a Missing Fonts dialog box displays and offers the option to Sync Fonts. If Typekit font syncing is disabled, a Turn Typekit On button is displayed in the Missing Fonts dialog box.

Online content

Your purchase of this Classroom in a Book includes online materials provided by way of your Account page on peachpit.com. These include:

Lesson files

To work through the projects in this book, you will need to download the lesson files from peachpit.com. You can download the files for individual lessons, or it may be possible to download them all in a single file.

Web Edition

The Web Edition is an online interactive version of the book providing an enhanced learning experience. Your Web Edition can be accessed from any device with a connection to the Internet, and it contains:

* The complete text of the book
* Hours of instructional video keyed to the text
* Interactive quizzes

In addition, the Web Edition may be updated when Adobe adds significant feature updates between major Creative Cloud releases. To accommodate the changes, sections of the online book may be updated or new sections may be added.

Accessing the lesson files and Web Edition

If you purchased an eBook from peachpit.com or adobepress.com, your Web Edition will automatically appear under the Digital Purchases tab on your Account page. Click the **Launch** link to access the product. Continue reading to learn how to register your product to obtain access to the lesson files.

If you purchased an eBook from a different vendor or you bought a print book, you must register your purchase on peachpit.com in order to access the online content:

1 Go to www.peachpit.com/register.

2 Sign in or create a new account.

3 Enter the ISBN: 9780134852508.

4 Answer the questions as proof of purchase.

5 The **Web Edition** will appear under the Digital Purchases tab on your Account page. Click the **Launch** link to access the product.

 The **lesson files** can be accessed through the Registered Products tab on your Account page. Click the Access Bonus Content link below the title of your product to proceed to the download page. Click the lesson file links to download them to your computer.

Saving and restoring the InDesign Defaults file

● **Note:** Each time you begin working on a new lesson, some panels may remain open even if you restore your InDesign Defaults file. If this occurs, you can close the panels manually if you want.

The InDesign Defaults file stores program preferences and default settings, such as tool settings and the default unit of measurement. To ensure that the preferences and default settings of your Adobe InDesign program match those used in this book, move the current InDesign Defaults file to a different location before you begin working on the lessons. When you have finished the book, you can return the saved InDesign Defaults file to its original folder, which restores the preferences and default settings used before you started working on the lessons.

Moving the current InDesign Defaults file

Moving the InDesign Defaults file to another location prompts InDesign to automatically create a new one with all preferences and defaults set to their original factory settings.

● **Note:** If you can't find the InDesign Defaults file, either you haven't started Adobe InDesign CC yet or you have already moved the preferences file. The preferences file is created after you launch the program the first time and is updated thereafter.

1 Quit Adobe InDesign.

2 Locate the InDesign Defaults file on Windows or macOS as described below.

3 If you want to restore customized preferences, move the file to another folder on your hard drive. Otherwise, you can delete the file.

4 Start Adobe InDesign CC.

Locating the InDesign Defaults file on Windows

The InDesign Defaults file is located in the folder [startup drive]\Users\[*username*]\ AppData\Roaming\Adobe\InDesign\Version 13.0\en_US*\InDesign Defaults.

● **Note:** If hidden files are visible and you still cannot locate the preferences file, use your operating system's Find File feature and search for "InDesign Defaults."

- The AppData folder is hidden by default on Windows 7, Windows 8, and Windows 10. To display the AppData folder, click Appearance And Personalization in the Control Panel, and then click Folder Options (Windows 7 and Windows 8) or File Explorer Options (Windows 10).

- Click the View tab in the Folder Options/File Explorer Options dialog box, select Show Hidden Files, Folders, And Drives, and then click OK.

Locating the InDesign Defaults file on macOS

The InDesign Defaults file is located in the folder [startup drive]/Users/[*username*]/ Library/Preferences/Adobe InDesign/Version 13.0/en_US*/InDesign Defaults.

- The folder name may be different depending on the language version you have installed.

- In macOS 10.9 and later, the Library folder is hidden. To access this folder, choose Go > Go To Folder from the Finder menu. Type ~/**Library** in the Go To The Folder box, and then click OK or Go.

Restoring the saved InDesign Defaults file

If you want to restore your customized InDesign Defaults file that you moved to another location:

1 Quit Adobe InDesign.

2 Locate your saved InDesign Defaults file, drag it back into its original folder, and replace the current InDesign Defaults file.

Training resources

Adobe InDesign CC Classroom in a Book is not meant to replace documentation that comes with the program or to be a comprehensive reference for every feature. Only the commands and options used in the lessons are explained in this book. For comprehensive information about program features and tutorials, refer to these resources:

Note: Adobe periodically provides updates to software. You can easily obtain these updates through Creative Cloud.

Adobe InDesign Learn & Support: helpx.adobe.com/indesign.html is where you can find and browse Help and Support content on Adobe.com. Adobe InDesign Help and Adobe InDesign Support Center are accessible from the Help menu in InDesign.

Adobe Forums: forums.adobe.com lets you tap into peer-to-peer discussions, questions, and answers on Adobe products.

Adobe InDesign CC product home page: adobe.com/products/indesign provides information about new features and intuitive ways to create professional layouts for print, tablets, and e-readers.

Adobe Add-ons: creative.adobe.com/addons is a central resource for finding tools, services, extensions, code samples, and more to supplement and extend your Adobe products.

Resources for educators: adobe.com/education and edex.adobe.com offer a treasure trove of information for instructors who teach classes on Adobe software. Find solutions for education at all levels, including free curricula that use an integrated approach to teaching Adobe software and can be used to prepare for the Adobe Certified Associate exams.

Adobe Authorized Training Centers: Adobe Authorized Training Centers offer instructor-led courses and training on Adobe products, employing only Adobe Certified Instructors. A directory of AATCs is available at training.adobe.com/trainingpartners.

1 INTRODUCING THE WORKSPACE

Lesson Overview

In this lesson, you'll learn how to do the following:

- Open documents.

- Select and use tools.

- Use the Application bar and Control panel.

- Manage document windows.

- Work with panels.

- Customize the workspace.

- Change the magnification of a document.

- Navigate through a document.

- Use context menus and panel menus.

- Change Interface preferences.

 This lesson will take about 45 minutes to complete.

Please log in to your account on peachpit.com to download the lesson files for this chapter, or go to the "Getting Started" section at the beginning of this book and follow the instructions under "Accessing the Lesson Files and Web Edition." Store the files on your computer in a convenient location.

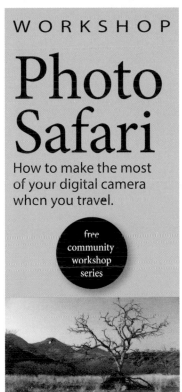

WORKSHOP

Photo Safari

How to make the most
of your digital camera
when you travel.

free
community
workshop
series

The intuitive InDesign interface makes it easy to
create compelling layouts. It is important to under-
stand the InDesign work area to make the most of
its powerful layout and design capabilities. The work
area consists of the Application bar, Control panel,
document window, menus, pasteboard, Tools panel,
and other panels.

Getting started

In this lesson, you'll practice using tools and panels, and navigating through a simple layout. The lesson file represents the final version of the document—you will not make permanent changes to objects, add graphics, or modify text. You will use this document only to explore the InDesign work area.

● **Note:** If you have not already downloaded the project files for this lesson to your computer from your Account page, make sure to do so now. See "Getting Started" at the beginning of the book.

1 To ensure that the preferences and default settings of your Adobe InDesign program match those used in this lesson, move the InDesign Defaults file to a different folder following the procedure in "Saving and restoring the InDesign Defaults file" on pages 4–5.

2 Start Adobe InDesign.

3 The InDesign Start Screen displays. Click Open at the left. (If the Start Screen does not display, choose File > Open from the InDesign menu bar.)

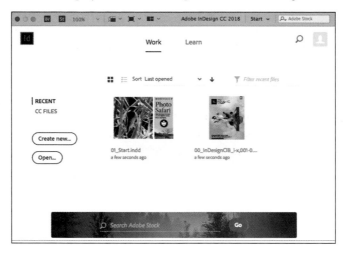

● **Note:** If the Missing Fonts dialog box displays, click Sync Fonts to access any missing fonts through Adobe Typekit. Click Close when font syncing is complete. For more information on using Adobe Typekit, see "Getting Started" at the beginning of this book.

4 Open the 01_Start.indd file in the Lesson01 folder, located inside the Lessons folder within the InDesignCIB folder on your hard disk.

5 Choose File > Save As, rename the file **01_Introduction.indd**, and save it in the Lesson01 folder.

6 To ensure that the panels and menu commands match those used in this lesson, choose Window > Workspace > [Advanced], and then choose Window > Workspace > Reset Advanced.

7 To display the document at a higher resolution, choose View > Display Performance > High Quality Display.

8 Using the scroll bars on the document window, scroll down to see the second page of the postcard, and then scroll back up to the first page of the postcard.

● **Note:** The screen captures in this book show the Medium Light interface. Interface elements such as panels and dialog boxes will be darker on your screen. You will learn to change this interface preference later in the lesson.

Looking at the workspace

The InDesign work area encompasses everything you see when you first open or create a document.

- Menu bar, Application bar, and Control panel, at the top of the screen
- Tools panel, docked at the left side of the screen
- Commonly used panels, docked at the right side of the screen

The configuration of the work area is referred to as the "workspace." You can save your custom workspace setup or choose among special-purpose configurations such as Digital Publishing, Printing And Proofing, and Typography.

▶ **Tip:** You can customize the InDesign work area to suit your work style. For example, you can choose to display only the panels you frequently use, minimize and rearrange panel groups, resize windows, and so on.

Menu bar Control panel Default panels in the Advanced workspace

Application bar

Tools panel

Document window

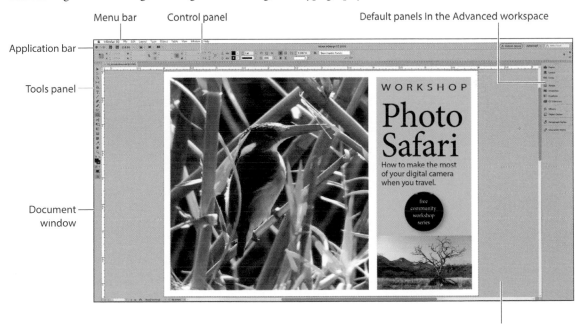

Pasteboard (work area)

Selecting and using tools

The Tools panel contains tools for creating and modifying page objects, adding and formatting text and images, and working with color. By default, the Tools panel is docked to the upper-left corner of the work area. In this exercise, you will select and experiment with several tools.

Using the Selection tool

▶ **Tip:** The building blocks of InDesign pages are objects, which include frames (for containing text and graphics) and lines.

The Selection tool lets you move and resize objects, and it lets you select objects for formatting, such as applying color. You will click to select the Selection tool. Later, you will experiment with other methods of selecting tools.

1 Locate the Tools panel at the far-left side of the screen.

2 Point at each tool in the Tools panel to see its name.

3 Click the Selection tool (▶), the top tool on the Tools panel.

4 Click near the bird's beak to select the graphics frame containing the bird photograph.

● **Note:** If you click and hold the mouse button before you start to drag, you can see a ghosted preview of the object as you drag it.

5 Drag the frame up and to the right to see how frames move.

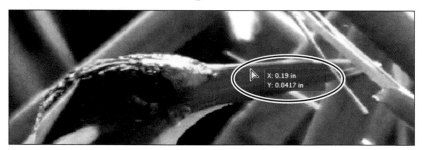

6 After you release the mouse button, press Ctrl+Z (Windows) or Command+Z (macOS) to undo the move.

7 With the Selection tool still selected, click other objects on the page, and drag them to new locations. The page contains another image in a graphics frame, a rectangular text frame, and an elliptical text frame. Undo each move immediately after you do it.

Using the Type tool

Now you will switch to the Type tool, which lets you enter, edit, and format text. Rather than clicking to select it, you will use its keyboard shortcut.

1 Point at the Type tool (**T.**) to display its tool tip. The letter shown in parentheses indicates a single-letter keyboard shortcut for selecting this tool. In this case, the letter is T.

2 Point at various other tools to see their single-letter keyboard shortcuts.

3 Press T on the keyboard to select the Type tool. Click after the word "travel" and the period on the right side of the postcard.

4 Type a space and a few characters to get a feel for the Type tool.

● **Note:** The single-letter shortcuts do not work when the text insertion bar is in text.

5 Press Ctrl+Z (Windows) or Command+Z (macOS) to undo any changes to the postcard text.

6 With the Type tool still selected, click in other words and revise the text. Undo each change immediately after you do so.

▶ **Tip:** As you learn InDesign and experiment with designs, remember that you can undo as many changes as you want.

Using the Line tool and Hand tool

Now you will switch to the Line tool, which lets you create horizontal, vertical, and diagonal lines. Once you have experimented with the Line tool, you will select the Hand tool temporarily by holding its keyboard shortcut: H. When you release the keyboard shortcut, InDesign reverts to the previously selected tool. This technique is useful for quickly using a tool—for example, you might use the Hand tool to move to another area of a page and then create a line there.

1 Click the Line tool (╱) to select it.

Tip: To constrain the Line tool to creating horizontal, vertical, or 45° lines, press the Shift key as you draw.

2 Click and drag to create a line anywhere on the page. Press Ctrl+Z (Windows) or Command+Z (macOS) to undo the line creation.

3 With the Line tool still selected, press and hold the H key on the keyboard. While you hold the H key, the Hand tool (✋) is selected.

4 Drag the Hand tool around to view another area of the page. When you release the H key, the Line tool remains selected.

Using the Rectangle Frame tool and the Ellipse Frame tool

So far, you have selected tools that display on the Tools panel in three ways: (1) clicking them, (2) pressing a keyboard shortcut, and (3) holding a keyboard shortcut to select the tool temporarily. Now, you will select a tool that is not visible on the Tools panel. A small triangle in the lower-right corner of a tool indicates a menu of additional hidden tools.

In this exercise, you will select and use the Rectangle Frame tool, and then you will select and use the Ellipse Frame tool. You would create these frames to contain imported graphics and text.

1 Choose View > Screen Mode > Normal so you can see the frames that contain graphics and text.

2 Press F on the keyboard to select the Rectangle Frame tool (⊠).

Tip: To easily create a square or circle, press the Shift key while you draw with the Rectangle Frame tool or with the Ellipse Frame tool.

3 Scroll to the left to view the pasteboard surrounding the document. (See "Reviewing the document window and pasteboard" later in this chapter.) Click and drag to create a rectangular graphics frame.

4 Press Ctrl+Z (Windows) or Command+Z (macOS) to undo the frame creation.

5 To see the Ellipse Frame tool, click and hold on the Rectangle Frame tool to display additional hidden tools.

6 Select the Ellipse Frame tool (⊗), and notice how it replaces the Rectangle Frame tool.

7 Click and drag to create an oval graphics frame anywhere on the page. Press Ctrl+Z (Windows) or Command+Z (macOS) as many times as necessary to undo the frame creation.

8 Click and hold the Ellipse Frame tool to display the menu, and choose the Rectangle Frame tool to display it again. This is the default tool that displays.

9 Review the remaining hidden tools: Click each tool with a triangle and hold down the mouse button to see its menu of additional tools. The tools with menus for hidden tools include the following:

- Type tool
- Pen tool
- Pencil tool
- Rectangle Frame tool
- Rectangle tool
- Free Transform tool
- Color Theme tool

▶ **Tip:** You can Alt-click (Windows) or Option-click (macOS) a tool in the Tools panel to alternate between the tools in a menu.

Reviewing the Control panel

The Control panel displays immediately below the Application bar and offers quick access to options for editing selected objects.

1 Choose View > Screen Mode > Normal so you can see the frames that contain graphics and text.

2 In the Tools panel, select the Selection tool (▶).

3 Click the bird image. The Control panel provides options for controlling the position, size, and other attributes of the selected object (a graphics frame).

▶ **Tip:** You can also move and resize objects by entering values in these fields and by dragging objects with the mouse.

4 In the Control panel, click the X, Y, W, and H up and down arrows to see how you can reposition the selected text frame and change its dimensions. Press Ctrl+Z (Windows) or Command+Z (macOS) to undo any changes

5 In the Tools panel, select the Type tool (T.).

6 Click in the word "Safari." The Control panel now provides options for controlling paragraph and character formatting.

7 Double-click to select the word "Safari" and click once on the down arrow on the Font Size field, as shown, to decrease the size of the type.

8 Press Ctrl+Z (Windows) or Command+Z (macOS) to undo the change.

9 Click the pasteboard (the blank area outside the pages) to deselect the text.

Reviewing the Application bar

At the top of the default workspace is the Application bar, which provides quick access to the most-used layout aids. These include options for changing a document's zoom level, showing and hiding guides, and managing multiple document windows. The Application bar also provides access to Adobe resources such as Adobe Stock art.

To get familiar with the controls in the Application bar, point at each to display its tool tip.

InDesign groups the Application bar, document windows, and panels into a single unit called the Application frame. In macOS, you can ungroup these components as follows:

* To deactivate the Application frame, choose Window > Application Frame.

* When the Application frame is not in use, macOS users can hide the Application bar by choosing Window > Application Bar.

* When you hide the Application bar in macOS, the zoom level controls display in the lower-left corner of the document window.

Reviewing the document window and pasteboard

The document window and pasteboard make up your work area and have the following characteristics:

* Controls for displaying different pages in the document are in the lower-left corner of the document window.

* Each page or spread is surrounded by its own pasteboard.

* You can use the pasteboard as a work area or a storage area—for example, to place design elements not yet included in the page layout.

▶ **Tip:** You can change the size of the pasteboard in Preferences > Guides & Pasteboard.

Now, you will look at the pasteboard and review features on the document window.

1 To see all the pages in the document and the document's pasteboard, choose 50% from the Zoom Level menu on the Application bar.

2 In the Tools panel, select the Selection tool (▶).

3 Click the text frame containing the words "free community workshop series." Drag the frame to the pasteboard to see how easy it is to use the area for storage.

4 Press Ctrl+Z (Windows) or Command+Z (macOS) to undo the change.

5 Choose View > Fit Page In Window.

6 In the lower-left corner of the document window, click the arrow next to the Page Number box to display a menu of document pages and master pages.

7 Choose 2 from the menu to display page 2 in the document window.

8 Click the arrow to the left of the Page Number box to turn back to page 1.

9 Choose View > Screen Mode > Preview to hide the frame guides.

Working with multiple document windows

When you open multiple documents, each document displays in its own tab of the main document window. You can also open multiple windows for a single document so you can see different parts of the layout at one time. Here, you'll create a second window so you can see how changes to the headline affect the entire page. The techniques you use here for arranging document windows can be used with different views of the same document and for any other open documents.

1 Choose Window > Arrange > New Window For 01_Introduction.indd.

A new window, titled 01_Introduction.indd:2, opens. The original window is now titled 01_Introduction.indd:1.

2 Select the Zoom tool (Q) in the Tools panel.

3 In the second window, 01_Introduction.indd:2, drag to draw a marquee around the box containing the word "WORKSHOP" to zoom in on the text.

Notice that the other window stays at its original magnification.

4 Press T on the keyboard to select the Type tool (T).

5 In the second window, click at the end of the word "WORKSHOP" and add an "S" to make it plural: WORKSHOPS.

Notice the change in the first window.

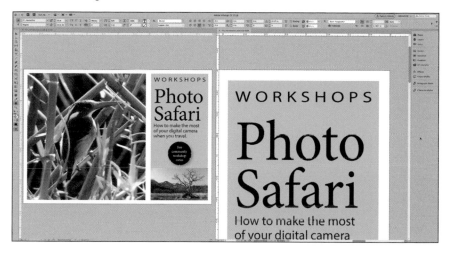

6 Press Ctrl+Z (Windows) or Command+Z (macOS) to restore the word "WORKSHOP."

7 Choose Window > Arrange > Consolidate All Windows. This creates a tab for each window.

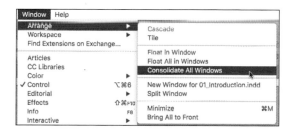

8 Click the tabs in the upper-left corner (below the Control panel) to control which document window to display.

● **Note:** The two windows displaying the document may be in reverse order on your screen. This does not affect the steps.

9 Close the 01_Introduction.indd:2 window by clicking the Close Window button on the tab. The original document window remains open.

10 If necessary, choose View > Fit Page In Window.

Working with panels

▶ **Tip:** As you become comfortable with InDesign, experiment with configuring the panels and workspace to best meet your needs. You will soon find out which panels you use the most, where you like to keep them, and what size is best for your needs.

Panels provide quick access to commonly used tools and features. By default, various useful panels are docked at the right side of the screen. (Think of a dock as a collection of panels "glued" together.) The panels that display are different depending on the selected workspace, and each workspace remembers its panel configuration.

You can reorganize panels in various ways. Here, you'll experiment with opening, collapsing, and closing the default panels in the Advanced workspace.

Opening and closing panels

To display a hidden panel, choose the panel name from the Window menu (or a submenu of the Window menu). If the panel name has a check mark, it is already open and in front of any other panels in its panel group. In this exercise, you will open, use, and close the Info panel, which provides feedback about anything you select in the document.

1 Choose Window > Info to open the Info panel.

2 In the Tools panel, select the Selection tool (▶).

3 Point at and click various objects on the page to view its details.

▶ **Tip:** When a panel is floating, you can click its close box (✖) to close it.

4 Choose Window > Info again to close the Info panel.

Expanding and collapsing panels

In this exercise, you will expand and collapse a panel, hide the panel names, and expand all the panels in the dock.

1 In the default dock to the right of the document window, click the Pages panel icon to expand the Pages panel.

This technique is handy if you want to open a panel, use it briefly, and then close it.

2 When you've finished using the Pages panel, click the double arrow (⟫) to the right of the panel names or click the Pages panel icon again to collapse the panel.

Tip: The double arrow button expands and collapses panels.

3 To reduce the width of the panel dock, drag the left edge of the panel dock to the right until the names are hidden.

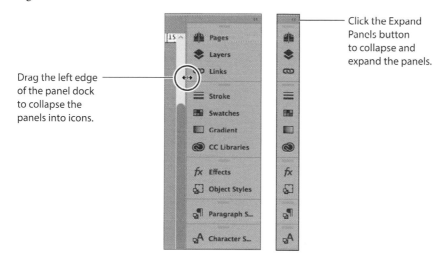

Click the Expand Panels button to collapse and expand the panels.

Drag the left edge of the panel dock to collapse the panels into icons.

4 To expand all the panels in the dock so you can see all their controls, click the double arrow (⟪) in the upper-right corner of the dock.

For the next exercise, you will leave the panels expanded.

Rearranging and customizing panels

In this exercise, you will drag a single panel out of the dock to create a free-floating panel. Then, you will drag another panel into that panel to create a custom panel group. You will also ungroup the panels, stack them, and minimize them.

Note: If necessary, click the double arrow (**≫**) in the upper-right corner of the dock to expand all of the panel.

1 Locate the Paragraph Styles panel toward the bottom of the default panels docked at the right. You will detach this from the dock to create a floating panel.

2 Drag the tab of the Paragraph Styles panel away from the dock to remove the panel from the dock.

 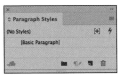

Now you will add the Character Styles panel to the floating Paragraph Styles panel to create a panel group.

Tip: Grouping the Character Styles and Paragraph Styles panels can be helpful for formatting text. You can put this panel group in a handy location while leaving the remaining panels collapsed and out of the way.

3 Locate the Character Styles panel toward the bottom of the panel dock. Drag its tab into the gray area to the right of the Paragraph Styles panel tab.

4 Release the mouse button when the blue line appears along the perimeter of the Paragraph Styles panel.

 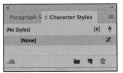

5 To ungroup the panels, drag one of the panel tabs out of the panel group.

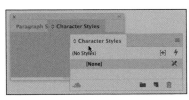

You can also stack floating panels in a vertical arrangement. You'll try that now.

6 Drag the tab of the Character Styles panel to the bottom of the Paragraph Styles panel. Release the mouse button when a blue line appears.

The panels are now stacked rather than grouped. Stacked panels attach vertically to each other. You can move the panels as a unit by dragging the topmost title bar. Next, you'll experiment with resizing the stacked panels.

7 Drag the lower-right corner of a panel to resize it.

8 Regroup the panels by dragging the tab of the Character Styles panel up next to the Paragraph Styles panel tab.

 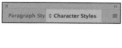

9 Minimize the panel group by double-clicking the gray area to the right of a panel's tab. Double-click the area again to expand the panels.

Leave the panels this way to be saved with a workspace in a later exercise.

Tip: A detached panel is called a floating panel. Click the double arrow on a floating panel's title bar to expand or minimize it.

Tip: For floating panels, you can change the width and height by dragging the lower-right or lower-left corner, change the height by dragging the bottom, and change the width by dragging the left or right edge of the panel. For docked panels, you can change the width and height by dragging the lower-left corner, change the width by dragging the left edge, or change the height by dragging the bottom of the panel.

Moving the Tools panel and Control panel

In general, you will keep the Tools panel and the Control panel open all the time. However, like all other panels, you can move them to best suit your own work style. Here, you will experiment with moving these two panels.

▶ **Tip:** To undock the Tools panel, you can drag either the title bar or the gray dotted bar just below the title bar.

1 To undock the Tools panel and make it float in the workspace, drag the panel by its dotted bar to pull it into the pasteboard.

When the Tools panel is floating, it can be a two-column vertical panel, a single-column vertical panel, or a single-column horizontal row. The Tools panel must be floating (not docked) to display horizontally.

2 With the Tools panel floating, click the double arrow (»») at the top of the Tools panel.

The Tools panel becomes one horizontal row.

3 Click the double arrow (⚇) in the Tools panel to turn it into a two-column vertical panel. Click the double arrow again to return to the default Tools panel.

4 To dock the Tools panel again, drag the dotted bar (⁞⁞⁞⁞⁞⁞⁞⁞) at the top of the Tools panel to the far-left edge of the screen.

5 Release the Tools panel when a blue line appears along the edge of the workspace.

The Control panel can be moved if you don't like it docked at the top of the document window.

▶ **Tip:** To customize the options showing in the Control panel, click the gear icon (⚙) at the far right side of the panel.

6 In the Control panel, drag the vertical dotted bar (⁞) at the left into the document window. Release the mouse button to make the panel float.

▶ **Tip:** You can also dock the Control panel by dragging the dotted bar until a horizontal blue line appears at the docking position.

7 To dock the panel again, click the Control panel menu button (☰) at the far right and choose Dock At Top.

Customizing the workspace

A workspace is a configuration of panels and menus. (The configuration of document windows is not saved in workspaces.) InDesign provides a variety of workspaces for special purposes, such as Digital Publishing, Printing And Proofing, and Typography. You cannot modify the provided workspaces, but you can save your own. In this exercise, you will save the panel customizations from the previous exercises. In addition, you will customize the appearance of the interface.

1 Choose Window > Workspace > New Workspace.

2 In the New Workspace dialog box, type **Styles** in the Name box. If necessary, select Panel Locations and Menu Customization. Click OK.

3 Choose Window > Workspace to see that your custom workspace is selected.

4 The name of the selected workspace also displays in a menu at the far right of the Control panel. Click this menu and select a different workspace.

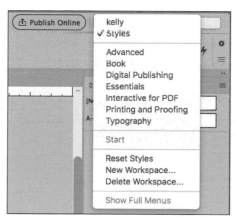

5 Choose each workspace from the Window > Workspace submenu or the Control panel Workspace menu to see the different panel and menu configurations.

6 Choose Window > Workspace > Advanced, and then choose Window > Workspace > Reset Advanced.

> **Tip:** To further customize the workspace, you can control which commands appear in the InDesign menus by choosing Edit > Menus. For example, you might prefer shorter menus for use on a smaller laptop screen, or you might want to streamline the commands available to a new user. You can save the menu customization with your saved workspaces.

Changing the magnification of a document

▶ **Tip:** Keyboard shortcuts let you quickly change the view to 200%, 400%, and 50% magnification. In Windows, press Ctrl+2 for 200%, Ctrl+4 for 400%, and Ctrl+5 for 50%. In macOS, press Command+2 for 200%, Command+4 for 400%, and Command+5 for 50%.

Controls in InDesign let you view documents at any zoom level from 5% to 4000%. When a document is open, the current magnification percentage is displayed in the Zoom Level box in the Application bar and next to the filename in the document's tab or title bar.

> ✕ *01_Introduction.indd @ 258%

In a document's title bar, the percentage next to the name indicates the zoom level.

Using the view commands

You can easily enlarge or reduce the view of a document by doing any of the following:

- Choose View > Zoom In to enlarge the display by one preset increment.

- Choose View > Zoom Out to reduce the display by one preset increment.

- Choose View > Fit Page In Window to center and display the page in the window.

- Choose View > Fit Spread In Window to center and display the targeted spread in the window.

- Choose View > Actual Size to display the document at 100%.

- Choose a percentage from the Zoom Level menu in the Application bar to enlarge or reduce the display by any preset increment.

- Type a percentage in the Zoom Level box by clicking in the box, typing the desired viewing percentage, and then pressing the Enter or Return key.

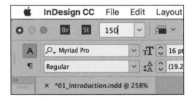

- Press Ctrl+= (Windows) or Command+= (macOS) to increase the magnification by one preset increment.

- Press Ctrl+– (Windows) or Command+– (macOS) to decrease the magnification by one preset increment.

Using the Zoom tool

In addition to the view commands, you can use the Zoom tool to magnify and reduce the view of a document. In this exercise, you will experiment with the Zoom tool.

1 Choose View > Actual Size to view the document at 100%.

2 Select the Zoom tool (🔍) in the Tools panel and position it over the tree image in the lower-right corner on the first page. Notice that a plus sign appears in the center of the Zoom tool.

3 Click three times. The view changes to the next preset magnification, centered on the point where you clicked.

▶ **Tip:** When clicking with the Zoom tool to increase the zoom level, target the item you want to zoom into to avoid zooming into random areas of a page.

Now you'll reduce the view.

4 Position the Zoom tool over the tree image and hold down the Alt (Windows) or Option (macOS) key. A minus sign appears in the center of the Zoom tool.

5 While holding the Alt or Option key, click three times to reduce the view scale.

 To magnify a specific area, you can drag the Zoom tool around that area. The percentage by which the area is magnified depends on the size of the marquee: the smaller the marquee, the larger the degree of magnification.

6 Scroll as necessary to view the black elliptical text frame containing the words "free community workshop series."

● **Note:** If you have a Mac with a compatible Graphics Processing Unit (GPU) card, your Zoom tool offers Animated Zoom. See the sidebar on the next page for details.

7 With the Zoom tool still selected, hold down the mouse button to drag a marquee around the text frame, and then release the mouse button.

8 Choose View > Fit Page In Window.

● **Note:** Your Windows or macOS system preferences may override some InDesign keyboard shortcuts. If a shortcut is not working, review your system preferences.

9 Because the Zoom tool is used frequently during the design and editing processes, you can temporarily select it from the keyboard at any time without deselecting the tool you are using. To do so:

- Click the Selection tool (▶) in the Tools panel and position it anywhere in the document window.

- Hold down Ctrl+spacebar (Windows) or Command+spacebar (macOS) so that the Selection tool icon becomes the Zoom tool icon, and then click the bird to magnify the view.

- When you release the keys, the pointer returns to the Selection tool.

10 Choose View > Fit Page In Window to center the page again.

Using Animated Zoom

If you have a Mac with a compatible Graphics Processing Unit (GPU) card, InDesign provides enhanced view features. The Display Performance (View menu) is set to High Quality by default and you can enable Animated Zoom (InDesign CC > Preferences > GPU Performance).

Animated Zoom offers smooth, animated displays when using the Zoom tool:

- Press and hold: Zoom in to the center.
- Press Option and hold: Zoom out from the center.
- Press and drag to the right: Zoom in.
- Press and drag to the left: Zoom out.
- Press Shift while dragging: Access standard marquee zoom.

Navigating through a document

InDesign offers several different ways to navigate through a document, including using the Pages panel, the Hand tool, the Go To Page dialog box, and controls in the document window. As you work with InDesign, you will find that you prefer certain methods over others. Once you find a method you like, remember any shortcuts to make that method easier. For example, if you prefer to enter a page number in the Go To Page dialog box, memorize its keyboard shortcut.

▶ **Tip:** To navigate pages, you can also use commands in the Layout menu: First Page, Previous Page, Next Page, Last Page, Next Spread, and Previous Spread.

Navigating pages

You can navigate document pages using the Pages panel, the page buttons at the bottom of the document window, the scroll bars, or a variety of other methods. The Pages panel displays an icon for each page in the document. Double-clicking any page icon or page number in the panel brings that page or spread into view. In this exercise, you will experiment with turning pages.

1 Click the Pages panel icon to expand the Pages panel, if necessary.

2 Double-click the page 2 icon to display it in the document window.

3 Double-click the page 1 icon to center the first page in the document window.

4 To return to the second page of the document, use the menu in the lower-left corner of the document window. Click the down arrow, and choose 2.

You will now use the buttons at the bottom of the document window to display a different page.

● **Note:** When View > Fit Spread In Window is selected, the navigation controls in the document window are for spreads rather than pages.

5 Click the Previous Page button (left-facing arrow) next to the Page Number box to switch pages until the first page is displayed.

6 Click the Next Page button (the right-facing arrow) next to the Page Number box until the second page is displayed.

▶ Tip: The keyboard shortcut for Layout > Go To Page is Ctrl+J (Windows) or Command+J (macOS).

7 Choose Layout > Go To Page.

8 In the Page box, type **1** or select 1 from the menu. Click OK.

Using the Hand tool

The Hand tool in the Tools panel lets you "push" the pages of a document around until the area you want to view is visible. In this exercise, you will experiment with the Hand tool.

▶ Tip: When you're using the Selection tool, you can press the spacebar to temporarily access the Hand tool. When you're using the Type tool, press the Alt (Windows) or Option (macOS) key to use the Hand tool.

1 Choose 400% from the Zoom Level menu on the Application bar.

2 Select the Hand tool (✋).

3 Click and drag in any direction to move the page around, and then drag upward in the document window to display page 2.

4 With the Hand tool still selected, click the page and hold the mouse button down to display a view rectangle.

- Drag the rectangle to view a different area of the page or a different page.

- Release the mouse button to display the area that the view rectangle encompasses.

- When the view rectangle is displayed, press the arrow keys on the keyboard to increase and decrease the rectangle's size.

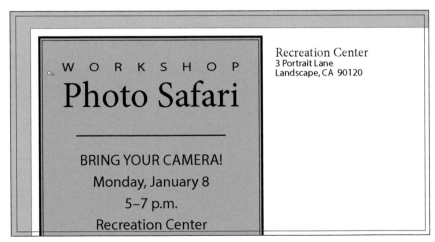

5 Double-click the Hand tool in the Tools panel to fit the page in the document window.

Using context menus

In addition to the menus at the top of your screen, you can use context menus to display commands relevant to the active tool or selection. To display context menus, position the pointer over a selected object or anywhere in the document window and click with the right mouse button (Windows) or press Control and hold down the mouse button (macOS).

1 Using the Selection tool (▶), click any object on the page, such as the text frame containing the postcard's return address starting with "Recreation Center."

2 Right-click (Windows) or Control-click (macOS) the text frame. Note the available options; a partial list is shown here.

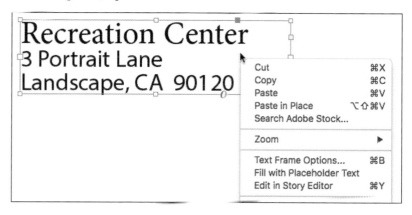

3 Select different types of objects on the page and display their context menus to see the available commands.

▶ **Tip:** You can display a context menu when entering or editing text. The Type context menu lets you insert special characters, check spelling, and perform other text-related tasks.

Using panel menus

Most panels have additional panel-specific options. Clicking the panel menu button displays a menu with additional commands and options for the selected panel.

In this exercise, you will change the display of the Swatches panel.

1 Choose Window > Color > Swatches to display the Swatches panel. Drag the Swatches panel out of the dock at the right to create a free-floating panel.

2 In the upper-right corner of the Swatches panel, click the panel menu button (≡) to display the panel menu.

You can use the Swatches panel menu to create new color swatches, load swatches from another document, and more.

● **Note:** If necessary, click the double arrow (≫) in its title bar to expand the Swatches panel.

3 Choose Large Swatch from the Swatches panel menu.

Modifying interface preferences

You can customize the InDesign interface by changing the overall color, the way various tools work, and how the panels are configured through preferences. Some settings in the Preferences dialog box affect the application (InDesign itself), while others affect only the active document. If you change the document-specific preferences while no documents are open, the changes affect all new documents (without affecting existing documents). Here, you will look at Interface preferences, which affect the application.

1 Choose Edit > Preferences > Interface (Windows) or InDesign CC > Preferences > Interface (macOS) to customize the appearance of InDesign.

2 In the Appearance area, click the Light box at far right.

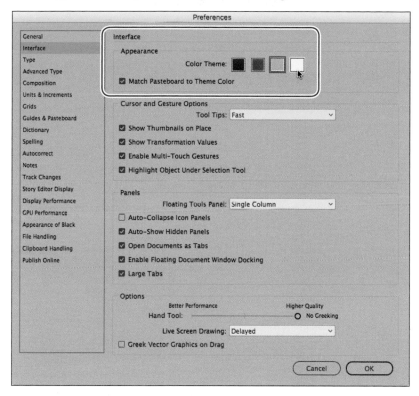

3 Experiment with the other options, and then choose the default, Medium Dark, again.

4 Click through the panels in the Preferences dialog box to see other options for customizing InDesign. For example, the Display Performance preference lets you specify how images display in all your InDesign documents (Fast, Typical, or High Quality).

- You changed the Display Performance at the beginning of this exercise through the View menu, but the change is temporary and not saved with the document.

- Changing this preference when no documents are open would affect all documents.

5 When you are finished reviewing Preferences, click OK.

▶ **Tip:** If your computer has a compatible GPU card, InDesign automatically displays documents using the GPU and sets the default Display Performance to High Quality.

Exploring on your own

▶ **Tip:** For complete and up-to-date information about using InDesign panels, tools, and other application features, use the Help menu.

Now that you have explored the work area, try some of the following tasks using either the 01_Introduction.indd document or your own document.

- Choose Window > Utilities > Tool Hints to display information about the selected tool. Select various tools to learn more about them.

- Choose Window > Editorial > Notes to display the Notes panel group, which includes the Assignments panel and the Track Changes panel. You can use these panels to collaborate on documents.

- Learn more about existing key commands and how you can change them by exploring the Keyboard Shortcuts dialog box (Edit > Keyboard Shortcuts).

- Review the menu configurations and how you can edit them in the Menu Customization dialog box (Edit > Menus).

- Try organizing your panels to meet your needs, and create your own workspace by choosing Window > Workspace > New Workspace.

Review questions

1 What are some ways you can change the magnification (zoom level) of a document?

2 How do you select tools in InDesign?

3 What are three ways to display a panel?

4 How do you create a panel group?

Review answers

1 You can choose commands from the View menu to zoom in, zoom out, fit the page to the window, and more. You can also use the Zoom tool in the Tools panel and click or drag over a document to enlarge or reduce the view. In addition, you can use keyboard shortcuts to increase or reduce the magnification. You can also use the Zoom Level box in the Application bar.

2 You can click to select a tool in the Tools panel. Or, if the Type tool is not selected, you can press the tool's keyboard shortcut. For example, you can press V to select the Selection tool from the keyboard; press and hold the keyboard shortcut to temporarily select the tool. You select hidden tools by positioning the pointer over a tool in the Tools panel and holding down the mouse button. When the menu appears, select the tool.

3 To make a panel appear, click its icon, click its tab, or choose its name from the Window menu. For example, choose Window > Object & Layout > Align. You can also access type-specific panels from the Type menu. For example, choose Type > Glyphs.

4 Drag a panel off the dock to create a free-floating panel. Drag the tab of any other panel into the tab bar of the new, free-floating panel. A panel group can be moved and resized as one panel.

2 GETTING TO KNOW INDESIGN

Lesson Overview

In this lesson, you'll learn how to do the following:

- View layout aids.

- Check on potential production issues with the Preflight panel.

- Type and style text.

- Import text and thread text frames.

- Import a graphic.

- Move, rotate, stroke, and fill an object.

- Automate formatting with paragraph, character, and object styles.

- Preview a document in Presentation mode.

 This lesson will take about 60 minutes to complete.

Please log in to your account on peachpit.com to download the lesson files for this chapter, or go to the "Getting Started" section at the beginning of this book and follow the instructions under "Accessing the Lesson Files and Web Edition." Store the files on your computer in a convenient location.

Amuse-Bouche

Bakery & Bistro

Relax in our elegant dining room and enjoy handcrafted artisan breads, irresistable appetizers, seasonal entrées, and homemade desserts. Our chef's inspired amuse-bouches tantalize your tastebuds and are the talk of the town.

Starters & Small Plates

Try *baked garlic, home-made tater tots, hummus, mussels* and more for appetizers. Share small plates such as *portobello sliders, seared scallops and jumbo lump crab cakes.*

Entrées & Desserts

Indulge in our chef's daily creations, such as *pesto cavatappi or grilled organic chicken,* and be sure to leave room for *scrumptious croissant bread pudding or lemon mousse.*

The building blocks of an InDesign layout are objects, text, and graphics. Layout aids such as guides help with size and placement, and styles let you format page elements automatically.

Getting started

The document for this lesson is a standard-size postcard designed to be printed and mailed. In addition, the postcard can be exported as a PDF to use in email marketing. As you will see in this lesson, the building blocks of an InDesign document are the same, regardless of the output media. In this lesson, you will add the text, images, and formatting necessary to finish the postcard.

● **Note:** If you have not already downloaded the project files for this lesson to your computer from your Account page, make sure to do so now. See "Getting Started" at the beginning of the book.

1 To ensure that the preferences and default settings of your Adobe InDesign program match those used in this lesson, move the InDesign Defaults file to a different folder following the procedure in "Saving and restoring the InDesign Defaults file" on pages 4–5.

2 Start Adobe InDesign.

3 The InDesign Start Screen displays. Click Open at left. (If the Start Screen does not display, choose File > Open from the InDesign menu bar.)

4 Open the 02_Start.indd file in the Lesson02 folder, located inside the Lessons folder within the InDesignCIB folder on your hard disk.

5 If the Missing Fonts dialog box displays, click Sync Fonts to access any missing fonts through Adobe Typekit. Click Close when font syncing is complete. For more information on using Adobe Typekit, see "Getting Started" at the beginning of this book.

● **Note:** For higher contrast in the printed manual, the screen captures in this book show the Medium Light interface. Interface elements such as panels and dialog boxes will be darker on your screen.

6 To ensure that the panels and menu commands match those used in this lesson, choose Window > Workspace > [Advanced], and then choose Window > Workspace > Reset Advanced.

7 To display the document at a higher resolution, choose View > Display Performance > High Quality Display (if it's not already enabled).

8 Choose File > Save As, rename the file **02_Postcard.indd**, and save it in the Lesson02 folder.

9 If you want to see what the finished document looks like, open the 02_End.indd file in the same folder. You can leave this document open to act as a guide as you work.

10 When you're ready to resume working on the lesson document, display it by clicking its tab in the upper-left corner of the document window.

Viewing guides

Revising or completing an existing document, as you will do in this lesson, is typical work for entry-level InDesign users. Currently, the postcard document is displayed in Preview mode, which displays artwork in a standard window, hiding nonprinting elements such as guides, grids, frame edges, and hidden characters. To work on this document, you will view guides and hidden characters (such as spaces and tabs). As you become comfortable working with InDesign, you will discover which view modes and layout aids work best for you.

▶ **Tip:** The other view modes are Bleed, for reviewing the predefined bleed area for objects that extend beyond the page boundaries; Slug, for displaying the area outside the bleed area that can contain information such as printer instructions or job sign-off information; and Presentation, which fills the screen and works well for presenting design ideas to clients.

1 Click and hold down the Screen Mode button at the bottom of the Tools panel, and choose Normal (⊡) from the menu.

 Enabled layout aids now display. For example, light blue, nonprinting lines now indicate existing text frames and objects because Frame Edges were displayed (View > Extras > Show Frame Edges). You will now enable other layout aids.

2 In the Application bar, click the View Options menu (▦ ⌄) and select Guides. Be sure Guides is checked in the menu.

 When guides are displayed, it's easy to position objects with precision, including automatically snapping them into place. The guides do not print and do not limit the print or export area.

3 From the same View Options menu, choose Hidden Characters. Be sure Hidden Characters is checked in the menu.

 Displaying hidden (nonprinting) characters, such as tabs, spaces, and paragraph returns, helps you precisely select and style text. In general, it's a good idea to show hidden characters whenever you are editing or formatting text.

▶ **Tip:** The commands in the Application bar are available in the main InDesign menus as well. These include View > Grids & Guides > Show Guides and Type > Show Hidden Characters.

4 As you work on this document, use the skills you learned in Lesson 1 to move panels, rearrange panels, scroll, and zoom as necessary.

Preflighting as you work

Anytime you start working on a document for the first time—whether you're creating a document from scratch or revising an existing document—you will need to keep an eye on output issues. For example, are all the rules (lines) in the document thick enough to print, or will the colors display properly? You will learn more about all of these issues throughout the lessons in this book.

In publishing, the process of evaluating a document for potential output issues is known as *preflighting*. The InDesign Live Preflight feature lets you monitor documents as you're working to prevent problems from occurring. To customize Live Preflight, you can create or import production rules (called preflight profiles) against which InDesign checks your documents. The default profile supplied with InDesign flags issues such as missing fonts (fonts that are not active on your system) and overset text (text that does not fit in its frame).

▶ **Tip:** Keep an eye on the lower-left corner of the document window to see if any errors arise. You can double-click the word "error" to open the Preflight panel for details on any errors.

1 Choose Window > Output > Preflight to open the Preflight panel.

Using the [Basic] (Working) preflight profile, InDesign finds one error, as indicated by the red Preflight icon (●), which displays in the lower-left corner of the Preflight panel and the document window. According to the Error list in the Preflight panel, the problem is in the TEXT category.

2 To view the error, click the arrow next to TEXT in the Preflight panel.

3 Click the arrow next to Overset Text, and then click Text Frame.

4 To display details for the error, click the arrow next to Info at the bottom of the Preflight panel.

5 Double-click Text Frame to locate and select the problem text frame on the page, or click the page number link to the right in the Page column.

The text frame containing the headline, subhead, and body text is selected. The overset text is indicated by a red plus sign (+) in the frame's out port (the small square just above the lower-right corner of the frame).

6 Using the Selection tool (▶), drag the handle at the bottom of the text frame down so the frame height is approximately 12p10.

▶ **Tip:** A quick way to expand the overset text frame is to double-click the bottom (center) handle of the text frame. You can handle overset text by revising the text, reducing the font size, and using the Auto-Size feature for the text frame (Object > Text Frame Options > Auto-Size) as well.

7 Click the pasteboard to deselect the text frame.

8 Choose View > Fit Page In Window.

InDesign now reports No Errors in the Preflight panel and in the lower-left corner of the document window.

9 Close the Preflight panel. Choose File > Save to save your work.

Adding text

With InDesign, most text is contained by a text frame. (Text can be contained in table cells and flow along paths as well.) You can type text directly into a text frame or import text files from word-processing programs. When importing text files, you can add the text to existing frames or create frames to contain the text. If text doesn't fit within a single frame, you can "thread," or link, multiple text frames.

Typing and styling text

You're ready to start working on the incomplete postcard. To get started, you'll edit and style the text under the headline.

1 Select the Type tool (T) and click immediately after the word "Cafe."

2 Press Backspace (Windows) or Delete (macOS) four times to delete the word "Cafe."

▶ **Tip:** Use the Type tool to edit text, format text, and create new text frames.

3 Type **Bistro** in the text frame so the restaurant's descriptor is changed from "Bakery & Cafe" to "Bakery & Bistro."

4 With the insertion point still in the text, click three times to select "Bakery & Bistro".

● **Note:** If necessary, use the Selection tool to drag the bottom of the text frame so all the text fits.

5 If necessary, click the Character Formatting Controls icon (**A**) in the Control panel. From the Font Style menu, select Bold.

6 Choose File > Save to save your work.

Options for styling and placing text

InDesign provides options for formatting characters and paragraphs and for positioning text within a frame. Common options are listed here.

- **Character formats:** Font, Font Style, Size, Leading, All Caps
- **Paragraph formats:** Alignment such as Center, Indents, Space Before/After
- **Text Frame Options:** Columns, Inset Spacing, Vertical Justification

The Control panel, Paragraph panel (Type > Paragraph), and Character panel (Type > Character) provide all the controls you need to style text. To control positioning of the text within its frame, choose Object > Text Frame Options; many of these options are on the Control panel as well.

Importing and flowing text

In most publishing workflows, writers and editors use word processors. When the text is almost final, they send the files to graphic designers. To complete the postcard, you will import a Microsoft Word file into a text frame at the bottom of the page using the Place command. You will then link the first text frame to the second frame using a process called "threading."

1 Using the Selection tool (▶), click a blank area of the pasteboard to make sure no objects are selected.

2 Choose File > Place. At the bottom of the Place dialog box, make sure that Show Import Options is not selected.

3 Navigate to the Lesson02 folder, in the Lessons folder, and double-click the Amuse.docx file.

The pointer changes to a loaded text icon (▤). You'll add this text to the text frame in the lower-left quadrant of the postcard. (The text frames are outlined by light blue nonprinting lines.)

4 Position the loaded text icon in the text frame, and then click.

Starters & Small Plates
Try baked garlic, homemade
tater tots, hummus, mussels
and more for appetizers.
Share small plates such as
portobello sliders, seared

Starters·&·Small·Plates¶

Try·baked·garlic,·
homemade·tater·tots,·
hummus,·mussels·and·
more·for·appetizers.·
Share·small·plates·such·
as·portobello·sliders,·

An out port on the text frame; the red plus sign indicates overset text.

The text in the Word file fills the frame, but it doesn't all fit. A red plus sign (+) in the out port of the frame (in the frame's lower-right corner) indicates overset text. You will thread the two bottom text frames so the text flows through them.

5 Using the Selection tool, select the text frame that now contains the text.

▶ **Tip:** When the loaded text icon is displayed, you have several choices: You can drag to create a new text frame, click inside an existing frame, or click to create a new text frame within the page's column guides.

● **Note:** To see where to place the body copy text, consult the finished lesson document, 02_End.indd.

6 Click the out port of the selected frame to select it. Click the out port again to display the loaded text icon. Click in the text frame immediately to the right.

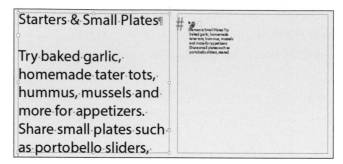

Note: Due to variations in font versions, you may see slightly different text in your frames.

At this point, text is still overset. You will resolve this problem by formatting the text with styles later in this lesson.

Starters & Small Plates¶	seared scallops and jumbo lump crab cakes.¶
Try baked garlic, homemade tater tots, hummus, mussels and more for appetizers. Share small plates such as portobello sliders,	Entrées & Desserts¶ Indulge in our chef's daily creations, such as pesto cavatappi or

7 Choose File > Save.

Working with styles

Tip: A paragraph style can include nested styles that format the beginning of a paragraph and lines within a paragraph. This automates common paragraph formatting, such as starting a paragraph with a drop cap followed by all capital letters on the first line.

InDesign provides paragraph styles, character styles, and object styles for quickly and consistently formatting text and objects and—more important—easily making global changes by simply editing the style. Styles work as follows:

- A paragraph style includes all text formatting attributes—such as font, size, and alignment—that apply to all the text in a paragraph. You can select a paragraph by simply clicking in it, highlighting any part it, or highlighting all of it.

- A character style includes only character attributes—such as font style (bold or italic) or font color—that apply only to selected text within a paragraph. Character styles are generally applied to call attention to specific text within a paragraph.

- An object style lets you apply formatting—such as fill and stroke color, stroke styles and corner effects, transparency, drop shadows, feathering, text frame options, and text wrap—to selected objects.

You will now format the text with paragraph and character styles.

Applying paragraph styles

Because the postcard is almost finished, all the paragraph styles you need are already created. You will first apply the Body Copy style to all the text in the two threaded text frames, and then you will apply the Subhead style to the box headings.

1 Using the Type tool (T), click in one of the text frames containing the newly imported text.

2 Choose Edit > Select All to select all the text in the threaded frames.

3 Choose Type > Paragraph Styles to display the Paragraph Styles panel.

4 In the Paragraph Styles panel, click the Body Copy style to format the entire story with the Body Copy style.

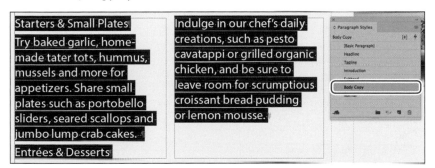

5 Using the Type tool, click in the first line of text in the story: "Starters & Small Plates."

As you can see from the hidden character (the paragraph return) at the end of the line, this line is actually its own paragraph. Therefore, it can be formatted with a paragraph style.

6 Click the Subhead style in the Paragraph Styles panel.

7 Apply the Subhead paragraph style to "Entrées & Desserts" as well.

8 Choose File > Save.

Tip: In many publishing environments, including marketing and advertising, the text in a publication is referred to as "copy," which is why the writers and editors are called "copywriters" and "copyeditors."

Note: If a plus sign (+) displays next to the applied style (Body Copy), it indicates that the text formatting does not precisely match the style's formatting. To resolve this, click Clear Overrides (¶*) at the bottom of the Paragraph Styles panel. You will learn more about styles in Lesson 9.

Formatting text for the character style

▶ **Tip:** Remember that as you work, you can tear off panels, resize them, and move them to suit your needs. The configuration of your panels is largely dependent on the amount of screen space available. Some InDesign users have a second monitor for managing panels.

Highlighting a few key words in a paragraph can draw readers into the text. For the postcard copy, you will format a few words to make them "pop" and then create a character style based on those words. You can then quickly apply the character style to other selected words.

1 Using the Zoom tool (🔍), zoom in on the first text frame in the lower-left quadrant of the postcard. This frame contains the subhead "Starters & Small Plates."

2 Using the Type tool (T.), select the words "baked garlic, homemade tater tots, hummus, mussels" in the first paragraph of body copy.

3 If necessary, click the Character Formatting Controls icon (A) in the Control panel.

4 Display the Type Style menu on the far-left side of the Control panel. Select Italic, leaving the font as Myriad Pro.

5 In the Control panel, click the arrow next to the Fill menu. Click the arrow next to Colorful_Theme to open the folder of swatches.

6 Choose the red swatch named C=23 M=97 Y=99 K=16 to apply the color to the text.

7 Click once to deselect the text and view your changes. Choose File > Save.

Creating and applying a character style

Now that you have formatted the text, you are ready to create a character style based on that formatting.

1 Using the Type tool (T.), select the words "baked garlic, homemade tater tots, hummus, mussels" again.

2 If necessary, choose Type > Character Styles to display the Character Styles panel.

3 Hold down the Alt (Windows) or Option (macOS) key and click the Create New Style button, at the bottom of the Character Styles panel.

Note: Pressing Alt (Windows) or Option (macOS) while you click the Create New Style button opens the New Character Style dialog box so you can immediately name the style. This feature works in the Paragraph Styles and Object Styles panels as well.

A new character style, named Character Style 1, is created in the New Character Style dialog box. This new style includes the characteristics of the selected text, as indicated in the Style Settings area of the dialog box.

4 In the Style Name box, type **Red Italic.**

5 At the bottom of the New Character Style dialog box, select Apply Style To Selection.

6 In the lower-left corner, deselect Add To CC Library (if necessary). Click OK.

Note: If the New Character Style dialog box does not open immediately, double-click Character Style 1 in the Character Styles panel.

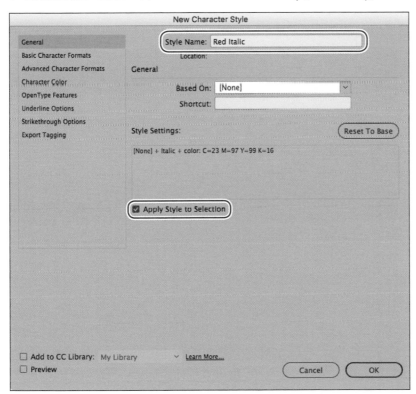

7 Using the Type tool, select the words "portobello sliders, seared scallops and jumbo lump crab cakes" and the period after "cakes" in the first text frame.

8 Click Red Italic in the Character Styles panel.

Because you applied a character style instead of a paragraph style, the formatting affected only the selected text, not the entire paragraph.

9 Using the Type tool, select the words "pesto cavatappi or grilled organic chicken" and the comma after "chicken" in the text frame at the right.

10 Click Red Italic in the Character Styles panel.

11 Repeat the process to apply the Red Italic character style to "croissant bread pudding or lemon mousse."

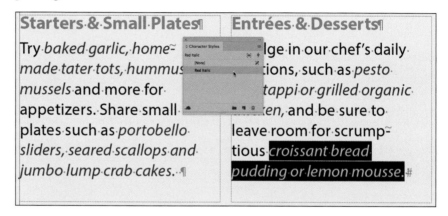

12 Choose File > Save.

Working with graphics

To add the final design element to the postcard, you'll import, resize, and position a graphic. Graphics used in InDesign documents are placed inside frames. Use the Selection tool (▶) to resize a graphics frame and to position the graphic within the frame. You will learn more about working with graphics in Lesson 10, "Importing and Modifying Graphics."

1 Choose View > Fit Page In Window.

You will position the graphic in the upper-right quadrant of the postcard.

2 Make sure that no objects are selected by choosing Edit > Deselect All.

3 Choose File > Place. In the Place dialog box, make sure that Show Import Options is not selected.

4 Navigate to the Lesson02 folder in the Lessons folder, and double-click the DiningRoom.jpg file.

The loaded graphics icon () displays a preview of the graphic. If you click the page, InDesign places the graphic at full size, inside an identically sized graphics frame. In this case, however, you will scale the graphic as you add it to the page. The resulting graphics frame will have the same dimensions as the graphic.

5 Position the loaded graphics icon at the intersection of the light blue and pink guides in the upper-right quadrant of the postcard.

● **Note:** To see where to place the graphic, consult the finished lesson document, 02_End.indd.

6 Drag down and to the right until the pointer touches the guide on the right side of the page.

When you release the mouse button, the graphic is added to the page and a graphics frame is created automatically. The width and height of the graphics frame are determined by the graphic's dimensions.

▶ **Tip:** When you create a frame while placing a graphic on the page, the graphic is automatically scaled to fit within the frame. You can use the scaling controls on the Control panel to precisely adjust the graphic size. You will learn more about sizing in Lesson 10.

7 Using the Selection tool (▶), select the middle handle at the bottom of the graphics frame and drag it up. You can crop the image by dragging any of its eight resizing handles.

Use the Selection tool to crop a graphic by reducing the size of its frame.

8 Press Ctrl+Z (Windows) or Command+Z (macOS) to undo the crop.

9 Still using the Selection tool, position the pointer over the graphic to display the content grabber (⊚) in the center of the graphic.

10 Click the content grabber to select the graphic, and then drag up to position the image within the frame as you please.

11 Press Ctrl+Z (Windows) or Command+Z (macOS) to undo the image move. The eventual position of the graphic should be where you placed it in step 6.

12 Choose File > Save.

Working with objects

The building blocks of InDesign pages are objects: text frames, graphics frames, rules (lines), and more. In general, you move and resize objects with the Selection tool. Objects can have a fill color (background color) and a stroke color (outline or border), which you can customize by specifying the width and style. You can move objects around freely, snap them to other objects, and place them with precision according to guides or values you enter. In addition, you can resize and scale objects and specify how text wraps around them. You will learn more about objects in Lesson 4, "Working with Objects." Here, you will experiment with a few object-related features.

Moving and rotating an object

A fork-and-knife graphic created with InDesign drawing tools is on the pasteboard to the left of the page. You will move this graphic to the right of the restaurant name, "Amuse-Bouche." Then, you will rotate the object.

1 Choose View > Fit Page In Window to center the page in the document window. If necessary, scroll left to see the white graphic on the pasteboard.

2 If necessary, use the Selection tool (▶) to click the fork-and-knife graphic.

3 Drag the graphic to the right of the headline, "Amuse-Bouche."

4 To fine-tune the object's placement, type the following values in the Control panel:

X: **11p5**

Y: **3p**

5 To rotate the object, type **30** in the Rotation Angle field.

<aside>
● **Note:** When you enter values in the Control panel X and Y fields, the object is repositioned according to its reference point. You can view and change the reference point (▦) by clicking a box immediately to the left of the X and Y fields.
</aside>

6 Choose File > Save.

Changing the object stroke and fill

When an object is selected, you can change its stroke (outline or border) weight and color. In addition, you can apply a fill (or background) color.

1 Using the Selection tool (▶), select the white fork-and-knife graphic object.

2 Choose Window > Stroke to open the Stroke panel. Type **1 pt** in the Weight field and press Enter (Windows) or Return (macOS).

3 With the graphic object still selected, click the Swatches panel icon at the right.

● **Note:** If necessary, drag the lower-right corner of the Swatches panel to resize it and view the Colorful theme.

4 Click the Stroke box () at the top of the panel to ensure that you apply the color to the stroke (rather than the fill). The Stroke box is the lower right of the two overlapping boxes.

5 Click the arrow next to the Colorful_Theme folder to see the swatches, and then click the green swatch named C=61 M=28 Y=100 K=9.

6 With the graphic object still selected, click the Fill box () at the top of the panel to indicate that you want to apply color to the fill of the object.

▶**Tip:** To quickly revert the default stroke color to Black and the fill to None, choose Edit > Deselect All and press D on the keyboard.

7 Click the red swatch named C=23 M=97 Y=99 K=16.

8 Click the pasteboard to deselect all objects.

9 Choose File > Save.

Working with object styles

As with paragraph and character styles, you can quickly and consistently format objects by saving attributes as styles. In this exercise, you will apply an existing object style to the two threaded text frames containing the body copy.

1 Choose View > Fit Page In Window.

2 Choose Window > Styles > Object Styles to display the Object Styles panel.

3 Using the Selection tool (▶), click the text frame at the left containing the "Starters & Small Plates" subhead.

4 Click the Green Stroke And Drop Shadow style in the Object Styles panel.

5 Click the second text frame, which contains the "Entrées & Desserts" subhead.

6 Click the Green Stroke And Drop Shadow style in the Object Styles panel.

7 Choose File > Save.

Viewing the document in Presentation mode

In Presentation mode, the InDesign interface is hidden entirely, and the document fills the whole screen. This mode works well for presenting design ideas to clients.

▶ **Tip:** You cannot edit documents in Presentation mode, but you can make changes in any other screen mode.

1 Click and hold down the Screen Mode button (▦) at the bottom of the Tools panel, and select Presentation (▢).

2 After viewing the document, press Esc (Escape) to exit Presentation mode. The document displays in its previous screen mode, Normal.

3 To view the document without layout aids, choose View > Screen Mode > Preview.

4 Choose View > Actual Size to see the document at its output size.

5 Choose File > Save.

Congratulations! You've completed the InDesign tour.

InDesign best practices

While completing the postcard in this lesson, you experimented with the basic building blocks of a document and the best practices for creating a document. When you create a document following best practices, the document is easy to format, revise, and replicate consistently. Some of these techniques are listed here.

- **Start with preflight.** As soon as you receive a document to work on, use the Live Preflight feature to make sure the document will output correctly. For example, if the document is missing a font, you will need to acquire that font before you continue working on the document.

- **Avoid stacking objects.** Format one object rather than using multiple objects. For example, the two text frames containing the postcard's body text have a text inset, stroke weight, stroke color, and drop shadow applied. A new InDesign user might be tempted to create this look by stacking multiple frames. Using multiple objects creates extra work when moving and aligning objects or changing the formatting.

- **Thread text frames.** New InDesign users are often tempted to place or paste text into separate, freestanding text frames. The text in these frames needs to be selected and formatted individually. If you flow the text through threaded frames, it remains as a single body of text called a "story." Among other benefits of working with a story as opposed to disjointed frames of text, you can select all the text in a story for formatting, and limit the use of Find/Change and Check Spelling to the text in a story. When working on a longer document, such as a book, threading text frames is crucial to controlling the text placement and entering revisions.

- **Use styles for all formatting.** InDesign provides styles for formatting objects, paragraphs, lines within paragraphs, characters, tables, and table cells. With styles, you can quickly and consistently format everything in a document. In addition, if you decide to change a format, you can update the style to make a global change. For example, in the postcard, if you wanted to change the font used in the body copy, all you would need to do is edit the Character Formats of the Body Text paragraph style. Styles can easily be updated to reflect new formatting, and styles can be shared among documents as well.

You will learn more about all these features as you work through the lessons.

Exploring on your own

To learn more about InDesign, try the following within the postcard layout:

- Change the text formatting by choosing other options in the Control panel.

- Apply different paragraph and character styles to text. Apply the object style to different objects.

- Move and resize objects and graphics.

- Double-click a paragraph, character, or object style and change its formatting. Notice how the change affects the text or objects to which the style is applied.

Review questions

1 How can you tell if an aspect of a layout will cause output problems?

2 What tool allows you to create text frames?

3 What tool allows you to thread text frames?

4 What symbol indicates that a text frame has more text than it can display—that is, overset text?

5 What tool allows you to move both frames and graphics within frames?

6 What panel provides options for modifying selected frames, graphics, and text?

Review answers

1 The Preflight panel reports errors when something in the layout does not comply with the selected preflight profile. For example, if a text frame has overset text (text that doesn't fit in the frame), an error is reported. Preflight errors are also reported in the lower-left corner of the document window.

2 You create text frames with the Type tool.

3 You thread text frames with the Selection tool.

4 A red plus sign in the lower-right corner of a text frame indicates overset text.

5 The Selection tool lets you drag a graphics frame (and its graphic) to move it or move a graphic within its frame.

6 The Control panel provides options for modifying the current selection: characters, paragraphs, graphics, frames, tables, and more.

3 SETTING UP A DOCUMENT AND WORKING WITH PAGES

Lesson Overview

In this lesson, you'll learn how to do the following:

- Save custom document settings as a document preset.
- Create a new document and set document defaults.
- Lay out a master page.
- Create an additional master page.
- Apply a master page to document pages.
- Add pages to a document.
- Rearrange and delete pages.
- Change the size of pages.
- Create sections and specify page numbering.
- Lay out document pages.
- Prepare to print to the edge of the paper.
- Rotate a document page.

 This lesson will take approximately 90 minutes to complete.

Please log in to your account on peachpit.com to download the lesson files for this chapter, or go to the "Getting Started" section at the beginning of this book and follow the instructions under "Accessing the Lesson Files and Web Edition." Store the files on your computer in a convenient location.

Preserving habitat

Of the more than 400 species of birds found in the Carolinas, perhaps the most majestic are the colonial wading birds. Characterized by long legs, long necks and long, pointed bills, these charismatic and graceful denizens of shores, lagoons, and wetlands search for food—fish, frogs, and small invertebrates, such as shrimp, crabs, and crayfish.

Herons and egrets both belong to the Ardeidae family, however, there is no clear distinction between the two. In general, species that are white or have ornate plumage are called egrets. You can identify herons and egrets in flight because of their retracted necks, unlike their cousin the ibis, which flies with an outstretched neck. In the late 1800s, Great Egrets were hunted nearly to extinction for their feathers. This led to the first laws protecting endangered birds.

Amazing migration

As a result of what researchers assert is a "catastrophic drop" in the number of monarchs migrating from the northern part of the United States and Canada to Mexico, a number of conservation efforts are under way. Mexican authorities have redoubled efforts to stop illegal logging in the mountain area where the butterflies spend the winter. In August 2014, scientists from a number of organizations filed a petition with the U.S. Fish and Wildlife Service requesting that monarchs be listed as "threatened."

Perhaps the most significant efforts are being made with respect to the monarchs' most important food source and larval host—milkweed plants. The world's struggle against weeds may be succeeding, but in winning that war, the battle to save the monarch is being lost. Milkweed loss means monarch loss. Experts today are studying ways to restore milkweed growth in the areas frequented by migrating butterflies. Even citizen scientists and backyard gardeners can help by planting milkweed, but caution is also required because not every variety of milkweed is appropriate for monarch purposes.

By taking advantage of features that help you set up the publications you create, you can ensure consistent page layout, simplify your production process, and work as quickly and efficiently as possible.

Getting started

In this lesson, you'll set up an eight-page newsletter with a four-page insert and then place text and graphics on one of the document's facing-page spreads.

● **Note:** If you have not already downloaded the project files for this lesson to your computer from your Account page, make sure to do so now. See "Getting Started" at the beginning of the book.

1 To ensure that the preferences and default settings of your Adobe InDesign program match those used in this lesson, move the InDesign Defaults file to a different folder following the procedure in "Saving and restoring the InDesign Defaults file" on pages 4–5.

2 Start Adobe InDesign. To ensure that the panels and menu commands match those used in this lesson, choose Window > Workspace > [Advanced], and then choose Window > Workspace > Reset Advanced. To begin working, you'll learn how to create a new document.

● **Note:** If an alert informs you that the document contains links to sources that have been modified, click Update Links.

3 To see what the finished document looks like, open the 03_End.indd file in the Lesson03 folder, located inside the Lessons folder within the InDesign CIB folder on your hard drive. (If the Missing Fonts dialog box displays, click Sync Fonts, and then click Close after the fonts have successfully synced from Typekit.)

4 Scroll through the document to view other pages. To see the guidelines and placeholder frames on the pages, choose View > Screen Mode > Normal. Navigate back to pages 2–3, which are the only document pages you'll lay out in this lesson. You will also lay out a pair of master page spreads.

5 Close the 03_End.indd file after you have finished examining it, or you can leave this document open for reference.

Creating and saving custom document settings

InDesign lets you save frequently used document settings, including the number of pages, page size, columns, and margins. Choosing one of these saved document parameters, called document presets, when creating a new document saves time and ensures consistency.

1 Choose File > Document Presets > Define.

2 Click New in the Document Presets dialog box.

3 In the New Document dialog box, set the following:

- In the Document Preset box, type **Newsletter**.

- In the Number of Pages box, type **8**.

- Make sure that the Facing Pages option is selected.

- Use the default Page Size (Letter).

- In the Columns section, type **3** for Number, and leave the Gutter at 1p0.

- In the Margins section, make sure that the Make All Settings The Same icon in the center of the margin settings is deselected (⟨⟩) so that you can enter custom settings for each margin. Type **6p** for Top; type **4p** for the Bottom, Inside, and Outside margins.

▶ **Tip:** You can use any supported unit of measurement in any dialog box or panel. If you want to use a measurement unit that differs from the default, simply type the indicator for the unit you want to use, such as *p* for picas, *pt* for points, *cm* for centimeters, *mm* for millimeters, and either *in* or " (inch marks) for inches, after the value you enter into a box. You can change the default units by choosing Edit > Preferences > Units & Increments (Windows) or InDesign CC > Preferences > Units & Increments (macOS).

4 Click the triangle to the left of Bleed And Slug to display additional controls. Highlight or delete the text (0p0) in the Top box of the Bleed option, and then enter **.125"**. Then ensure that the Make All Settings The Same icon is selected (unbroken) so that the same value is used for the Bottom, Inside, and Outside boxes. Click inside the Bottom box and notice that InDesign automatically converts measurements expressed using other measurement units (in this

case, inches) to the pica and point equivalents. (The default Bleed value is 0p9, or one-eighth of an inch.)

The bleed values specify an area outside the perimeter of each page that can be printed and is used to print design elements, such as pictures or a colored background, that extend to the edge of the paper. The bleed area is trimmed and discarded after the printing process.

5 Click OK in both dialog boxes to save the document preset.

Creating a new document

Each time you create a new document, the New Document dialog box lets you choose a document preset as the starting point, or you can use this dialog box to specify several document settings, including the number of pages, the page size, the number of columns, and more. In this section, you'll use the Newsletter preset that you just created.

1 Choose File > New > Document.

2 In the New Document dialog box, choose the Newsletter preset, which you'll see when you click Saved at the top of the dialog box.

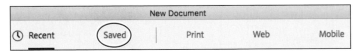

Tip: You can also create a new document based on a document preset by choosing File > Document Presets > [Preset_Name]. If you press the Shift key when selecting a preset, the New Document dialog box is bypassed and a new document that uses those presets opens.

3 Click Create.

InDesign creates a new document using all of the specifications from the document preset, including the page size, margins, columns, and number of pages.

4 Open the Pages panel by clicking its panel icon or choosing Window > Pages. If necessary, drag the bottom of the panel downward until all eight document page icons are visible.

In the Pages panel, the icon for page 1 is highlighted, and the page number below the icon is displayed within a highlighted rectangle to indicate that page 1 is currently displayed in the document window.

About page numbering

There are two kinds of page numbering in any kind of multi-page publication. One is the physical structure of the folded paper that creates the physical pages. The other is the label placed on the pages. The label, or *folio*, can have sections, begin new numbering with each section, in many possible configurations. Here we are concerned with the physical structure.

Any printed material that has a spine, such as a magazine or a book, follows a structure dictated by folding paper. The simplest example is to fold a piece of paper in half. Each resulting rectangle is a page. If you nest two folded pieces of paper into each other and staple them at the fold (the spine), you have created an 8-page booklet. The first page (the cover) of this booklet is to the right of the fold (the spine). Open the first page and you have one page to the left of the spine (or fold), page 2, and one page to the right of the spine, page 3.

When you create a document with facing pages, InDesign shows you this structure in the Pages panel. Page 1 is to the right of the center line, which represents the spine. Page 2 is to the left. All odd number pages are to the right, and all even number pages to the left. To begin a document to the left of the spine, you must enter an even number in the Start Page # box in the Document Setup dialog box.

spine
(fold)

The Pages panel is divided into two sections by a horizontal line. The upper section displays thumbnails of the document's master pages. A master page is like a background template that you can apply to any page in a document. Master pages contain elements, such as headers, footers, and page numbers, that appear on all document pages. (You'll work with master pages later in this lesson.) The lower section of the Pages panel displays thumbnails of document pages.

In this document, the default master page (which is automatically given the default name "A-Master") consists of a two-page spread of facing pages.

— Master page icon

— Document page icon

— Center line (spine)

— Letter of applied master page

Even numbered pages are left of the spine

Odd numbered pages are right of the spine

5 Choose File > Save As, name the file **03_Setup.indd**, navigate to the Lesson03 folder, and click Save.

Switching between open InDesign documents

As you work, you may want to switch between your new document and the supplied finished document for reference. If both documents are open, you can bring one or the other to the front.

▶ **Tip:** The keyboard shortcut for switching among open InDesign documents is Ctrl+` (Windows) or Command+` macOS). (The ` character is located above the Tab key.)

1 Choose the Window menu. A list of currently open InDesign documents is displayed at the bottom.

2 Choose the document you want to view. That document now appears in front. Choose the 03_Setup.indd document when you're ready to continue.

The names of all open documents are also displayed in tabs along the top of the document window, starting on the left with the first document opened. Clicking a document's name displays that document.

Working with master pages

Before you add graphics and text frames to a document, you may want to set up the master pages, which serve as backgrounds for your document pages. Any object that you add to a master page automatically appears on the document pages to which the master page has been applied.

In this document, you'll create two master page spreads—one that contains a grid of guidelines and footer information, and a second that contains placeholder frames for text and graphics. By creating multiple master pages, you allow for variation while ensuring consistent design.

Adding guides to the master page

Guides are nonprinting lines that help you lay out a document precisely. Guides placed on a master page appear on any document pages to which that master is applied. For this document, you'll add several guides that, along with the existing column guides, act as a grid to help you position graphics frames, text frames, and other objects.

▶ **Tip:** If the two pages of the master page spread are not centered in the document window, double-click the Hand tool in the Tools panel to center them.

1 In the upper section of the Pages panel, double-click the name A-Master. The master spread's left and right pages are displayed in the document window.

2 Choose View > Fit Spread In Window to display both pages of the master spread.

3 Choose Layout > Create Guides.

4 Select Preview to display your changes as you make them.

5 For the Rows option, type **4** in the Number box and **0** in the Gutter box.

6 For the Columns option, type **2** in the Number box and **0** in the Gutter box.

7 For Fit Guides To, select Margins and notice how the horizontal and vertical guides appear on your master pages, along with the margin and column guides that you established when you created the Newsletter preset.

● **Note:** *Gutter* is the term for the space between columns.

Selecting Margins instead of Page causes the guides to fit within the margin boundaries rather than the page boundaries. When you lay out document pages, you can use these guides to help you position and align objects.

8 Click OK.

Dragging guides from rulers

You can drag guides from the horizontal (top) and vertical (left side) rulers at the edge of the document window to provide additional alignment assistance on individual pages. Pressing Ctrl (Windows) or Command (macOS) while dragging a horizontal guide applies the guide to the entire spread. Pressing Alt (Windows) or Option (macOS) while dragging a guide from the horizontal ruler changes it to a vertical guide and, likewise, changes a vertical guide to a horizontal guide when dragging a guide from the vertical ruler.

In this lesson, you will place headers above the top margin of the page and footers below the bottom margin. To position the headers and footers accurately, you will manually add two horizontal guides and two vertical guides.

1 Open the Transform panel (Window > Object & Layout > Transform). Without clicking in your document, move the pointer around the document window and watch the horizontal and vertical rulers as the pointer moves. Notice how the

▶ **Tip:** Guides can also be added to a spread in a facing-page document by using the Create Guides command (Layout menu) when working on a document page rather than a master page.

▶ **Tip:** A header is text placed at the top of a page and is separate from the main body text. A header can include information such as page number, publication name, or issue date. When placed at the bottom of a page, such text is called a footer.

hairline indicators in the rulers correspond to the pointer's position. Also notice that the dimmed X and Y values in the Control panel and the Transform panel indicate the position of the pointer.

▶ **Tip:** You can also drag a ruler guide without the Ctrl or Command key and release the guide over the pasteboard to have a guide appear across all pages in a spread as well as on the pasteboard.

2 Press Ctrl (Windows) or Command (macOS) and position your pointer on the horizontal ruler anywhere above the spread. Drag a ruler guide down to 2p6. The Y value is displayed next to the pointer while you drag and is also displayed in the Y box in the Control panel and the Transform panel. Pressing Ctrl (Windows) or Command (macOS) when you create a guide causes the guide to extend across both pages of the spread, as well as across the pasteboard on either side. If you don't press Ctrl or Command, the guide will extend only across the page on which you release the mouse button.

● **Note:** The controls in the Transform panel are similar to those in the Control panel. You can use either panel to make many common modifications, such as changing position, size, scale, and angle of rotation.

3 Press Ctrl (Windows) or Command (macOS) and drag two more ruler guides from the horizontal ruler: one to 5p and the other to 63p.

4 Press Ctrl (Windows) or Command (macOS) and drag a ruler guide from the vertical ruler to the 17p8 position. Watch the X value in the Control panel as you drag. The guide snaps to the column guide at that location. If the X value doesn't display 17p8 as you drag, place the guide as close as you can, and then—with the guide still selected—highlight the X value in the Control panel or Transform panel, enter **17p8**, and then press Enter or Return.

5 Press Ctrl (Windows) or Command (macOS) and drag another guide from the vertical ruler to the 84p4 position.

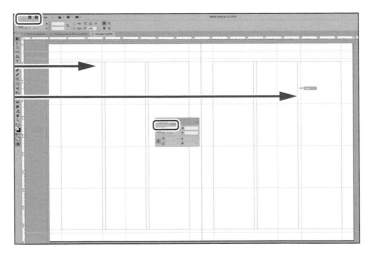

6 Close or dock the Transform panel, and then choose File > Save.

Step and repeat, paste, and delete guides

A key concept to understand about guides in InDesign is that they behave like other objects. You can use many of the same techniques with guides that you use for working with any objects. One powerful technique is Step and Repeat.

In this lesson, you step and repeat guides, copy and paste guides, and delete guides.

1 Navigate to page 6 by double-clicking the icon for page 6 in the Pages panel. Drag a guide from the vertical ruler to 3p.

2 With the Selection tool, drag across the guide to select it. When selected, the color of the guide will be darker.

3 Open the Step and Repeat dialog box (Edit > Step and Repeat). Enter **3** for the repeat count and **3p** for the Horizontal offset. Click Preview to see the changes while you work. Hold down the Shift key and click the up arrow in the Horizontal measurement four times until you get an offset of 7p, or just type **7p**. (If you don't hold down the Shift key, InDesign will change the measurement in increments of one point, or p1.) Click OK.

4 Use the Selection tool and drag across all four guides you just created to select the guides. Choose Copy from the Edit menu.

5 Double-click page 8 in the Pages panel. Choose Paste In Place from the Edit menu. The guides will be in the exact same place on page 8 as they are on page 6. This technique can be useful when you want to duplicate a design, but not on enough pages to create another master page. You can also copy and paste guides between documents.

6 If you decide to change your layout, it's often helpful to delete guides you no longer need. Again, use the Selection tool and drag across the four guides you just pasted onto page 8 to select them. Choose Edit > Clear, or press the Delete key.

Creating a text frame on the master page

Any text or graphic that you place on a master page appears on document pages to which the master is applied. To create a footer, you'll add a publication title ("Flora & Fauna of the Coastal Carolinas") and a page number marker to the bottom of the verso (left) and recto (right) pages of the document's facing-page master spread.

Note: When you draw a frame with the Type tool, the frame starts at the point of the black arrowhead that's displayed in the upper-left corner of the I-beam pointer. The arrowhead turns white when it's over a guideline.

1 Navigate to the left master page, and make sure that you can see the bottom of the page. If necessary, zoom in and use the scroll bars or Hand tool (✋).

2 Select the Type tool (T,) in the Tools panel. On the left master page, click where the two ruler guides intersect below the leftmost column and drag to create a text frame, as shown below. A white arrowhead is displayed next to the crosshair pointer when you drag over a guideline.

3 With the insertion point in the new text frame, choose Type > Insert Special Character > Markers > Current Page Number.

The letter A appears in your text frame. On document pages based on this master page, the correct page number is displayed, such as "2" on the document's page 2.

Tip: An em space is the width of the current font size. For example, when working with 12-point text, an em space is 12 points wide. The term originated in the days of metal type and described the width of the capital letter M.

4 To add an em space after the page number, right-click (Windows) or Control-click (macOS) with the insertion point in the text frame to display a context menu, and then choose Insert White Space > Em Space. Or you can choose this same command from the Type menu.

5 Type **Flora & Fauna of the Coastal Carolinas** after the em space.

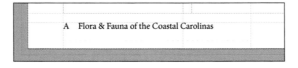

6 Click a blank area of your document window or choose Edit > Deselect All to deselect the text frame.

Next, you'll duplicate the footer on the left master page, position the copy on the right master page, and adjust the text so that it's a mirror opposite of the other footer.

7 Choose View > Fit Spread In Window to display both master pages.

Tip: If you also press the Shift key while Alt-dragging (Windows) or Option-dragging (macOS) a text frame, movement is constrained to vertical, horizontal, and 45-degree angles.

8 Using the Selection tool (▶), select the footer text frame on the left master page. Hold down the Alt key (Windows) or Option key (macOS), and drag the text frame to the right master page so that it snaps to the guides, mirroring the left master page as shown below.

9 Select the Type tool (**T**), and click anywhere inside the text frame on the right master page, creating an insertion point.

10 Click Paragraph Formatting Controls (**¶**) in the Control panel, and then click the Align Right button.

▶ **Tip:** Depending on the size of your monitor, the paragraph formatting controls in the Control panel may be visible (to the right of the character formatting controls) without having to click the Paragraph Formatting Controls button.

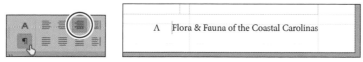

Click Paragraph Formatting Controls at the left side of the Control panel to see the alignment options.

The text is now right-aligned within the footer frame on the right master page. Now you'll modify the footer text on the right master page, placing the page number on the right side of the words "Flora & Fauna of the Coastal Carolinas."

11 Delete the em space and page number at the beginning of the footer.

12 Place the insertion point at the end of "Flora & Fauna of the Coastal Carolinas" and then choose Type > Insert White Space > Em Space. (Note: You won't see this change until you add the Current Page Number character in the next step.)

13 Choose Type > Insert Special Character > Markers > Current Page Number to insert the Current Page Number character after the em space.

Left footer and right footer.

14 Choose Edit > Deselect All, and then choose File > Save.

Renaming the master page

When a document contains multiple master pages, you may want to assign a descriptive name to each master page to make them all easier to identify. You will rename this first master page "3-column Layout."

1 Choose Window > Pages if the Pages panel is not open. Confirm that the A-Master page is still selected. Choose Master Options For "A-Master" from the Pages panel flyout menu (≡).

2 In the Name box, type **3-column Layout**, and click OK.

▶ **Tip:** In addition to changing the names of master pages, you can use the Master Options dialog box to change other properties of a master page, such as the prefix, number of pages in the master page spread, and whether or not the master page is based on another master.

Adding placeholder frames for text

▶ **Tip:** To set up a master page spread with different margin and column settings for the left and right pages, you can double-click the individual page in the master page spread and then change the selected page's settings by choosing Layout > Margins And Columns.

Each document page in the newsletter will contain text and graphics. The main text frame and graphics frame are the same on each page, so you'll create a placeholder text frame and a placeholder graphics frame on the left and right pages of the A-3-column Layout master page.

1 To center the left page in the document window, double-click the left page icon of the A-3-column Layout master in the Pages panel.

2 Select the Type tool (**T**). Click where the horizontal and vertical margin guides intersect in the upper-left corner of the page, and drag to create a text frame that extends horizontally across two columns and vertically from the top margin to the bottom margin.

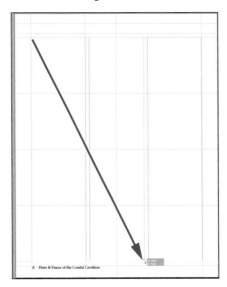

3 Double-click the right page icon of the A-3-column Layout master in the Pages panel to center it in the document window.

4 With the Type tool (**T**), create another text frame on the right page that's identical to the text frame you just created on the left page. Make sure the upper-left corner of the frame aligns with the intersection of the margin guides in the upper-left corner of the page.

5 Click a blank area of the page or pasteboard, or choose Edit > Deselect All.

6 Choose File > Save.

Adding placeholder frames for graphics

You have now created placeholder text frames for the main text on each page. Next, you'll add two graphics frames to the A-3-column Layout master. Similar to the text frames you created, these frames act as placeholders for graphics you'll later place on document pages, helping you to maintain a consistent design.

Although the Rectangle tool (▢) and the Rectangle Frame tool (⊠) are more or less interchangeable, the Rectangle Frame tool, which includes nonprinting diagonal lines within, is commonly used to create placeholders for graphics.

1 Select the Rectangle Frame tool (⊠) in the Tools panel.

2 Position the crosshair pointer at the intersection of the top margin guide and the right margin guide on the right page.

Drag down and to the left to create a frame that extends horizontally one column width and vertically to the next ruler guide below.

3 Create an identical placeholder graphics frame in the same position on the left page.

4 Use the Selection tool to click a blank area of the page or pasteboard, or choose Edit > Deselect All.

5 Choose File > Save.

● **Note:** It's not necessary to add placeholder frames to every document you create. For example, one-page documents, such as posters, business cards, and ads, may not benefit from master pages and placeholder frames.

Creating an additional master page

▶ Tip: The ability to create parent/child master pages is ideal for publications like newsletters and magazines with folios that include the date of publication. Each time you create a new publication, begin by changing the date on the parent master page, which automatically changes the date on all children master pages.

You can create multiple master pages within a document. You can build them independently or base one master page on another master page. If you base a master page on another master, any change made to the parent master is automatically applied to the child master.

For instance, the A-3-column Layout master page is useful for most pages in the newsletter and can be used as the basis for another set of master pages that share key layout elements, such as margins and the current page number character.

To accommodate different layouts, you will create a separate master page spread that uses a two-column format, and then you'll modify the two-column layout.

1 In the Pages panel, choose New Master from the Pages panel flyout menu.

2 In the Name box, type **2-column Layout**.

3 From the Based On Master menu, choose A-3-column Layout, and click OK.

 Notice that the letter A is displayed on the B-2-column Layout master page thumbnails at the top of the Pages panel. This letter indicates that the A-3-column Layout master serves as the foundation for the B-2-column Layout master. If you were to change the A-3-column Layout master, the changes would also be reflected in the B-2-column Layout master. You may also notice that you cannot easily select objects, such as the footer frames, from parent master pages. You'll learn about selecting and overriding master page items later in this lesson.

● Note: If all of the master page icons are not visible in the Pages panel, click the horizontal bar that separates the master page icons from document page icons and drag down until the other master page icons are visible.

4 Choose Layout > Margins And Columns.

5 In the Margins And Columns dialog box, set the number of columns to **2**, and then click OK.

Overriding master items

The document pages that will use the two-column layout do not require placeholder frames, which means that only the footer text frames and the ruler guides from the A-3-column Layout master are required. Next, you'll remove the placeholder frames from the B-2-column Layout master.

1 Using the Selection tool (▶), click within the graphics frame on the left page of the B-2-column Layout master. Nothing happens. Because this frame is inherited from the parent master, you can't select it with a simple click.

2 Hold down Shift+Ctrl (Windows) or Shift+Command (macOS), and then click within the graphics frame. The frame is now selected, and you have overridden its status as a master item. Press Backspace or Delete to delete the frame.

3 Use the same method to delete the placeholder graphics frame on the right page, as well as the placeholder text frame on the left and right pages.

4 Choose File > Save.

▶ **Tip:** To override multiple master page items, hold down Shift+Ctrl (Windows) or Shift+Command (macOS) and with the Selection tool, drag a marquee around the objects you want to override.

Modifying a parent master

To complete your work laying out the newsletter's master pages, you'll add several header elements to the top of the A-3-column Layout master and another footer element to the right page. Then you'll view the B-2-column Layout master and see how the new objects are automatically added to that master page spread.

Rather than manually laying out the additional header and footer frames, you'll import a *snippet*. A snippet is a file that contains InDesign objects, including their location relative to one another on a page or spread, and can be imported into a layout with the Place command (File menu) the same way you import graphic files. InDesign lets you export selected objects as a snippet file and place snippets into documents. (You'll use snippets again later in this lesson, and you'll learn more about snippets in Lesson 10, "Importing and Modifying Graphics.")

1 Double-click the name of the A-3-column Layout master in the Pages panel to display the spread.

2 Choose File > Place. Open the Links folder in the Lesson03 folder, located inside the Lessons folder within the InDesign CIB folder. Click the file named Snippet1.idms, and then click Open.

3 Position the loaded snippet icon (⌐) outside the upper-left corner of the spread, where the red bleed guides meet. Click to place the snippet.

● **Note:** You'll learn more about creating and modifying text frames, graphics frames, and other kinds of objects in Lesson 4, "Working with Objects."

Tip: To create a snippet, select one or more objects on a page or spread. Choose File > Export, and then choose InDesign Snippet from the Save As Type menu (Windows) or the Format menu (macOS). Choose the location of the file, assign a name, and then click Save.

The snippet places a header at the top of each page, as well as an imported graphic at the bottom of the right page. Each header includes an empty blue graphics frame and a text frame with white placeholder text.

4　Double-click the name of the B-2-column Layout master in the Pages panel. Notice how the new elements you just applied to the A-3-column Layout master have been automatically applied to this child master.

Tip: The parent–child master structure enables you to quickly apply design changes to common elements, without having to make the same change to several items.

5　Navigate back to the A-3-column Layout master. Click the left blue graphics frame to select it. Open the Swatches panel, and click the green swatch. Now navigate to the B-2-column Layout master in the Pages panel again, and see that the color of the left header box is now green as well.

6　Choose File > Save.

Applying master pages to document pages

Now that you have created all of the master pages, it's time to apply them to the pages in the document. By default, all of the document pages are formatted with the A-3-column Layout master. You will apply the B-2-column Layout master to

several pages in the newsletter, and then you'll apply the None master page to the cover page, which doesn't require header or footer information and thus does not require a master page.

You can apply master pages to document pages by dragging master page icons onto document page icons in the Pages panel or by using an option in the Pages panel menu.

▶ **Tip:** In large documents, you may find it easier to display the page icons horizontally in the Pages panel. To do this, choose View Pages > Horizontally from the Pages panel flyout menu.

1 Double-click the name of the B-2-column Layout master in the Pages panel. Make sure that all master pages and document pages are visible in the panel.

2 Drag either the highlighted master page name or the accompanying spread icon of the B-2-column Layout master onto the icon of document page 4. When page 4 is displayed with a black border, indicating it's the page to which the selected master will be applied, release the mouse button.

3 Drag either the highlighted master page name or the accompanying spread icon of the B-2-column Layout master onto the icon of document page 5 and then onto document page 8.

4 Double-click the page numbers 4–5 (below the page icons) in the Pages panel to display this spread. Notice that the two pages of this spread have the two-column layout of the applied master page, as well as the header and footer elements that you placed on the parent master page. Also notice that the correct page numbers are displayed on each page as a result of the Current Page Number characters you placed on the A-3-column Layout master page spread.

5 Double-click the icon for document page 1. Because it's based on the A-3-column Layout master, it includes header and footer elements, which aren't required on the cover of the newsletter.

6 Choose Apply Master To Pages from the Pages panel flyout menu. In the Apply Master dialog box, choose [None] from the Apply Master menu and make sure that 1 is the page number in the To Pages box. Click OK.

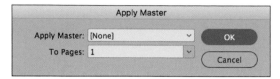

7 Choose File > Save.

Adding new document pages

You can add new pages to your existing document. Next, you'll add six additional pages to your newsletter. Later in this lesson, you'll use four of these pages for a "special section" within your newsletter that uses a different page size and separate page numbering.

1 In the Pages panel flyout menu, choose Insert Pages.

2 In the Insert Pages dialog box, type **6** in the Pages box, choose After Page from the Insert menu, and enter **4** in the accompanying (page number) box, and then choose [None] from the Master menu.

3 Click OK. Six blank pages are added in the middle of the document. Lengthen the Pages panel so that you can see as many document pages as possible.

Rearranging and deleting document pages

You can use the Pages panel to rearrange the sequence of pages and delete extra pages.

1 In the Pages panel, click page 12 to select it. Notice that it's based on the A-3-column Layout master. Drag the page 12 icon upward onto the icon for page 11, which is based on the B-2-column Layout master. When the small arrow inside the hand is pointing to the right, indicating that page 11 will be "pushed" in that direction, release the mouse button.

Notice that page 11 is now based on the A-3-column Layout master, and the page that had previously been page 11 is now page 12. Pages 13 and 14 remain unchanged.

2 Click page 5, and then press the Shift key and click page 6.

3 Click the Delete Selected Pages button icon (🗑) at the bottom of the panel. Pages 5 and 6 are deleted from the document, leaving it with 12 pages.

4 Choose File > Save.

Changing the size of pages

Next, you'll create an insert within the newsletter by changing the size of four pages in a "special section" of the publication. You'll then quickly lay out the two spreads that make up this section.

1 Select the Page tool (▢). Click page 5 in the Pages panel, and then press the Shift key and click page 8. The icons for pages 5–8 are highlighted in the panel. These are the pages whose size you will change.

2 In the Control panel, enter **36p** in the Width box; enter **25p6** in the Height box. Press Enter or Return each time you enter a value to apply it to the selected pages. (These values produce a 6" x 4.25" insert—the size of a standard postcard.)

3 Double-click page 4 in the Pages panel, and then choose View > Fit Spread In Window. Notice that the spread now contains pages of unequal size.

4 Use the Page tool to select pages 5–8 in the Pages panel.

5 To set new margin and column guides for the selected pages, choose Layout > Margins And Columns to display the Margins And Columns dialog box. In the Margins section, make sure that the Make All Settings The Same icon (🔳) in the center is selected (unbroken) so that you can enter one setting for all four margins. Enter **1p6** in the Top box. In the Columns section, enter **1** in the Number box, and then click OK.

6 Choose File > Save.

Adding sections to change page numbering

The special section you just created will use its own page-numbering system. You can use different kinds of page numbering within a document by creating sections. Next, you'll start a new section on the first page of the special section, and then you'll adjust the page numbering of the subsequent newsletter pages so that they're numbered correctly.

1 Choose the Selection tool (▶). In the Pages panel, double-click the page 5 icon to select and display it.

2 Choose Numbering & Section Options from the Pages panel flyout menu, or choose Layout > Numbering > Section Options. In the New Section dialog box, make sure that Start Section and Start Page Numbering At are selected and that the Start Page Numbering At value is 1.

3 Choose i, ii, iii, iv… from the Style menu in the Page Numbering section of the dialog box. Click OK.

The triangle above the page i page icon indicates the start of a section.

4 Examine the page icons in the Pages panel. Starting with the fifth document page, the numbers below the page icons now appear as Roman numerals. The numbers in the footers of the remaining document pages that contain footers also appear as Roman numerals.

Now you'll specify for the document to use Arabic numerals for the newsletter pages that follow the special section and to continue the numbering from the page prior to the first page of the special section (page 4).

5 Select page v in the Pages panel by clicking its icon once.

6 Choose Numbering & Section Options from the Pages panel flyout menu.

7 In the New Section dialog box, make sure that Start Section is selected.

8 Select Start Page Numbering At and specify a value of **5** in the accompanying box to start section numbering on page 5 and resume the numbering of the document pages (1–4) that precede the special section.

9 Make sure that 1, 2, 3, 4… is selected in the Style menu, and then click OK.

● **Note:** Single-clicking a master page icon or a document page icon targets the page for editing purposes but does not cause that page to be displayed in the document window. If you want to navigate to a page, double-click its icon in the Pages panel.

Now your pages are correctly renumbered. Notice that a small triangle is displayed above pages 1, i, and 5 in the Pages panel, indicating the start of a new section. In this document, the page numbering at page 5 continues the numbering from the first section, but the numbering could be another pattern. The important point to note is that whenever you see the triangle above a page in the Pages panel, it indicates a section change, regardless of the particular numbering pattern in that file.

10 Choose File > Save.

Overriding master page items and placing text and graphics

Now that the framework of the 12-page publication (the eight-page guide and four-page insert) is in place, you're ready to lay out document pages. To see how the work you've done setting up the document's master pages affects the document pages, you'll add text and graphics to the spread on pages 2 and 3. You'll learn more about creating and modifying objects in Lesson 4, so for this lesson, we've simplified the layout process to minimize your work.

1 Choose File > Save As, name the file **03_Newsletter.indd**, navigate to the Lesson03 folder, and click Save.

2 In the Pages panel, double-click the page 2 icon (not page ii), and then choose View > Fit Spread In Window.

 Notice that because the A-3-column Layout master is assigned to pages 2 and 3, these pages include the guides, headers and footers, and placeholder frames from the A-3-column Layout master.

 To import text and graphics created with other applications, such as a text file from Microsoft Word or an image from Adobe Photoshop, you use the Place command.

3 Choose File > Place. If necessary, open the Links folder in the Lesson03 folder, located inside the Lessons folder within the InDesign CIB folder. Click the Article1.txt file, and then Ctrl-click (Windows) or Command-click (macOS) Article2.txt, Graphic1.jpg, and Graphic2.jpg to select these four files. Click Open.

 The pointer changes to a loaded text icon (⌷), with a preview of the first few lines of the Article1.txt text file that you are placing.

● **Note:** Parentheses are displayed when InDesign recognizes a preexisting frame beneath the loaded text icon or the loaded graphics icon when importing text or graphics into a layout. If you click within an existing frame, InDesign uses that frame rather than creating a new text or graphics frame.

4 Position the loaded text icon over the placeholder text frame on page 2, and then click to place the Article1.txt text into the frame. Notice the (4) after the loaded text icon, indicating that you have loaded four items to place.

5 To place the three remaining files, click within the text frame on page 3 to place the Article2.docx text, click within the graphics frame on page 2 to place Graphic1.jpg, and click within the graphics frame on page 3 to place Graphic2.jpg.

6 Choose Edit > Deselect All.

You'll import a snippet to complete the layout of the spread.

7 Choose File > Place. Click the Snippet2.idms file, and then click Open.

8 Position the loaded snippet icon () outside the upper-left corner of the spread, where the red bleed guides meet. Click to place the snippet.

9 Choose Edit > Deselect all, or click an empty area of the page or pasteboard to deselect all objects.

10 Choose File > Save.

Next, you'll override two master items on your spread—the two text frames that contain the header text—and then replace the placeholder text with new text.

Replacing placeholder text

1 Select the Type tool (T.). Hold down Shift+Ctrl (Windows) or Shift+Command (macOS), and then click within the placeholder text frame on page 2 that contains "Placeholder Text." Replace the placeholder text with **Egrets and Herons**.

2 Repeat step 1 to change the header text on page 3 to **Monarch Butterflies**.

3 Choose Edit > Deselect All.

4 Choose File > Save.

Printing to the edge of the paper: using the bleed guides

A very important concept to keep in mind when setting up a document is whether any elements will print all the way to the edge of the paper. If so, you need to account for how that is accomplished in commercial printing. The bleed guides that we set up in the newsletter template are there to enable you to do that.

Pages are printed on larger paper, not single sheets as is familiar on an office printer. For example, the pages could be 2-up as on a small digital press, or 8-up on a typical large offset press. Throughout the printing process, tolerances are built in to allow for slight variations, and one of those tolerances is bleed. Sheets of printed material are cut in large stacks, and even with a very sharp blade, it's impossible to cut exactly to the edge of an image hundreds or thousands of times. So to get a perfect edge every time, allowing for the mechanics of cutting paper in stacks, any artwork that will print to the edge must actually extend past where the blade will cut the printed sheet.

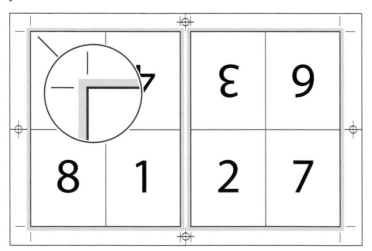

Diagram of a press sheet. The pink line is where the blade will cut the piece to the final size. The blue represents the bleed. Notice that the bleed extends past where the blade will cut.

To create a finished piece with photos or other elements that print right to the edge of the page, you actually must extend those items past where the blade will cut the sheet to the final size. That produces a clean edge because the blade cuts through printed image, not unprinted paper. It's best to do this while you are building a file because you may have a photo or other art that is not big enough to extend past the page edge, and it's better to deal with that early in the process. You will now learn how to check that items extend sufficiently beyond the page edge, and fix them if they do not.

1 Using the Selection tool (▶), double-click the page 2 icon in the Pages panel to display it.

2 Choose View > Screen Mode > Normal and focus on the red bleed guides.

3 First look at the bottom photos on the left and right. Notice that the photo on the left of the eggs in the nest extends to the red bleed guide, which means there is enough image to get a clean edge when the paper is cut.

4 Now look at the photo of the butterfly on the right. See that the box ends exactly at the edge of the page. This needs to be extended at least up to the red bleed guide. Click this photo with the Selection tool. Pull the right handle farther to the right to make the picture box big enough to meet or pass the red bleed guide.

Close-up of butterfly image with no bleed: image ends at the page edge.

Image extending past the bleed guide.

5 Next look across the top of the spread. See how the green graphics frame on the left is lower than the blue graphics frame on the right. Click it with the Selection tool. You won't be able to select it since this item is on a master spread. Navigate to the A-3-column Layout master by clicking it in the Pages panel. Now you can select the green box. Pull the center handle upwards to make the box bigger. Stop either at the red bleed guide or slightly past it.

6 Navigate back to page 2 and notice that the green box is now big enough to bleed off the top. Every document page that uses this master page will now bleed correctly without you having to fix each one.

7 Choose File > Save.

Viewing the completed spread

At this point you're ready to hide guides and frames and see what the completed spread looks like.

▶ **Tip:** To hide all panels, including the Tools panel and Control panel, press Tab. Press Tab again to redisplay all panels. (You can't do this when you're working with text using the Type tool.)

1 Choose View > Fit Spread In Window, and hide any panels if necessary.

2 Choose View > Screen Mode > Preview to hide the pasteboard and all guides, grids, and frame edges. Preview is the closest onscreen view that best shows how the pages will look when printed and trimmed to size.

You have formatted enough of the 12-page document to see how adding objects to the master pages helps you maintain a consistent design throughout your document.

3 Choose File > Save.

Congratulations. You have finished the lesson.

Rotating spreads

In some cases, you may want to rotate a page or spread to make it easier to view and work on its content. For example, a standard-sized magazine with portrait-oriented pages might require a calendar page with a landscape orientation. You could lay out such a page by rotating all objects 90 degrees, but then you would have to turn your head or rotate your monitor to modify the layout and edit text. To make editing easier, you can rotate—and unrotate—spreads. For an example of this feature, open the 03_End.indd document in the Lesson03 folder (if it's not already open).

1 In the Pages panel, double-click page 4 to display it in the document window.

2 Choose View > Fit Page In Window to center the page within the document window.

3 Choose View > Rotate Spread > 90° CW, and then choose View > Fit Spread In Window.

After you rotate the spread (clockwise), it's easier to work with the objects on the page.

4 Choose View > Rotate Spread > Clear Rotation.

5 Close the document without saving changes.

Exploring on your own

▶ **Tip:** Choose View > Screen Mode > Normal to return to your normal display as you explore on your own.

A good way to reinforce the skills you've learned in this lesson is to experiment with them. Try some of the following exercises. They'll give you more practice with InDesign techniques.

1 Place another photograph in the third column on page 3. Use the GraphicExtra. jpg image inside the Links folder in the Lesson03 folder. After you click Open in the Place dialog box, click where the horizontal ruler guide intersects with the left margin of the third column. Hold down the Shift key and drag until the frame is as wide as the column, and then release the mouse button. Choose Object > Fitting > Fill Frame Proportionally.

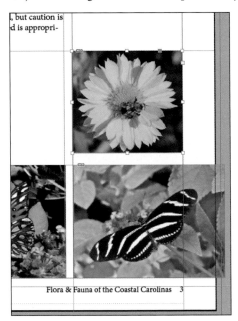

2 Create another master page for the document. Base it on the A-3-column Layout master, name it **C-4-column Layout**, and then modify it so that it contains four columns instead of three. Apply the new master page to any of the document's full-sized pages that don't contain objects (1 or 5–8).

Review questions

1 What are the advantages of adding objects to master pages?

2 How do you change the page-numbering scheme within a document?

3 How do you select a master page item on a document page?

4 What's the advantage of basing a new master page on an existing master page?

5 How do you override a master page item?

6 How do you handle items that print to the edge of the paper?

Review answers

1 By adding objects such as guides, footers, and placeholder frames to master pages, you can maintain a consistent layout on the pages to which the master is applied.

2 In the Pages panel, select the page icon where you want new page numbering to begin. Then, choose Numbering & Section Options from the Pages panel flyout menu, or choose Layout > Numbering > Section Options and specify the new page-numbering scheme.

3 Hold down Shift+Ctrl (Windows) or Shift+Command (macOS), and then click the object to override it from the master page and select it. You can then edit, delete, or manipulate the object.

4 By basing a new master page on an existing master page, you create a parent–child relationship between the new master page and the existing one. Any changes you make to the parent master page are automatically applied to the child master.

5 Hold down Shift+Ctrl (Windows) or Shift+Command (macOS), and then click the item you want to change.

6 Items that will print up to the edge of paper must extend past the edge of the page in the file and into the pasteboard area. The bleed guides show the minimum amount they must extend.

4 WORKING WITH OBJECTS

Lesson Overview

In this lesson, you'll learn how to do the following:

- Work with layers.
- Create and edit text frames and graphics frames.
- Import graphics into graphics frames.
- Crop, move, and scale graphics.
- Adjust the space between frames.
- Add captions to graphics frames.
- Place and link graphics frames.
- Change the shape of frames.
- Wrap text around an object or graphic.
- Create complex frame shapes.
- Convert frame shapes to other shapes.
- Modify and align objects.
- Select and modify multiple objects.
- Add arrowheads to a line.
- Create a QR code.

 This lesson will take approximately 90 minutes.

Please log in to your account on peachpit.com to download the lesson files for this chapter, or go to the "Getting Started" section at the beginning of this book and follow the instructions under "Accessing the Lesson Files and Web Edition." Store the files on your computer in a convenient location.

InDesign frames can contain text, graphics, or color. As you work with frames, you'll discover that Adobe InDesign provides you with a great amount of flexibility and control over your design.

Getting started

In this lesson, you'll work on a pair of spreads that make up a four-page newsletter. You'll add text and images and make several modifications to the objects on the two spreads.

1 To ensure that the preferences and default settings of your Adobe InDesign program match those used in this lesson, move the InDesign Defaults file to a different folder following the procedure in "Saving and restoring the InDesign Defaults file" on pages 4–5.

2 Start Adobe InDesign. To ensure that the panels and menu commands match those used in this lesson, choose Window > Workspace > [Advanced], and then choose Window > Workspace > Reset Advanced. To begin working, you'll open an InDesign document that is already partially completed.

● **Note:** If an alert is displayed when you open the sample document, click Update Links.

3 Choose File > Open, and open the 04_Start.indd file in the Lesson04 folder, located inside the Lessons folder within the InDesignCIB folder on your hard drive. (If the Missing Fonts dialog box displays, click Sync Fonts, and then click Close after the fonts have successfully synced from Typekit. If the Update Links message displays, click Update Links.)

4 Choose File > Save As, rename the file **04_Objects.indd**, and save it in the Lesson04 folder.

● **Note:** As you work through the lesson, move panels or change the zoom level to a magnification that works best for you.

5 To see what the finished document looks like, open the 04_End.indd file in the same folder. You can leave this document open to act as a guide as you work. When you're ready to resume working on the lesson document, choose Window > 04_Objects.indd or click its tab at the top of the document window.

The newsletter that you will work on in this lesson contains two spreads: The spread on the left contains page 4 (the back page on the left) and page 1 (the cover on the right); the spread on the right contains pages 2 and 3 (the center spread). Keep this page arrangement in mind as you navigate from page to page. Here you see the finished newsletter.

Working with layers

Before you begin creating and modifying objects, you should understand how layers work in InDesign. By default, every new InDesign document contains one layer (named Layer 1). You can rename this layer and add more layers at any time as you work on a document. Placing objects on different layers lets you organize them for easy selection and editing. In the Layers panel, you can select, display, edit, and print different layers individually, in groups, or all together.

Tip: Turn on Paste Remembers Layers, found in the Layers Panel flyout menu. When you copy and paste items to a different page or a different document, the layer structure remains intact rather than all items pasting onto the topmost layer.

About layers

Think of layers as transparent sheets stacked on top of each other. When you create an object, you can place it on the layer of your choice, and you can move objects between layers. Each layer contains its own set of objects.

The Layers panel (Window > Layers) displays a list of a document's layers and lets you create, manage, and delete layers. The Layers panel also lets you display the names of all objects on a layer and show, hide, or lock individual objects. Click the triangle to the left of a layer name to alternately display and hide the names of the objects on the layer.

The order displayed in the layer panel is the stacking order in the file. The topmost layer in the panel is the topmost layer in the file, and so on. The objects within each layer follow the same logic. One way to move an object in front of (above) or behind (below) another object is to move it up or down in the Layers panel.

By using multiple layers, you can create and edit specific areas or kinds of content in your document without affecting other areas or kinds of content. For example, you can drag-select and move items on one layer without affecting other items, such as selecting and moving text boxes without moving the backgrounds. Another example: If a document prints slowly because it contains many large graphics, you can use one layer for only the text in the document; then, when it's time to proofread the text, you can hide all other layers and quickly print only the Text layer. You can also use layers to display alternate design ideas for the same layout or different versions of an advertisement for different regions.

The 04_Objects.indd document has two layers. You'll experiment with these layers to learn how the arrangement of the layers and the placement of objects on layers can affect the design of your document, and you'll add a new layer.

1 Click the Layers panel icon or choose Window > Layers to open the Layers panel.

2 If the Text layer is not selected in the Layers panel, click to select it. The layer is highlighted to indicate that it's selected. Notice that a pen icon (✏) appears to the right of the layer name. The pen icon indicates that this layer is the target layer, and while it's selected, anything you import or create is placed on this layer.

3 Click the small triangle to the left of the Text layer name. All the groups and objects on this layer are now displayed below the layer name. Use the panel's scroll bar to view the names in the list, and then click the triangle again to hide them.

4 Click the eye icon (👁) to the far left of the Graphics layer name. All the objects on the Graphics layer are hidden. The eye icon lets you hide or display individual layers. When you turn off the visibility of a layer, the eye disappears. Click the empty box again to display the layer contents.

Click to hide layer contents.

The spread with the Graphics layer hidden.

5 Use the Zoom tool (🔍) to zoom in on the dark blue frame on the front page (page 1).

6 Using the Selection tool (▶), move the pointer within the Yield sign graphic. Notice the blue frame edge on the graphics frame. This blue border indicates that the frame is on the Text layer, which has been assigned a blue color. A transparent doughnut shape, otherwise known as the content grabber, is displayed in the center of the frame. When you move the pointer within the content grabber, it changes to a hand.

Click and drag when the arrow pointer is displayed to move the frame along with the graphic.

Click and drag when the hand pointer is displayed to move only the graphic within the frame.

▶ **Tip:** Frames are also called "Containers" and the graphic within "Content." You can choose the content when you have the container selected and vica versa: go to Object >Select.

7 Now move the pointer within the circular graphics frame below the Yield sign. Notice that this frame's edge is red, the color assigned to the Graphics layer.

8 Move the pointer back to the frame with the Yield sign, make sure the arrow pointer is displayed, and then click within the graphics frame to select it.

In the Layers panel, you'll notice that the Text layer is selected, and a small blue square appears to the right of the layer name. This indicates that the selected object belongs to this layer. You can move objects from one layer to another by dragging this square between layers in the panel.

9 In the Layers panel, drag the small blue square from the Text layer up to the Graphics layer, and then release the mouse button. The image now belongs to the Graphics layer and is now the topmost object on the top layer. Notice that the small square in the Layers panel turns red, corresponding to the layer color.

▶ **Tip:** To see the position of the Yield sign in the Graphics layer relative to other objects in the layer, expand the Graphics layer by clicking the triangle to the left of the layer name. The topmost item in the list is the topmost item in the layer.

Select the image and drag its icon in the Layers panel.

Result.

10 Note that the Object > Arrange commands operate within each layer, and not between layers. To see this in action, choose Object > Arrange > Send To Back. The Yield sign does not move behind the blue background as you expect. This is because the Yield sign is on the Graphics layer, which is above the Text layer that contains the blue box. Now move the small red square in the Layers panel back to the Text layer and choose Object > Arrange > Send To Back again. Now the Yield sign moves behind the blue box because they are on the same layer. To move the Yield sign back to the Graphics layer, choose Edit > Undo twice.

Creating and reordering layers

1 Click the empty layer lock box to the left of the Graphics layer to lock the layer.

2 Choose View > Fit Spread In Window.

Next, you will make a new layer and move existing content to it.

3 At the bottom of the Layers panel, click the Create New Layer button (▤). Because the Graphics layer was selected when you created the new layer, the new layer is positioned above the Graphics layer in the Layers panel.

► **Tip:** You can also rename a layer by selecting the layer in the Layers panel and then clicking its name.

4 Double-click the name of the new layer (Layer 3) to open the Layer Options dialog box. Change the name to **Background**, and click OK.

5 In the Layers panel, drag the Background layer to the bottom of the layer stack. A horizontal line appears when you move the pointer below the Text layer, indicating that the layer will be moved to the bottom when you release the mouse button.

 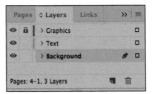

Move items to the Background layer

Now you'll move the background colored boxes to the Background layer and lock that layer so that you can work with objects on the Text and Graphics layers without accidentally selecting or moving the backgrounds.

1 Choose View > Fit Spread In Window. Click the light blue background on the left-hand page with the Selection Tool (▶).

2 In the Layers panel, drag the blue square down from the Text layer to the Background layer.

3 Navigate to the next spread (pages 2–3) by clicking the Next Spread arrow in the lower left of the document window.

4 Select both the green box on the left and the blue box on the right by dragging a small area starting in the pasteboard above where the two boxes meet, down and across a small section of each box. This is a quick way to select multiple items while being careful not to select too many items.

5 In the Layers panel, drag the blue square down to the Background layer, moving both items to the Background layer at the same time.

6 Click the lock box to the left of the Background layer.

7 Choose File > Save.

Creating and modifying text frames

In most cases, text is placed inside a frame. (You can also use the Type On A Path tool [✎] to flow text along a path.) The size and location of a text frame determine where the text appears on a page. Text frames can be created with the Type tool and can be modified using a variety of tools—as you'll do in this part of the lesson.

Creating and resizing text frames

Now you'll create your own text frame, adjust its size, and then resize another frame.

1 In the Pages panel, double-click the icon for page 4 to center it in the document window.

2 In the Layers panel, click the Text layer to select it. Any content created when the Text layer is selected will be placed on that layer.

3 Select the Type tool (T) in the Tools panel. Position the pointer where the left edge of the first column meets the horizontal guide at 3p0 on the vertical ruler. Drag to create a frame that snaps to the right edge of the second column and has a height of about 8p.

4 Use the Zoom tool (🔍) to magnify the text frame, and then select the Type tool.

5 In the new text frame, type **Customer**, press Shift+Enter (Windows) or Shift+Return (macOS) to create a forced line break (without creating a new paragraph), and then type **Testimonials**. Click anywhere within the text to select the paragraph.

Now you'll apply a paragraph style to the text.

▶ **Tip:** It isn't necessary to highlight an entire paragraph before applying a paragraph style to it. You can select a paragraph by clicking anywhere within it.

6 Click the Paragraph Styles panel icon (◨) or choose Type > Paragraph Styles to open the panel. Click the style named Testimonials to apply it to the selected paragraph.

Read more about paragraph styles in Lesson 9, "Working with Styles."

7 Using the Selection tool (▶), double-click the center-bottom handle of the selected text frame to fit the frame to the text vertically.

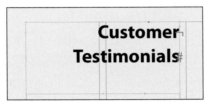

Double-click to fit the frame to its content.

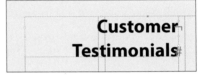

Result.

8 Choose View > Fit Spread In Window, and then press Z to temporarily access the Zoom tool and magnify the rightmost column on the front page (page 1). Use the Selection tool (▶) to select the text frame below "the BUZZ." The frame contains the text "NEW Day & Evening Classes."

The red plus sign (+) at the lower-right corner of the text frame indicates that the frame contains overset text. Overset text is not visible because the frame is too small to display it. You'll fix this by changing the size and shape of the text frame.

9 Drag the center-bottom handle of the selected text frame downward to resize the height of the frame until the bottom edge snaps to the ruler guide at 48p0 on the vertical ruler. When the pointer approaches the ruler guide, the arrows change in appearance from black to white, indicating that the frame edge is about to snap to the guide. The text remains overset. You'll fix that later in this lesson.

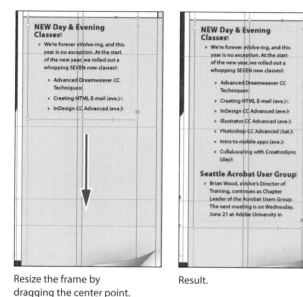

Resize the frame by dragging the center point.

Result.

10 Choose Edit > Deselect All, and then choose File > Save.

Reshaping a text frame

So far, you've resized a text frame with the Selection tool by dragging a handle. Now you'll reshape the frame using the Direct Selection tool to move one of the frame's anchor points.

1 In the Tools panel, select the Direct Selection tool (▷), and then click within the text frame you just resized. Four very small anchor points now appear at the corners of the selected text frame. The anchor points are all hollow, indicating that none of them is selected.

Tip: To resize a text frame and the text characters inside it simultaneously, select the frame, and then double-click the Scale tool (⊞), which is combined with the Free Transform, Rotate, and Shear tools in the Tools panel. You can then specify values in the Scale dialog box. You can also choose the Selection tool, hold down Shift+Ctrl (Windows) or Shift+Command (macOS), and drag a text frame handle. Including the Shift key ensures that the object and content are scaled proportionally.

2 Select the anchor point at the lower-left corner of the text frame, and pause for a moment until the arrow pointer turns black. Drag straight down until the point touches the margin guide at the bottom of the page and release the mouse button. As you drag, the text reflows simultaneously to give you a real-time view. After you release the mouse button, notice that the overset text indicator (the red plus sign) is no longer displayed, and all of the story's text is now visible.

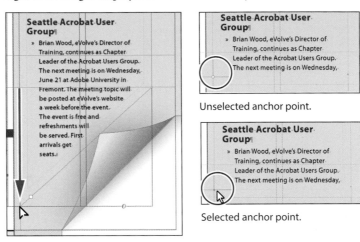

Unselected anchor point.

Selected anchor point.

Be sure to drag only the anchor point—if you drag just above or to the right of the anchor point, you'll move other corners of the text frame, too. If you accidentally move the frame, choose Edit > Undo Move and try again.

3 Press the V key to switch to the Selection tool.

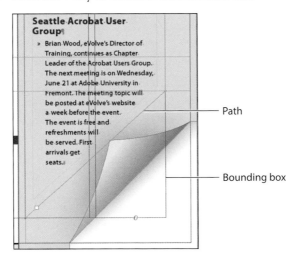

Path

Bounding box

4 Deselect all objects, and then choose File > Save.

Using Smart Guides

The Smart Guides feature gives you great flexibility in precisely creating and positioning objects. With Smart Guides, you can snap objects to the edges and centers of other objects, to the vertical and horizontal centers of pages, and to the midpoints of columns and gutters. Plus, Smart Guides appear dynamically as you work to provide instant visual feedback.

You can enable four Smart Guide options in the Guides & Pasteboard preferences (Edit > Preferences > Guides & Pasteboard [Windows] or InDesign CC > Preferences > Guides & Pasteboard [macOS]):

- **Align To Object Center.** Causes object edges to snap to the center of other objects on a page or spread when you create or move an object.
- **Align To Object Edges.** Causes object edges to snap to the edge of other objects on a page or spread when you create or move an object.
- **Smart Dimensions.** Causes the width, height, or rotation of an object to snap to the dimensions of other objects on a page or spread when you create, resize, or rotate an object.
- **Smart Spacing.** Lets you quickly arrange objects so that the space between them is equal.

The Smart Guides command (View > Grids & Guides > Smart Guides) lets you turn Smart Guides on and off. You can also enable/disable Smart Guides from the View Options menu in the Application bar. Smart Guides are enabled by default.

To familiarize yourself with Smart Guides, create a new multicolumn one-page document. (In the New Document dialog box, specify a value greater than 1 in the Columns Number field.)

1 In the Tools panel, select the Rectangle Frame tool (⊠). Click the left margin guide and drag to the right margin. As the pointer moves across the page, notice that a guide is displayed when the pointer reaches the middle of a column, the midpoint within a gutter, and the vertical center of the page. Release the mouse button when a Smart Guide appears.

2 With the Rectangle Frame tool still selected, click the top margin guide and drag downward to the bottom margin. Notice that when the pointer reaches the top edge, center, and bottom edge of the first object you created, as well as the horizontal center of the page, a Smart Guide appears.

3 In an empty area of the page, create one more object with the Rectangle Frame tool. Drag the mouse slowly and watch carefully. Smart Guides appear when the pointer reaches the edge or center of any other objects. Also, when the height or width of the new object equals the height or width of either of the other two objects, a vertical or horizontal (or both) line with arrows at both ends appears next to the object you're creating and the object with the matching height or width.

4 Close the document without saving changes.

Creating multi-column text frames

Now you'll take an existing text frame and convert it to a multiple-column text frame.

1 Choose View > Fit Spread In Window, and then use the Zoom tool (🔍) to display the middle-right portion of the back page (page 4). Use the Selection tool (▶) to select the text frame that begins with "Shauneen H."

2 Choose Object > Text Frame Options. In the Text Frame Options dialog box, type **3** in the Number box and **p11** (11 points) in the Gutter box if necessary. The gutter controls the distance between the columns. Click OK.

3 Choose Type > Show Hidden Characters to see the break characters. (If Hide Hidden Characters is displayed—rather than Show Hidden Characters—at the bottom of the Type menu, hidden characters are already showing.)

▶ **Tip:** You can also display hidden characters by choosing Hidden Characters from the View Options menu in the Application bar.

4 To begin each column with a heading, select the Type tool (T) and place the cursor before the "S" in "Sylvia B.," and then choose Type > Insert Break Character > Column Break. This forces "Sylvia B." to the top of the second column. Insert a column break before the name "Jeff G."

The small blue downward-pointing triangles within the red circles above are the Column Break characters.

5 Choose Type > Hide Hidden Characters.

Adjusting text inset and vertical alignment

You'll now finish the red title bar on the cover by fitting the text nicely into the frame. By adjusting the space between the edge of the frame and the text, you make the text easier to read.

1 Choose View > Fit Spread In Window, and then use the Zoom tool (🔍) to magnify the red text frame near the top of the front page (page 1) with the text "arrive smart. leave smarter." Using the Selection tool (▶), select the text frame with a red fill and white text at the top of the page.

2 Choose Object > Text Frame Options. If necessary, drag the Text Frame Options dialog box aside so that you can still see the selected text frame as you set options.

3 In the Text Frame Options dialog box, make sure that the Preview option in the lower-left corner of the Text Frame Options dialog box is selected. Then, in the Inset Spacing section, click the Make All Settings The Same icon (🔘) to disable it so that you can change the Left setting independently. Change the Left value to **3p** to move the left margin of the text frame 3 picas to the right and away from the left edge of the frame, and then change the Right value to **3p9**.

4 In the Vertical Justification section of the Text Frame Options dialog box, choose Center from the Align menu. Click OK.

5 Select the Type tool (T), and then click to the left of "www.evolveseattle.com" to establish an insertion point. To move the URL text so that it aligns with the right inset you specified earlier, choose Type > Insert Special Character > Other > Right Indent Tab.

6 Choose Edit > Deselect All, and then choose File > Save.

Creating and modifying graphics frames

Now you're ready to add the company logo and the employees' images to the spread. In this section, you'll focus on different techniques for creating and modifying graphics frames and their contents.

Because you'll be working on graphics rather than text, your first step is to make sure that the graphics appear on the Graphics layer rather than on the Text layer. Isolating objects on different layers streamlines your workflow and makes it easier to find and edit elements of your design.

Drawing a new graphics frame

To begin, you'll create a frame for the logo at the top of the cover page (the page on the right in the first spread).

1 If the Layers panel is not visible, click the Layers panel icon or choose Window > Layers.

2 In the Layers panel, click the lock icon (🔒) to unlock the Graphics layer. Lock the Text layer by clicking the box to the left of the layer name. Select the Graphics layer by clicking the name of the layer so that the new elements are assigned to this layer.

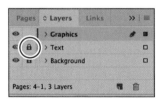

3 Choose View > Fit Spread In Window, and then use the Zoom tool (🔍) to zoom in on the upper-left corner of the front page (page 1).

4 In the Tools panel, select the Rectangle Frame tool (⊠). Move the pointer to the corner where the top and left margin guides intersect, drag down until the pointer reaches the horizontal guide, and then drag across to the right edge of the first column.

Drag to create a graphics frame.

5 Switch to the Selection tool (▶) and make sure that the graphics frame is still selected.

Placing a graphic within an existing frame

Now you'll place the company logo within the selected frame.

1 Choose File > Place, and then double-click logo_paths.ai in the Links folder in the Lesson04 folder. The image appears in the graphics frame.

2 To ensure that the graphic is displayed at the highest possible resolution, choose Object > Display Performance > High Quality Display.

● **Note:** If a graphics frame isn't selected when you place an image, the pointer changes to the loaded graphics icon (⊡). In this case, you could click within the graphics frame to place the image within the frame.

Resizing a graphics frame to crop a graphic

The graphics frame you created isn't quite wide enough to show the entire logo, so you'll widen it to reveal the hidden portion.

1 Using the Selection tool (▶), drag the center-right handle until the entire logo is visible. If you pause just after you start to drag, you'll see the cropped portion of the image as you drag—a feature called Dynamic Preview—and easily determine when the frame edge is beyond the edge of the logo. Make sure you drag the white handle and not the yellow one. The yellow handle lets you add corner options, and you'll learn more about them later in this lesson.

▶ **Tip:** You can also reveal the cropped portion of the graphic by choosing Object > Fitting > Fit Frame To Content.

2 Choose Edit > Deselect All, and then choose File > Save.

Placing a graphic without an existing frame

The design of the newsletter uses two versions of the logo—one on the front cover and one on the back cover. You could simply use the logo you just placed and the Copy and Paste commands (Edit menu) to add the logo to the back cover, and you'll do that later in this lesson, but instead you'll import the logo graphic without first creating a graphics frame.

1 Choose View > Fit Spread In Window, and then use the Zoom tool (🔍) to display the lower-right quarter of the back page (page 4).

2 Choose File > Place, and then double-click logo_paths.ai in the Links folder in the Lesson04 folder. The pointer changes to a thumbnail of the graphic you have chosen with a loaded graphics icon in the upper-left corner. (The icon changes depending on the file format of the graphic.)

▶ **Tip:** If you click—rather than click and drag—an empty area of the page when you place an image, the image is placed at 100 percent of its original size. The upper-left corner of the image is placed where you click.

3 Position the loaded graphics icon at the left edge of the rightmost column slightly below the rotated text frame that contains the return address. Drag until the pointer reaches the right edge of the column, and then release the mouse button. Notice that as you drag, a rectangle is displayed. This rectangle is proportional to the logo image.

You don't need to resize the frame as you did earlier because the frame already shows the entire image. The graphic still needs to be rotated, but you'll do that later in the lesson.

4 Choose Edit > Deselect All, and then choose File > Save.

Placing multiple graphics in a grid of frames

The back cover of the newsletter should contain six photos. You could place the photos one by one and then position each one individually, but because they will be arranged in a grid, you can place all the photos and arrange them in a grid at the same time.

1 Choose View > Fit Spread In Window.

2 Choose File > Place. Navigate to the Links folder in the Lesson04 folder, click the graphic file named 01ShauneenH.tif to select it, and then press Shift and click the file named 06HannahB.tif to select all six photos. Click Open.

3 Position the loaded graphics icon () at the intersection of the horizontal ruler guide at the top margin and the left edge of the third column.

▶ **Tip:** When using any of the frame creation tools (Rectangle, Polygon, Type, and so on), you can create multiple and equally spaced frames by using the same arrow key gestures as you drag with the tool.

4 Drag down and toward the right margin. As you drag, press the up arrow key once and the right arrow key twice. As you press the arrows, the proxy image changes to a grid of rectangles to indicate the layout of the grid.

5 Continue dragging until the pointer snaps to the intersection of the right margin guide and the lower horizontal ruler guide, and then release the mouse. A grid of six graphics frames displays the six photos you placed.

6 Choose Edit > Deselect All, and then choose File > Save.

Resizing and moving images within frames

Now that you've placed the six photos, you need to resize and reposition them so that they fill the graphics frames and are cropped correctly.

The image and the frame for any placed graphic are separate elements. Unlike text frames, a graphics frame and its content each have their own bounding box. To resize the image (without resizing the frame), select the content by choosing Object > Select > Content, or use the content grabber (◎), which displays as you hover over the graphic. You can see the different bounding boxes when either the content or the frame is selected.

1 Using the Selection tool (▶), position the pointer over the content grabber within the image of Shauneen H. (the top-left photo). When the pointer is within the content grabber, a hand icon (✋) is displayed. Click to select the frame's contents (the image itself).

Note: If you want, you can use the Zoom tool to magnify the area you're working on as you perform the tasks in this lesson.

Before clicking.

Result.

Tip: When resizing an image with the Selection tool, press Shift+Alt (Windows) or Shift+Option (macOS) to size the image proportionately from the center outward.

2 While holding down the Shift key, drag the center-bottom handle to the bottom edge of the graphics frame. Do the same with the center-top handle and drag it to the top edge of the frame. The Shift key maintains the proportions of the graphic so that it is not distorted. Remember that if you pause briefly just after you start dragging, you'll see a ghosted image of the cropped graphic contents. Make sure that the image entirely fills the graphics frame.

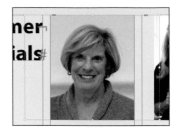

3 The image in the middle frame on the top row is too narrow to fill the frame. Click the content grabber with the Selection tool to select the image. While holding down the Shift key, drag the center-left handle to the left edge of the graphics frame. Do the same with the center-right handle and drag to the right edge of the frame. Make sure that the image entirely fills the graphics frame. Notice that the handles of the image bounding box extend beyond the frame's bounding box. This tells you that the image is bigger than the frame.

4 The image now fills the frame but is poorly cropped. To fix this, position the pointer over the content grabber within the image, and while holding down the Shift key, drag downward until the top of the photo aligns with the top of the frame.

5 Repeat step 2 for the remaining photo in the top row to fill the frame with the image.

You'll use a different method to resize the other three photos.

Tip: You can also access the fitting commands from the context menu by right-clicking (Windows) or Control-clicking (macOS), and you can click the fitting controls in the Control panel.

6 Use the Selection tool to select the graphic on the left of the second row. You can select either the frame or its content.

7 Choose Object > Fitting > Fill Frame Proportionally. This increases the scale of the graphic so that the frame is filled. Small portions of the graphic are now cropped by the left and right edges of the frame.

8 Repeat steps 6 and 7 for the remaining two photos in the bottom row.

9 Choose Edit > Deselect All, and then choose File > Save.

You can simultaneously resize a graphics frame and its content by selecting the frame (rather than the content) and holding down Shift+Ctrl (Windows) or Shift+Command (macOS) as you drag a handle of the frame. The Shift key maintains the proportions of the bounding box so that the graphic is not distorted. Using the Shift key is optional if distorting the graphic doesn't matter to your design.

▶ **Tip:** If you enable the Auto-Fit option for a graphics frame, the image within will automatically resize when you resize the frame. To enable Auto-Fit for a selected graphics frame, choose Object > Fitting > Frame Fitting Options, and then select Auto-Fit or select Auto-Fit in the Control panel.

Next, you'll adjust the space between some of the photos to give the grid arrangement a visual tweak.

Adjusting the space between frames

The Gap tool (⊢⊣) lets you select and adjust the space between frames. You'll use it to adjust the space between two of the photos in the top row and then two of the photos in the bottom row.

1 Choose View > Fit Page In Window. Hold down the Z key to temporarily access the Zoom tool (🔍), zoom in on the two photos at the top left, and then release the Z key to return to the Selection tool.

2 Select the Gap tool (⊢⊣), and then move the pointer into the vertical gap between the two pictures. The gap is highlighted—all the way down to the bottom of the two photos below.

3 Hold down the Shift key and drag the gap one gutter width to the right, making the graphics frame on the left one gutter width wider and the one on the right one gutter width narrower. (If you don't hold Shift while dragging, you'll move the gap between the two photos below as well.)

4 Choose View > Fit Page In Window.

5 Using the Selection tool (▶), drag-select the pictures in the top row. Set the Reference Point in the Control panel to the lower left (▦). Click after the number in the Y: entry, type **–p4**, and then press Enter. InDesign does the subtraction for you, and by selecting the reference point you control the direction of the move. In this case, the photos move up by 4 points.

6 Choose View > Fit Page In Window, and then choose File > Save.

You've completed the grid of images on the back page (page 4).

Adding metadata captions to graphics frames

You can automatically generate captions for placed graphics based on metadata information stored in the original graphic files. Next, you'll use the metadata captions feature to automatically add photographer credits to the pictures using metadata information.

InDesign lets you create either static captions, which generate caption text from a graphic's metadata and must be updated manually, or live captions, which are variables that retain links to a graphic's metadata and can be automatically updated.

1 With the Selection tool (▶), drag-select the six graphics frames by dragging across a portion of all six photos (you don't have to select all the way around them).

2 Click the Links panel icon to display the Links panel, and then choose Captions > Caption Setup from the panel flyout menu.

3 In the Caption Setup dialog box, specify the following settings:

- In the Text Before box, type **Photo by** . (Make sure to enter a space character after **by**. Don't add a period after the space character.)

- Choose Author from the Metadata menu; leave the Text After box blank.

- Choose Below Image from the Alignment menu.

- Choose Photo Credit from the Paragraph Style menu.

- In the Offset box, enter **p2**.

4 Click OK to save the settings and close the Caption Setup dialog box.

5 With the photos still selected, from the Links panel menu, choose Captions > Generate Static Captions.

Each of the graphic files contains a metadata element named "Author," which stores the name of the photographer. This metadata information is used when the photo credit caption is generated.

6 Choose Edit > Deselect All, and then choose File > Save.

Placing and linking graphics frames

The two imported graphics on the cover page within the "IN THIS ISSUE" frame are used again on page 3 of the newsletter to accompany articles. Next, you'll use the Place and Link feature to create copies of these two graphics and place them on page 3.

Unlike the Copy and Paste commands, which simply create a duplicate of the original object, the Place and Link feature creates a parent–child relationship between the original object and the copy. If you make changes to the parent object, you have the option to update the child object.

1 Choose View > Fit Spread In Window.

▶ **Tip:** In addition to placing and linking objects within a document, you can place and link objects between documents.

Tip: You can also add objects to the Content Conveyor by selecting them and then choosing Edit > Place And Link.

2 Select the Content Collector tool (). Notice that an empty Content Conveyor is now displayed at the bottom of the window.

3 Move the pointer over the Yield sign graphic on page 1. Notice that a heavy red border is displayed around the image, indicating that this graphics frame is on the Graphics layer (because red was chosen as the color for the Graphics layer). Click within the frame. The graphics frame is added to the Content Conveyor.

4 Click within the circular graphics frame below the Yield sign to add it to the Content Conveyor.

5 Open the Pages panel, and double-click page 3 to center it in the document window.

Note: Creating a link when placing content not only creates a link to the parent graphic but also links the object's appearance. Link Options can be set from the Links panel menu.

6 Select the Content Placer tool (). (It's paired with the Content Collector tool in the Tools panel, and it's also available in the lower-left corner of the Content Conveyor.) The pointer changes to a loaded graphics icon with the Yield sign graphic active. Both graphics are loaded.

7 Select Create Link at the lower-left corner of the Content Conveyor. If you don't select Create Link, you will simply create copies of the original objects without any parent–child relationships.

8 Click the pasteboard to the right of the top article to place a copy of the Yield sign graphic, and then click the pasteboard to the right of the bottom article to place a copy of the circular graphic.

9 Click the close box in the Content Conveyor to close it, or choose View > Extras > Hide Conveyor.

Modifying and updating parent–child graphics frames

Now that you've placed and linked the two graphics frames, you'll see how the parent–child relationships work between the original objects and the copies.

Tip: When you select the Content Placer tool, it is loaded with all objects in the Content Conveyor. Press the arrow keys to move between objects in the Content Conveyor. To remove an object from the Content Conveyor, press Esc.

1 Open the Links panel and adjust the panel so that all the filenames of the imported graphics are visible in the scroll list. The selected circular graphic (<ks88169.jpg>) is highlighted in the list. The other graphic you placed and linked (<yield.ai>) is the next filename in the list. The greater than and less than

characters (<>) that bracket the filenames indicate that these graphics are linked to parent objects. Notice that these two graphic files—the parent objects—are also listed higher up in the scroll list.

2 Use the Selection tool (▶) to position the circular graphics frame to the left of the "CSS Master Class" article. Align the top of the graphics frame with the top of the article's text frame; align the right edge of the graphics frame with the column guide to the left of the article's text frame.

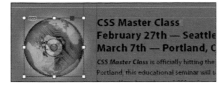

> **Tip:** A Smart Guide appears when the top of the circular graphics frame is aligned with the top of the text frame.

3 Navigate to page 1 (the front cover page), and then select the circular graphics frame.

4 Use the Control panel to apply a 5-point white [Paper] stroke to the frame.

5 In the Links panel, notice that the status of the <ks88169.jpg> graphic on page 3 has changed to Modified (⚠). That's because its parent object has been modified.

▶ **Tip:** You can also click the modified link badge on the circular graphics frame on page 3 to update the link or double-click the modified link icon to the right of <ks88169.jpg> in the Links panel.

6 Navigate to page 3. Notice that the circular graphics frame no longer matches the version on the cover, and its link badge (the yellow triangle with the exclamation mark) also indicates it's been modified. Select the circular graphics frame, and then click the Update Link button (↻) in the Links panel. The frame now matches its parent.

Next, you'll replace the Yield sign graphic with a newer version and then update its child frame.

7 Navigate to page 1, and then select the red Yield sign graphic with the Selection tool.

8 Choose File > Place. Make sure Replace Selected Item is selected in the lower-left quadrant of the Place dialog box, and then double-click yield_new.ai in the Links folder in the Lesson04 folder.

In the Links panel, notice that the status of the file named <yield_new.ai> that's on the pasteboard of page 3 is Modified. That's because you replaced the parent graphic on page 1.

9 Select <yield_new.ai> in the scroll list, and then click the Update Link button (↻) in the Links panel. If you want, navigate to page 3 to see the updated graphic on the pasteboard, and then return to page 1.

10 Click the pasteboard to deselect all objects, choose View > Fit Spread In Window, and then choose File > Save.

Changing the shape of a frame

When you resized a graphics frame using the Selection tool, the frame maintained its rectangular shape. Now you'll use the Direct Selection tool and the Pen tool to reshape a frame on page 3 (the right page of the center spread).

1 Choose 3 from the page box at the bottom of the document window. Choose View > Fit Page In Window.

2 Click the Layers panel icon, or choose Window > Layers. In the Layers panel, click the lock icon for the Background layer to unlock it, click the Graphics layer to lock it, and click the Background layer to select it if it's not selected.

Next, you'll change the shape of a rectangular frame and, by doing so, change the background of the page.

3 Press the A key to switch to the Direct Selection tool (▷). Move the tip of the pointer over the right edge of the green frame that covers the page, and click when the pointer appears with a small diagonal line (▷). This selects the path and reveals the four anchor points and the center point of the frame. Leave the path selected.

4 Press the P key to switch to the Pen tool (✒).

5 Carefully position the pointer over the top edge of the frame path where it intersects with the vertical ruler guide in the first column on page 3. When a plus sign is displayed at the lower right of the pointer, click. A new anchor point is added. The Pen tool automatically changes to the Add Anchor Point tool when it moves over an existing path.

6 Move the pointer to where the horizontal guide below the two-column text frame intersects with the bleed guide. Using the Pen tool, click again to add another new anchor point, and then choose Edit > Deselect All.

This anchor point and the anchor point you created in the previous step will form the corners of the irregular shape you're creating. Repositioning the anchor point at the upper-right corner of the green frame will complete the reshaping of the frame.

7 Switch to the Direct Selection tool (▷). Click to select the upper-right corner point of the green frame. Drag the point down and to the left. When the anchor point snaps into place at the intersection of the right edge of the first column and the first horizontal guide from the top of the page (at 40p9 on the vertical ruler), release the mouse button.

The graphics frame is now properly shaped and sized for the design.

8 Choose File > Save.

Wrapping text around a graphic

With InDesign, you can wrap text around the rectangular bounding box of any object, around objects of any shape, and around the contours of imported images. As you wrap text around the Yield sign in this exercise, you'll see the difference between wrapping around its bounding box and around the shape of the graphic.

Your first task is to move the Yield sign graphic. For precise positioning, you can use the Smart Guides that are displayed dynamically when you create, move, or resize objects.

1 Unlock the Graphics layer. Then, using the Selection tool (▶), select the graphics frame with the image of a Yield sign on the pasteboard to the right of page 3. Make sure to click when the arrow pointer is displayed. If you click when the hand pointer is displayed, you'll select the graphic instead of the graphics frame.

2 Being careful not to select one of the handles, drag the frame to the left so that the center point of the frame is aligned with the center point of the text frame that contains the article text. When the two center points align, you should see a purple vertical Smart Guide and a green horizontal Smart Guide appear. When these guidelines appear, release the mouse button.

Make sure that you have moved the frame onto the page without changing its size. Notice that the graphic overlaps the text. You'll change this by applying a text wrap.

3 Use the Zoom tool to zoom in on the frame you just moved. Choose Window > Text Wrap. In the Text Wrap panel, select Wrap Around Bounding Box (▦) to wrap the text around the bounding box. If necessary, choose Show Options from the panel menu to display all the controls in the Text Wrap panel.

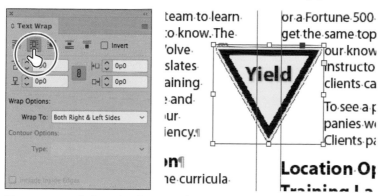

Wrap text around a bounding box. Result.

This option leaves too much white space for your desired design, so you'll try another Text Wrap option.

4 Select Wrap Around Object Shape (▦). In the Wrap Options section, choose Both Right & Left Sides from the Wrap To menu if it isn't already selected. In the Contour Options section, choose Detect Edges from the Type menu. Enter **1p**

● **Note:** The Wrap To menu in the Text Wrap panel is available only if you select Wrap Around Bounding Box or Wrap Around Object Shape at the top of the panel.

in the Top Offset box to add space between the edge of the graphic and the text, and press Enter or Return. Click a blank area to deselect all, or choose Edit > Deselect All.

Wrap text around an object shape. Result.

5 Close the Text Wrap panel, and choose File > Save.

Modifying the shape of frames

In this section, you'll use various features that allow you to create nonrectangular frames. To begin, you'll subtract the area of one shape from another. After that, you'll create a polygon-shaped frame, and then you'll add rounded corners to a frame.

Working with compound shapes

You can change the shape of an existing frame by adding other shapes to or subtracting other shapes from its area. The shape of a frame can also be changed, even if the frame already contains text or graphics. Now you'll subtract a shape from the green background on page 3 to create a white background for the article at the bottom of the page.

1 Choose View > Fit Page In Window to fit and center page 3 in the document window.

2 Using the Rectangle Frame tool (⊠), draw a frame around the story in the lower right. Start from where the right edge of the first column meets the horizontal guide at 46p6 on the vertical ruler past the intersection of the bleed guides that meet outside the lower-right corner of the page. Look ahead to the illustrations in Step 4 for guidance.

3 With the Selection tool (▶), hold down the Shift key and click the blue shape you modified earlier (outside of the frame you just created) that covers a good part of page 3 to simultaneously select the new rectangle and the background box. Two frames are now selected.

4 Choose Object > Pathfinder > Subtract to subtract the top shape (the new rectangle) from the blue shape. The text frame at the bottom of the page is now on a white background.

Both rectangles selected, Pathfinder dialog box. Subtract the front object.

5 Open the Layers panel and lock the Background layer again to avoid accidental repositioning of the frame.

6 Choose File > Save.

Converting shapes

You can change the shape of an existing frame, even if the frame already contains text or graphics. You'll try this out by creating a perfect square and then converting it to a perfect circle in one step.

1 Click the Layers panel icon or choose Window > Layers to open the Layers panel.

2 Click the Graphics layer to select it.

3 Select the Rectangle tool (□.)

4 Click in the blue area between the stories on page 3. Hold down the Shift key and drag up and to the left until the Width and Height are 4p. Holding down the Shift key constrains the rectangle to a perfect square.

5 Open the Swatches panel, click the fill color icon (▨), and choose Paper (White).

6 With the square still selected, choose Object > Convert Shape > Ellipse. You now have a perfect circle. Check this by looking at the measurements in the Control Panel. They are still 4p for both Width and Height.

Repeating shapes

1 With the circle still selected, choose Edit > Step And Repeat.

2 Under Offset, enter **5p6** for Horizontal and enter **8** for the Count above. (Enter the Offset number first because the default value may be too large to have enough room for eight repeats). Leave Vertical at Zero. Click OK.

3 Now delete the third circle and the eighth circle.

4 Drag-select across all of the circles (make sure you locked the Background layer so that you select only the circles).

5 Choose Distribute Horizontal Centers (♦♦) from the Align area of the Control Panel, or from the Align panel.

The circles are evenly distributed once again, with equal space between them.

Adding rounded corners to frames

Next, you'll modify a text frame by rounding its corners.

1 Navigate to page 1 by choosing 1 from the page box at the bottom of the document window. Choose View > Fit Page In Window. Unlock the Text layer.

2 With the Selection tool (▶) still selected, hold down the Z key to temporarily access the Zoom tool (Q), zoom in on the dark blue text frame on page 1, and then release the Z key to return to the Selection tool.

▶ **Tip:** If the yellow square is not visible when selecting the frame, choose View > Extras > Show Live Corners. Also ensure that Screen Mode is set to Normal (View > Screen Mode > Normal).

3 Select the dark blue text frame, and then click the small yellow square that's slightly below the resizing handle at the upper-right corner of the frame. Four small yellow diamonds replace the four resizing handles at the corners of the frame.

Click the yellow square.

Result.

4 Drag the diamond at the upper-right corner of the frame to the left and release the mouse button when the live radius (R:) value is approximately 2p0. As you drag, the other three corners change, too. (If you hold down the Shift key when dragging, only the corner you are working on changes.)

▶ **Tip:** After you create rounded corners, you can Alt-click (Windows) or Option-click (macOS) any of the diamonds to cycle through several different corner effects.

5 Choose Edit > Deselect All to exit live corner edit mode, and then choose File > Save.

Transforming and aligning objects

Various tools and commands in InDesign let you modify an object's size or shape and change its orientation on the page. All transformations—rotating, scaling, shearing, and flipping—are available in the Transform and Control panels, where you can precisely specify transformations. You can also align or distribute objects horizontally or vertically along the selection, margins, page, or spread.

You'll experiment with some of these features now.

Rotating an object

InDesign offers several methods for rotating objects. In this part of the lesson, you'll use the Control panel to rotate one of the logos you imported earlier in the lesson.

1 Use either the page box at the bottom of the document window or the Pages panel to display page 4 (the first page of the document; the back page of the newsletter). Choose View > Fit Page In Window.

2 Using the Selection tool (▶), select the "evolve" logo you imported earlier in the lesson. (Make sure you select the graphics frame and not the graphic within.)

3 At the left end of the Control panel, make sure that the center point is selected on the Reference Point locator (▒) so that the object rotates around its center. Choose 180° from the Rotation Angle menu in the Control panel.

Rotating an image within its frame

▶ **Tip:** You can also rotate a selected object by choosing Object > Transform > Rotate and entering a value in the Angle field of the Rotate dialog box.

You can rotate the content of a graphics frame with the Selection tool.

1 Using the Selection tool (▶), select the image of Jeff G. (top right) by clicking within the content grabber. The arrow pointer changes to a hand when it's within the doughnut shape.

2 Move the pointer slightly outside the resizing handle at the upper-right corner of the picture. The rotate pointer (�ъ) is displayed.

3 Click and drag clockwise to rotate the image until the head is approximately vertical (about −25°), and then release the mouse button. As you drag, the angle of rotation is displayed along with the image.

4 In the Control panel, make sure that the center point is selected in the reference point locator (◈).

5 After being rotated, the image no longer fills the frame. To fix this, first make sure that the Constrain Proportions For Scaling icon (▣) to the right of the Scale X and Scale Y Percentage boxes in the Control panel is selected, and then enter **55** in the Scale X Percentage box and press Enter or Return.

6 Choose Edit > Deselect All, and then choose File > Save.

Aligning multiple objects

Precise alignment is made easy when you use the Align panel. Next, you'll use the Align panel to horizontally center multiple objects on a page, and then you'll align multiple images.

1 Choose View > Fit Page In Window, and then choose page 2 in the page box at the bottom of the document window.

2 Using the Selection tool (▶), click the text frame at the top of the page containing the "Partial Class Calendar" text and Shift-click the "evolve" logo above it. (Unlike the two logos you imported earlier, this logo is a group of InDesign objects. You'll work with this group later in the lesson.)

3 Choose Window > Object & Layout > Align to open the Align panel.

4 In the Align panel, choose Align To Page from the Align To menu, and then click the Align Horizontal Centers button (▦). The objects are now aligned to the center of the page.

Align the objects dialog box. Result.

5 Click a blank area or choose Edit > Deselect All.

6 Use the scroll bar at the bottom of the document window to show more of the pasteboard on the left of page 2. You'll see seven software application icons.

7 Using the Selection tool (▶), select the graphics frame at the upper-left corner of the calendar, and then Shift-drag-select the seven graphics frames in the pasteboard.

8 In the Align panel, choose Align To Key Object from the Align To menu. Notice that the first graphics frame you selected now has a thick blue border, indicating it's the key object.

9 Click the Align Right Edges button (▟).

10 Choose Edit > Deselect All, and then choose File > Save.

● **Note:** When you specify a key object, the alignment of the other selected objects will be relative to the key object's position.

▶ **Tip:** InDesign automatically assigns the object you selected first as the key object. To change the key object once you've selected all objects to be aligned, click the object that should be the key object. A thicker selection border will then appear around that object.

Scaling multiple objects

InDesign lets you scale multiple selected objects.

Next you'll select two of the icons and resize both of them at once.

1 Use the Zoom tool (🔍) to zoom in on the two Acrobat icons on the left side of the page.

2 Using the Selection tool (▶), click the first of the icons to select it, and then Shift-click the second icon to select both.

● **Note:** If you press only the Shift key, the frames will scale proportionally, but the graphics within will not scale.

3 Press Shift+Ctrl (Windows) or Shift+Command (macOS), and then drag the handle at the upper-left corner down and to the right to make the two icons the same width as the Adobe Photoshop icon above or the Adobe Illustrator icon below the selected icons. A Smart Guide is displayed when the left edges of the selected frames align with the frame above. Note that you may have to repeat the scaling more than once to get the size correct.

Shift-drag to resize Result.
the selected icons.

4 Choose Edit > Deselect All, and then choose File > Save.

Transforming multiple objects

InDesign lets you apply a transformation to multiple selected objects.

Next, you'll duplicate the icons, apply a transformation to one of them, and then apply the same transformation to the rest of them at once.

1 Choose View > Fit Page In Window.

2 Using the Selection tool (▶), select the InDesign logo and press Alt (Windows) or Option (macOS) while dragging it up to the area between the table and the calendar headline. This technique makes a copy of the object. Align the left edge of the graphic with the vertical guide above the word "Class."

3 Drag-copy the Photoshop, Illustrator, and Acrobat icons to the same area. Align the Acrobat icon with the vertical guide on the right above the word "Platform." Notice how the Smart Guides show you when the objects are aligned.

4 Select the InDesign icon again. Set the Reference Point in the Control Panel to the center position. Choose 200% for the scale and then choose 30° for the angle.

5 Drag across the other three icons (because the Background layer is locked, you won't select the background box). Then choose Object > Transform Again > Transform Sequence Again Individually. InDesign applies the same scale and angle that you applied to the InDesign icon to the other three icons without you having to apply them one at a time to each object. A sequence of many transformations can be applied to other objects using this command.

6 Select all four icons and nudge all four icons up or down using the keyboard arrow keys so that they are approximately centered between the table and the calendar headline. Then, in the Align panel, choose Align To Selection and choose Distribute Horizontal Centers ().

7 Choose Edit > Deselect All, and then choose File > Save.

Selecting and modifying grouped objects

Earlier you aligned the "evolve" logo at the top of page 2 to the center of the page. Now you'll change the fill color of some of the logo's shapes. Because they're grouped, you can select and modify them as a unit. You'll now change the fill color of just a few of the shapes without ungrouping or changing the other objects of the group.

The Direct Selection tool, or a set of commands in the Object menu (Object > Select), lets you select individual objects in a grouped object.

1 Choose View > Fit Spread In Window.

2 With the Selection tool (), click the "evolve" logo at the top of page 2. If you want, use the Zoom tool () to magnify the area you're working on.

3 Click the Select Content button () in the Control panel to select one object in the group without ungrouping.

Select the group with Choose Result.
the Selection tool. Select Content.

Tip: You can also select an object in a group by double-clicking the object with the Selection tool, by selecting the group and choosing Object > Select > Content, or by right-clicking (Windows) or Control-clicking (macOS) the group and choosing Select > Content from the context menu.

4 Click the Select Previous Object button () in the Control panel six times to select the first "e" in the word "evolve." Note that the Select Next Object button selects in the opposite direction.

Click Select Previous Object Result.
six times.

5 Using the Direct Selection tool (▷), hold down the Shift key and click the "v," "l," "v," and "e" letters in the logo to simultaneously select them.

6 Click the Swatches panel icon or choose Window > Color > Swatches. Click the Fill box at the top of the Swatches panel and choose [Paper] to fill the letter shapes with a white color.

Change the fill of the selected Result.
shapes to [Paper].

7 Choose Edit > Deselect All, and then choose File > Save.

Drawing lines and modifying arrowheads

InDesign has the ability to scale arrowheads independently of line size. Next, you'll use this feature to complete the design of the newsletter.

1 Select the Line tool (╱). Position the pointer on the left margin guide on page 4, slightly below the text frame with the "Customer Testimonials" text.

2 With the Line tool selected, change the Fill color to None and the Stroke color to Black.

3 While pressing the Shift key, drag horizontally from the left margin guide to the vertical column guide at the right of the second column. The Shift key constrains the line to be perfectly horizontal.

4 Click the Stroke panel icon or choose Window > Stroke to open the Stroke panel. Choose 4 from the Weight menu, CircleSolid from the Start Arrowhead menu, and Curved from the End Arrowhead menu.

5 Make sure Link Start And End Arrowhead Scales is not selected (⧉) so that you can independently scale the start and end arrowheads. Enter **75** in the Scale Factor For Start Arrowhead box; enter **150** in the Scale factor for end arrowhead box, and press Enter or Return.

▶ **Tip:** In addition to adding arrowheads to straight lines created with the Line tool, you can also add arrowheads to curved lines created with the Pen tool.

6 Choose File > Save.

Creating a QR code

InDesign lets you quickly generate and edit high-quality quick response (QR) code graphics. QR codes are machine-readable printed representations of data for various industry uses and have become common in consumer advertising. A consumer with a smartphone can install a QR-code scanner app that can read and decode the URL information and redirect the phone's browser to a company website. After scanning QR codes, users may receive text, add a business card contact to their devices, open a web hyperlink, or compose an email or text message.

The QR code generated in InDesign is a high-fidelity graphic object that behaves exactly like other InDesign objects. You can easily scale the object and fill it with color, apply transparency effects, or copy and paste the object as a vector graphic into a standard graphics editor tool such as Adobe Illustrator.

Next, you'll add a QR code to the back page of the newsletter and configure it to open a web page.

1 Navigate to page 4 of the document (the back cover), and then choose View > Fit Page In Window to center the page.

2 Choose Object > Generate QR Code.

3 Choose each of the options in the Type menu to see the possiblities, and then choose Web Hyperlink for this lesson.

4 In the URL field, enter **http://www.adobe.com** (or the complete URL for any website you want).

▶ **Tip:** Click the Color tab in the Generate QR Code dialog box to apply a swatch color to the code.

▶ **Tip:** To edit a QR code, right-click (Windows) or Control-click (macOS) the code with the Selection tool, and then choose Edit QR Code from the context menu or choose Object > Edit QR Code.

5 Click OK to close the dialog box.

6 Click above the caption "SCAN for the latest information from Adobe." The automatically generated graphic is placed. Adjust its position to left align with the caption.

Finishing up

Now it's time to admire your work.

1 Choose Edit > Deselect All.

2 Choose View > Fit Spread In Window.

3 At the bottom of the Tools panel, hold down the current screen mode button (▨) and choose Preview from the menu that appears. Preview mode is an ideal way to see what a document will look like when printed. Preview mode displays artwork as if it were printed and trimmed, with all nonprinting elements suppressed (grids, guides, frame edges, nonprinting objects) and the pasteboard set to the preview color defined in Preferences.

4 Press the Tab key to close all the panels at the same time. Press the Tab key again when you are ready to show all the panels.

5 Choose File > Save.

Congratulations. You have finished the lesson.

Exploring on your own

One of the best ways to learn about frames is to experiment on your own.

In this section, you'll learn how to nest an object inside a frame. Follow these steps to learn more about selecting and manipulating frames:

1 Create a new (Print) document using the default settings in the New Document dialog box.

2 Use the Ellipse Frame tool (⊗) to create a small circular text frame, approximately 12p0 x 12p0. (Press the Shift key as you drag to constrain the shape to a circle.)

3 Select the Type tool and then click within the frame to convert it to a text frame.

4 Choose Type > Fill With Placeholder Text to fill the frame with text.

5 Press the Esc key to switch to the Selection tool, and then use the Swatches panel to apply a fill color to the text frame.

6 Select Edit > Deselect All, and then select the Polygon tool (◯). Draw a shape on the page. (Before creating the polygon, you can double-click the Polygon tool to specify the number of sides and optionally a star inset value if you want to create a starburst shape.)

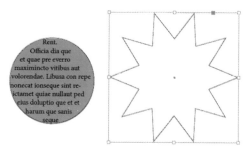

7 Using the Selection tool (▶), select the text frame you created earlier, and then choose Edit > Copy.

8 Select the polygon frame, and then choose Edit > Paste Into to nest the blue text frame inside the polygon frame. (If you choose Edit > Paste, the copied text frame is not pasted inside the selected frame.)

9 Use the Selection tool to move the text frame by positioning the pointer within the content grabber in the center of the polygon frame and then dragging.

10 Use the Selection tool to move the polygon frame and its content by positioning the pointer outside the content grabber and then dragging.

11 Choose Edit > Deselect All.

12 Use the Direct Selection tool (▷) to select the polygon frame, and then drag any of the handles to change the shape of the polygon.

13 When you have finished experimenting, close the document without saving.

Review questions

1 When should you use the Selection tool to select an object, and when should you use the Direct Selection tool to select an object?

2 How do you resize a graphics frame and its content simultaneously?

3 How do you rotate the graphic within a graphics frame without rotating the frame?

4 Without ungrouping objects, how do you select an object within a group?

Review answers

1 Use the Selection tool for general layout tasks, such as positioning, rotating, and resizing objects. Use the Direct Selection tool for tasks involving editing paths or frames, such as moving an anchor point on a path or selecting an object within a group and then changing the object's fill or stroke color.

2 To resize a graphics frame and its content simultaneously, select the frame with the Selection tool, hold down Shift+Ctrl (Windows) or Shift+Command (macOS), and then drag a handle. This keyboard combination ensures that objects and contents will be scaled proportionally. (If you don't include the Shift key while dragging, the object's and content's proportions are not maintained.) Alternatively, you can enable the Auto-Fit feature for a selected graphics frame and resize it without the need to hold down the Ctrl (Windows) or Command (macOS) key.

3 To rotate a graphic within a frame, use the Selection tool to select the graphic within the frame by clicking within the content grabber. Then position the pointer slightly outside any of the four corner handles and drag to rotate the graphic. Add the Shift key while dragging to constrain rotation to increments of 45°. You can also rotate a selected graphic by changing the Rotation Angle value in the Control panel.

4 To select an object within a group, use the Selection tool (▶) to select the group, and then click the Select Content button (⊕) in the Control panel to select one object in the group. You can then click the Select Previous Object or Select Next Object button to select different objects in the group. You can also select an object in a group by clicking the object with the Direct Selection tool (▷) or double-clicking it with the Selection tool.

5

FLOWING TEXT

Lesson Overview

In this lesson, you'll learn how to do the following:

- Import and flow text into existing text frames.

- Resize text frames automatically.

- Link text frames to flow text across columns and pages.

- Create linked frames automatically.

- Add pages and linked frames automatically while flowing text.

- Apply paragraph styles to text.

- Control column breaks.

- Make a jump line to indicate where an article continues.

This lesson will take approximately 45 minutes to complete.

Please log in to your account on peachpit.com to download the lesson files for this chapter, or go to the "Getting Started" section at the beginning of this book and follow the instructions under "Accessing the Lesson Files and Web Edition." Store the files on your computer in a convenient location.

I thought that the light drizzle on this crisp fall day might be a deterrent.

Hot Spot: Urban Museum

Location: 1 Main St., Meridien

Hours: 10 a.m.–6 p.m., Daily

Cost: Free

When I asked Alexis, director of Meridien's Urban Museum, to give me her personal tour of the city she's resided in since her teenage years, she accepted, but only if we did it by bicycle.

I'm not a fitness freak and Meridien is known for its formidable hills, so when 6 a.m. rolled around, when I noted damp streets outside my apartment window and my cell phone started buzzing, I was hoping it was Alexis calling to tell me that we were switching to Plan B.

"Sorry, Charlie. We're not going to let a little misty air ruin our fun. Anyway, the forecast says it will clear up by late morning."

So much for Plan B.

We met at the Smith Street subway station, a mid-century, mildly brutalist concrete cube designed by archi-

Museum continued on 2

Adobe InDesign provides methods for flowing text into existing frames, creating frames while flowing text, and adding frames and pages while flowing text. This makes it easy to flow copy for anything from a catalog to a magazine article to an ebook.

Getting started

In this lesson, you'll work on a booklet in progress. The design of the opening spread of the article is almost finished, and several pages are ready for text. While working on this article, you will experiment with various text-flow methods and create a "jump line" to indicate the page on which an article continues.

● **Note:** If you have not already downloaded the project files for this lesson to your computer from your Account page, make sure to do so now. See "Getting Started" at the beginning of the book.

1 To ensure that the preferences and default settings of your Adobe InDesign program match those used in this lesson, move the InDesign Defaults file to a different folder following the procedure in "Saving and restoring the InDesign Defaults file" on pages 4–5.

2 Start Adobe InDesign.

3 The InDesign Start Screen displays. Click Open at left. (If the Start Screen does not display, choose File > Open from the InDesign menu bar.)

4 Open the 05_Start.indd file in the Lesson05 folder, located inside the Lessons folder within the InDesignCIB folder on your hard disk.

5 If the Missing Fonts dialog box displays, click Sync Fonts to access any missing fonts through Adobe Typekit. Click Close when font syncing is complete.

● **Note:** For higher contrast in the printed manual, the screen captures in this book show the Medium Light interface. Interface elements such as panels and dialog boxes may be darker on your screen.

6 To ensure that the panels and menu commands match those used in this lesson, choose Window > Workspace > [Advanced], and then choose Window > Workspace > Reset Advanced.

7 To display the document at a higher resolution, choose View > Display Performance > High Quality Display (if it's not already enabled).

8 Choose File > Save As, rename the file **05_FlowText.indd**, and save it in the Lesson05 folder.

9 If you want to see what the finished document looks like, open the 05_End.indd file in the same folder. You can leave this document open to act as a guide as you work.

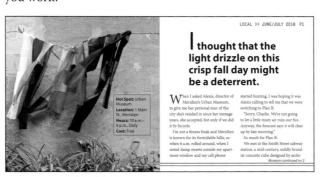

10 When you're ready to resume working on the lesson document, display it by clicking its tab in the upper-left corner of the document window.

Flowing text into an existing frame

When you import text, you can flow it into a new frame or an existing frame. If the frame is empty, you can click the loaded text icon in the frame to flow the text. On the left page of the opening spread of this booklet, an empty sidebar box is ready for text to be inserted. You will import a Microsoft Word document into this frame, apply a paragraph style, and automatically adjust the height of the text frame.

Importing text into an existing text frame

1 Choose Type > Show Hidden Characters to see paragraph returns, spaces, tabs, and other hidden characters onscreen. This helps you place and format text.

2 Zoom in to comfortably view the sidebar text frame on the left page of the opening spread. The frame has a stroke and a sage green background.

3 Make sure no objects are selected.

4 Choose File > Place. At the bottom of the Place dialog box, make sure the three options are deselected: Show Import Options, Replace Selected Item, and Create Static Captions. (If necessary, click Options on macOS to see the options.)

5 Locate 05_MuseumStats.docx, in the Lesson05 folder, and then double-click it.

 The pointer becomes a loaded text icon (▤), previewing the first few lines of text in the article you are placing. When you move the loaded text icon over an empty text frame, parentheses enclose the icon (▤).

6 Position the loaded text icon over the placeholder text frame.

7 Click to place the text.

8 Choose File > Save.

The text does not fit in the text frame and is considered "overset." Overset text is indicated by a red plus sign (+) in the out port, which is in the lower-right corner of the text frame. You will resolve the overset text later in this exercise.

▶ **Tip:** InDesign provides many features for automatically and manually controlling how text flows through columns and frames. These include the paragraph Keep Options (Keep With Previous, Keep With Next, and Keep Lines Together), along with Column Break and Frame Break characters (Type > Insert Break Character).

▶ **Tip:** You edit text with the Type tool and thread (link) text frames with the Selection tool, but it does not matter what tool is selected when you import text.

Applying a paragraph style

Now you will apply a paragraph style to the sidebar text. The paragraph style includes a nested style that automatically applies bold to the beginning of a paragraph until InDesign encounters the first colon.

1 Using the Type tool (T.), click in the sidebar text frame so you can format the text. Choose Edit > Select All to select all the text in the frame.

2 Choose Type > Paragraph Styles to open the Paragraph Styles panel.

▶ **Tip:** Style groups help you organize styles in panels such as the Paragraph Styles and Swatches panels. When the group is expanded, you can select options in the group.

3 Click the triangle to the left of the Body Text style group to open it.

4 Click the paragraph style Sidebar Text.

5 Click in the text to deselect it. Choose File > Save.

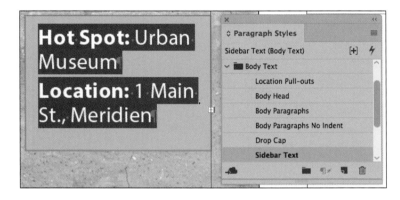

After formatting, the text is still overset, so you will resolve that in the next exercise.

Resizing text frames automatically

While adding, deleting, and editing text, you often end up resizing text frames. With the Auto-Size feature, you can specify that a text frame resize itself automatically according to your specifications. You will now use the Auto-Size feature to automatically adjust the size of the sidebar text frame based on the length of the text.

▶ **Tip:** The Auto-Size feature is ideal for individual text frames with a stroke and/or fill providing a boundary for the text (for example, a sidebar or coupon). If the text is shortened, the frame becomes smaller as well. If the text is lengthened, the frame bcomes bigger so text is not overset.

1 Using the Selection tool (▶), click the text frame containing the sidebar text starting with "Hot Spot."

2 Choose Object > Text Frame Options. In the Text Frame Options dialog box, click the Auto-Size tab.

3 Choose Height Only from the Auto-Sizing menu.

4 If necessary, click the center icon in the top row (⬍) to indicate that you want the text frame to "grow down" as if you were manually dragging the bottom handle of the text frame down.

5 Click OK.

6 Click the pasteboard to deselect objects on the page, and then choose View > Screen Mode > Preview to see how the sidebar looks.

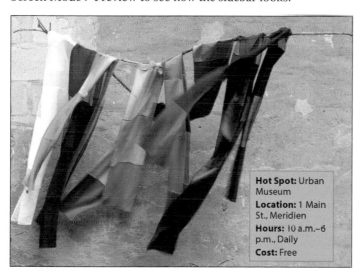

Hot Spot: Urban Museum
Location: 1 Main St., Meridien
Hours: 10 a.m.–6 p.m., Daily
Cost: Free

7 Choose View > Screen Mode > Normal to restore the layout aids, such as guides and hidden characters.

8 Choose File > Save.

Flowing text manually

▶ **Tip:** You can create columns by threading individual text frames or by dividing text frames into multiple columns using the General tab of the Text Frame Options dialog box (Object menu). Some designers prefer separate text frames for more layout flexibility.

The process of taking an imported text file and flowing it across several connected text frames is called threading text. InDesign lets you flow text manually for greater control, flow text automatically to save time, and flow text while automatically adding enough pages to hold all the text.

In this exercise, you will flow the feature article text into the two columns at the bottom of the right page. First, you will select a Word file to import into the existing text frame in the first column. Second, you will thread the first text frame to the second text frame. Finally, you will create new text frames on the third page of the document to contain more text.

1 Choose View > Fit Spread In Window to locate the two text frames at the bottom of the right page under the sentence ending with "deterrent."

2 Zoom in as necessary to view these text frames.

▶ **Tip:** To prepare to import text, you can pre-thread empty text frames. Using the Selection tool, click a frame's out port, and then click anywhere in the next frame. Repeat this process until all the frames are threaded.

3 Using the Type tool (**T**), click in the text frame at the left as shown below.

4 Choose File > Place.

5 Locate and select 05_Feature_2018.docx, in the Lesson05 folder.

6 Select Replace Selected Item at the bottom of the Place dialog box. (If necessary, click Options on macOS to see this option.) Click Open.

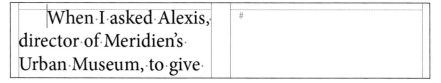

The text flows into the existing frame in the left column. Notice that the text frame includes an out port in the lower-right corner. The red plus sign (+) indicates that some of the text you imported is overset, meaning that not all of the text fits into the existing text frame. You will now flow the additional text into another text frame in the second column.

7 Using the Selection tool (▶), click in the text frame's out port to load the text icon. (If necessary, first click the frame to select it, and then click the out port.)

8 Move the loaded cursor over the text frame to the right and click once in the frame as shown.

▶ **Tip:** As you flow text, the Selection tool's cursor changes to various loaded text icons.

> When·I·asked·Alexis, director·of·Meridien's· Urban·Museum,·to·give· me·her·personal·tour·of· the·city·she's·resided·in· since·her·teenage·years,· she·accepted,·but·only·if· we·did·it·by·bicycle.·¶

> When I asked Alexis, director of Meridien's Urban Museum, to give me her personal tour of the city she's resided in since her teenage years, she accepted, but

9 The text flows into the second column. The out port in the text frame at the right contains a red plus sign (+), indicating that there is still overset text.

▶ **Tip:** If you change your mind and decide you don't want to flow overset text, you can press Esc or click any tool in the Tools panel to cancel the loaded text icon. No text will be deleted.

> When·I·asked·Alexis, director·of·Meridien's· Urban·Museum,·to·give· me·her·personal·tour·of· the·city·she's·resided·in· since·her·teenage·years,· she·accepted,·but·only·if· we·did·it·by·bicycle.·¶

> I'm·not·a·fitness· freak·and·Meridien·is· known·for·its·formida= ble·hills,·so·when·6·a.m.· rolled·around,·when· I·noted·damp·streets· outside·my·apartment· window·and·my·cell·

10 Choose File > Save. Leave the page in this position for the next exercise.

Loading the Type tool with multiple text files

In the Place dialog box, you can "load" the Type tool with multiple text files and then place them individually. Loading the Type tool works as follows:

- First, choose File > Place to open the Place dialog box.
- Ctrl-click (Windows) or Command-click (macOS) to select multiple noncontiguous files. Shift-click to select a contiguous range of files.
- When you click Open, the loaded text icon shows in parentheses how many files are loaded, such as (4).
- Press the arrow keys on the keyboard to change which text file is loaded for placement, and press Esc to remove a text file from the loaded text icon.
- Click to place the text files one at a time.

▶ **Tip:** You can also "load" the Type tool with graphics files and text files at the same time.

Creating text frames while flowing text

▶ **Tip:** The loaded text icon changes slightly in appearance, depending on whether you are threading text manually or using semi-autoflow or autoflow.

Now, you will try two different text flow methods. First, you will use semi-autoflow to place text into a column. Semi-autoflow lets you create threaded text frames one at a time. The pointer becomes a loaded text icon that automatically reloads after each column of text is placed. After that, you will use the loaded text icon to manually create a text frame.

Note that the success of these exercises relies on holding the correct modifier keys on the keyboard and clicking in the correct place. Therefore, it may help to read all the steps in each exercise before you perform them. If anything goes wrong, be sure to choose Edit > Undo, and then repeat the step.

● **Note:** The success of these exercises relies on holding the correct modifier keys on the keyboard and clicking in the correct place. Therefore, it may help to read all the steps in each exercise before you perform them. If anything goes wrong, be sure to choose Edit > Undo, and then repeat the step.

1 Using the Selection tool (▶), click the out port of the text frame in the second column on the right page (page 1). This loads the text icon with the overset text.

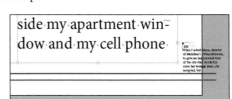

You will create new text frames on page 2 to contain more of the text. Guides indicate where to place the text frames.

2 Choose Layout > Next Spread to display pages 2 and 3, and then choose View > Fit Spread In Window.

When the loaded text icon is active, you can still navigate to different document pages or add new pages.

3 On the page at left, position the loaded text icon (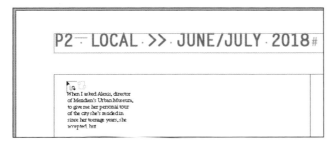) in the upper-left corner where the guides intersect. For proper placement, watch for the black arrow in the loaded text icon to turn white.

4 Hold down the Alt (Windows) or Option (macOS) key and click.

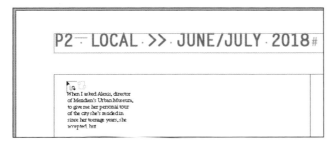

▶ **Tip:** When the loaded text icon is over an empty text frame, a chain icon indicates that you can thread to that frame. You can also flow overset text into an empty graphics frame; the graphics frame is automatically converted to a text frame.

The text flows into the first column. Because you held down Alt or Option, the pointer is still a loaded text icon, ready for you to flow text into another frame.

5 Release the Alt or Option key, and position the loaded text icon (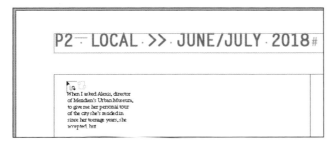) in the second column indicated by the guides.

6 Click to create a frame within the column guides in the right column.

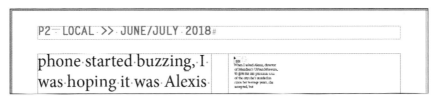

Clicking the loaded text icon creates text frames within the column guides and flows the text.

▶ **Tip:** When you create a text frame by clicking with the loaded text icon, InDesign creates the new text frame as wide as the column where you click. Although these frames are placed within the column guides, you can move, resize, and reshape these text frames as necessary.

Text remains overset, as indicated by the red plus sign (+) in the lower-right corner of the second text frame. You will fix this later.

7 Choose File > Save. Leave the page in this position for the next exercise.

Creating threaded frames automatically

To speed up the creation of column-width linked text frames, InDesign provides a shortcut. If you press the right arrow key as you drag the Type tool to create a new text frame, InDesign automatically divides the text frame into multiple threaded frames. For example, if you press the right arrow key once while creating a text frame, the text frame is divided into two text frames of equal width. If you press the right arrow key five times, the text frame is divided five times, resulting in six columns of equal width.

You will now create a two-column text frame on page 3. You can then thread the text frames to help contain the overset text.

1 Choose View > Fit Spread In Window to center pages 2 and 3 in the window.

2 Select the Type tool (**T**), and position it in the first column on the page at right, where the column guide (purple) and margin guide (pink) intersect.

● **Note:** If you accidentally press the right arrow key more than once— producing more than two threaded text frames—choose Edit > Undo, and then try again. You can also remove text frames by pressing the left arrow key as you drag.

3 Drag the Type tool down and to the right to create a text frame that spans the width of both columns. As you drag, tap the right arrow key once.

InDesign automatically subdivides the text frame into two threaded text frames of equal width.

W: 1.47 in
H: 0.7708 in

4 Continue to drag down to position the text frame within the column and margin guides. If necessary, use the Selection tool (▶) to adjust the text frames to fit within the guides as shown.

5 Using the Selection tool, click the text frame in the second column on page 2. Click the frame's out port in the lower-right corner to load the text icon with overset text.

6 Click the loaded text icon (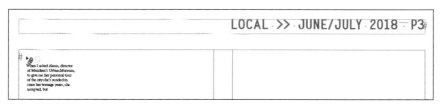) in the new text frame on page 3.

The text flows through the two columns.

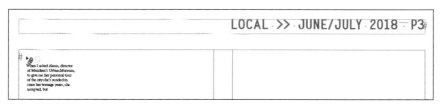

7 Choose File > Save. Leave the page in this position for the next exercise.

Flowing text automatically

You will now autoflow the remaining text into the booklet. When you autoflow text, InDesign automatically creates new text frames within column guides on subsequent pages until all of the overset text is placed. This is ideal for longer projects, such as books, but for this project it will end up obscuring some of the images that are already placed. You can fix that easily by deleting the text frames; the text flow is automatically rerouted through the remaining frames in the thread.

1 Using the Selection tool (▶), click the out port in the lower-right corner of the text frame in the second column on page 3. This loads the text icon with the overset text. (If necessary, first click the frame to select it, and then click the out port.)

2 Choose Layout > Next Spread to display pages 4 and 5.

3 Position the loaded text icon (⊞) in the first column on page 4, precisely where the column and margin guides intersect.

4 Hold down the Shift key and click.

Notice that new text frames are added to the remaining pages in the document, even on top of the photos. This is because you held down the Shift key to autoflow text.

▶ **Tip:** Shift-clicking the loaded text icon creates and flows text into automatically created text frames, adding pages as necessary to flow all the text into the document.

5 Using the Selection tool, Shift-click to select the two new text frames added to page 5 (the frame on top of the image of the man riding a bike).

6 Choose Edit > Clear to delete the text frames.

7 Choose Layout > Next Spread to display pages 6 and 7. As you can see, the text is flowing from page 4 to page 6 to page 7.

8 Using the Selection tool, Shift-click the two new text frames added to page 7 (the frames on top of the image of the rental bikes).

9 Choose Edit > Clear to delete the text frame.

Text is still overset, but you will resolve that with formatting in the next exercise.

10 Choose File > Save. Leave the page in this position for the next exercise.

Adding pages while flowing text

In addition to threading text frames on existing pages, you can add pages while flowing text. This feature, called Smart Text Reflow, is ideal for flowing long passages of text such as book chapters. With Smart Text Reflow, flowing text or typing into a primary text frame automatically adds pages and threaded text frames to contain all the text. If text becomes shorter through editing or reformatting, any extra pages can be automatically deleted as well. To experiment with Smart Text Reflow, follow these steps:

1 Choose File > New > Document. In the New Document screen:

- Click Print across the top.
- Click the Letter - Half icon.
- Click the Landscape icon for Orientation.
- Select Primary Text Frame.

2 Click Create.

3 Choose Edit > Preferences > Type (Windows) or InDesign > Preferences > Type (macOS) to open the Type preferences. The options in the Smart Text Reflow section of the Type preferences let you specify how pages are handled when you use Smart Text Reflow. Options include:

- Where pages are added (to the end of a story, section, or document)
- Whether Smart Text Reflow applies only to primary text frames or to other text frames in a document
- How pages are inserted into facing-page spreads
- Whether empty pages are deleted as text becomes shorter

4 Smart Text Reflow is selected by default, but confirm that it is selected. The Smart Text Reflow controls are at the bottom of the Type preferences. Click OK.

5 Choose File > Place. In the Place dialog box, locate and select 05_Feature_2018.docx, in the Lesson05 folder, and click Open.

6 On the first page of the new document, click the loaded text icon within the page margins to flow all the text into the primary text frame, adding pages as necessary. Note the number of pages (3) in the Pages panel.

7 Close the file without saving it.

Applying paragraph styles to text

Now that all the threaded text frames are in place and the text is flowing through them, you can format the text. This gives you a clear view of how the text fits and how it looks with the layout. Here, you will format the entire article with the Body Paragraphs style, and then you will format the opening paragraph and subheads.

1 Using the Type tool (T,), click in any text frame containing the main article you just imported.

2 Choose Edit > Select All to select all the text in the story (the text in the series of linked frames).

3 Choose Type > Paragraph Styles to open the Paragraph Styles panel.

4 Click the paragraph style Body Paragraphs. (If necessary, open the Body Text style group folder and scroll to locate the style.)

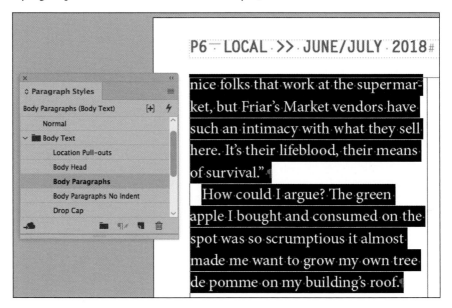

5 Choose Layout > Go to Page. Enter **1** in the Page field, and click OK.

6 On page 1, click in the first paragraph of the article, starting with "When I asked Alexis."

7 Click the Drop Cap paragraph style in the Paragraph Styles panel.

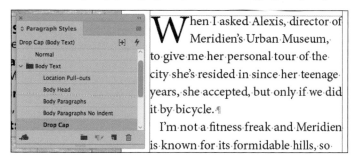

Now you will format the three subheads in the article.

8 Choose View > Fit Spread In Window, and then choose Layout > Next Spread to view pages 2 and 3.

9 Using the Type tool, click in the subhead that reads "B-Cycle" in the left column of page 2. This targets the paragraph for paragraph formatting.

10 Click the Body Head paragraph style in the Paragraph Styles panel.

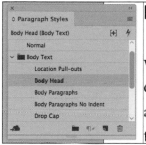

11 Follow steps 9–10 to apply the Body Head paragraph style to the remaining subheads in the story as follows:

- Page 3, left column: "Old Town"

- Page 3, right column: "Cobblestones, Gentrification and Local Produce"

- Page 4: "Farmers Market"

12 Choose File > Save. Remain on this page for the next exercise.

Adjusting columns

InDesign provides many methods for adjusting the length of columns of text. You might do this to suit the layout or to keep specific topics together. One way to do this is to resize the text frame with the Selection tool. Another method is to manually "bump" text to the next column with the Column Break character. Here, you will adjust the size of the text frames to suit the layout.

1 Double-click the page 4 icon on the Pages panel to center it in the document window.

2 Using the Selection tool (▶), click the text frame on the left containing the main article.

3 Drag the bottom of the text frame up so that the height of the frame shows approximately 2.1 in.

Note: If necessary, type **2.1 in** in the Height field on the Control panel and press Enter (Windows) or Return (macOS) to resize the frame.

4 Select the text frame at right, which contains the second column of text. Drag the bottom of the frame up to match the height of the text frame at left.

Resizing these text frames keeps the article text from obscuring the shaded sidebar box.

P4 · LOCAL · >> · JUNE/JULY · 2018

that was one of Old Town's first new businesses, to meet Scott G., Meridien's supervisor of urban renewal. He, too, arrives on a HUB bicycle, stylishly dressed for the weather in a medium-length Nehru-style jacket and knit cap, the ensemble nicely complemented by a pair of stylish spectacles and a worn leather shoulder bag.

"There are some hard-core purists who dismiss this development as negative—gentrification to ease the fears of yuppies who wouldn't come near here before," Scott remarks,

"but I find their argument difficult to support in light of all the good that has come to Old Town. We didn't move the blight out and then hide it somewhere else. We helped the people who needed assistance and let them stay as long as they weren't committing any violent crimes. They receive housing and there has been phenomenal success in getting many back into the workforce and making them part of the community again. How can this be bad?"

The old area of the city until recently was a haven for homeless people and addicts after the federal government suspended welfare aid in 1980. Since 2000, Meridien has opened 30 homeless shelters and a clinic specializing in substance abuse, promoting Old Meridien's recent development of live/work housing, boutique stores, and cafes.

5 Choose Layout > Next Spread to see pages 6 and 7. The "Farmers Market" subhead is now at the top of page 6.

6 Using the Selection tool, click the text frame at left. Drag the bottom of the text frame up so the height of the frame shows 2.1 in.

7 Click the pasteboard to deselect all objects on the page, and choose File > Save.

▶ **Tip:** To adjust how text flows within frames, you can enter break characters such as Column Break and Frame Break (Type > Insert Break Character).

Adding a jump line page number

When an article continues across multiple pages, forcing readers to turn pages, it helps to add a jump line, such as "(Continued on page x)." You can create jump lines in InDesign that automatically reflect the number of the next page in the text flow (that is, the next page to which the text frame is linked).

1 Double-click the page 1 icon in the Pages panel to center the page in the document window. Scroll to the right to view a portion of the pasteboard. Zoom in as necessary to see the text.

2 Using the Type tool (**T**,) and working on the pasteboard, drag to create a text frame approximately 1.5 inches by 0.25 inches.

3 Using the Selection tool (▶), drag the new text frame to the bottom of the second column on page 1. Be sure the top of the new text frame touches the bottom of the existing text frame.

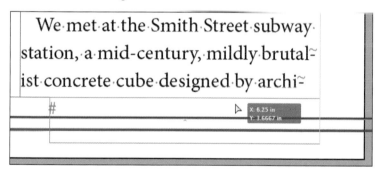

4 Using the Type tool, click to place an insertion point in the new frame. Type **Museum continued on** followed by a space.

5 Right-click (Windows) or Control-click (macOS) to display a context menu, and then choose Insert Special Character > Markers > Next Page Number. The jump line now reads "Museum continued on 2."

● **Note:** For the Next Page Number character to work properly, the text frame containing the jump line must touch or overlap the threaded frame.

6 Choose Type > Paragraph Styles to open the Paragraph Styles panel. With the
 text insertion point still in the jump line, click the Continued From/To Line
 paragraph style to format the text according to the template.

7 Choose File > Save.

8 Choose View > Fit Spread In Window.

9 Choose Preview from the Screen Mode menu in the Application bar
 at the top of the screen.

Congratulations, you have finished the lesson.

Exploring on your own

▶ **Tip:** Experiment
with text-flowing
options to find out what
threading methods
work best for you
and your projects. For
example, if you are
creating a template for
a catalog, you might
thread several small
text frames for item
descriptions and then
flow the text later.

In this lesson, you learned how to create a jump line that indicates the page number
on which an article continues. You can also create a jump line that indicates the
page number from which a continued article originated.

1 Choose View > Screen Mode > Normal to see the frame edges.

2 Using the Selection tool (▶), duplicate the text frame containing the jump line
 on page 1. (To duplicate an object, select it and choose Edit > Copy.)

3 Paste the jump line text frame on page 2. Drag the text frame so that it touches
 the top of the text frame in the first column. (Drag the top of the main text frame
 down as necessary so the jump line isn't touching the page header.)

4 Using the Type tool (T), change the words in the text frame from "Museum
 continued on" to "Museum continued from."

5 Select the page number, 3, in the jump line.

 At this point, you need to replace the Next Page Number character with the
 Previous Page Number character.

6 Choose Type > Insert Special Character > Markers > Previous Page Number.

 The jump line now reads "Museum continued from 2."

Review questions

1 Which tool lets you thread text frames?

2 How do you load the text icon?

3 What happens when you click the loaded text icon between column guides?

4 Which key do you press to automatically divide a text frame into multiple threaded frames?

5 What is the name of the feature that automatically adds pages and threaded text frames to contain all the text in an imported text file?

6 What feature automatically adjusts the size of a text frame based on the length of the text?

7 What do you need to do to ensure that the Next Page Number and Previous Page Number characters work in a jump line?

Review answers

1 The Selection tool.

2 Choose File > Place and select a text file, or click in an out port that contains overset text. You can also drag text files from the desktop onto a page.

3 InDesign creates a text frame where you click; the frame fits within the vertical column guides.

4 Press the right arrow key as you drag with the Type tool. (You can also press the left arrow key to decrease the number of threaded text frames.)

5 Smart Text Reflow.

6 The Auto-Size feature, found in the Text Frame Options dialog box (Object menu).

7 The text frame containing the jump line must touch the threaded text frame containing the story.

6

EDITING TEXT

Lesson Overview

In this lesson, you'll learn how to do the following:

- Sync fonts from Typekit.

- Handle a missing font.

- Enter and import text.

- Find and change text and formatting.

- Check the spelling in a document.

- Edit a spelling dictionary.

- Automatically correct misspelled words.

- Use the Story Editor.

- Move text by dragging and dropping.

- Track changes.

 This lesson will take about 60 minutes to complete.

Please log in to your account on peachpit.com to download the lesson files for this chapter, or go to the "Getting Started" section at the beginning of this book and follow the instructions under "Accessing the Lesson Files and Web Edition." Store the files on your computer in a convenient location.

We rush past the pastiche of architectural styles and eras that characterize Meridien's eclectic urbanism, something Alexes has made a career of celebrating. "A real city is never homogenous," she remarks.

One of Meridien's urban success stories is the rejuvenation of the Old Town district. Just five years ago, the area's cobblestone streets were strewn with trash and drug paraphernalia. The city's homeless would congregate here, and the historical buildings, some dating back to the 18th century, were primarily abandoned. But with the election of Mayor Pierre H. in 2016, the government allocated funds for a renewal project that provided new businesses and nonprofits with startup funding to renovate and occupy these empty structures. Before long, artists were occupying the upper floors, and boutiques, galleries, and cafés began to spring up to fit their lifestyles. Combine this with more robust social service programs that provided housing and drug counseling programs, and the area underwent a speedy, remarkable renaissance.

The bumpy roads result in a precarious ride that makes steering the shared hub bikes in a straight line virtually impossible. Luckily, auto traffic is mostly banned from Old Town, making it a favorite destination for those who disdain cars and much safer for our own clumsy veering.

We stop in front of Frugal Grounds, an airy café/gallery/performance space hybrid that was one of Old Town's first new businesses, to meet Scott G., Meridien's supervisor of urban renewal. He, too, arrives on a hub bicycle, stylishly dressed for the weather in a medium-length Nehru style jacket and knit cap, the ensemble nicely complemented by a pair of stylish spectacles and a worn leather shoulder bag.

"There are some hard-core purists who dismiss this development as negative—pentrification to ease the fears of yuppies who wouldn't come near here before," Scott remarks, "but I find their argument difficult to support in light of all the good that has come to Old Town. We didn't move the blight out and then hide it somewhere else. We helped the people who needed assistance. They receive housing and there has been phenomenal success in getting many back into the workforce and making them part of the community again."

Our next stop is Friar's Market—an open-air agora for Meridien's local farmers and produce growers to sell their fresh organic sustenance to residents weary of the old supermarket model. "The best part of the experience here is that I get to converse with the people who actually grew this stuff," beams Alexes. "Friar's Market vendors have such an intimacy with what they sell here. It's their lifeblood, their means of survival."

How could I argue? The green apple I bought and consumed on the spot was so scrumptious it made me want to grow my own tree de pomme.

We cut up Grayson Boulevard towards the "Green Light" district, Meridien's center of provincial haute couture and cuisine, where rustic cafes huddle alongside boutiques offering hemp clothing and hipster hot spots that sell art, books, and the latest designer accessories. After a whirlwind browse through almost ten different retailers, we greet the setting sun by settling at Alexes's favorite evening hangout spot, Le Bon Mot.

"I'll always be pushing for Meridien to promote thoughtful development by using our best and brightest creative minds," she says.

city

Urban Renewal with Respect

THE PASTICHE OF ARCHITECTURAL STYLES AND ERAS CHARACTERIZE MERIDIEN'S ECLECTIC URBANISM.

InDesign offers many of the text-editing features you find in dedicated word-processing software, including the ability to search and replace text and formatting, check spelling, automatically correct spelling as you type, and track changes as you edit.

Getting started

In this lesson, you will perform editorial tasks commonly expected of a graphic designer. These include importing a new story and using the editorial features in InDesign to search and replace text and formatting, check spelling, enter and track text changes, and more.

Note: If you have not already downloaded the project files for this lesson to your computer from your Account page, make sure to do so now. See "Getting Started" at the beginning of the book.

1 To ensure that the preferences and default settings of your Adobe InDesign program match those used in this lesson, move the InDesign Defaults file to a different folder following the procedure in "Saving and restoring the InDesign Defaults file" on pages 4–5.

2 Start Adobe InDesign.

3 The InDesign Start Screen displays. Click Open at left. (If the Start Screen does not display, choose File > Open from the InDesign menu bar.)

4 Open the 06_Start.indd file in the Lesson06 folder, located inside the Lessons folder within the InDesignCIB folder on your hard disk.

Note: If the Goudy Old Style and Urbana Light fonts happen to be active on your system, this alert will not display. You can review the steps on replacing a missing font and then move on to the next section.

5 When the Missing Fonts alert displays, click Sync Fonts. Click Close when font syncing is complete. (If necessary, click "Turn Typekit On" in the upper-right corner.)

The Adobe Typekit online service will locate, download, and activate the missing Urbana Light font. The Goudy Old Style font is not available through Adobe Typekit and will remain missing for now.

You will fix the problem of the missing Goudy Old Style font in the next section by replacing it with a font installed on your system.

6 To ensure that the panels and menu commands match those used in this lesson, choose Window > Workspace > [Advanced], and then choose Window > Workspace > Reset Advanced.

7 If necessary, choose View > Display Performance > High Quality Display to display the document at a higher resolution.

8 Choose File > Save As, rename the file **06_Text.indd**, and save it in the Lesson06 folder.

9 If you want to see what the finished document looks like, open the 06_End.indd file in the same folder. You can leave this document open to act as a guide as you work.

▶ **Tip:** In general, it is not necessary to display images at full resolution when working with text. If you are working on a slower computer, you can leave the display at Typical Display or even gray out the images with Fast Display.

10 When you're ready to resume working on the lesson document, 06_Text.indd, display it by clicking its tab in the upper-left corner of the document window.

● **Note:** For higher contrast in the printed manual, the screen captures in this book show the Medium Light interface. Interface elements such as panels and dialog boxes may be darker on your screen.

Finding and changing a missing font

When you opened the document in the previous exercise, the Goudy Old Style font may have been listed as missing. If this font is active on your computer, you did not receive an alert message, but you can still follow the steps for future reference. You will now search for text formatted with the Goudy Old Style font and replace it with the Minion Pro Regular font.

1 Choose View > Screen Mode > Normal so you can see layout aids such as guides.

Notice that once you leave Preview mode, the word "city" on the right-facing page is highlighted in pink. This indicates a missing font.

2 Choose Type > Find Font. The Find Font dialog box lists the fonts used in the document. An alert icon (⚠) appears next to any missing fonts.

3 Select Goudy Old Style in the Fonts In Document list.

4 For the Replace With option at the bottom of the dialog box, choose Minion Pro from the Font Family menu.

5 Choose Regular from the Font Style menu.

▶ **Tip:** If you select Redefine Style When Changing All in the Find Font dialog box, any character styles or paragraph styles that specify the missing font will be updated to include the Replace With font as well. This can be handy for quickly updating documents and templates—as long as you're sure the font change is appropriate.

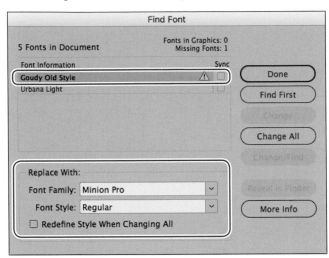

▶ **Tip:** To display more information about a missing font (such as character count, page where it is used, and font type), click More Info in the Find Font dialog box.

6 Click Change All.

7 Click Done to close the dialog box and see the replaced font in the document.

8 Choose File > Save.

Adding missing fonts

For most projects, you need to add the missing font to your system instead of substituting a different font. This maintains the original design and the way the text fits and flows. You can do this in the following ways:

- If you have the font, activate it on your system.

- If you do not have the font, you can purchase it.

- If you are a Creative Cloud member, you can see whether the font is available for use through Adobe's Typekit font library (click Sync Fonts in the Find Font dialog box).

Once you have the font, you can use font management software to activate it. You can also add the font to your InDesign Fonts folder or a Document Fonts folder in the folder containing the InDesign document.

For more information on acquiring and using fonts, see Chapter 6, "Fonts," in *Real World Print Production with Adobe Creative Cloud,* by Claudia McCue (Peachpit, 2014).

Entering and importing text

You can enter text directly into your InDesign documents, or you can import text prepared in other applications, such as word-processing software. To type text, you need to use the Type tool and select a text frame or text path. Options for importing text include dragging files from the desktop, "loading" the cursor with one or more text files to import, or importing text into a selected text frame.

Entering text

While graphic designers are not generally responsible for the text in all their layouts, they are often asked to enter edits from a marked-up hard copy or Adobe PDF. In this exercise, you will use the Type tool to revise the headline.

1 Choose View > Extras > Show Frame Edges. The text frames are outlined in gold so you can see them. Locate the text frame on the left-facing page under the images containing the headline "Urban Renewal."

2 Using the Type tool (**T**), click in the text frame next to "Urban Renewal."

3 Type a space and the words **with Respect.**

● **Note:** If you cannot see the frame edges, be sure that the screen mode is set to Normal (View > Screen Mode > Normal).

4 Choose File > Save.

Importing text

When working with a template for a project such as a magazine, designers generally import article text into existing text frames. In this exercise, you will import a Microsoft Word file and apply body-copy formatting to it.

1 Using the Type tool (**T**), click in the first column of the text frame on the right-facing page.

▶ **Tip:** In the Place dialog box, you can Shift-click to select multiple text files. When you do this, the cursor is "loaded" with those files. You can then click in text frames or on the page to import the text from each file. This works well with content such as long captions that are saved in different text files.

2 Choose File > Place. In the Place dialog box, make sure Show Import Options is not selected.

3 Navigate to and select the Feature_February2018.docx file in the Lesson06 folder, located inside the Lessons folder within the InDesignCIB folder on your hard disk.

4 Click Open. If the Missing Fonts dialog box displays, click Close to dismiss it. You will apply a different font through a paragraph style.

The text flows from column to column, filling the three columns.

5 Choose Edit > Select All to select all the text in the story.

6 Click the Paragraph Styles panel icon at the right to display the panel.

7 Click the Body Paragraph style to apply it to the selected paragraphs. If a plus sign displays next to Body Paragraph, click Clear Overrides (¶⁄) at the bottom of the Paragraph Styles panel.

8 Click in the first body paragraph starting with "We rush past." Click the First Body Paragraph Style in the Paragraph Styles panel to apply a style that includes a drop cap.

● **Note:** Now that you have changed the formatting, the story may no longer fit. In the lower-right corner of the text frame on the right-facing page, a red plus sign (+) will indicate overset text (additional text). Later, you will use the Story Editor to resolve this.

We rush past the pastiche of architectural styles and eras that characterize Meridien's eclectic urbanism, something Alexis has made a career of celebrating. "A real city is never homogenous," she remarks.

One of Meridien's urban success stories is the rejuvenation of the Old Town district. Just eight years ago, the

9 Choose Edit > Deselect All to deselect the text.

10 Choose View > Extras > Hide Frame Edges.

11 Choose File > Save.

Finding and changing text and formatting

Like most popular word-processing software, InDesign lets you search and replace text and formatting. Often, while graphic designers are working on layouts, the copy is still being revised. When editors request global changes, Find/Change helps ensure accurate and consistent changes.

Finding and changing text

For this article, the fact checker discovered that the tour guide's name is not spelled as "Alexis"—it's "Alexes." You will change all instances of her name in the document.

1 Using the Type tool (**T**), click at the beginning of the story before "We rush past" (on the right-facing page in the far left column).

2 Choose Edit > Find/Change.

3 Click the menu in the Query field to see the built-in Find/Change options. Click each tab across the top to view other options: Text, GREP, Glyph, and Object.

4 Click the Text tab for a simple search and replace of text.

5 Click Forward for the search Direction.

6 Type **Alexis** in the Find What box.

Press Tab to navigate to the Change To box. Type **Alexes**.

Using the Search menu in the Find/Change dialog box, you can choose to search All Documents, Document, Story, To Beginning Of Story, To End Of Story, or Selection (when text is selected).

7 Select Story from the Search menu, which defines the scope of the search.

▶ **Tip:** You can toggle the search direction by pressing Ctrl+Alt+ Enter (Windows) or Command+Option+ Return (macOS).

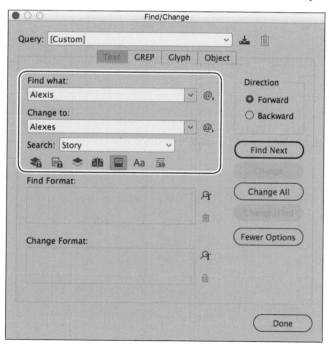

When using the Find/Change dialog box, it's always a good idea to test your settings. Find one instance of the search criterion, replace it, and review the text before you make global changes. (Alternatively, you may opt to look at each instance with Find as you make the changes so you can see how each change affects surrounding copy and line breaks.)

8 Click Find Next. When the first instance of "Alexis" is highlighted, click Change.

9 Click Find Next, and then click Change All. When the alert indicates that two additional replacements were made, click OK.

10 Leave the Find/Change dialog box open for the next exercise.

Finding and changing formatting

The editors request one more global edit to this article; this one concerns formatting rather than spelling. The city's HUB bike program prefers to see its name in small caps rather than lowercase.

1 Type **hub** in the Find What box. Press Tab to select the text in the Change To field and press Backspace or Delete.

2 Point at each icon in the row below the Search menu to view its tool tip and see how it affects the Find/Change operation. For example, clicking the Whole Word icon (≣) ensures that instances of the Find What text within another word will not be found or changed. Do not change any of the settings.

3 If necessary, click the More Options button to display formatting options for the found text.

4 In the Change Format section at the bottom of the dialog box, click the Specify Attributes To Change icon (♀).

5 On the left side of the Change Format Settings dialog box, select Basic Character Formats.

> **Tip:** When the Find/Change dialog box is open, you can still click in the text and make edits with the Type tool. The Find/Change dialog box remains open so you can resume your search after editing the text.

> **Tip:** For acronyms and abbreviations, designers often prefer to use Small Caps style (abbreviated versions of capital letters) rather than All Caps style (all capital letters). The small caps are generally the same height as lowercase characters, and they blend into body copy better.

6 In the main part of the Change Format Settings dialog box, choose Small Caps from the Case menu.

▶ **Tip:** If you are unhappy with the results of Find/Change, you can choose Edit > Undo to undo the last "change" operation, whether it was Change, Change All, or Find/Change.

7 Leave the other options blank, and then click OK to return to the Find/Change dialog box.

Notice the alert icon () that appears above the Change To box. This icon indicates that InDesign will change text to the specified formatting.

8 Test your settings by clicking Find Next and then clicking Change. Once you confirm that "hub" changes to "HUB," click Change All.

9 When the alert indicates that two changes were made, click OK. Click Done to close the Find/Change dialog box.

10 Choose File > Save.

Checking spelling

Tip: Be sure to discuss with your client or editor whether you should be the one checking spelling in InDesign. Many editors strongly prefer to check spelling themselves.

InDesign has features for checking spelling similar to the options in word-processing programs. You can check the spelling in selected text, an entire story, all the stories in a document, or all the stories in several open documents at once. To customize which words are flagged as possible misspellings, you can add words to your document's dictionary. In addition, you can have InDesign flag possible spelling issues and correct spelling as you type.

The Check Spelling dialog box provides the following buttons to handle the words shown in the Not In Dictionary field (otherwise known as suspect words):

- **Skip:** Click Skip when you are confident of the spelling of the current suspect word but would like to review any other instances of the spelling in context.

- **Change:** Click Change to change the spelling of the current instance of the suspect word to the spelling in the Change To field.

- **Ignore All:** Click Ignore All when you are confident that the spelling of the suspect word is appropriate for use througout the selection, story, or document.

- **Change All:** Click Change All when you are confident that changing the spelling of the suspect word is appropriate for the entire selection, story, or document.

Checking spelling in the document

Note: Depending on the InDesign preferences set for Dictionary and Spelling, or whether you've added words to a custom dictionary, different words may be flagged. Simply experiment with the various Check Spelling options to get familiar with them.

Before a document is ready for print or electronic distribution, it's a good idea to check spelling. In this case, we suspect the newly imported story may be a little sloppy, so you will check the spelling now.

1 If necessary, choose View > Fit Spread In Window to view both pages of the document.

2 Using the Type tool (**T**), click before the first word of the article you've been working on: "We."

3 Choose Edit > Spelling > Check Spelling.

 Using the Search menu in the Check Spelling dialog box, you can choose to check All Documents, Document, Story, To End Of Story, or Selection.

4 Select Story from the Search menu at the bottom of the dialog. The spell check starts automatically.

5 InDesign highlights various words that do not match the spelling dictionary.

Handle the flagged words as follows:

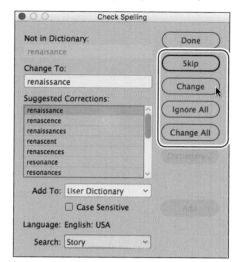

- Meridien's, Alexes, nonprofits: Click Ignore All.

- renaisance: Select "renaissance" in the Suggested Corrections list and click Change.

- Nehru: Click Ignore All.

- recieve: Type **receive** in the Change To field and click Change.

- pomme, Grayson, Meridien: Click Ignore All.

6 Click Done.

7 Choose File > Save.

Adding words to a document-specific dictionary

With InDesign, you can add words to your user dictionary or to a document specific dictionary. If you work with multiple clients who may have different spelling preferences, for example, it is better to add words to a document-specific dictionary. In this case, you will add "Meridien" to the document's dictionary.

1 Choose Edit > Spelling > User Dictionary to display the User Dictionary dialog box.

2 Select 06_Text.indd from the Target menu.

3 Type **Meridien** in the Word box.

4 Select Case Sensitive to add only "Meridien" to the dictionary. This ensures that a lowercase use of "meridien" is still flagged when you check spelling.

5 Click Add.

6 Type Meridien's in the Word box.

7 Make sure Case Sensitive is still selected, and then click Add.

8 Click Done, and then choose File > Save.

► **Tip:** If a word is not specific to one language—such as a person's name—you can choose All Languages to add the word to every language's spelling dictionary.

Checking spelling dynamically

It's not necessary for you to wait until a document is finished before checking the spelling. Enabling dynamic spelling allows you to see misspelled words in text. To see how this works:

1 Choose Edit > Preferences > Spelling (Windows) or InDesign CC > Preferences > Spelling (macOS) to display Spelling preferences.

2 In the Find section, select the possible errors you want highlighted.

3 Select Enable Dynamic Spelling.

4 In the Underline Color section, use the menus to customize how possible errors are signified.

 You can customize what the Check Spelling dialog box flags as possible errors: Misspelled Words, Repeated Words, Uncapitalized Words, and Uncapitalized Sentences. For example, if you're working on a directory with hundreds of names, you might want to select Uncapitalized Words but not Misspelled Words.

5 Click OK to close the Preferences dialog box and return to your document.

 Words that may be misspelled (according to the default user dictionary) are now underlined.

6 Right-click (Windows) or Control-click (macOS) a word flagged by dynamic spelling to display a contextual menu from which you can select an option to change the spelling.

Automatically correcting misspelled words

Autocorrect takes the concept of dynamically checking spelling to the next level. With Autocorrect activated, InDesign automatically corrects misspelled words as you type them. Changes are made based on an internal list of commonly misspelled words. You can add other commonly misspelled words, including words in other languages, to this list if you like.

1 Choose Edit > Preferences > Autocorrect (Windows) or InDesign CC > Preferences > Autocorrect (macOS) to display Autocorrect preferences.

2 Select the Enable Autocorrect option. By default, the list of commonly misspelled words is for English: USA.

3 Change the language to French and note the commonly misspelled words in that language. Try other languages, if you'd like. Change the language back to English: USA before proceeding.

The editors have realized that the name of their city, "Meridien," is frequently typed as "Meredien," with an "e" in the middle rather than an "i." You will prevent this mistake by adding the misspelling and correct spelling to the Autocorrect list.

4 Click Add. In the Add To Autocorrect List dialog box, type **Meredien** in the Misspelled Word box and **Meridien** in the Correction box.

5 Click OK to add the word, and then click OK again to close the Preferences dialog box.

6 Using the Type tool (T), type the word **Meredien** followed by a space anywhere in the text.

7 Notice that Autocorrect changes the spelling from "Meredien" to "Meridien," and then choose Edit > Undo until the word you added is deleted.

8 Choose File > Save.

► **Tip:** Words are autocorrected as soon as you finish a word, as indicated by typing a space, period, comma, or forward slash.

Editing text by dragging and dropping

To quickly cut and paste words in your document, InDesign allows you to drag and drop text within the same story, between frames, and between documents. You'll now use drag and drop to move text from one paragraph to another in the magazine layout.

1 Choose Edit > Preferences > Type (Windows) or InDesign CC > Preferences > Type (macOS) to display Type preferences.

Tip: When you drag and drop text, by default InDesign automatically adds and deletes spaces before and after words as necessary. If you need to turn off this feature, deselect Adjust Spacing Automatically When Cutting And Pasting Words in Type preferences.

2 In the Drag And Drop Text Editing section, select Enable In Layout View. This option lets you drag and drop text in Layout view in addition to the Story Editor. Click OK.

> Drag and Drop Text Editing
> ☑ Enable in Layout View
> ☑ Enable in Story Editor

3 Locate the subhead below the "Urban Renewal with Respect" headline. Adjust the zoom level as necessary so you can read the subhead text.

4 Using the Type tool (T), double-click in the word "ECLECTIC" to select it.

5 Position the I-bar pointer over the selected word until the pointer changes to the drag and drop icon (⬥).

> THE PASTICHE OF ARCHITECTURAL STYLES AND ERAS
> CHARACTERIZE ▆ECLECTIC▆ MERIDIEN'S URBANISM.

Tip: If you want to copy a selected word instead of moving it, hold down the Alt (Windows) or Option (macOS) key after you start dragging.

6 Drag the word to its correct location before "URBANISM."

> THE PASTICHE OF ARCHITECTURAL STYLES AND ERAS
> CHARACTERIZE ▆ECLECTIC▆ MERIDIEN'S |URBANISM.

> THE PASTICHE OF ARCHITECTURAL STYLES AND ERAS
> CHARACTERIZE MERIDIEN'S ▆ECLECTIC▆ URBANISM.

7 Choose File > Save.

Using the Story Editor

If you need to enter many text edits, rewrite a story, or cut a story, you can isolate the text with the Story Editor. The Story Editor window works as follows:

• Text displays without formatting—with the exception of the styles bold, italic, and bold italic. Any graphics and other nontext elements are omitted to make editing easier.

• The column to the left of the text displays a vertical depth ruler and the name of the paragraph style applied to each paragraph.

• Dynamic spelling (if enabled) highlights misspelled words, just like in the document window.

• If the Enable In Story Editor option is selected in Type preferences, you can also drag and drop text in the Story Editor, just as you did in the previous exercise.

• In Story Editor Display preferences, you can customize the font, size, background color, and more for the Story Editor window.

The article on the right-facing page is too long to fit in the text frame. You will delete a sentence in the Story Editor to help it fit.

1 Choose View > Fit Spread In Window.

2 Using the Type tool (T), click in the first full paragraph in the third column of the article.

3 Choose Edit > Edit In Story Editor. Position the Story Editor window next to the far-right column on the spread.

Note: If the Story Editor window goes behind the document window, you can bring it to the front by choosing its name from the bottom of the Window menu.

4 Drag the vertical scroll bar in the Story Editor to the end of the story. Note the line that indicates the overset text.

5 In the Story Editor, scroll up to locate and select the following sentence: "The long arcade is a kaleidoscope of nature's colors—fruits, vegetables, and meats meticulously arranged in bins by their growers and producers." Be sure to select the final period.

| Body Paragraph | Our next stop is Friar's Market—an open-air agora for Meridien's local farmers and produce growers to sell their fresh organic sustenance to residents weary of the old supermarket model. The long arcade is a kaleidoscope of nature's colors—fruits, vegetables, and meats meticulously arranged in bins by their growers and producers. "The | Our next stop is Friar's Market—an open-air agora for Meridien's local farmers and produce growers to sell their fresh organic sustenance to residents weary of the old supermarket model. The long arcade is a kaleidoscope of nature's colors—fruits, vegetables, and meats meticulously arranged in bins by their growers and producers. "The best part of the |

6 Press Backspace or Delete. Leave the Story Editor open for the next set of steps.

7 Choose File > Save.

Tracking changes

For some projects, it's important to see what changes are made to the text throughout the design and review process. In addition, reviewers may suggest changes that another user can accept or reject. As with a word-processing program, you can track text that is added, deleted, or moved using the Story Editor.

In this document, you will edit a few words. When the final edits are made, the text frame should no longer have overset text.

Tip: In Track Changes preferences, you can customize which changes are tracked and how the changes display in the Story Editor.

1 Choose Type > Track Changes > Track Changes In Current Story.

2 In the Story Editor, scroll up to the second paragraph of the story starting with "One of Meridien's."

3 Using the Type tool (T) in the Story Editor, make the following changes in the second paragraph:

- Change "eight" to "five"
- Delete "controversial"
- Insert "more" before "robust social service programs"

Notice how the changes are marked in the Story Editor window.

4 With the Story Editor window still open, choose Type > Track Changes, and review the options for accepting and rejecting changes. Once you have reviewed the possibilities, choose Accept All Changes > In This Story.

5 When the alert dialog box displays, click OK.

6 Click the Story Editor window's close box. If necessary, choose Edit > Spelling > Dynamic Spelling to disable this feature.

7 Choose File > Save.

Congratulations. You have finished the lesson.

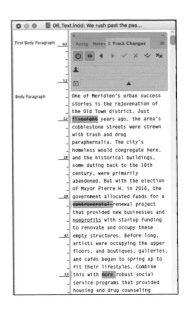

Exploring on your own

Now that you have tried the basic text-editing tools in InDesign, experiment with them more to edit and format this document.

1 Using the Type tool (T), add subheads to the story and format them with options in the Control panel.

2 If you have additional text files on your system, try dragging them from the desktop to the layout to see how they're imported. Choose Edit > Undo if you don't want to keep them in the document.

3 Use the Find/Change dialog box to find all em dashes in the story and replace them with an em dash with a space on either side of it. Click the @ icon next to the Find What box to search for special characters such as em dashes.

4 Edit the story using the Story Editor and Track Changes. See how the different changes are marked, and experiment with accepting and rejecting the changes.

Review questions

1 Which tool lets you edit text?

2 Where are most of the commands for editing text?

3 What is the InDesign search-and-replace feature called?

4 While checking the spelling in a document, InDesign flags words that are not in the dictionary—but they may not actually be misspelled. How can you fix this?

5 If you seem to continually type a word incorrectly, what can you do?

Review answers

1 The Type tool allows you to edit text.

2 Most commands for editing text are in the Edit menu and the Type menu.

3 InDesign uses the term Find/Change (Edit menu).

4 Add those words to the document's or InDesign's default spelling dictionary for the language or languages of your choice (Edit > Spelling > User Dictionary).

5 Add the word to your Autocorrect preferences.

7 WORKING WITH TYPOGRAPHY

Lesson Overview

In this lesson, you'll learn how to do the following:

- Customize and use the baseline grid.

- Adjust vertical and horizontal text spacing.

- Change fonts and type styles.

- Insert special characters from OpenType fonts.

- Create a headline that spans multiple columns.

- Balance the text in columns.

- Hang punctuation outside a margin.

- Add and format a drop cap.

- Adjust line breaks.

- Specify a tab with a leader and create a hanging indent.

- Add a rule and shading to a paragraph.

 This lesson will take approximately 60 minutes to complete.

Please log in to your account on peachpit.com to download the lesson files for this chapter, or go to the "Getting Started" section at the beginning of this book and follow the instructions under "Accessing the Lesson Files and Web Edition." Store the files on your computer in a convenient location.

Restaurant**Profile**

Assignments Restaurant

Sure, you can get Caesar salad prepared tableside for two at any of the higher-end restaurants in town—for $25 plus another $40 (just for starters) for a single slab of steak. Or, you can visit Assignments Restaurant, run by students of the international Culinary School at The Art Institute of Colorado, where tableside preparations include Caesar salad for $4.50 and steak Diane for $19. No, this isn't Elway's, but the chefs in training create a charming experience for patrons from start to finish.

Since 1992, the School of Culinary Arts has trained more than 4,300 chefs—all of whom were required to work in the restaurant. Those chefs are now working in the industry all over the country, says Chef Instructor Stephen Kleinman, CEC, AAC. "Whether I go to a restaurant in Manhattan or San Francisco, people know me," Kleinman says, describing encounters with former students. Although he claims to be a "hippie from the '60s," Kleinman apprenticed in Europe, attended a culinary academy in San Francisco and had the opportunity to cook at the prestigious James Beard House three times. He admits that his experience lends him credibility, but it's his warm, easygoing, approachable style that leads to his success as a teacher.

IF YOU GO

Name Assignments Restaurant
Address 675 S. Broadway, Denver
Reservations . . . call 303-778-6625 or visit
 www.opentable.com
Hours Wednesday–Friday, 11:30
 a.m.–1:30 p.m. and 6–8 p.m.

THE RESTAURANT

Assignments Restaurant, tucked back by the Quest Diagnostics lab off South Broadway near Alameda Avenue, seats 71 at its handful of booths and tables. The blissful quiet, a welcome change from the typical hot spot, is interrupted only by solicitous servers

dressed in chef attire. Despite decor that is on the edge of institutional with its cream-colored walls, faux cherry furniture and kitschy cafe artwork, this is a spot that welcomes intimate conversation with friends and family.

A perusal of the menu, while munching fresh bread and savoring a glass of wine, tempts you with its carefully planned variety. "The menu is all designed to teach cooking methods," says Kleinman. "It covers 80 to 85 percent of what students have been learning in class—saute, grill, braise, make vinaigrettes, cook vegetables, bake and make desserts." In a twist on "some of the best restaurants in the world serve tableside, chefs are more grounded this way," claims Kleinman, who would never be mistaken for a snob. "By having the students come to the front of the house—serving as waitpeople and preparing dishes tableside—we break a lot of barriers."

For our "test dinner," an amuse bouche, a crab-stuffed mushroom cap, arrives followed by an appetizer of chorizo-stuffed prawns wrapped in applewood-smoked bacon. The tableside Caesar preparation is a wonderful ritual that tastes as good as it looks. Entrees, all under $20, include grilled trout, sweet and sour spareribs, spinach

lasagna, seared duck breast, flatiron steak, steak Diane prepared tableside and pesto-crusted lamb chops. We opted for a succulent trout and tender spareribs, and notice that a $10 macaroni and cheese entree makes Assignments kid-friendly for special occasions.

THE GOALS

The purpose of this unique restaurant is to give students practical experience so they can hit the ground running. "The goal is to make the students comfortable, thinking on their feet, getting

"Maybe the next celebrity chef to hit town will whip up a tableside bananas Foster for you."

ready for reality," says Kleinman. He wants students to be able to read tickets, perform, and recover and learn getting valuable front-of-the-house and business experience in addition to cooking.

Five to seven students work in the Assignments kitchen at one time. Students at the School of Culinary Arts work toward an associate of applied science degree in culinary arts or a bachelor of arts degree in culinary management.

With degree in hand, the school places 99 percent of its students. While

many students are placed at country clubs and resorts that prefer formal training, chefs from all over town—Panzano, Jax Fish House, Julia's, St. Mark's—have trained at Assignments as well. Or try O's Restaurant, whose recent media darling chef Ian Kleinman is not just a former student but Stephen Kleinman's son. Make a reservation and maybe the next celebrity chef to hit town will whip up a tableside bananas Foster for you.

Julia Pippin is a writer, editor and hockey mom who wishes that her assignments involved lighting bananas on fire. For now, she celebrates any evening that doesn't involve a hockey game and a sports bar.

TRY IT @ HOME

CAESAR SALAD
2 cloves garlic
Taste kosher salt
2 anchovy fillets, chopped
1 coddled egg
½ lemon
½ Tbsp Dijon mustard
¼ cup red wine vinegar
¼ cup virgin olive oil
¼ tsp Worcestershire
Romaine lettuce heart, washed and dried
¼ cup croutons
¼ cup Parmesan cheese
Taste cracked black pepper

Grind together the garlic and salt. Add the chopped

anchovies. Stir in the egg and lemon. Add the vinegar, olive oil and Worcestershire sauce, and whip briefly. Pour over lettuce and toss with croutons, Parmesan and black pepper.

CHORIZO-STUFFED PRAWNS
3 prawns, butterflied
3 Tbsp chorizo sausage
3 slices bacon, blanched
1 bunch parsley, fried
2 oz morita mayonnaise (recipe follows)
½ oz olive oil

Heat oven to 350°. Stuff the butterflied prawns with chorizo. Wrap a piece of the blanched bacon around each prawn and place in the oven. Cook until the chorizo is done. Place the fried parsley on a plate and place the prawns on top. Drizzle with the morita mayonnaise.

MORITA MAYONNAISE
1 pint mayonnaise
1 tsp morita powder
1 Tbsp lemon juice
Salt and pepper to taste

Mix ingredients and serve.

InDesign offers many features for fine-tuning typography, including drop caps for leading the eye into a paragraph, easy access to OpenType features such as fractions, precision line-spacing and character-spacing controls, and the ability to automatically balance text in columns.

Getting started

In this lesson, you'll fine-tune the typography in a restaurant review for a high-end lifestyles magazine. For the rich look of the magazine, the type is precisely spaced and formatted: It uses a baseline grid for aligning text across columns, correctly formatted fractions in the recipes, and decorative touches, such as drop caps and pull quotes.

Note: If you have not already downloaded the project files for this lesson to your computer from your Account page, make sure to do so now. See "Getting Started" at the beginning of the book.

1 To ensure that the preferences and default settings of your Adobe InDesign program match those used in this lesson, move the InDesign Defaults file to a different folder following the procedure in "Saving and restoring the InDesign Defaults file" on pages 4–5.

2 Start Adobe InDesign.

3 The InDesign Start Screen displays. Click Open at left. (If the Start Screen does not display, choose File > Open from the InDesign menu bar.)

4 Open the 07_Start.indd file in the Lesson07 folder, located inside the Lessons folder within the InDesignCIB folder on your hard disk.

5 If the Missing Fonts dialog box displays, click Sync Fonts to access any missing fonts through Adobe Typekit. Click Close when font syncing is complete.

Note: For higher contrast in the printed manual, the screen captures in this book show the Medium Light interface. Interface elements such as panels and dialog boxes may be darker on your screen.

6 To ensure that the panels and menu commands match those used in this lesson, choose Window > Workspace > [Advanced], and then choose Window > Workspace > Reset Advanced.

7 To display the document at a higher resolution, choose View > Display Performance > High Quality Display (if it's not already enabled).

8 Choose File > Save As, rename the file **07_Type.indd**, and save it in the Lesson07 folder.

9 If you want to see what the finished document looks like, open the 07_End.indd file in the same folder. You can leave this document open to act as a guide as you work.

In this lesson, you will work intensively with text. You can use the character-formatting controls and paragraph-formatting controls in the Control panel, or you can use the Character panel and Paragraph panel. Using the individual Character and Paragraph panels can be easier for formatting text because you can drag the panels to where you want them.

● **Note:** Drag the Paragraph panel tab Into the Character panel tab to create a panel group, if you prefer.

10 Choose Type > Character and Type > Paragraph to open the two primary text-formatting panels. Leave these panels open until you finish this lesson.

11 Choose Type > Show Hidden Characters so you can see spaces, paragraph returns, tabs, and the like while you work on this lesson.

Adjusting vertical spacing

InDesign provides several options for customizing and adjusting the vertical spacing of text in a frame. You can do the following:

- Set the space between lines of paragraphs using a baseline grid.

- Set the space between lines using the Leading menu in the Character panel.

- Set the space between paragraphs using the Space Before and Space After options in the Paragraph panel.

- Use the Vertical Justification and Balance Columns options in the Text Frame Options dialog box to align text within a frame.

- Control how paragraphs flow from one column to the next using the Keep Lines Together, Keep With Previous, and Keep With Next settings available in the Keep Options dialog box (choose Keep Options from the Paragraph panel menu).

In this section of the lesson, you will use the baseline grid to align text.

Using the baseline grid to align text

Once you've decided on the font size and leading for your document's body text, you may want to set up a baseline grid (also called a leading grid) for the entire document. The baseline grid represents the leading (line spacing) for your document's body text and is used to align the baseline of type in one column of text with the baseline of type in neighboring columns and pages.

Before you set up the baseline grid, you need to check the margin value for the top of your document and the leading value for the body text. These elements work together with the grid to create a cohesive design.

▶ **Tip:** You can set up a baseline grid at the text frame level, which is ideal for situations in which different stories have different leading values. Choose Object > Text Frame Options, and then click the Baseline Options tab.

1 To view the top margin value for the page, choose Layout > Margins And Columns. The top margin is set to 6p0 (6 picas, 0 points). Click Cancel.

2 To view the leading value for the body text, select the Type tool (T) in the Tools panel. Click to place an insertion point in the first full paragraph of the story, which starts with "Sure." Look at the leading value () in the Character panel. The leading is set to 14 pt (14 points).

3 Choose Edit > Preferences > Grids (Windows) or InDesign CC > Preferences > Grids (macOS) to set the baseline grid options.

4 In the Baseline Grid section, type **6p** in the Start box to match your top margin setting of 6p0.

 This option sets the location of the first grid line for the document. If you use the default value of 3p0, the first grid line would appear above the top margin.

5 In the Increment Every box, type **14 pt** to match the leading.

▶ **Tip:** By customizing the View Threshold value, you can view the grid while zoomed in to edit text but have it hidden while you zoom out and view the whole page.

6 Choose 100% from the View Threshold menu.

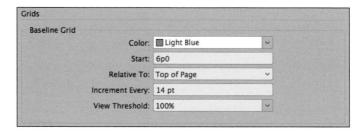

 The View Threshold menu sets the minimum zoom level at which you can see the grid onscreen. When this setting is 100%, the grid appears in the document window only at magnifications of 100% or higher.

7 Click OK.

8 Choose File > Save.

Viewing the baseline grid

Now you'll make the new grid visible onscreen.

1 To view the baseline grid in the document window, choose View > Grids & Guides > Show Baseline Grid, and then choose View > Actual Size.

Sure, you can get Caesar salad prepared tableside for two at any of the higher-end res-	welcomes intimate conversation with
taurants in town—for $25 plus another $40 (just for starters) for a single slab of steak.	friends and family.¶
Or, you can visit Assignments Restaurant, run by students of the International Culinary	A perusal of the menu, while
School at The Art Institute of Colorado, where tableside preparations include Caesar	munching fresh bread and savoring a
salad for $4.50 and steak Diane for $19. No, this isn't Elway's, but the chefs in training	glass of wine, tempts you with its care-
create a charming experience for patrons from start to finish.¶	fully planned variety. "The menu is all
Since 1992, the School of Culinary Arts has trained more than 4,300 chefs—all	designed to teach cooking methods,"
of whom were required to work in the restaurant. Those chefs are now working in	says Kleinman. "It covers 80 to 85 per-

You can align one paragraph, selected paragraphs, or all the paragraphs in a story to the baseline grid. (A story is all the text in a series of threaded text frames.) In the following steps, you will use the Paragraph panel to align the main story to the baseline grid.

2 Using the Type tool (T), click to place an insertion point anywhere in the first paragraph on the spread, and then choose Edit > Select All to select all the text in the main story.

3 If the Paragraph panel isn't visible, choose Type > Paragraph.

If necessary, choose Show Options from the Paragraph panel menu to see all the options.

4 In the Paragraph panel, click Align To Baseline Grid (≡≡). The text shifts so that the baselines of the characters rest on the grid lines.

▶ **Tip:** As with most other paragraph-formatting controls, the baseline grid controls are also available on the Control panel.

5 Click the pasteboard to deselect the text. Choose File > Save.

Changing the spacing between paragraphs

When you apply space before or after a paragraph aligned to the baseline grid, the space before/after values are ignored, and the first line of the paragraph is placed on the next baseline grid line. For example, if you apply Space Before (greater than 0 and less than 14 pt) to a paragraph aligned to a 14-pt baseline grid, the paragraph will automatically start on the next available baseline. If you apply Space After, the following paragraph will automatically jump to the next available baseline. This creates a 14-pt space between the paragraphs.

Here, you'll make the subheads in the main story stand out more by inserting space before (above) them. Then, you'll update the Subhead paragraph style to automatically apply the new spacing to all the subheads.

1 Choose View > Fit Spread In Window to see the full-page spread.

2 Using the Type tool (T), click anywhere in the subhead "THE RESTAURANT" on the left page.

▶ **Tip:** When applying paragraph attributes, it isn't necessary to select an entire paragraph with the Type tool. Just select part of the paragraph or paragraphs you want to format. If you are formatting only one paragraph, you can simply click in the paragraph to place an insertion point.

3 In the Paragraph panel, type **6 pt** in the Space Before box (✱≣), and press Enter or Return.

The points are automatically converted to picas, and the text in the subhead shifts automatically to the next grid line.

4 Click Paragraph Styles in the list of docked panels at right.

5 With the insertion point still in the "The Restaurant" subhead, notice that a plus sign (+) appears after the Subhead style name in the panel.

This sign indicates that the formatting of the selected text has been modified from the original formatting of the applied paragraph style. Differences between a style and actual formatting are referred to as "overrides."

▶ **Tip:** If you're working on a redesign of a publication, often you will experiment with already-formatted text. The ability to redefine styles makes it easy to save new specifications in styles that are then saved with updated templates.

6 Choose Redefine Style from the Paragraph Styles panel menu. The Subhead style takes on the formatting—specifically, the new Space Before setting and the Align To Baseline Grid setting—of the selected paragraph.

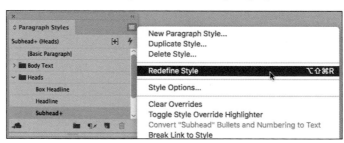

Notice that the plus sign (+) no longer appears after the style name and that space is added above the "The Goals" subhead on the right page as well.

▶ **Tip:** You can also choose Baseline Grid from the View Options menu on the Application bar to view and hide the baseline grid.

7 Choose View > Grids & Guides > Hide Baseline Grid.

8 Choose Edit > Deselect All.

9 Choose File > Save.

Working with fonts, type styles, and glyphs

Changing the fonts and type styles of text can make a dramatic difference in the appearance of your document. InDesign automatically installs a few fonts, including several styles of Letter Gothic and Myriad Pro. Creative Cloud members can access additional fonts through the Adobe Typekit website, which offers select fonts for free and others for licensing. Once a font is installed, you can apply it to text and change its size, select a style (such as bold or italic), and more. In addition, you can access all the glyphs (every form of each character) in the font.

OpenType fonts

OpenType fonts, such as Adobe Caslon Pro, may display many more glyphs than you are accustomed to seeing. OpenType fonts can contain many more characters and glyph alternates than other font formats. For more information on OpenType fonts, visit www.adobe.com/products/type.html.

Adding a font from Adobe Typekit

This exercise uses Adobe Caslon Pro Bold Italic, which is available for free from the Adobe Typekit website. If the font is already installed on your system, follow the steps to see how you can add another font.

1 Choose Type > Add Fonts From Typekit. This launches your preferred browser and takes you to https://typekit.com.

> **Tip:** Each style of a font, such as bold or italic, is actually installed as a different font file on your system.

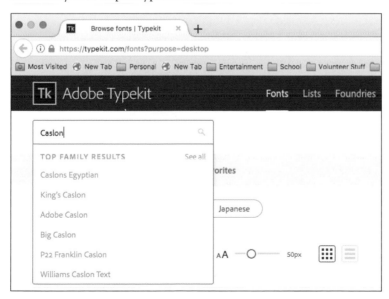

2 Click in the Search box at the top of the screen, type **Caslon**, and press Enter or Return.

3 When the search results display, click Adobe Caslon.

4 Scroll down to locate Adobe Caslon Pro Bold Italic and, if necessary, click Sync.

5 Switch back to InDesign.

Applying a font, style, size, and leading

Here, you'll use the Font Similarity feature to apply a different font to the headline. Then, you'll change the font family, style, size, and leading for the text in the pull quote on the right page. A pull quote is an interesting quote copied from the main text and formatted in an eye-catching way to draw readers into an article.

▶ **Tip:** The Font Similarity feature lets you quickly experiment with different fonts with similar characteristics.

1 Using the Type tool (T), select the story headline, "Assignments Restaurant," at the top of the left page.

2 Click the Font menu on the Control panel or on the Character panel. Click Show Similar Fonts above the menu.

InDesign filters the Font menu to show typefaces similar to the current font, Minion Pro Bold Italic.

3 Select the font you synced from Adobe Typekit: Adobe Caslon Pro Bold Italic.

Now you will work on the pull quote starting with "Maybe the next celebrity chef" on the right page.

4 Zoom in on the pull quote, and choose View > Hide Guides to better concentrate on the text.

5 If the Character panel isn't visible, choose Type > Character.

6 Using the Type tool (T), click inside the pull quote's text frame. To select the entire paragraph, quadruple-click (click four times rapidly).

7 In the Character panel, set the following options:

- Font: Adobe Caslon Pro (alphabetized under "C")

- Style: Bold Italic

- Size: 14 pt

- Leading: 30 pt

Tip: To quickly select a font, you can type the first few letters in the Font Name field until it is recognized.

8 Choose Edit > Deselect All.

9 Choose File > Save.

Finding fonts

InDesign provides four ways to quickly find fonts:

- **Name Search:** A quick way to find a font is to start typing the font name in the Font box. For example, as you type "Cas" for Adobe Caslon Pro, all fonts with those three characters in it are listed. By default, InDesign searches by the entire font name. You can click the search icon (🔍) to the left of the font name to search by first word only. In that case, you would need to type "Adobe Cas" for the same result.

- **Filter by Class:** Select a font class from the Filter menu, such as Serif or Script.

- **Favorites:** For quick access to fonts you use frequently, click the star to the left of a font name in any Font menu. Then, click Apply Favorite Filter (★) at the top of the menu.

- **Font Similarity:** Click Show Similar Fonts to filter the Font menu to display fonts visually similar to the current font.

Replacing a character with an alternate glyph

▶ **Tip:** The Glyphs panel features many controls for filtering the options available within a font—such as Punctuation or Ornaments. Some fonts may have hundreds of alternates available, while others will have only a few.

Because Adobe Caslon Pro is an OpenType font, which typically provides multiple glyphs for standard characters, you can select alternatives for many characters. A glyph is a specific form of a character. For example, in certain fonts, the capital letter "A" is available in several forms, such as small cap. You can use the Glyphs panel to select alternatives and locate any glyph in a font. In addition, InDesign offers an on-the-fly method for replacing a glyph. You will try both methods here.

1 Using the Type tool (T), select the first "M" in the pull quote.

2 Choose Type > Glyphs.

3 In the Glyphs panel, choose Alternates For Selection from the Show menu to see the alternate glyphs available. Depending on the active version of Adobe Caslon Pro, your options may look different.

4 Double-click the more script-like "M" to replace the original character.

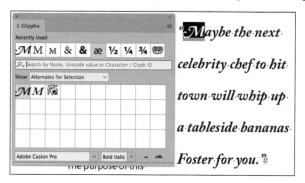

▶ **Tip:** From the Character panel menu, choose the OpenType option. Options in the OpenType menu displayed in brackets are not available for the selected font.

If alternate glyphs, or other OpenType features, are available for the combination of selected characters, InDesign displays a small menu that lets you select from OpenType glyph options.

5 Select the last word in the pull quote, "you," to see the OpenType badge. If you click this badge, it indicates OpenType Properties Are Not Applicable.

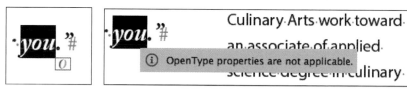

6 In the last line of the pull quote, select the letter "F" in "Foster." A blue highlight appears below the selected character and a contextual menu displays the OpenType glyph. Click the "F" in the menu to replace the existing "F."

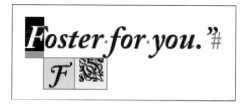

7 Choose Edit > Deselect All.

8 Choose File > Save.

Adding a special character

Now you'll add a right-indent tab followed by a decorative font character to the end of the story—also known as an "end-of-story character." This lets the reader know that the story is finished.

Tip: You can access
some of the more
commonly used glyphs,
such as the copyright
and trademark
symbols, in the Type
menu (Insert Special
Character > Symbols)
and the context menu.
To access the context
menu, right-click
(Windows) or Control-
click (macOS) at the
insertion point.

1 Scroll or zoom to see the last body paragraph of the story, ending with the words "bananas Foster for you."

2 Using the Type tool (**T**), click to place an insertion point in the last paragraph, just after the final period.

3 If the Glyphs panel is not open, choose Type > Glyphs.

 You can use the Glyphs panel to view and insert OpenType attributes, such as ornaments, swashes, fractions, and ligatures.

4 At the bottom of the panel, delete the name of the selected font. Type the first few letters of "Adobe Caslon Pro" until the font is recognized. Press Enter or Return to select the font.

5 In the Glyphs panel, choose Ornaments from the Show menu.

6 From the scrollable list, select any decorative character you prefer and double-click to insert it. The character appears at the insertion point in the document.

7 Using the Type tool, click to place an insertion point between the final period and the decorative character.

Tip: To quickly insert
a right-indent tab, press
Shift+Tab.

8 Right-click (Windows) or Control-click (macOS) to display the context menu, and choose Insert Special Character > Other > Right Indent Tab.

> Make·a·reservation·and·maybe·the·next·
> celebrity·chef·to·hit·town·will·whip·up·a·
> tableside·bananas·Foster·for·you. ⸱ 🏵

9 Choose File > Save.

Inserting fraction characters

The recipes in this article do not use actual fraction characters—rather, the 1/2 is built with a numeral 1, a slash, and a numeral 2. Most fonts contain individual characters for common fractions such as ½, ¼, and ¾. When available, these elegant fractions look much more professional than using numerals and slashes.

1 Scroll to the recipes at the bottom of the right-facing page and zoom as necessary to see the fractions in the recipe.

2 Using the Type tool (**T**), select the first instance of 1/2 ("1/2 lemon" in the Caesar Salad recipe).

3 If the Glyphs panel is not open, choose Type > Glyphs.

4 Choose Numbers from the Show menu.

5 Locate the ½ fraction. If necessary, resize the panel and scroll to see more characters.

6 Double-click the ½ fraction to replace the selected 1/2 in the text.

▶ Tip: If you are working on a cookbook or other document that requires a variety of fractions, the fractions built into most fonts will not cover all the values you need. You will need to research numerator and denominator formatting options, which are available in some OpenType fonts, or purchase a specific fraction font.

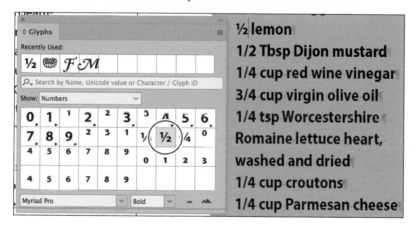

Notice that the ½ fraction is stored in the Recently Used boxes at the top of the Glyphs panel. Now you'll change instances of the 1/4 and 3/4 fractions.

7 In the Caesar Salad recipe, locate and select 1/4 ("1/4 cup red wine vinegar").

8 In the Glyphs panel, locate and double-click the ¼ fraction.

9 Repeat the steps above, locating and selecting 3/4 ("3/4 cup virgin olive oil") and replacing it with the ¾ fraction in the Glyphs panel.

10 If you want, replace the remaining instances of 1/2 and 1/4 in the recipes by selecting the text and double-clicking the respective glyphs in the Recently Used boxes or selecting from the OpenType badge next to the characters.

11 Close the Glyphs panel, and choose Edit > Deselect All.

12 Choose View > Grids & Guides > Show Guides.

13 Choose File > Save.

Fine-tuning columns

In addition to adjusting the number of columns in a text frame, the width of the columns, and the space between them, you can create a headline that spans multiple columns (also known as a "straddle head") and automatically balance the amount of text across the columns.

Creating a straddle head

The headline for the sidebar box needs to span the three columns. You can do this with a paragraph format rather than by placing the headline in its own text frame.

1 If necessary, zoom out to see the entire sidebar containing the recipes.

2 Using the Type tool (**T**), click in the "TRY IT @ HOME" headline.

3 Click the Paragraph Formatting Controls icon (¶) in the Control panel.

4 Locate the Span Columns menu in the Control panel. Select Span All from the menu.

▶ **Tip:** You can also access the Span Columns controls in the Paragraph panel menu.

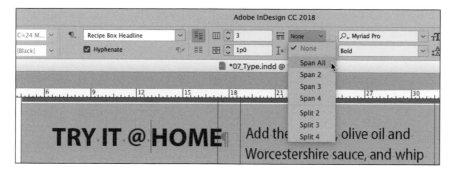

5 To see the controls for fine-tuning how the head spans the columns, Alt-click (Windows) or Option-click (macOS) the Span Columns button on the Control panel (⊟).

6 Select Preview and then experiment with any of the controls to see how they work. When you're finished, click Cancel.

▶ **Tip:** You can open the Span Columns dialog box by selecting Span Columns from the Paragraph panel menu or the Control panel menu.

> ### TRY IT @ HOME
>
> **CAESAR SALAD**
> **2 cloves garlic**
> **Taste kosher salt**
> **2 anchovy fillets, chopped**
> **1 coddled egg**
>
> Add the vinegar, olive oil and Worcestershire sauce, and whip briefly. Pour over lettuce and toss with croutons, Parmesan and black pepper.
>
> bacon around each prawn and place in the oven. Cook until the chorizo is done. Place the fried parsley on a plate and place the prawns on top. Drizzle with the

7 With the insertion point still in the "TRY IT @ HOME" subhead, choose Redefine Style from the Paragraph Styles panel menu. The Recipe Box Headline style is updated to reflect the Span Columns setting.

8 Choose File > Save.

Balancing columns

Now that the headline is added, you can complete the fine-tuning of the sidebar by balancing the amount of text in each column. You can do this manually by inserting a column break character (Type > Insert Break Character > Column Break). The break characters, however, remain if the text reflows, often forcing text into the wrong column. Instead, you will balance the columns automatically.

1 Choose View > Fit Page In Window to center the second page in the document window.

2 Using the Selection tool (▶), click to select the text frame containing the recipes.

3 Choose Object > Text Frame Options. In the General tab, in the Columns area, select the Balance Columns box. Click OK.

Note that any Keep With Next and Keep Lines Together settings for the paragraphs are honored when balancing columns.

4 Choose File > Save.

Balanced Columns is set for the sidebar box's text frame. The paragraphs flow according to the Keep With Next and Keep Lines Together paragraph formats.

Changing paragraph alignment

You can easily manipulate how a paragraph fits within its text frame by changing the horizontal alignment. You can align text with one or both edges of a text frame, or you can apply inset spacing. In this exercise, you'll align the author's biographical information—otherwise known as the "bio"—with the right margin.

1 On the right page, scroll and zoom as necessary to view the author's bio under the last paragraph of the story.

2 Using the Type tool (T), click to place an insertion point in the bio text.

Because the text in the bio is so small, the line spacing from the baseline grid looks too big. To fix this, you will unlock this paragraph from the grid.

3 With the insertion point still in the bio paragraph, in the Paragraph panel, click Do Not Align To Baseline Grid (☰☰).

4 In the Paragraph panel, click Align Right (≣|).

5 Choose Edit > Deselect All.

6 Choose File > Save.

Hanging punctuation outside the margin

Sometimes, particularly with punctuation at the beginning and end of lines, margins
that are in fact even may appear uneven. To fix this visual discrepancy, designers use
optical margin alignment to "hang" punctuation and swashes on characters slightly
outside the text frame.

● **Note:** When you
select Optical Margin
Alignment, it applies
to all of the text in a
story—defined as all
the text in a frame or
a series of threaded
text frames.

In this exercise, you will apply optical margin alignment to the pull quote.

1 Scroll and zoom as necessary to view the pull quote on the right page.

2 To see how the characters align with the margins, choose View > Extras >
Show Frame Edges.

3 Using the Selection tool (▶), click to select the text frame containing the
pull quote.

4 Choose Type > Story to open the Story panel.

5 Select Optical Margin Alignment. Enter **14 pt**
in the field and press Enter (Windows) or
Return (macOS).

▶ **Tip:** When using
Optical Margin
Alignment, specifying
an Align Based On Size
setting that matches
the point size of the text
in the frame produces
the best results.

Without (left) and with
(right) optical margin
alignment. Notice the
alignment of the quota-
tion marks. The text looks
more visually aligned.

6 Choose View > Extras > Hide Frame Edges. Choose Edit > Deselect All.
Choose File > Save.

Creating a drop cap

▶ **Tip:** Drop caps can be saved with paragraph styles so you can apply them quickly and consistently.

You can add creative touches to your document using InDesign typographic features. For example, you can make the first character or word in a paragraph a drop cap, apply a gradient or color fill to text, or create superscript and subscript characters, along with ligatures and old-style numerals. Here, you'll create a drop cap out of the first character in the first paragraph of the story.

1 Scroll to view the first paragraph in the left page. Using the Type tool (T), click to place an insertion point anywhere in that paragraph.

2 In the Paragraph panel, type **3** in the Drop Cap Number Of Lines box (ⁱᴀ≣) to make the letter drop down three lines. Press Enter or Return.

3 Note the 1 in the Drop Cap One Or More Characters box (ᴬ±≣) to see how you would increase the number of characters that drop.

4 Using the Type tool, select the drop-cap character.

Now, you can apply any character formatting you want.

5 Choose Type > Character Styles to open the Character Styles panel.

6 Click the Drop Cap style to apply it to the selected text.

▶ **Tip:** You can create a drop cap and apply a character style in one step using the Drop Caps And Nested Styles dialog box (Paragraph panel menu). You can then save that formatting in a paragraph style.

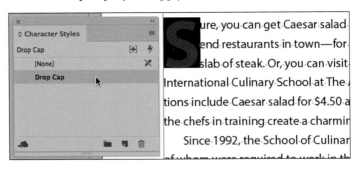

7 Click the pasteboard to deselect the text and view the drop cap. Choose File > Save.

Applying a stroke to text

Next, you'll add a stroke to the drop-cap character you just created.

1 With the Type tool (**T**.) still selected, select the drop-cap character.

2 Choose Window > Stroke. In the Stroke panel, type **1 pt** in the Weight box, and press Enter or Return.

 A stroke appears around the selected character. Now you'll change the color of the stroke.

3 Choose Window > Color > Swatches. In the Swatches panel, do the following:

 • Select the Stroke box (⊞).

 • Click the rust-colored swatch named C=24 M = 98 Y= 99 K = 18.

 • Type **100** in the Tint field and press Enter or Return.

4 Press Shift+Ctrl I A (Windows) or Shift I Command+A (macOS) to deselect the text so that you can view the stroke effect.

5 Choose File > Save.

Adjusting the drop cap alignment

You can adjust the alignment of drop-cap characters as well as scale the size of the drop cap if it has a descender, such as the "tail" on a "y." In this section, you'll adjust the drop cap so that it aligns better with the left margin.

► **Tip:** Selecting Align Left Edge is particularly helpful for better typographical positioning of a sans serif drop cap.

1 Using the Type tool (**T**.), click to place an insertion point anywhere in the first paragraph with the drop cap.

2 Choose Type > Paragraph. In the Paragraph panel, choose Drop Caps And Nested Styles from the panel menu.

3 Select Preview to view your changes as they occur.

4 Select Align Left Edge to move the drop cap so that it aligns better to the left edge of the text.

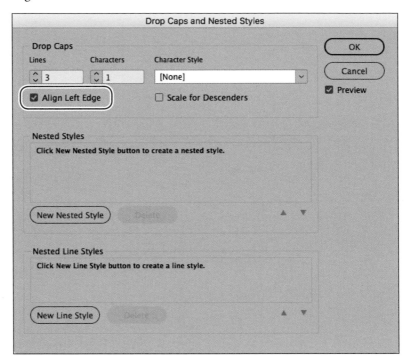

5 Click OK.

6 Choose File > Save.

Adjusting letter and word spacing

You can change the spacing between letters and words using kerning and tracking. You can also control the overall spacing of text in a paragraph by using the Adobe Single-Line Composer and the Adobe Paragraph Composer.

Adjusting the kerning and tracking

By adjusting kerning, you can add or subtract space between specific letter pairs. Tracking increases or decreases spacing across a range of letters. You can use both kerning and tracking on the same text.

Here, you'll manually kern the space between the drop cap "S" and the remainder of the word, "ure." Then you'll track the heading "IF YOU GO" in the box.

1 To see the results of the kerning more clearly, select the Zoom tool (🔍) in the Tools panel, and drag a marquee around the drop cap.

2 Using the Type tool (T), click to place an insertion point between the "S" drop cap and the "u" after it.

3 Press Alt+right arrow (Windows) or Option+right arrow (macOS) on the keyboard two times to increase the amount of space between the drop cap and the letter "u."

The Kerning field (VA) on the Character panel and Control panel lets you see and adjust the amount of space between characters.

Now you'll set a tracking value for the entire "If You Go" heading to increase the overall spacing between the letters. To set tracking, you must first select the entire range of characters you want to track.

4 Choose Edit > Deselect All. Scroll down to view the "If You Go" heading in the brown box below the word "Sure."

5 Using the Type tool, click in "If You Go" three times to select the entire heading.

6 In the Character panel, choose 50 from the Tracking menu (VA).

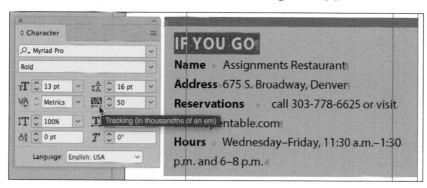

7 Click the pasteboard to deselect the text.

8 Choose View > Fit Spread In Window to see your latest changes.

9 Choose File > Save.

▶ **Tip:** When you kern text, the right arrow key adds space and the left arrow key removes space when combined with the Alt (Windows) or Option (macOS) key. To change the amount of kerning applied using the shortcuts, you can edit the Keyboard Increments value in Preferences (Units & Increments).

● **Note:** If you have trouble selecting the "IF YOU GO" text, first use the Selection tool to select the text frame.

Adjusting line breaks

▶ **Tip:** For justified text, Justification settings combine with the Paragraph Composer and hyphenation settings to control how dense paragraphs look. To adjust these settings for a selected paragraph, choose Justification from the Paragraph panel menu.

When text is not justified, the breaks at the end of each line affect readability and impact. For example, when paragraphs are aligned left, the right edge remains ragged. Too much "rag" can make the text easier or harder to read based on many factors, including the font, size, leading, column width, and more. Three other paragraph formats affect the readability of the text:

- The Adobe Paragraph Composer, which automatically determines line breaks

- Hyphenation settings, such as whether to hyphenate capitalized words

- The Balance Ragged Lines feature

Typically, a graphic designer will experiment with a combination of settings until a few paragraphs of sample text look just right. Then, all these options can be saved in paragraph styles and applied with one click. The body paragraph styles used in the lesson document use the Adobe Paragraph Composer and fine-tuned hyphenation settings, so you will only compare the Composers and then apply the Balanced Ragged Lines feature.

Adobe Single-Line Composer	Adobe Paragraph Composer	Adobe Paragraph Composer with Balance Ragged Lines
A perusal of the menu, while munching fresh bread and savoring a glass of wine, tempts you with its carefully planned variety. "The menu is all designed to teach cooking methods," says Kleinman. "It covers 80 to 85 percent of what students have been learning in class—saute, grill, braise, make vinaigrettes, cook vegetables, bake and make desserts." In a twist on "You have to know the rules to break them," Kleinman insists that students need to first learn the basics before they can go on to create their own dishes.	A perusal of the menu, while munching fresh bread and savoring a glass of wine, tempts you with its carefully planned variety. "The menu is all designed to teach cooking methods," says Kleinman. "It covers 80 to 85 percent of what students have been learning in class—saute, grill, braise, make vinaigrettes, cook vegetables, bake and make desserts." In a twist on "You have to know the rules to break them," Kleinman insists that students need to first learn the basics before they can go on to create their own dishes.	A perusal of the menu, while munching fresh bread and savoring a glass of wine, tempts you with its carefully planned variety. "The menu is all designed to teach cooking methods," says Kleinman. "It covers 80 to 85 percent of what students have been learning in class—saute, grill, braise, make vinaigrettes, cook vegetables, bake and make desserts." In a twist on "You have to know the rules to break them," Kleinman insists that students need to first learn the basics before they can go on to create their own dishes.

Note the difference in line breaks with successive applications of line break methods. The first column shows a paragraph with the Adobe Single-Line Composer applied. The middle column shows the same paragraph with the Adobe Paragraph Composer applied. As you can see, the right edge is much less ragged. The column on the right shows the paragraph with both Adobe Paragraph Composer and Balance Ragged Lines applied, which helps balance the length of the last line of the paragraph.

Applying the Adobe Paragraph and Single-Line Composers

The density of a paragraph (sometimes called its color) is determined by the composition method used. InDesign's composition methods consider the word spacing, letter spacing, glyph scaling, and hyphenation options you've selected and then determine the best line breaks. InDesign provides two options for composing text: the Adobe Paragraph Composer, which examines all of the lines in a paragraph before composing each line, and the Adobe Single-Line Composer, which composes text one line at a time starting with the first line.

When you use the Paragraph Composer, InDesign composes a line while considering the impact on other lines in the paragraph to set the best overall arrangement of the paragraph. As you change type in a given line, previous and subsequent lines in the same paragraph may break differently, making the overall paragraph appear more evenly spaced. When you use the Single-Line Composer, which is the standard for other layout and word-processing software, InDesign recomposes only the lines following the edited text.

The text in this lesson was composed using the default, the Adobe Paragraph Composer. To see the difference between the two, you'll recompose the body text using the Adobe Single-Line Composer.

1 Using the Type tool (**T**), click to place an insertion point anywhere in the main story.

2 Choose Edit > Select All.

3 In the Paragraph panel, choose Adobe Single-Line Composer from the panel menu. If necessary, increase the view scale to see the difference.

Note: The Adobe World-Ready Single-Line Composer and the Adobe World-Ready Paragraph Composer are intended for use with Middle Eastern languages. With these composers, you can enter text in a combination of Arabic, Hebrew, English, French, German, Russian, and other Latin languages.

Tip: As a last resort, you can adjust line breaks manually by inserting the Forced Line Break (Shift+Return) character or a Discretionary Line Break character at the end of a line. Both characters are available in the Type > Insert Break Character submenu. Because the line break characters remain as text reflows, it's best to add them when the text and formatting are final.

The Single-Line Composer handles each line individually. As a result, some lines in a paragraph appear denser or more sparse than others. Because the Paragraph Composer looks at multiple lines at once, it makes the density of the lines in a paragraph more consistent.

4 Click a blank area of the page to deselect the text, and view the different spacing and line endings.

5 To restore the story to the Adobe Paragraph Composer, choose Edit > Undo.

6 Choose Edit > Deselect All.

Hyphenation settings

Whether and how words are hyphenated at the ends of lines is a paragraph format. In general, hyphenation settings are editorial decisions, not design decisions. A publication's style guide, for example, may specify that capitalized words should not be hyphenated.

- **Hyphenation Settings:** To customize hyphenation for selected paragraphs, choose Hyphenation from the Paragraph panel menu. You can also adjust hyphenation settings in the Paragraph Style Options dialog box.

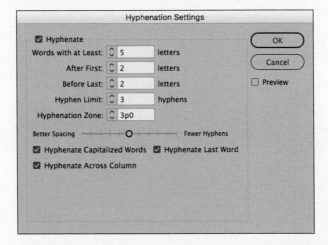

- **Toggle hyphenation:** When you're editing text, you can use the Hyphenate check box on the Control panel or Paragraph panel to quickly enable and disable hyphenation for selected paragraphs.

- **Customize hyphenation:** You may have specific words, such as trademarked words, that you prefer not to hyphenate or to hyphenate at specific points. You can specify the preferred hyphenation in Edit > Spelling > User Dictionary.

Balancing ragged lines

When paragraphs are not justified, the line endings can sometimes look too ragged, with some lines much longer or shorter than others. Using the Adobe Paragraph Composer and adjusting hyphenation can help, as can the Balance Ragged Lines feature. You will apply that here.

▶ **Tip:** The Balance Ragged Lines feature also works well for balancing multi-line headlines.

1 Using the Type tool (**T**), click to place an insertion point anywhere in the author's bio. (The bio, which starts with "Julia Pépin," is on the right page in the last paragraph of the last column.)

2 In the Paragraph panel, choose Balance Ragged Lines from the panel menu.

3 Choose Edit > Deselect All.

4 Choose File > Save.

Setting tabs

You can use tabs to position text in specific horizontal locations in a column or frame. In the Tabs panel, you can organize text and create tab leaders, indents, and hanging indents.

Aligning text to tabs and adding tab leaders

Here, you'll format the tabbed information in the "If You Go" box on the left page. The tab markers have already been entered in the text, so you will specify the final location of the text.

1 Scroll and zoom as necessary to view the "IF YOU GO" box.

2 To view the tab markers in the text, make sure that hidden characters are showing (Type > Show Hidden Characters) and that Normal Mode (⊞) is selected in the Tools panel.

▶ **Tip:** When working with tabs, it helps to view the tab characters by choosing Type > Show Hidden Characters. It is common to receive word-processing files in which the writer or editor has entered multiple tabs to align the text onscreen—or worse, entered spaces rather than tabs. The only way to see what you're dealing with (and fix it) is to view hidden characters.

3 Using the Type tool (**T**), click in the "If You Go" box, and select from the second line (starting with "Name") to the last line (ending with "6–8 p.m.)."

4 Choose Type > Tabs to open the Tabs panel.

When a text frame has an insertion point and enough space at the top, the Tabs panel snaps to the top of the frame so that the measurements in the panel's ruler exactly match the text. Regardless of the position of the Tabs panel, you can enter values to set tabs with precision.

5 In the Tabs panel, click Left-Justified Tab (↓). This specifies that text aligns to the left of the tab stop.

6 Type **5p5** in the X (tab stop) box, and press Enter or Return.

The information following each tab marker in the selected text now aligns to the new tab stop, which is positioned just above the ruler in the Tabs panel.

7 With the text still selected and the Tabs panel still open, click the new tab stop in the tab ruler to select it. Type a period (.) and a space in the Leader box.

The Leader box specifies the character or characters that fill the space between the text and the tab stop. Tab leaders are commonly used in tables of contents. Using a space between periods creates a more open dot sequence in the tab leader.

8 Press Enter or Return to apply the tab leader. Leave the Tabs panel open and in position for the next exercise.

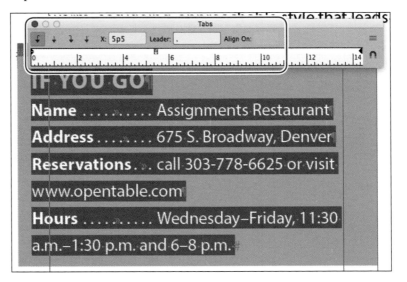

9 Choose Edit > Deselect All.

10 Choose File > Save.

Working with tabs

The controls for creating and customizing tabs in InDesign are similar to those in a word processor. You can precisely position tabs, repeat tabs across a column, create leaders for tabs, specify how text aligns with tabs, and easily modify the tabs you've created. Tabs are paragraph formats, so they apply to the paragraph containing the text insertion point or any selected paragraphs. All the controls are in the Tabs panel, which you open by choosing Type > Tabs. Here's how the tabs controls work:

- **Enter tabs:** To enter a tab in text, press the Tab key.

- **Specify tab alignment:** To specify how text aligns with a tab stop—for example, to the left of the tab stop (the traditional setting) or on a decimal point—click one of the tab buttons in the upper-left corner of the Tabs panel: Left-Justified Tab, Center-Justified Tab, Right-Justified Tab, or Align To Decimal (Or Other Specified Character) Tab.

- **Position tabs:** To position a tab stop, click one of the tab buttons, type a value in the X box, and press Enter or Return. You can also click a tab button, and then click just above the ruler.

- **Repeat tabs:** To create multiple tab stops the same distance apart, select a tab on the ruler. Choose Repeat Tab from the Tabs panel menu. This creates tab stops across the column based on the distance between the selected tab stop and the previous tab stop (or the left indent).

- **Specify a character on which to align text:** To align text on a specific character—for example, a decimal point—click the Align To Decimal (Or Other Specified Character) Tab button at left, and then type or paste the character into the Align On box. (If the text does not contain that character, text will align to the left of the tab stop.)

- **Create a tab leader:** To fill the white space between text and tabs—for example, to add periods between text and page numbers in a table of contents—enter up to eight characters to repeat in the Leader box.

- **Move tabs:** To change the position of a tab stop, select the tab on the ruler, and type a new position in the X box. On Windows, press Enter on the keyboard; on macOS, press Return. Or, drag the tab on the ruler to a new location.

- **Delete tabs:** To delete a tab, drag it off the tab ruler. Or, select the tab on the ruler, and choose Delete Tab from the Tabs panel menu.

- **Reset default tabs:** To return to the default tab stops, choose Clear All from the Tabs panel menu. The default tab stop positions vary depending on the document's settings in the Units & Increments panel of the Preferences dialog box. For example, if the Horizontal Ruler is set to Inches, default tab stops are placed at every half-inch.

- **Change tab alignment:** To change a tab stop's alignment, select it on the ruler, and then click a different tab button. Or, press the Alt (Windows) or Option (macOS) key while clicking the tab on the ruler to cycle through the four alignment options.

Creating a hanging indent

In a "hanging indent," text before the tab marker hangs to the left—as you will often see in a bulleted or numbered list. To create a hanging indent for the information in the "If You Go" box, you will use the Tabs panel. You can also use the Left Indent and First Line Left Indent boxes in the Paragraph panel.

1 Using the Type tool (T,), click in the "If You Go" box, and select from the second line (starting with "Name") to the last line (ending with "6–8 p.m.").

● **Note:** If the Tabs panel has moved, click its Position Panel Above Text Frame button (⋒) at the right.

2 Make sure that the Tabs panel is still aligned directly above the text frame.

3 In the Tabs panel, drag the bottom indent marker on the left side of the ruler to the right until the X value is 5p5.

Dragging the bottom marker moves both the Left Indent and First Line Indent markers at once. Notice how all the text shifts to the right, and the Left Indent value in the Paragraph panel changes to 5p5.

Keep the text selected. Now you'll bring just the category headings back to their original location in the frame to create a hanging indent.

▶ **Tip:** You can also adjust the first-line indent for selected paragraphs by dragging the top indent marker on the tab ruler. However, it can be difficult to select the marker without accidentally creating or modifying a tab stop.

4 In the Paragraph panel, type **–5p5** in the First Line Left Indent (⁺≣) box.

5 Press Enter or Return to apply the setting.

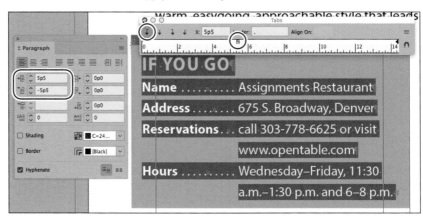

6 Deselect the text, and view the hanging indent. Close the Tabs panel.

7 Choose File > Save.

Hanging indents and bulleted lists

You can adjust paragraph indents—including the Left Indent, Right Indent, First Line Left Indent, and Last Line Right Indent—using controls in the Control panel, the Paragraph panel (Type > Paragraph), and the tab ruler (Type > Tabs). In addition to specifying values, you can create hanging indents in the following ways:

- Press the Shift key while dragging the indent markers on the tab ruler. The Shift key lets you drag the indent markers independently.

- Insert an Indent To Here character to hang all the subsequent lines in the paragraph to the right of the character. To do this, press Control+\ (Windows) or Command+\ (macOS), or choose Type > Insert Special Character > Other > Indent To Here.

You can use a combination of hanging indents and bullet characters or numerals to create bulleted or numbered lists. A quicker way to do this, however, is to use the Bullets And Numbering feature in the Paragraph panel menu or the Bulleted & Numbered Lists submenu of the Type menu. You can save bulleted list and numbered list formatting as part of a paragraph style.

Adding a rule above a paragraph

You can add a horizontal rule (line) above or below a paragraph. The advantage of using rules rather than simply drawing a line is that rules can be applied with a paragraph style, and they travel with the paragraph when text reflows. For example, you might use both a rule above and rule below in a paragraph style for pull quotes. Or, you might use a rule above a subhead. Paragraph rules can be the width of the column or the text, as follows:

- When Width is set to Column, the paragraph rule will have the same length as the text column—minus any paragraph indent settings. To extend a rule beyond the paragraph indents, you can enter negative Left Indent and Right Indent values in the Paragraph Rules dialog box.

- When Width is set to Text, the paragraph rule will have the same length as the line of text to which it applies. For Rule Above, that is the first line of a multi-line paragraph; for Rule Below, it's the last line of the paragraph.

Here you'll add a rule above the author bio at the end of the story.

1 Scroll to view the third column on the right page, which contains the author bio.

2 Using the Type tool (T), click to place an insertion point in the author bio.

3 Choose Paragraph Rules from the Paragraph panel menu.

4 At the top of the Paragraph Rules dialog box, choose Rule Above from the menu, and select Rule On to activate the rule.

5 Select the Preview option. Move the dialog box so that you can see the paragraph.

6 In the Paragraph Rules dialog box, set these options:

- From the Weight menu, choose 1 pt.
- From the Color menu, choose the brown-colored swatch (C=20 M=70 Y=100 K=8).
- From the Width menu, choose Column.

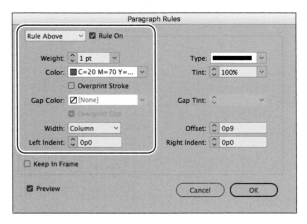

7 Click OK to apply the changes.

A rule now appears above the author bio.

8 Choose File > Save.

Working with paragraph shading

To call attention to text within a story, you can apply shading to a paragraph. InDesign provides many options for fine-tuning the shading, including the tint of the shading and its offset from the paragraph. To allow enough space above or below a paragraph for shading, apply a Space Before or Space After setting for the paragraph. To quickly and consistently apply shading, you can include paragraph shading in a paragraph style.

Applying shading to a paragraph

First, you will apply shading to the paragraph containing the author's bio, which is at the end of the story. Later, you will save this effect as part of the paragraph style.

1 Using the Type tool (T), click to place an insertion point in the author biography at the end of the magazine article. This targets the paragraph for formatting.

2 Choose Type > Paragraph to display the Paragraph panel.

3 Select Shading in the lower-left corner of the Paragraph panel.

4 To select the color of the shading, click the Shading Color menu to the right of the Shading box. Select the color swatch named C=65 M=35 Y=100 K=20.

▶ **Tip:** The paragraph-shading controls are available in the Control panel as well.

5 To fine-tune the shading, choose Paragraph Borders & Shading from the Paragraph panel menu, and click the Shading tab at the top.

6 Select the Preview option. Move the dialog box so that you can see the paragraph.

7 Type **50** in the Tint field.

8 In the Offsets area, confirm that the Same Settings icon (🔒) is selected and the Offset is set to 0p6 to indent the text from the shading.

▶ **Tip:** You can also open the Paragraph Shading dialog box by Alt-clicking (Windows) or Option-clicking (macOS) the Shading Color button on the Control panel or Paragraph panel.

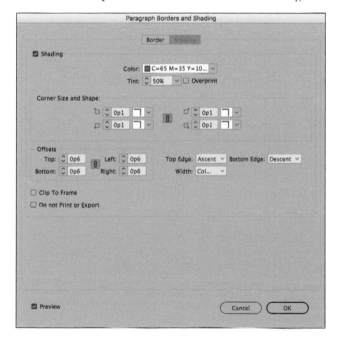

9 Choose Text from the Width field to see how the shading adjusts to the longest line of text. Then, choose Column again.

10 Click OK to apply the changes.

The paragraph is now shaded to match the other tints used on the page.

11 To view your results, choose Presentation from the Screen Mode menu (■) in the Application bar at the top of the screen.

12 When you're finished viewing the document, press Esc.

Congratulations, you have finished the lesson. To finalize this article, you would likely spend time with an editor or proofreader to fix any tight or loose lines, awkward line breaks, widows, and orphans.

Exploring on your own

Now that you have learned the basics of formatting text in an InDesign document, you're ready to apply these skills on your own. Try the following tasks to improve your typographic skills.

1 Place an insertion point in various paragraphs and experiment with turning hyphenation on and off in the Paragraph panel. Select a hyphenated word and choose No Break from the Character panel menu to stop an individual word from hyphenating.

2 Experiment with different hyphenation settings. First, select all the text in the main story. Then, choose Hyphenation from the Paragraph panel menu. In the Hyphenation Settings dialog box, select Preview, and then experiment with the settings. For example, Hyphenate Capitalized Words is selected for this text, but an editor would probably want to turn it off to prevent the chef's name from hyphenating.

3 Experiment with different justification settings. First, select all the text, and then click Justify With Last Line Aligned Left (≡) in the Paragraph panel. Choose Justification from the Paragraph panel menu. In the Justification dialog box, select Preview and experiment with the settings. For example, look at the difference that the Adobe Single-Line Composer and the Adobe Paragraph Composer make when applied to justified (rather than left-aligned) text.

4 Choose Type > Insert Special Character and view all the options available, such as Symbols > Bullet Character and Hyphens And Dashes > Em Dash. Using these characters rather than hyphens significantly enhances how professional the typography looks. Choose Type > Insert White Space and notice the Nonbreaking Space. Use this to "glue" two words together so they cannot split at the end of a line (such as "et al.").

Review questions

1 How do you view the baseline grid?

2 When and where do you use a right-indent tab?

3 How do you hang punctuation outside the edges of a text frame?

4 How do you balance text across the columns in multicolumn text frames?

5 What is the difference between kerning and tracking?

6 What is the difference between the Adobe Paragraph Composer and the Adobe Single-Line Composer?

Review answers

1 To view the baseline grid, choose View > Grids & Guides > Show Baseline Grid. The current document view must be at or above the View Threshold value set in the baseline grid preferences. By default, that value is 75%.

2 A right-indent tab, which automatically aligns text with the right paragraph indent, is useful for placing end-of-story characters.

3 Select the text frame and choose Type > Story. Select Optical Margin Alignment, which will apply to all the text in the story.

4 Select the text frame with the Selection tool, and then click the Balance Columns button in the Control panel or select the Balance Columns option in the Text Frame Options dialog box (Object > Text Frame Options).

5 Kerning adjusts the space between two characters; tracking adjusts the space between a range of selected characters. Kerning controls are available when the text insertion point is flashing; tracking controls are available when a range of text is selected. The controls are available on the Control panel and the Character panel.

6 The Paragraph Composer evaluates all lines in a paragraph when determining the best possible line breaks. The Single-Line Composer evaluates only one line at a time when determining line breaks.

8 WORKING WITH COLOR

Lesson Overview

In this lesson, you'll learn how to do the following:

- Set up color management.
- Specify output requirements.
- Create color swatches.
- Create color themes and add them to CC Libraries.
- Apply colors to objects, strokes, and text.
- Create and apply a tint.
- Create and apply a gradient swatch.
- Work with color groups.

This lesson will take approximately 60 minutes to complete.

Please log in to your account on peachpit.com to download the lesson files for this chapter, or go to the "Getting Started" section at the beginning of this book and follow the instructions under "Accessing the Lesson Files and Web Edition." Store the files on your computer in a convenient location.

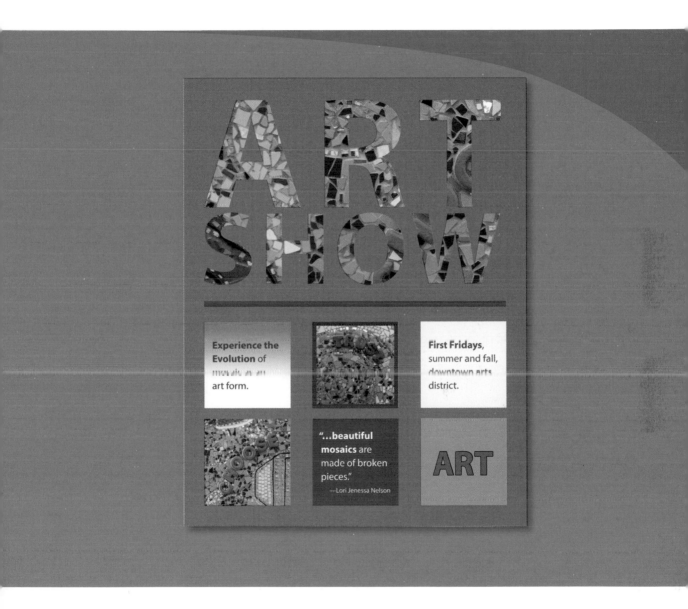

You can create and apply process and spot color swatches to objects, strokes, and text. Color themes make it easy to achieve color harmony in layouts. For consistent color usage across projects and workgroups, you can add color themes to CC Libraries. Using a preflight profile helps ensure that colors output properly.

Getting started

In this lesson, you'll add colors, color themes, tints, and gradients to a flyer for an art show. The flyer consists of CMYK colors and a spot color along with imported CMYK images. (You'll learn more about CMYK later in this chapter.) Before you get started, however, you will do two things to ensure that the document looks as good in print as it does onscreen: You will review color management settings and use a preflight profile to review the color modes of the imported images. When the flyer is finished, you will organize the colors into a color group.

● **Note:** If you have not already downloaded the project files for this lesson to your computer from your Account page, make sure to do so now. See "Getting Started" at the beginning of the book.

1 To ensure that the preferences and default settings of your Adobe InDesign program match those used in this lesson, move the InDesign Defaults file to a different folder following the procedure in "Saving and restoring the InDesign Defaults file" on pages 4–5.

2 Start Adobe InDesign.

3 The InDesign Start Screen displays. Click Open at left. (If the Start Screen does not display, choose File > Open from the InDesign menu bar.)

4 Choose File > Open, and open the 08_Start.indd file, in the Lesson08 folder, located inside the Lessons folder in the InDesignCIB folder on your hard disk.

5 If an alert informs you that the document contains links to sources that have been modified, click Update Links.

6 If the Missing Fonts dialog box displays, click Sync Fonts. Click Close when font syncing is complete.

7 To ensure that the panels and menu commands match those used in this lesson, choose Window > Workspace > [Advanced], and then choose Window > Workspace > Reset Advanced.

8 Choose File > Save As, rename the file **08_Color.indd**, and save it in the Lesson08 folder.

9 If you want to see what the finished document looks like, open the 08_End.indd file located in the same folder. You can leave this document open to act as a guide as you work.

10 When you're ready to resume working on the lesson document, click its tab in the upper-left corner of the document window.

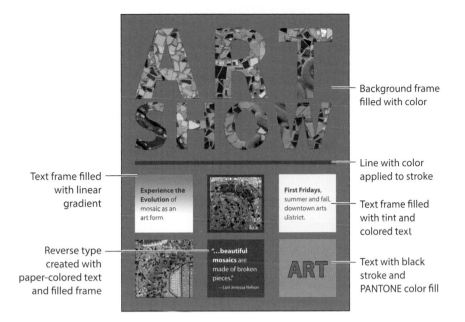

Background frame filled with color

Line with color applied to stroke

Text frame filled with tint and colored text

Text with black stroke and PANTONE color fill

Text frame filled with linear gradient

Reverse type created with paper-colored text and filled frame

Managing color

Color management works to reproduce colors consistently across a range of output devices, such as monitors, tablets, color printers, and offset presses. InDesign gives you easy-to-use color management features that help you achieve good, consistent color without needing to become a color management expert. With color management enabled out of the box, you'll be able to view colors consistently while ensuring more accurate color from edit to proof to final print or display output.

The need for color management

No screen, film, printer, copier, or printing press can produce the full range of color visible to the human eye. Each device has specific capabilities and makes different kinds of compromises in reproducing color images. The unique color-rendering abilities of a specific output device are known collectively as its "gamut." InDesign and other graphics applications, such as Adobe Photoshop CC and Adobe Illustrator CC, use color numbers to describe the color of each pixel in an image. The color numbers correspond to the color model, such as the RGB values for red, green, and blue, or the CMYK values for cyan, magenta, yellow, and black.

Color management is simply a way of translating the color numbers for each pixel from the source (the document or image stored on your computer) to the output device (such as your monitor, laptop, tablet, smartphone, color printer, or high-resolution printing press). Because each source and output device has its own specific gamut (or range) of colors it is capable of reproducing, the aim of the color translation is color accuracy across devices.

● **Note:** The screen captures in this book show the Medium Light interface. Interface elements such as panels and dialog boxes may be darker on your screen.

▶ **Tip:** You can find additional information about color management in the InDesign Help file, online at adobe.com (search for "color management") and in DVDs/videos such as Peachpit's *Color Management for Photographers and Designers: Learn by Video.*

Creating a viewing environment for color management

Your work environment influences how you see color on your monitor and on printed output. For best results, control the colors and light in your work environment by doing the following:

- View your documents in an environment that provides a consistent light level and color temperature. For example, the color characteristics of sunlight change throughout the day and alter the way colors appear onscreen, so keep shades closed or work in a windowless room.

- To eliminate the blue-green cast from fluorescent lighting, you can install D50 (5000° Kelvin) lighting. You can also view printed documents using a D50 light box.

- View your document in a room with neutral-colored walls and ceiling. A room's color can affect the perception of both monitor color and printed color. Neutral gray is the best color for a viewing room.

- The color of your clothing reflecting off your monitor may affect the appearance of colors onscreen.

- Remove colorful background patterns on your monitor desktop. Busy or bright patterns surrounding a document interfere with accurate color perception. Set your desktop to display neutral grays only.

- View document proofs in the real-world conditions under which your audience will see the final piece. For example, you might want to see how a housewares catalog looks under the typical light bulbs used in homes, or view an office furniture catalog under the fluorescent lighting used in offices.

- Always make final color judgments under the lighting conditions specified by the legal requirements for contract proofs in your country.

—From InDesign Help

Displaying images at full resolution

▶ **Tip:** You can specify Display Performance defaults in the Preferences dialog box, and you can change the display of an individual object using the Object > Display Performance menu.

In a color management workflow, even using default color settings, you should display images at high quality for the best possible color representation that your monitor is capable of showing. When you use lower-resolution image displays, graphics are displayed more quickly, but the colors are less precise.

To see the difference in one of your documents, experiment with the options in the View > Display Performance menu.

- Fast Display (ideal for quick text editing because images do not display)

- Typical Display (the default)

- High Quality Display (displays raster and vector graphics at high resolution)

For this lesson, choose View > Display Performance > High Quality Display.

Specifying color settings in InDesign

For consistent color in InDesign, you can specify a color settings file (CSF) with preset color management policies and default profiles. The default setting is North America General Purpose 2, which is the best option for beginners.

In this section, we review some of the preset color settings in Adobe InDesign that you can use to help achieve consistent color in your projects. However, you will not change any color settings.

1 Choose Edit > Color Settings. These settings apply to the InDesign application rather than to individual documents.

2 Click the various options in the Color Settings dialog box to see what is available.

3 Point at the Working Spaces title to see a description of this feature in the Description box at the bottom of the dialog box.

4 Point at various other features to see their descriptions.

▶ **Tip:** According to Adobe, "For most color-managed workflows, it is best to use a preset color setting that has been tested by Adobe Systems. Changing specific options is recommended only if you are knowledgeable about color management and very confident about the changes you make."

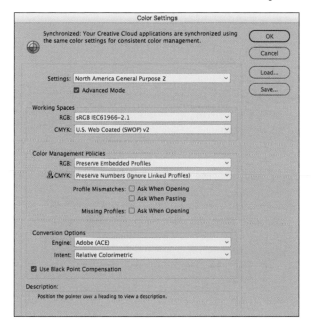

5 Click Cancel to close the Color Settings dialog box without making changes.

Proofing colors onscreen

When you proof colors onscreen, also known as "soft proofing," InDesign attempts to display colors according to specific output conditions. The accuracy of the simulation depends on various factors, including the lighting conditions of the room and whether your monitor is calibrated. To experiment with soft proofing, do the following:

1 Choose Window > Arrange > New Window for 08_Color.indd to open a second window for your lesson document.

2 If necessary, click the 08_Color.indd:2 window to activate it.

3 Choose View > Proof Colors. You can see a soft proof of the colors according to the current settings under View > Proof Setup.

▶ **Tip:** SWOP stands for Specifications for Web Offset Publications.

The current setting is Document CMYK - U.S. Web Coated SWOP V2, which reflects the typical output method for print documents in the United States.

4 To customize the soft proof, choose View > Proof Setup > Custom.

5 In the Customize Proof Condition dialog box, click the Device To Simulate menu and review the available presses, desktop printers, and output devices such as monitors.

6 Scroll down in the menu and select Dot Gain 20% from the Device To Simulate menu, and click OK.

Grayscale profiles such as Dot Gain 20% let you preview how a document will print in black and white. Notice that the InDesign document's title bar shows which device is being simulated, such as (Dot Gain 20%) or (Document CMYK).

7 Try different soft proofing options.

8 When you're finished reviewing the various soft proofing options, click 08_Color.indd:2's close box to close the second window. Resize and reposition the 08_Color.indd window as necessary.

About monitor calibration

Profiling software can both *calibrate* and *characterize* your monitor. Calibrating your monitor brings it into compliance with a predefined standard—for example, adjusting your monitor so that it displays color using the graphics arts standard white point color temperature of 5000° K (Kelvin). Characterizing your monitor simply creates a profile that describes how the monitor is currently reproducing color.

Monitor calibration involves adjusting the following video settings: brightness and contrast (the overall level and range of display intensity), gamma (the brightness of the midtone values), and white point (the color and intensity of the brightest white the monitor can reproduce).

When you calibrate your monitor, you are adjusting it so it conforms to a known specification. Once your monitor is calibrated, the profiling utility lets you save a color profile. The profile describes the color behavior of the monitor—what colors can or cannot be displayed on the monitor and how the numeric color values in an image must be converted so that colors are displayed accurately.

For details, see "Calibrate and profile your monitor" in InDesign Help.

—Condensed from InDesign Help

Defining printing requirements

Whether you are working on a document for delivery in a print or digital format, it's a good idea to know the output requirements before you start working. For example, for a print document, meet with your printer and discuss your document's design and use of color. Because printers understand the capabilities of their equipment, they may suggest ways for you to save time and money, increase quality, and avoid potentially costly printing or color problems. The flyer used in this lesson was designed to be printed by a commercial printer using CMYK colors. (Color modes are described in more detail later in this lesson.)

To confirm that your document matches the printing requirements, you can check it against a preflight profile, which contains a set of rules regarding the document's size, fonts, colors, images, bleeds, and more. The Preflight panel can alert you to anything in the document that does not follow the rules set in the profile. In this exercise, you will import a preflight profile, select it in the Preflight panel, and resolve an issue with the document.

▶ **Tip:** Your commercial printer may provide a preflight profile with all the necessary specifications for output. You can import the profile and use it to check your work against these criteria.

Loading a preflight profile

First, you will load a preflight profile provided by the printer.

1 Choose Window > Output > Preflight.

2 Choose Define Profiles from the Preflight panel menu button (≡).

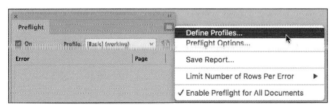

3 In the Preflight Profiles dialog box, click the Preflight Profile Menu button (≡) below the list of preflight profiles at left. Choose Load Profile.

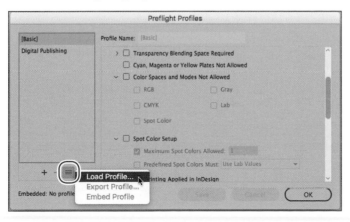

4 Select the Flyer Profile.idpp file, in the Lesson08 folder, located inside the Lessons folder within the InDesignCIB folder on your hard disk. Click Open.

5 With the Flyer Profile selected, look through the settings specified for the output of this ad. Click the arrows next to the other categories to see all the options you can include in a preflight profile.

Checked options are those that InDesign will flag as incorrect. For example, under Color > Color Spaces And Modes Not Allowed, RGB is selected. As a result, all uses of RGB colors will be reported as errors.

6 Click OK to close the Preflight Profiles dialog box.

Selecting a preflight profile

Now, you will select the Flyer Profile and review any errors that it flags.

1 From the Profile menu in the Preflight panel, choose Flyer Profile. Notice that the profile detects one issue with the colors that currently exist in the document.

2 To view the error, click the triangle next to COLOR (1).

3 Click the triangle next to Color Space Not Allowed (1).

▶ **Tip:** The lower-
left corner of the
document window
displays the number
of preflight errors in a
document (provided
that On is selected in
the upper-left corner
of the Preflight panel).
If you start to see a
lot of errors, open the
Preflight panel to see
more information.

4 Double-click Text Frame to select the frame that is triggering the error.

5 If necessary, click the triangle next to Info below to see details on the problem. Leave this panel open for the next exercise.

Because this document is destined for CMYK printing, colors in the RGB color mode are not allowed. The fill color of the text frame is in the RGB color model.

Converting a color mode for a swatch

Now, you will resolve the preflight error by converting the color mode of the swatch applied to the text frame.

1 Choose Window > Color > Swatches to display the Swatches panel.

2 In the list of colors in the Swatches panel, double-click the sage color swatch (R=133 G=155 B=112) to open the Swatch Options dialog box.

3 Select CMYK from the Color Mode menu, and then click OK.

▶ **Tip:** When you package a document for final output (File > Package), InDesign may flag issues with color models. You will change the color mode in the same way as shown here.

5 Notice that the error no longer displays in the Preflight panel.

6 Close the Preflight panel, and choose File > Save.

Creating colors

For maximum design flexibility, InDesign provides a variety of methods for creating colors. Once you create colors and color swatches, you can apply them to objects, strokes, and text in the layout. For consistent color usage, you can share colors among documents and users.

- Create colors on-the-fly using the Color panel.
- Create named color swatches for repeated and consistent usage with the Swatches panel.
- Select a color from an image using the Eyedropper tool.
- Use the Color Theme tool to choose among color themes generated from images or objects.
- Create and select themes from the Adobe Color Theme panel.

● **Note:** As you work through the lesson, you can move panels around and change the zoom level to a setting that works best for you. For more information, see "Working with panels" and "Changing the magnification of a document" in Lesson 1.

- Use the CC Libraries feature to share colors with Photoshop and Illustrator, with other members of your workgroup, and with other documents.

You can define colors in a variety of color modes, including RGB, CMYK, and "spot color" modes such as PANTONE. The difference between spot and process (CMYK) colors is discussed in detail later in this exercise.

This flyer will be printed by a commercial printer using CMYK color, which requires four separate plates for printing—one each for cyan, magenta, yellow, and black. However, the CMYK color mode has a limited range of colors, which is where spot colors are useful. Spot colors are used to add colors beyond the range of CMYK (for example, metallic and pastel inks) and to ensure consistent color (for example, for use in company logos).

In this exercise, you will use the Swatches panel to create a PANTONE color for a logo. You will then use the Eyedropper tool, Color panel, and Swatches panel to create a CMYK color swatch for the flyer's background color. Finally, you will use the Color Theme tool to create a set of complementary colors from one of the mosaic images in the document. The selected color theme is added to the Swatches panel and to your CC Library.

> **Tip:** Many corporate identities, including logos, specify a PANTONE color. When working on projects for clients, it's a good idea to ask about any PANTONE colors and fonts required to reproduce their corporate identity.

Creating a PANTONE color swatch

In this flyer, the ART logo in the lower-right corner calls for a PANTONE spot color ink. You'll now add a spot color from a color library. In a real-world scenario, you would need to notify the printer that you plan to use a PANTONE spot color.

1 Using the Selection tool (▶), click the pasteboard surrounding the page to make sure nothing is selected.

2 If necessary, choose Window > Color > Swatches to display the Swatches panel.

3 Choose New Color Swatch from the Swatches panel menu button (≡).

4 In the New Color Swatch dialog box, choose Spot from the Color Type menu.

5 Select PANTONE+ Solid Coated from the Color Mode menu.

6 In the PANTONE C box, type **265** to automatically scroll the list of Pantone swatches to the color you want for this project, which is PANTONE 265 C.

7 Deselect Add To CC Library in the lower-left corner.

▶ **Tip:** CC Libraries allow you to share assets, such as colors, among documents and users. You will learn about CC Libraries in Lesson 10, "Importing and Modifying Graphics."

8 Click OK. The spot color is added to your Swatches panel.

The icon (◙) to the right of the color name in the Swatches panel indicates that it is a spot color. New colors added to the Swatches panel are stored with the document in which they are created.

▶ **Tip:** When selecting PANTONE colors for print, it's a good idea to select them from a printed PANTONE color guide, available from www.pantone.com.

9 Choose File > Save.

You'll apply the newly added spot color to the "ART" text later in this lesson.

Creating CMYK color swatches

▶ **Tip:** Using the Swatches panel to name colors makes it easy to apply, edit, and update colors for objects in a document. Although you can also use the Color panel to apply colors to objects, there is no quick way to update these colors, which are considered "unnamed colors." Instead, if you want to change an unnamed color on multiple objects, you need to change each one individually.

To create a CMYK color swatch from scratch, you need an understanding of color mixing and color values. Alternatively, you can experiment with defining colors in the Colors panel and add a color as a color swatch. You can also use the Eyedropper tool to "pick up" a color from an image. In this exercise, you will use the Eyedropper tool to get a head start on creating a CMYK color swatch. Then, you will create two additional colors by simply entering color values.

1 Choose Window > Color > Color to display the Color panel.

2 On the Color panel, click the Fill box (⬚) in the upper-left corner.

3 Click the Color Theme tool (🖌) toward the bottom of the Tools panel. Hold the mouse button down to view the pop-out menu, and then select the Eyedropper tool (🖋).

4 Click the Eyedropper tool on the word "Choose" in the lower-left corner of the page as shown.

5 The color picked up from the image displays in the Color panel. The color values may differ depending on precisely where you clicked. To create the intended color, fine-tune the values as necessary:

- Cyan: **0**
- Magenta: **73**
- Yellow: **95**
- Black: **0**

6 Choose Add To Swatches from the Color panel menu button (≡).

A color swatch is added to the bottom of the list in the Swatches panel. It is automatically selected.

7 Click the New Swatch icon (▊) at the bottom of the Swatches panel. This makes a copy of any selected swatch.

8 Double-click the new swatch added to the bottom of the Swatches panel. This opens the Swatch Options dialog box so you can edit the swatch.

9 Make sure the Color Type is Process and the Color Mode is CMYK. Adjust the color by typing values in the following fields; you can tab from field to field.

- Cyan: **95**
- Magenta: **85**
- Yellow: **40**
- Black: **30**

10 Click OK to close the Swatch Options dialog box.

▶ **Tip:** When you know the color definition, as with the PANTONE color, it's easiest to use the Swatches panel and create a swatch. When you're trying to match a color in an image, it can work better to use the Eyedropper tool and Color panel.

11 Press Alt (Windows) or Option (macOS) while you click the New Swatch icon (▊) at the bottom of the Swatches panel. This creates a new swatch and automatically opens the New Color Swatch dialog box.

12 If necessary, select Name With Color Value. Make sure that Color Type is set to Process and Color Mode is set to CMYK. Enter the following values in the fields, tabbing between fields:

- Cyan: **35**
- Magenta: **90**
- Yellow: **95**
- Black: **0**

▶ **Tip:** If you want to give a color a recognizable name, such as Aqua or Forest Green, deselect Name With Color Value in the Swatch Options dialog box. You can then enter a name in the Swatch Name field.

13 Click OK to update the color, and then choose File > Save.

You have now created a spot color swatch and three process (CMYK) color swatches. Later, you will create color themes from an image. In the next exercise, you will apply colors to objects on the page.

About spot and process colors

▶ **Tip:** In addition to spot and process colors, InDesign provides Mixed Ink colors to expand the color palette of a publication that uses multiple spot colors. To use this feature, select New Mixed Ink Swatch from the Swatches panel menu. You can then mix a spot color and black to create an additional color, offering the tonal range you would see in a duotone image. If the New Mixed Ink Swatch option is not available, make sure that the document includes a spot color swatch.

A spot color is a special premixed ink used instead of, or in addition to, CMYK process inks. Each spot color requires its own printing plate on a printing press, so use spot colors when few colors are specified and color accuracy is critical. Spot color inks can accurately reproduce colors outside the gamut of process colors. However, the exact appearance of the printed spot color is determined by the combination of the ink as mixed by the commercial printer and the paper it's printed on, not by color values you specify or by color management.

A process color is printed using a combination of the four standard process inks: cyan, magenta, yellow, and black (CMYK). Use process colors when a job requires so many colors that using individual spot inks would be expensive or impractical, as when printing color photographs.

- For best results in a high-quality printed document, specify process colors using CMYK values printed in process color reference charts, such as those available from a commercial printer.

- The final color values of a process color are its values in CMYK, so if you specify a process color using RGB, those color values are converted to CMYK when you print color separations. These conversions differ based on your color-management settings and document profile.

- Don't specify a process color based on how it looks on your monitor, unless you are sure you have set up a color-management system properly and you understand its limitations for previewing color.

- Avoid using process colors in documents intended for onscreen viewing because CMYK has a smaller color gamut than that of a typical screen.

Sometimes it's practical to use process and spot inks in the same job. For example, you might use one spot ink to print the exact color of a company logo on the same pages of an annual report where photographs are reproduced using process color. You can also use a spot-color printing plate to apply a varnish over areas of a process color job. In both cases, your print job would use a total of five inks—four process inks and one spot ink or varnish.

Each spot color you create generates an additional spot-color plate for the press. In general, commercial printers produce either two-color (using black and one spot color) or four-color CMYK work, with the possibility of adding one or more spot colors. Using spot colors typically increases printing costs. It is a good idea to consult with your printer before using spot colors in a document.

—Condensed from InDesign Help

Applying colors

Once you create color swatches, you can apply them to objects, text, and more. The Swatches panel, Control panel, and CC Libraries panel offer the primary tools for applying colors. There are three general steps to applying a color:

1 Select the text or object.

2 Select the stroke or fill option, depending on what you want to change.

3 Select a swatch.

You use the Stroke/Fill box (⬚) to specify whether you want to apply color to a selection's stroke (outline) or fill (background). You can find the Stroke/Fill box on the Tools panel, the Swatches panel, the Color panel, and the Control panel. Whenever you apply colors, keep an eye on this box, as it's easy to apply color to the wrong part of an object.

InDesign provides many other options for applying colors, including dragging swatches onto objects, copying color from an object with the Eyedropper tool, and specifying colors in styles. As you work with InDesign, you will discover which methods work best for you.

In this exercise, you will apply color swatches to strokes, fills, and text using various panels and techniques.

Applying fill colors to objects

In this task, you will apply fill colors to various objects on the page by using the Swatches panel, dragging a swatch, and using the Eyedropper tool.

1 If necessary, choose Window > Color > Swatches to display the Swatches panel. Leave this panel open until you reach the end of this lesson.

2 Choose View > Screen Mode > Normal to see the frame edges.

3 Using the Selection tool (▶), click anywhere in the margin of the page (outside the margin guides) to select the large background frame.

> ▶ **Tip:** Clicking the small arrow on the Fill/Stroke box (⬚) swaps the stroke and fill colors of a selected object.

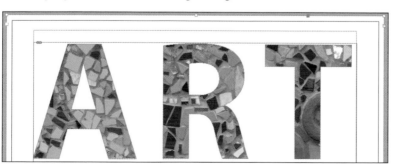

Click in the margins of the page to select the large text frame as shown above.

4 Click the Fill box () on the Swatches panel.

5 Click the orange color you created from the word "choose": C=0 M=73 Y=95 K=0.

6 Using the Selection tool, select the text frame at left containing the words "Experience the Evolution."

7 With the Fill box still selected, click the blue color swatch named C=65 M=40 Y=0 K=0.

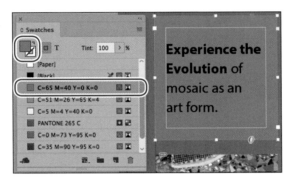

8 Click the pasteboard to make sure nothing is selected on the page.

9 In the Swatches panel, click the burgundy color swatch: C=35 M=90 Y=95 K=0.

10 Drag the swatch to the text frame centered at the bottom of the page containing the words "beautiful mosaics."

11 Click the pasteboard so no objects are selected.

The lower portion of the page should look something like this:

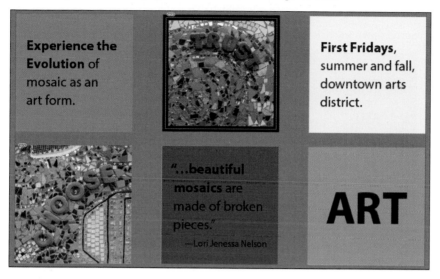

12 Choose File > Save.

Applying colors to strokes

The Stroke panel (Window > Stroke) lets you apply a border to lines, frames, and text. Here, you will apply color to an existing line and a graphics frame stroke using options on the Control panel.

1 Using the Selection tool (▶), click the horizontal line below the words "Art Show."

2 Click the Stroke menu on the Control panel.

3 Scroll down and select the burgundy color: C=35 M=90 Y=95 K=0.

● **Note:** If you apply color to the wrong object or the wrong part of an object, you can always choose Edit > Undo and try again.

4 Using the Selection tool, click the graphics frame containing the mosaic with the word "Trust." Be sure to click outside the content grabber to select the frame.

5 Click the Stroke box (⬛) on the Swatches panel.

6 Scroll down to click the dark blue color swatch named C=95 Y=85 M=40 K=0.

7 Choose File > Save.

Applying colors to text

▶ Tip: [Paper] is a special color that simulates the color of the paper on which you're printing.

You will now select text with the Type tool and apply a fill color to it using the Swatches panel and the Control panel. To create reverse type, which is lighter text on a dark background, you will apply InDesign's [Paper] color to text in one frame.

1 Using the Type tool (**T.**), click in the text frame starting with "Experience the Evolution." Drag to select all the text.

On the Swatches panel, notice that the Fill box has changed to indicate that text is selected: (⬛).

2 With the Fill box still selected, click the dark blue color swatch named C=95 Y=85 M=40 K=0.

3 Using the Type tool, click in the frame at right containing the words "First Fridays." Press Ctrl+A (Windows) or Command+A (macOS) to select all the text in the paragraph.

216 LESSON 8 Working with Color

4 With the Fill box still selected in the Swatches panel, click the burgundy color: C=35 M=90 Y=95 K=0.

Click the pasteboard to deselect the text, which should look something like this:

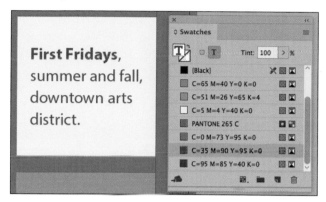

5 Using the Type tool, click in the text frame centered at the bottom of the page containing the words "beautiful mosaics." Choose Edit > Select All to select all the text.

6 With the Fill box still selected, click the [Paper] color on the Swatches panel.

Click the pasteboard to deselect the text and see the results.

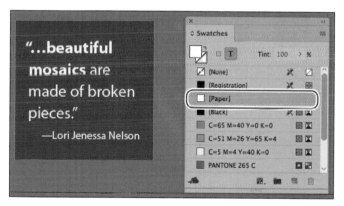

7 Using the Type tool, click in the text frame containing the word "Art" in the lower-right corner. Double-click in the word to select it.

8 With the Fill box still selected, click the PANTONE 265 C swatch.

9 With the word "Art" still selected, choose Window > Stroke.

10 Type **1 pt** in the Weight field, and press Enter or Return.

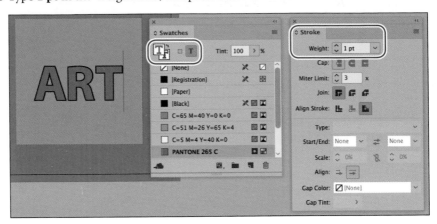

11 With the Stroke box (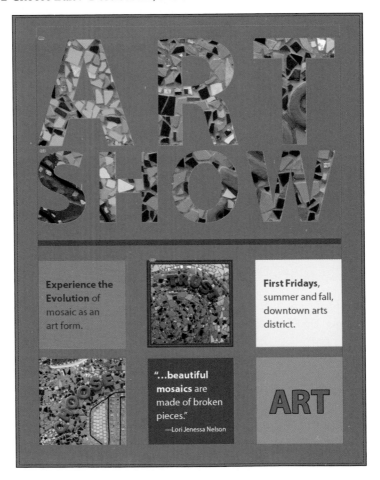) selected on the Swatches panel, click [Black].

12 Choose Edit > Deselect All, and then choose File > Save.

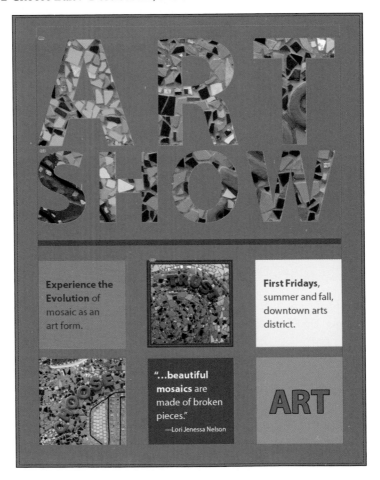

Working with tint swatches

A tint swatch is a screened (lighter) version of a color that you can apply quickly and consistently. The tint swatch is available on the Swatches panel and in other color menus, such as in the Control panel. You can share tint swatches with other documents through the Load Swatches command on the Swatches panel menu. You will now create a light-green tint swatch and apply it to the yellow text frame.

Creating a tint swatch

You create a tint swatch from an existing color swatch.

1 Choose View > Fit Page In Window to center the page in the document window.

2 Using the Selection tool (▶), click the pasteboard surrounding the page to make sure nothing is selected.

3 Select the yellow color swatch named C=5 M=4 Y=40 K=0.

4 Click the Fill box (⬚). Choose New Tint Swatch from the Swatches panel menu (≡).

5 In the New Tint Swatch dialog box, the Tint option at the bottom is the only option you can modify. Type **65** in the Tint box, and then click OK.

The new tint swatch appears at the bottom of the list of swatches. The top of the Swatches panel displays information about the selected swatch, with a Fill/Stroke box showing that the 65% tint is currently the selected fill color and a Tint box showing that the color is 65% of the original color.

> **Tip:** Tints are helpful because InDesign maintains the relationship between a tint and its parent color. So if you change the parent color swatch to a different color, the tint swatch becomes a lighter version of the new color.

Applying a tint swatch

You will apply the tint swatch as a fill color.

1 Using the Selection tool (▶), click the text frame at right containing the words "First Fridays."

2 Click the Fill box (▧) on the Swatches panel.

3 Click the new tint you just created in the Swatches panel. Its tint swatch name will be C=5 M=4 Y=40 K=0 65%. Notice how the color changes.

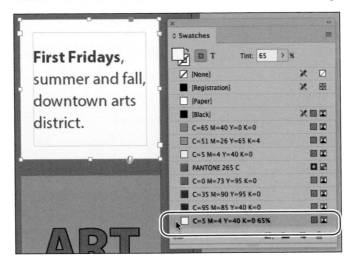

4 Choose File > Save.

Working with gradients

▶ Tip: It's a good idea to test gradients on the intended output device, whether it's a tablet, inkjet printer, or press.

A gradient is a graduated blend between two or more colors or between tints of the same color. You can create either a linear or a radial gradient. In this exercise, you will create a linear gradient swatch with the Swatches panel, apply it to several objects, and adjust the gradients with the Gradient Swatch tool.

Linear gradient.

Radial gradient.

Creating a gradient swatch

In the New Gradient Swatch dialog box, gradients are defined by a series of color stops in the gradient ramp. A stop is the point at which each color is at full intensity between the transitions; it is identified by a square below the gradient ramp. Every InDesign gradient has at least two color stops. By editing the color of each stop and adding additional color stops, you can create custom gradients.

1 Choose Edit > Deselect All to make sure no objects are selected.

2 Choose New Gradient Swatch from the Swatches panel menu (≡).

3 For Swatch Name, type **Blue/White**. Leave the Type menu set to Linear.

4 Click the left stop marker (🔒) on the Gradient Ramp.

5 From the Stop Color menu, select Swatches, and then scroll down the list and select the blue color swatch named C=65 M=40 Y=0 K=0.

> **Tip:** To create a gradient that uses a tint of a color, first create a tint swatch in the Swatches panel.

Notice that the left side of the gradient ramp is now blue.

6 With the left stop marker still selected, type **5** in the Location field.

7 Click the right stop marker (🔒), and make sure the Stop Color is set to [Paper]. Type **70** in the Location field.

The gradient ramp shows a color blend between blue and white.

8 Click OK. The new gradient swatch appears at the bottom of the list in the Swatches panel.

9 Choose File > Save.

Applying a gradient swatch

Now you'll replace the fill in one of the text frames with the gradient.

1 Using the Selection tool (▶), click the text frame at left containing the words "Experience the Evolution."

2 Click the Fill box (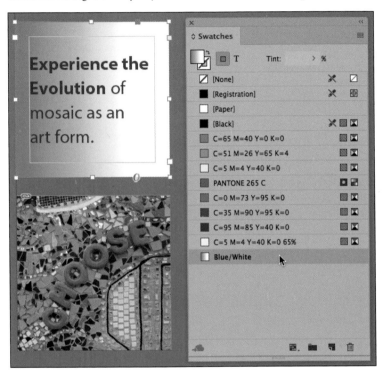) on the Swatches panel.

3 Click the new gradient you just created in the Swatches panel: Blue/White.

4 Choose File > Save.

Adjusting the direction of the gradient blend

> ▶ **Tip:** When using the Gradient Swatch tool, the farther away you start from the outer edges of the object, the more gradual the gradient blend will be.

Once you have filled an object with a gradient, you can modify the gradient by using the Gradient Swatch tool to "repaint" the gradient along an imaginary line that you draw. This tool lets you change the direction of a gradient and change its beginning point and end point. You'll now change the direction of the gradient.

1 Make sure the "Experience the Evolution" text frame is still selected, and then press G on the keyboard to select the Gradient Swatch tool (▪) in the Tools panel.

2 To create a more gradual gradient effect, position the cursor slightly outside the left edge of the selected text frame, and drag to the right as shown.

When you release the mouse button, you'll notice that the transition between blue and white is more gradual than it was before you dragged the Gradient Swatch tool.

▶ **Tip:** To constrain gradient angles to horizontal, vertical, or 45-degree angles, press the Shift key while dragging with the Gradient tool.

3 To create a sharper gradient, drag a short horizontal line in the center of the text frame using the Gradient Swatch tool. Continue to experiment with the Gradient Swatch tool so that you understand how it works.

4 When you are finished experimenting, drag from the top to the bottom of the text frame to form a gradient from top to bottom. That's how you'll leave the gradient for the "Experience the Evolution" text frame.

5 Press V on the keyboard to switch to the Selection tool (▶), and then click the pasteboard to make sure no objects are selected.

6 Choose File > Save.

Working with color groups

If a document contains many color swatches intended for specific purposes (such as chapter openers or divider pages), you can group the swatches in the Swatches panel. You can then easily share the color group with other documents and with other designers working on the campaign.

Adding colors to a color group

You will organize the colors in this document into a new color group.

1　To create a new color group, choose New Color Group from the Swatches panel menu (≡).

2　In the Edit Color Group dialog box, type **Art Show Campaign**. Click OK.

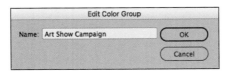

3　To add the color swatches, tint swatch, and gradient swatch to the Art Show Campaign color group, select and drag the colors to the group.

- To select the swatches, Shift-click the first and last swatch as shown. (You do not need to move [None], [Registration], [Paper], or [Black] into the group.)

- Drag the selected colors below the Art Show Campaign folder until a line displays.

4　Choose File > Save.

Previewing the final document

As a final step, you'll preview the document in its finished state.

1 Choose View > Screen Mode > Preview.

2 Choose View > Fit Page In Window.

3 Press Tab to hide all the panels and review the results of your work.

Congratulations! You have now completed this lesson.

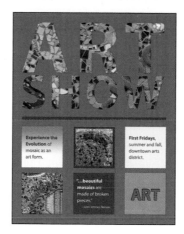

Exploring on your own

Follow these steps to learn more about working with color themes.

Creating a color theme

To create colors that complement an image you are using in a document, you can use the InDesign Color Theme tool. The tool analyzes an image or object, selects representative colors, and generates five different themes. You can select and apply swatches from a color theme, add a color theme's swatches to the Swatches panel, and share the color themes through CC Libraries. To use the Color Theme tool:

- Click an image or object with the Color Theme tool to create a color theme from a small area.

- Drag the Color Theme tool to marquee images and/or objects on a page from which to create a color theme.

- Alt-click (Windows) or Option-click (macOS) the Color Theme tool to clear the existing color theme and create a new one.

▶ **Tip:** As you design a document, you often create more color swatches than you use. When you settle on a final design and color palette, you will want to delete any unused colors to make sure they aren't applied accidentally. To do this, choose Select All Unused from the Swatches panel menu (≡). Click the Delete Selected Swatches/Groups button (🗑) at the bottom of the panel.

Viewing color themes

First, you will view the possible color themes from the mosaic image featuring the word "Choose." Then, you will select the color theme you want to use.

▶ **Tip:** To select the Color Theme tool from the keyboard, press the "i" key. If necessary, press the "i" key twice to cycle through the Eyedropper tool and the Color Theme tool. Note that you cannot use the keyboard shortcut while editing text.

1 On the Tools panel, click the Eyedropper tool (). Hold down the mouse button to view the pop-out menu, and then select the Color Theme tool ().

2 Locate the mosaic image containing the word "Choose" in the lower-left corner of the page.

3 Click the Color Theme tool anywhere on the image.

Notice that the Color Theme panel displays with a color theme picked up from the image.

4 On the Color Theme panel, click the Current Theme menu. Select the Deep theme.

You can select and use any of the swatches shown here, but instead you will add the entire color theme to the Swatches panel.

Adding a theme to the Swatches panel

▶ **Tip:** You can add a single color from a color theme to the Swatches panel in addition to adding an entire theme. To do this, select a swatch on the Color Theme panel, and then Alt-click (Windows) or Option-click (macOS) the Add To Swatches button.

The Deep color theme will work best for the flyer in progress. First, you will add it to the Swatches panel and then view it in the Adobe Color Themes panel, which helps you manage your themes. Then, you will share this color theme with others in your workgroup who are working on other pieces in the marketing campaign.

1 With the Deep theme selected on the Color Theme panel, click the Add This Theme To Swatches button ().

2 If necessary, choose Window > Color > Swatches to open the Swatches panel.

3 Scroll down as necessary to see the Deep theme added to the Swatches panel as a color group (organized in a folder).

Note: The CMYK color values in the Deep theme's colors may vary slightly. This will not affect your ability to complete this lesson.

4 Choose File > Save.

Adding a color theme to your CC Library

The InDesign Creative Cloud Libraries feature makes it easy to share assets, such as color swatches and themes, with a workgroup. If multiple designers are working on a magazine or marketing campaign, this ensures that everyone on the creative team has easy access to the same content. Here, you will add the Deep color theme to your Creative Cloud library. For more information about CC Libraries, see Lesson 10.

1 On the Color Theme panel, with the Deep theme still showing, click the Add This Theme To My Current CC Library button (🔾).

Note: To use the Creative Cloud Libraries features, make sure the Adobe Creative Cloud application is running on your system.

2 If necessary, choose Window > CC Libraries to see the Deep theme added to your CC Libraries panel.

3 Click the CC Libraries panel menu to see the collaboration options: Share Link and Collaborate.

4 The Deep theme is added to the Adobe Color Themes panel as well. To see it, choose Window > Color > Adobe Color Themes.

5 In the Adobe Color Themes panel, click My Themes, and then select My Library from the library menu.

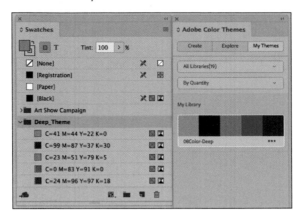

6 Choose Window > Color > Adobe Color Themes to close the panel.

7 Choose File > Save.

Managing color themes

InDesign users have many options for creating and managing color themes. These tools help you synchronize colors across your applications and projects and collaborate with other users.

- The Adobe Capture CC app for iPad, iPhone, and Android lets you create color themes from anything you point at with your device's camera.

- The Adobe Color CC website at https://color.adobe.com lets you create your own color themes, explore other users' themes, and review your themes.

- The Adobe Color Themes panel (Window > Color > Adobe Color Themes) lets you create and explore themes within InDesign and other Creative Cloud applications, such as Photoshop CC and Illustrator CC.

- The CC Libraries panel (Window > CC Libraries) allows you to share color themes with a workgroup and manage color themes by copying, moving, or deleting them.

For more information about any of these features, consult InDesign Help.

Review questions

1 What is the advantage of creating colors in the Swatches panel instead of the Color panel?

2 What are the three general steps involved in applying a swatch of color?

3 What are the pros and cons of using spot colors versus process colors?

4 After you create a gradient and apply it to an object, how do you adjust the direction of the gradient blend?

Review answers

1 If you use the Swatches panel to apply a color to text and objects, and then decide you want to use a different color, you don't need to update each use of the color individually. Instead, change the color's definition in the Swatches panel, and the color changes automatically throughout the layout.

2 The three general steps to applying a color swatch are: (1) selecting the text or object, (2) selecting the stroke or fill box, depending on what you want to change, and (3) selecting the color. You can access color swatches in the Swatches panel and the Control panel. The Tools panel provides quick access to the last color applied as well.

3 By using a spot color, you can ensure color accuracy. However, each spot color requires its own plate on the press, so using spot colors can be more costly. Use process colors when a job requires so many colors that using individual spot inks would be expensive or impractical, such as when printing color photographs.

4 To adjust the direction of the gradient blend, use the Gradient Swatch tool to repaint the fill along an imaginary line in the direction you want.

9 WORKING WITH STYLES

Lesson Overview

In this lesson, you'll learn how to do the following:

- Create and apply paragraph styles.

- Create and apply character styles.

- Nest character styles inside paragraph styles.

- Create and apply object styles.

- Create and apply cell styles.

- Create and apply table styles.

- Globally update paragraph, character, object, cell, and table styles.

- Import and apply styles from other InDesign documents.

- Create style groups.

This lesson will take approximately 60 minutes to complete.

Please log in to your account on peachpit.com to download the lesson files for this chapter, or go to the "Getting Started" section at the beginning of this book and follow the instructions under "Accessing the Lesson Files and Web Edition." Store the files on your computer in a convenient location.

Expedition Tea Company

TEA HOUSE & GIFT SHOP

unbelievable
elievable taste. A
hat results in a
te.

ka • English
body with
cing with milk.

hnauth region,
quor with nutty,
th milk.

Nuwara Eliya,
wn Ceylon with
excellent finish.
ear.

pe :: Darjeeling,
e distinctive
black currant

• This superb
long-fired oolong tea has a bakey, but sweet
fruity character with a rich amber color.

Orange Blossom Oolong :: *Taiwan, Sri
Lanka, India* • Orange and citrus blend with
toasty oolong for a "jammy" flavor.

Ti Kuan Yin Oolong :: *China* • A light "airy"
character with lightly noted orchid-like hints
and a sweet fragrant finish.

Phoenix Iron Goddess Oolong :: *China* • A
light "airy" character with delicate orchid-like
notes. A top grade oolong.

Quangzhou Milk Oolong :: *China* • A
unique character —like sweet milk with light
orchid notes from premium oolong peeking
out from camellia depths.

GREEN TEA

Dragonwell (Lung Ching) :: *China* •
Distinguished by its beautiful shape, emerald
color, and sweet floral character. Full-bodied
with a slight heady bouquet.

Genmaicha (Popcorn Tea) :: *Japan* • Green
tea blended with fire-toasted rice with a
natural sweetness. During the firing the rice
may "pop" not unlike popcorn.

Sencha Kyoto Cherry Rose :: *China* • Fresh,
smooth sencha tea with depth and body. The
cherry flavoring and subtle rose hints give the
tea an exotic character.

Superior Gunpowder :: *Taiwan* • Strong
dark-green tea with a memorable fragrance
and long lasting finish with surprising body
and captivating green tea taste.

4 Contains tea from Ethical Tea Partnership monitored estates.

With Adobe InDesign, you can create styles—sets of
formatting attributes—and apply them in one step to
text, objects, tables, and more. Any changes to a style
automatically affect all the text or objects to which
the style is applied. Styles offer a quick, consistent
method for formatting layouts.

Getting started

In this lesson, you'll create and apply styles for a few pages of a catalog for the Expedition Tea Company. Styles are collections of attributes that allow you to quickly and consistently apply formatting to text and objects throughout a document. (For example, a Body Text paragraph style specifies attributes such as font, size, leading, and alignment.) The catalog pages here contain text, tables, and objects that you will manually format and then use as the basis for creating styles. Later, if you were to place more catalog content, you could format the new text, tables, and objects with one click using styles.

● **Note:** If you have not already downloaded the project files for this lesson to your computer from your Account page, make sure to do so now. See "Getting Started" at the beginning of the book.

1 To ensure that the preferences and default settings of your Adobe InDesign program match those used in this lesson, move the InDesign Defaults file to a different folder following the procedure in "Saving and restoring the InDesign Defaults file" on pages 4–5.

2 Start Adobe InDesign.

3 The InDesign Start Screen displays. Click Open at left. (If the Start Screen does not display, choose File > Open from the InDesign menu bar.)

4 Open the 09_Start.indd file in the Lesson09 folder, located inside the Lessons folder within the InDesignCIB folder on your hard disk.

5 If the Missing Fonts dialog box displays, click Sync Fonts. Click Close when font syncing is complete.

6 Choose File > Save As, rename the file **09_Styles.indd**, and save it in the Lesson09 folder. Scroll to view all the pages.

● **Note:** The screen captures in this book show the Medium Light interface. Interface elements such as panels and dialog boxes may be darker on your screen.

7 To ensure that the panels and menu commands match those used in this lesson, choose Window > Workspace > [Advanced], and then choose Window > Workspace > Reset Advanced.

8 To display the document at a higher resolution, choose View > Display Performance > High Quality Display.

9 If you want to see what the finished document will look like, open the 09_End.indd file in the same folder. You can leave this document open to act as a guide as you work.

When you're ready to resume working on the lesson document, click its tab in the upper-left corner of the document window.

BLACK TEA

Earl Grey :: *Sri Lanka* • An unbelievable aroma that portends an unbelievable taste. A correct balance of flavoring that results in a refreshing true Earl Grey taste.

English Breakfast :: *Sri Lanka* • English Breakfast at its finest. Good body with satisfying full tea flavor. Enticing with milk.

Assam, Gingia Estate :: *Bishnauth region, India* • Bright, full-bodied liquor with nutty, walnut-like character. Try with milk.

Ceylon, Kenmare Estate :: *Nuwara Eliya, Sri Lanka* • A classic high grown Ceylon with expressive flavor that has an excellent finish. Kenmare was 'Estate of the Year.'

Darjeeling, Margaret's Hope :: *Darjeeling, India* • A delicate cup with the distinctive 'Muscatel' character. Hints of black currant for an almost wine-like taste.

OOLONG TEA

Formosa Oolong :: *Taiwan* • This superb long-fired oolong tea has a bakey, but sweet fruity character with a rich amber color.

Orange Blossom Oolong :: *Taiwan, Sri Lanka, India* • Orange and citrus blend with toasty oolong for a "jammy" flavor.

Ti Kuan Yin Oolong :: *China* • A light "airy" character with lightly noted orchid-like hints and a sweet fragrant finish.

Phoenix Iron Goddess Oolong :: *China* • A light "airy" character with delicate orchid-like notes. A top grade oolong.

Quangzhou Milk Oolong :: *China* • A unique character —like sweet milk with light orchid notes from premium oolong peeking out from camellia depths.

GREEN TEA

Dragonwell (Lung Ching) :: *China* • Distinguished by its beautiful shape, emerald color, and sweet floral character. Full-bodied with a slight heady bouquet.

Genmaicha (Popcorn Tea) :: *Japan* • Green tea blended with fire-toasted rice with a natural sweetness. During the firing the rice may "pop" not unlike popcorn.

Sencha Kyoto Cherry Rose :: *China* • Fresh, smooth sencha tea with depth and body. The cherry flavoring and subtle rose hints give the tea an exotic character.

Superior Gunpowder :: *Taiwan* • Strong dark-green tea with a memorable fragrance and long lasting finish with surprising body and captivating green tea taste.

4 Contains tea from *Ethical Tea Partnership monitored estates.*

Understanding styles

InDesign provides styles for automating nearly all text and object formatting. Creating, applying, modifying, and sharing styles works the same way for all types of styles: paragraph, character, object, table, and cell styles.

Basic styles

The default formatting of everything in a new InDesign document is determined by its respective "basic" style. For example, when you create a new text frame, its formatting is determined by the [Basic Text Frame] object style. Therefore, if you wanted to specify that all new text frames have a 1-pt stroke, you would modify [Basic Text Frame]. To create a new default for all new InDesign documents, modify the "basic" style when no documents are open. Whenever you find yourself repeating a formatting task, stop and think about whether it makes sense to modify the relevant basic style or create a new style.

Tip: On all the styles panels (Paragraph, Object, etc.), the panel menu provides a Load option for importing styles from other InDesign documents. You can also share paragraph styles and character styles with a workgroup through InDesign CC Libraries.

Applying styles

Applying a style is as simple as making a selection and then clicking a style name in the relevant Styles panel. For example, to format a table, you select the table and then click a style name in the Table Styles panel. If you are working with an extended keyboard, you can set up keyboard shortcuts for applying styles as well.

Overriding manual formatting with styles

In most cases, you will want an object, a table, or some text to match a style's specifications precisely. To do this, you need to override any manual formatting. If a selection does not precisely match its style, a plus sign appears next to the style name. This is referred to as a *style override*.

To see how the formatting varies from the style, point at the style name in the Styles panel; a tool tip describes the overrides applied. (To see text formatting overrides, you can choose Toggle Style Override Highlighter from the Character Styles or Paragraph Styles panel menu.) Each Styles panel has a Clear Overrides control at the bottom, indicated by an icon and a plus sign. Move your mouse over the icon to learn how to clear overrides in the selection. (Note that if you are having trouble clearing overrides while applying a paragraph style, check to see whether a character style is applied to the text.)

Tip: Keyboard shortcuts are especially handy for formatting text. A quick way to remember shortcuts is to sync them up to the style names and usage. For example, if you create a paragraph style named "1 Headline" with the shortcut Ctrl+1, it's easy to remember the shortcut because it's often the first style you apply.

Modifying and redefining styles

A primary benefit of using styles is the ability to apply formatting consistently and quickly make global changes. To modify a style, double-click its name in a Styles panel; this displays its Options dialog box so you can make changes. You can also modify the formatting of text, a table, or an object, and then choose Redefine Style from the Styles panel menu.

Creating and applying paragraph styles

Paragraph styles let you apply and globally update text formatting to speed up production and create a more consistent overall design. Paragraph styles incorporate all elements of text formatting, including character attributes such as font, size, style, and color, along with paragraph attributes such as indents, alignment, tabs, and hyphenation. They differ from character styles in that they are applied to entire paragraphs at once, not just to selected characters.

Creating a paragraph style

In this exercise, you'll create and apply a paragraph style to selected paragraphs. First, you will manually format the text in the document locally (that is, not based on a style). Then, you will have InDesign pick up this formatting and build it into a new paragraph style.

▶ **Tip:** When working on longer documents, such as books and catalogs, using styles can save hours of time in manual formatting. A common way to get started is to select all the text in a document and apply a "body text" paragraph style with one click. You can then go through the text and apply heading paragraph styles and character styles with keyboard shortcuts.

1 Navigate to page 2 of 09_Styles.indd. Adjust the view scale so you can easily see the text.

2 Using the Type tool (**T**), drag to select the "Loose Leaf Teas" subhead, which follows the introductory paragraph on page 2.

3 If necessary, click the Character Formatting Controls icon (**A**) in the Control panel. Specify the following:

 • Enter **18 pt** in the Font Size field.

 • Click the character Fill box (**T**) and select the burgundy swatch: K=24 M=93 Y=100 K=18.

▶ **Tip:** The easiest way to create a paragraph style is to format a sample paragraph using local (not style-based) formatting and then create a new style based on that sample paragraph. Effectively, this lets you see the style before you build it. You can then efficiently use the new style in the rest of the document.

4 In the Control panel, click Paragraph Formatting Controls (¶), and increase Space Before (⁺≣) to **p3**. Decrease the Space After (₊≣) to **p4**.

 Now you'll create a paragraph style using this formatting so that you can use it to format the other subheads in the document.

5 Make sure that the "Loose Leaf Teas" subhead is still selected. If it's not already visible, open the Paragraph Styles panel by choosing Type > Paragraph Styles.

6 In the Paragraph Styles panel, create a new paragraph style by choosing New Paragraph Style from the panel menu. The New Paragraph Style dialog box opens, displaying the formatting you just applied to the subhead in the Style Settings section.

● **Note:** In this document, the Paragraph Styles panel already has a few styles provided for you, including the default, [Basic Paragraph].

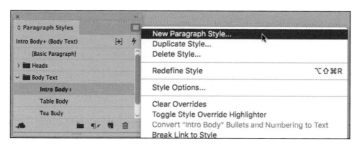

7 In the Style Name box at the top of the dialog box, type **Head 2** to name this style as the second largest headline.

Below the Style Name, notice that the new style is based on the Intro Body style. Since Intro Body was applied to the subhead when you created the style, the new style is automatically based on Intro Body. By using the Based On option in the General section of the New Paragraph Style dialog box, you can use an existing style as a starting point for a new style. In this case, the Intro Body formatting is unrelated to the heading style, so you will change the Based On style to No Style.

8 Select [No Paragraph Style] from the Based On menu.

To speed up text formatting while typing in InDesign, you can specify a Next Style for a paragraph style. Each time you press Enter or Return, InDesign automatically applies the Next Style. For example, your headline style might automatically be followed by your body paragraph style.

9 Select Intro Body from the Next Style menu, because this is the style used for the text following each Head 2 headline.

You can also create keyboard shortcuts for easily applying styles in InDesign.

10 Click in the Shortcut box, hold down Shift (Windows) or Command (macOS), and press 9 on the numeric keypad of your keyboard. (InDesign requires the use of a modifier key for style shortcuts.) Note that in Windows the Num Lock key on the keypad must be down to create or apply style shortcuts.

▶ **Tip:** If you change the Based On style—for example, by changing the font—the changes update all styles based on that style. Unique characteristics of styles based on other styles are maintained. Basing styles on other styles is helpful when creating a series of related styles, such as Body Copy, Bulleted Body Copy, and so on. If the font of the Body Copy style changes, InDesign updates the font in all related styles as well.

● **Note:** If your keyboard lacks a numeric keypad, you can skip this step.

11 Select Apply Style To Selection to apply this new style to the text you just formatted.

12 In the lower-left corner, deselect Add To CC Libraries.

13 Click OK to close the New Paragraph Style dialog box.

The new Head 2 style appears in the Paragraph Styles panel and is highlighted to indicate that it's applied to the selected paragraph.

14 In the Paragraph Styles panel, click the arrow next to the Heads style group to open it. Then, drag the Head 2 style up between Head 1 and Head 3.

15 Choose Edit > Deselect All, and then choose File > Save.

Applying a paragraph style

Now you'll apply your paragraph style to other paragraphs in the document.

1 If necessary, scroll to the right to see the right page of the spread.

2 Using the Type tool (T), click to place an insertion point anywhere within "Tea Gift Collections."

3 Click the Head 2 style in the Paragraph Styles panel to apply the style to the paragraph. The text attributes change to reflect the paragraph style.

4 Repeat steps 2 and 3 to apply the Head 2 style to "Teapots and Tea Accessories" on page 3.

5 Choose Edit > Deselect All, and then choose File > Save.

Creating and applying character styles

In the previous exercise, paragraph styles allowed you to apply character and paragraph formatting to text with a single click or a keystroke. Similarly, character styles are a way to apply multiple attributes—such as font, size, and color—to text using a single action. Unlike paragraph styles, which format the entire paragraph, character styles apply formatting only to selected characters such as a word or phrase.

Creating a character style

Now you will create and apply a character style to selected text in the document. This demonstrates how character styles can make your work more efficient and consistent.

1 Scroll to view the first paragraph on page 2 at left.

2 If it's not already visible, open the Character Styles panel by choosing Type > Character Styles. The only style listed in this panel is the default, [None].

As you did with the paragraph style in the previous section, you'll build a character style based on existing text formatting. This approach lets you see the formatting before you create the style. In this case, you'll format the Expedition Tea Company name and build it into a character style so that it can be reused efficiently throughout the document.

3 Using the Type tool (**T.**), select the words "Expedition Tea Company™" on page 2.

4 In the Control panel, click Character Formatting Controls (**A**).

 • Click Small Caps (Tr).

 • Click the character Fill box (T) and select the khaki swatch:
 K–43 M=49 Y=100 K=22.

Now that the text is formatted, you'll create a new character style.

▶ **Tip:** Character styles are helpful for lead-in characters such as bullet characters, numbers in numbered lists, and drop caps. They are also useful for emphasizing text within body copy—for example, the names of stocks (investments) are often formatted in bold and small caps.

▶ **Tip:** Character styles include only differences, such as italic, from the attributes specified in the paragraph style. The benefit of this is that you can use the same character style with different paragraph styles. For example, say that a newsletter's style is to italicize the names of books and movies. The newsletter has a body text style in Minion Pro and a sidebar body text style in Myriad Pro. You need only one character style that specifies Italic for use with both paragraph styles. InDesign will know to use the italic version of the correct font.

5 Click Create New Style at the bottom of the Character Styles panel.

6 Double-click the new Character Style 1 that displays in the Character Styles panel. The Character Style Options dialog box opens.

7 In the Style Name box at the top of the dialog box, type **Company Name** to define the style's purpose.

As you did for the paragraph style you created, now you'll create a keyboard shortcut for easy application of this character style.

● **Note:** If your keyboard lacks a numeric keypad, you can skip this step.

8 Click in the Shortcut box, hold down Shift (Windows) or Command (macOS), and press 8 on the numeric keypad of your keyboard. In Windows, be sure that the Num Lock key on the keypad is down.

9 Click Basic Character Formats and Character Color in the list at the left to see what the character style includes.

10 Click OK to close the Character Style Options dialog box. The new Company Name style appears in the Character Styles panel and is now applied to the text.

11 Choose Edit > Deselect All, and then choose File > Save.

▶ **Tip:** You can use Find/Change (Edit menu) to search for all instances of a word or phrase, and then apply a character style to it.

Applying a character style

You're ready to apply your character style to selected text already placed in the document. As with paragraph styles, using character styles prevents you from having to manually apply multiple type attributes to each instance of text.

1 Scroll to the right to view the right page of the first spread.

To maintain a consistent look for the company name, you'll apply the Company Name character style.

2 Using the Type tool (**T**), select the words "Expedition Tea Company" in the first paragraph of body text.

3 In the Character Styles panel, click the Company Name style to apply it to this text. You should see the text change to reflect the character style you created.

4 Using either the Character Styles panel or the keyboard shortcut, apply the Company Name style to the words "Expedition Tea Company" in the second body paragraph as well.

● **Note:** You can also use the keyboard shortcut you defined earlier (Shift+8 or Command+8) to apply the Company Name style.

Leave the Character Styles panel open for the next exercise.

5 Choose Edit > Deselect All, and then choose File > Save.

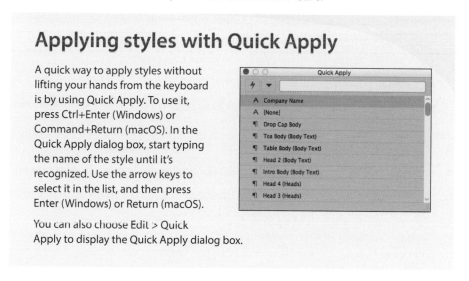

Applying styles with Quick Apply

A quick way to apply styles without lifting your hands from the keyboard is by using Quick Apply. To use it, press Ctrl+Enter (Windows) or Command+Return (macOS). In the Quick Apply dialog box, start typing the name of the style until it's recognized. Use the arrow keys to select it in the list, and then press Enter (Windows) or Return (macOS).

You can also choose Edit > Quick Apply to display the Quick Apply dialog box.

Nesting character styles inside paragraph styles

▶ **Tip:** You can use the powerful nested styles feature to automatically apply different formatting within a paragraph according to a specific set of rules. For example, in a table of contents, you can automatically apply bold to the text, change the tracking in the tab leader (the dots that lead to the page number), and change the font and color of the page number.

To make the use of styles more convenient and powerful, InDesign lets you nest character styles within paragraph styles. These nested styles allow you to apply distinct character formatting to specific portions of a paragraph—such as the first character, the second word, or the first line—at the same time you apply a paragraph style. This makes nested styles ideal for creating run-in headings, where the first portion of a line or paragraph is styled differently from the rest of the line or paragraph. In fact, anytime you can define a pattern of formatting within a paragraph, such as applying an italic type style until reaching the first period, you can probably automate the formatting with a nested style.

Creating character styles for nesting

To create a nested style, you need to first create both a character style and a paragraph style in which to nest it. In this section, you'll create two character styles for nesting and then nest them within the paragraph style Tea Body, which already exists.

1 Double-click page 4 in the Pages panel, and then choose View > Fit Page In Window. If the body copy is too small to view, zoom in to the first paragraph under the "Black Tea" heading, beginning with "Earl Grey."

2 Review the text and punctuation:

 - In this exercise, you'll create two nested styles to distinguish the tea name from the country where it was grown.

 - A pair of colons (::) separates the tea's name and country of origin.

 - A bullet (•) appears after the country.

 - These characters will be important when creating your nested styles later in this section.

3 Using the Type tool (T), select the words "Earl Grey" in the first column.

4 In the Character Styles panel, choose New Character Style from the panel menu.

5 In the Style Name box at the top of the dialog box, type **Tea Name** to define the text to which the style will be applied.

 To make the name of each tea stand out more, you will change the font, style, and color.

6 From the categories on the left side of the dialog box, click Basic Character Formats.

7 From the Font Family menu, select Myriad Pro. From the the Font Style menu, select Bold.

8 From the categories on the left side of the dialog box, click Character Color.

9 In the Character Color settings that appear on the right side of the dialog box, select the khaki color swatch (C=43, M=49, Y=100, K=22).

10 In the lower-left corner, deselect Add To CC Libraries.

11 Click OK to close the New Character Style dialog box. The new Tea Name style appears in the Character Styles panel.

Now you'll create a second character style for nesting.

12 To the right of the "Earl Grey" text you just formatted, select the text "Sri Lanka." Using the Character panel (Type menu) or the Control panel, change the Font to Myriad Pro and the Style to Italic.

13 With "Sri Lanka" still selected, choose New Character Style from the Character Styles panel menu. Type **Country Name** in the Style Name box. Click OK to create the character style based on the formatting applied in step 12.

14 Choose Edit > Deselect All, and then choose File > Save.

You have created two new character styles. Using these along with the existing Tea Body paragraph style, you are ready to create and apply your nested style.

Creating a nested style

▶ **Tip:** In addition to nested styles, InDesign provides nested line styles. These let you specify formatting for individual lines in a paragraph—such as a drop cap followed by small caps, which are common in the lead paragraphs of magazine articles. If the text reflows, InDesign adjusts the formatting to encompass only the specified lines. The controls for creating nested line styles are in the Drop Caps And Nested Styles panel of the Paragraph Style Options dialog box.

When you create a nested style within an existing paragraph style, you're basically specifying a secondary set of rules for InDesign to follow while formatting a paragraph. In this exercise, you'll build a nested style into the Tea Body style using one of the two character styles you created in the previous exercise.

1 If necessary, position page 4 in the center of the document window.

2 If the Paragraph Styles panel is not visible, choose Type > Paragraph Styles.

3 In the Paragraph Styles panel, double-click the Tea Body style to open the Paragraph Style Options dialog box.

4 From the categories on the left side of the dialog box, select Drop Caps And Nested Styles.

5 In the Nested Styles section, click the New Nested Style button to create a new nested style.

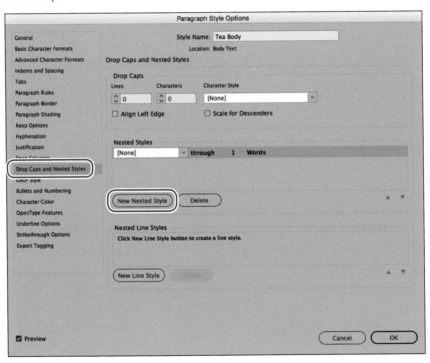

A nested style that applies the [None] character style through 1 Words appears.

6 Click the [None] style to display a menu. Select the Tea Name character style; this is the first nested style in the sequence.

7 Click the word "through" to reveal another menu. This menu contains only two choices: Through and Up To. The Tea Name character style needs to be applied up to the first colon (:) after Earl Grey, so select Up To.

8 Click the number 1 next to Up To to activate a text box into which you can type a number. The number defines how many elements the style applies Through or Up To. Although there are two colons, you only need to reference the first colon, so leave this as the default, 1.

9 Click Words to reveal a text box and menu. Click the menu button to the right of the box to view elements to which the style can be applied, including sentences, characters, and spaces. Select and delete the word "Words," and then type a colon (:) in the box.

10 In the lower-left corner, select Preview. Move the Paragraph Style Options dialog box so that you can see the columns of text.

11 The name for each tea should be bold and khaki up to (but not including) the first colon. Click OK.

12 Choose Edit > Deselect All, and then choose File > Save.

Adding a second nested style

Now you'll add another nested style, but first you need to copy a bullet character from the page. Within the nested style you are creating, the formatting switch takes place up until a bullet character is encountered—but you cannot always type a bullet within a dialog box, so you may need to paste it.

1 In the first column under "Black Tea," navigate to the bullet character after "Sri Lanka." Select it and choose Edit > Copy.

2 In the Paragraph Styles panel, double-click the Tea Body style. In the Drop Caps And Nested Styles section of the Paragraph Style Options dialog box, click the New Nested Style button to create another new nested style.

● **Note:** On a Mac, you can copy and paste the bullet or you can press Option+8 to insert a bullet in the field.

3 Repeat steps 6 through 9 of "Creating a nested style" to set up your new nested style with the following formatting:

- First option: Choose Country Name.

- Second option: Choose Up To.

- Third option: Leave as the default, 1.

- Fourth option: Select and delete "Words" and enter the bullet character by pasting the bullet you copied (Edit > Paste).

4 If necessary, select Preview in the lower-left corner. Drag the Paragraph Style Options dialog box out of the way so you can see that each country name is now italicized. Notice that the two colons between the tea name and country are also italicized—but this formatting is not specified in the design.

To fix the italicized colons, you'll create another nested style that applies the paragraph style's normal font to the colons. To do this, you select the [None] option as the character style.

5 Click the New Nested Style button to create another nested style.

6 Repeat steps 6 through 9 of "Creating a nested style" to set up your new nested style with the following formatting:

- First option: Choose [None].

- Second option: Choose Through.

- Third option: Type **2**.

- Fourth option: Type **:** [colon].

You now have a third nested style, but it needs to be placed between the Tea Name and Country Name nested styles to be in the proper position sequentially.

7 With the [None] nested style selected, click the up arrow button once to move the style between the other two.

8 Click OK to accept these changes. You have now finished creating a series of nested styles that apply the Tea Name and Country Name character styles to any paragraph styled with the Tea Body paragraph style.

▶ **Tip:** Using nested styles can automate some very tedious formatting. When making style decisions for longer documents, think about establishing a pattern that will enable automatic formatting through nested styles.

> **BLACK·TEA¶**
> **Earl·Grey**·::·*Sri·Lanka*·•·An·unbelievable·
> aroma·that·portends·an·unbelievable·taste.·A·
> correct·balance·of·flavoring·that·results·in·a·
> refreshing·true·Earl·Grey·taste.¶

9 Choose Edit > Deselect All, and then choose File > Save.

Creating and applying object styles

Object styles let you apply and globally update formatting to objects, such as frames. Combining formatting attributes—including fill, stroke, transparency, and text wrap options—into object styles helps create a more consistent overall design and speeds up tedious production tasks.

▶ **Tip:** All of the InDesign Styles panels (Character, Object, Table, and so on) let you group similar styles in folders called style groups. To create a style group, click the Create New Style Group button at the bottom of the panel. Click in the group's folder to name it. You can drag styles into the folder to organize them, and you can drag styles up and down in the list to organize them.

Formatting an object for a style

In this section, you will create and apply an object style to the black circles containing the "etp" symbols on the second spread of the catalog. (The "etp" stands for Ethical Tea Partnership.) You'll base the new object style on the formatting of the black circle. You'll start by changing the circle's color and adding a drop shadow to it; then you can define the new style.

1 Double-click page 4 in the Pages panel to center the page in the document window.

2 Select the Zoom tool (🔍) in the Tools panel and increase the magnification to better view the etp symbol near English Breakfast.

To format the symbol, you will fill it with a khaki color and apply a Drop Shadow effect. To make this task easier, the type and circle for all the etp symbols have been placed on separate layers—the type on the layer called etp Type and the circles on a layer called etp Circle.

3 Choose Window > Layers to view the Layers panel.

4 Click the empty box to the left of the etp Type layer's name to display a lock icon (🔒). This locks the layer so you cannot accidentally change the text while editing the object.

5 Using the Selection tool (▶), click the black etp symbol next to English Breakfast.

► Tip: In addition to formatting attributes, object styles can include size (Width, Height) and placement (X, Y) attributes.

6 Choose Window > Color > Swatches. In the Swatches panel, click the Fill box (), and then click the khaki color swatch (C=43, M=49, Y=100, K=22).

7 With the etp symbol still selected, choose Object > Effects > Drop Shadow. In the Position section, decrease X Offset and Y Offset to **p2**.

8 Select Preview to see the changes.

9 Click OK. Choose Edit > Deselect All to see the effect.

10 Choose File > Save.

Creating an object style

Now that the object is formatted properly, you are ready to create the object style from its formatting.

1　Using the Selection tool (▶), click the etp symbol.

2　Choose Window > Styles > Object Styles to open the Object Styles panel.

3　In the Object Styles panel, hold down the Alt (Windows) or Option (macOS) key while you click Create New Style in the lower-right corner.

▶ **Tip:** Just as with paragraph and character styles, you can base an object style on another object style. Changes made to the Based On style update all object styles based on that style. (Unique characteristics of styles based on other styles are maintained.) The controls for basing a style on another are in the General panel of the New Object Style dialog box.

When you Alt-click or Option-click the Create New Style button, the New Object Style dialog box opens automatically. The selected boxes on the left side of this dialog box indicate which attributes will be applied when this style is used.

4　In the Style Name box at the top of the New Object Style dialog box, type **ETP Symbol** to describe the purpose of the style.

5　Select Apply Style To Selection, and click OK.

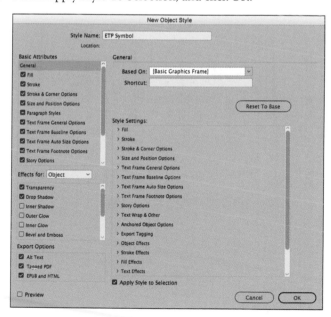

The new ETP Symbol style appears in the Object Styles panel.

Tip: When you modify a style, the text, table, or objects to which the style is applied will update automatically. If you have a specific instance of text, a table, or an object that you do not want to update, you can break its link to the style. Each styles panel (Paragraph Styles, Cell Styles, and so on) has a Break Link To Style command in the panel menu.

Now you'll change the color of the drop shadow and update the object style. You do not need to finalize design decisions before creating and applying styles because styles are easy to update based on new formatting.

6 With the symbol still selected, choose Object > Effects > Drop Shadow.

7 In the Blending area, click the color swatch to display a menu. Choose the burgundy swatch (C=24, M=93, Y=100, K=18) from the menu, and click OK.

8 Click OK to close the Effects dialog box.

Notice the plus sign next to the ETP Symbol style in the Object Styles panel. This indicates formatting that overrides the object style's formatting. To resolve this, you can update the style to match the new formatting.

9 Choose Redefine Style from the Object Styles panel menu. This updates the style to match the new formatting.

10 Choose Edit > Deselect All, and then choose File > Save.

Applying an object style

Now you'll apply your new object style to the other circles on the second spread. Applying the object style changes the formatting of the circles automatically; you don't have to manually apply the color and drop shadow to each circle individually.

1 With pages 4 and 5 displayed, choose View > Fit Spread In Window.

 To quickly select the etp objects, you will hide the layer containing the text.

2 Choose Window > Layers. In the Layers panel, click in the visibility box to the far left of Layer 1 to hide this layer.

3 Select the Selection tool (▶), and choose Edit > Select All.

4 With all of the etp circles selected, click the ETP Symbol style in the Object Styles panel.

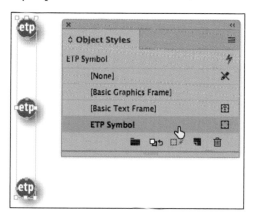

5 If the formatting does not match the new style, choose Clear Overrides from the Object Styles panel menu.

6 In the Layers panel, click in the column to the far left of Layer 1 to display the layer again.

7 Choose Edit > Deselect All, and then choose File > Save.

▶ **Tip:** Once you have even a rough idea of how you want text, objects, and tables to look, you can start creating styles and applying them. Then, as you experiment with a design and make changes, you can simply update the style definitions using the Redefine Style option, which automatically updates the formatting of anything to which the style is applied. The panel menus for all of the InDesign Styles panels, such as Paragraph Styles and Table Styles, provide the Redefine Style option.

Creating and applying table and cell styles

Table and cell styles let you format tables with the same convenience and consistency you get from styling text with paragraph and character styles. Table styles let you control the visual attributes of the table, including the table border, space before and after the table, row and column strokes, and alternating fill patterns. Cell styles let you control cell inset spacing, vertical justification, individual cell strokes and fills, and diagonal lines. You'll learn more about creating tables in Lesson 11, "Creating Tables."

In this exercise, you'll create and apply a table style and two cell styles to tables in the catalog document to help distinguish the different descriptions of tea.

Creating cell styles

You'll begin by creating cell styles for both the header row and body rows of the table at the bottom of page 3. Later, you'll nest these two styles inside the Table style, a process similar to how you nested character styles inside a paragraph style earlier in this lesson. You'll now create two cell styles.

1 Double-click page 3 in the Pages panel, and then choose View > Fit Page In Window.

2 Using the Zoom tool (🔍), drag around the table at the bottom of the page to make it easily visible.

3 Using the Type tool (T), drag to select the first two cells in the header row, containing the words "Tea" and "Finished Leaf."

TEA#	FINISHED LEAF#	COLOR#	BREWING DETAILS#
White #	Soft, grayish white#	Pale yellow or pinkish #	165° for 5-7 min.#
Green #	Dull to brilliant green#	Green or yellowish#	180° for 2-4 min.#
Oolong#	Blackish or greenish#	Green to brownish #	212° for 5-7 min.#
Black#	Lustrous black#	Rich red or brownish #	212° for 3-5 min.#

4 Choose Table > Cell Options > Strokes And Fills. For Cell Fill, select the pale yellow color swatch (C=4, M=15, Y=48, K=0). Click OK.

5 With the cells still selected, open the Cell Styles panel by choosing Window > Styles > Cell Styles.

6 From the Cell Styles panel menu, choose New Cell Style.

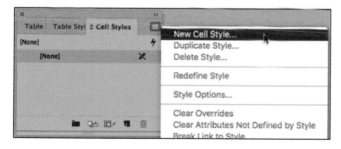

▶ **Tip:** You can create new styles from any InDesign Styles panel (Character, Object, Table, and so on) by choosing New Style from the panel menu or clicking the Create New Style button at the bottom of the panel.

The cell formatting you applied to the selected cells is displayed in the Style Settings box. You'll also notice additional cell formatting options on the left side of the dialog box. In this exercise, however, you will only set the desired paragraph style to use for the text within the header row.

7 In the Style Name box at the top of the New Cell Style dialog box, type **Table Head**.

8 From the Paragraph Style pop-up menu, choose Head 4. This paragraph style was already created in the document. Click OK.

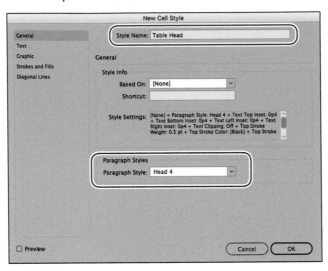

Now you will create a new cell style for the body rows.

9 Using the Type tool (**T**.), select the first two cells of the second row of the table. They contain the words "White" and "Soft, grayish white."

10 From the Cell Styles panel menu, choose New Cell Style.

11 In the Style Name box, name this style **Table Body Rows**.

12 From the Paragraph Style pop-up menu, choose Table Body. This paragraph style was already created in the document.

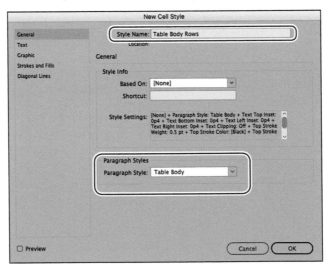

13 Click OK. The two new cell styles appear in the Cell Styles panel. Choose Edit > Deselect All.

14 Choose File > Save.

Creating a table style

Now you'll create a table style that formats the overall look of the table and applies the two cell styles you just created to the header and body rows.

1 With the table still easily visible onscreen, select the Type tool (T.). Click to place an insertion point anywhere in the table.

2 Choose Window > Styles > Table Styles. From the Table Styles panel menu, choose New Table Style.

3 In the Style Name box, type **Tea Table**.

4 In the Cell Styles section, choose the following options:

- Header Rows: Select Table Head

- Footer Rows: Leave at [Same as Body Rows]

- Body Rows: Select Table Body Rows

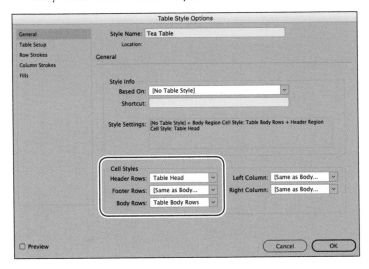

You'll now set up the table style to apply alternating rows of color to the body rows.

5 Select the Fills category on the left side of the New Table Style dialog box.

6 Choose Every Other Row from the Alternating Pattern pop-up menu. The options for alternating rows appear.

7 Specify the following Alternating options:

- For Color, select the pale yellow color swatch (C=4, M=15, Y=48, K=0).

- For Tint, type **30**%.

8 Click OK. The new table style, Tea Table, appears in the Table Styles panel.

9 Choose Edit > Deselect All, and then choose File > Save.

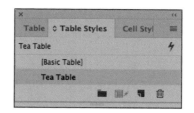

Applying a table style

Now you'll apply the table style you just created to the two tables in the document.

1 With the table still easily visible onscreen, select the Type tool (**T**). Click to place an insertion point anywhere in the table, and select Table > Select > Table.

2 In the Table Styles panel, click the Tea Table style. The table is reformatted with the table and cell styles you created.

▶ **Tip:** If you create a table from existing text (using Table > Convert Text To Table), you can apply a table style as you convert the text.

3 Double-click page 6 in the Pages panel, and then choose View > Fit Page In Window. Click to place an insertion point anywhere in the Tea Tasting Overview table, and then select Table > Select > Table.

4 In the Table Styles panel, click the Tea Table style. The table is reformatted with the table and cell styles you created.

5 Choose Edit > Deselect All, and then choose File > Save.

Globally updating styles

InDesign features two ways to update paragraph, character, object, table, and cell styles. The first way is to open a style options dialog box and make changes to the formatting options. The other way to update a style is to use local formatting to modify some formatting and then redefine the style based on the updated formatting. In either case, formatting is updated wherever the style is applied.

In this exercise, you'll make a change to the Head 3 style to include a paragraph rule below it.

1 Double-click page 4 in the Pages panel, and then choose View > Fit Page In Window.

2 Using the Type tool (T), drag to select the "Black Tea" subhead at the top of the first column.

3 If necessary, click the Character Formatting Controls icon (A) in the Control panel. Type **13** in the Font Size box, and press Enter (Windows) or Return (macOS).

4 Choose Type > Paragraph to display the Paragraph panel. Choose Paragraph Rules from the panel menu.

5 In the Paragraph Rules dialog box, choose Rule Below from the menu at the top of the dialog box, and select Rule On. Make sure that Preview is selected, and move the dialog box so you can see "Black Tea" on your screen.

6 Format the rule using the following settings:

- Weight: 1 pt

- Color: C=24, M=93, Y=100, K=18 (burgundy swatch)

- Offset: p2

Leave all other settings at their defaults.

7 Click OK. A thin burgandy line now appears below "Black Tea."

8 If it's not already visible, choose Type > Paragraph Styles to view the Paragraph Styles panel.

In the Paragraph Styles panel, notice that the Head 3 style is selected, indicating that it is applied to the selected text. You will also see a plus sign (+) next to the Head 3 style name. This indicates that the selected text has local formatting applied to it, which is overriding the applied style.

Now you'll redefine the paragraph style so that the local changes are incorporated in the paragraph style definition and automatically applied to all the headlines previously formatted with the Head 3 style.

9 In the Paragraph Styles panel menu, choose Redefine Style. The + should no longer appear next to the Head 3 style name. All headlines in the document that have been styled with Head 3 should globally update to reflect the changes you made.

Note: You can use the process in steps 8–9 to redefine any type of style based on local formatting.

10 Choose Edit > Deselect All, and then choose File > Save.

Loading styles from another document

▶ Tip: In addition to loading styles from another document, you can share paragraph and character styles among multiple documents through CC Libraries. To do this, select a style in the Paragraph Styles panel and click Add Selected Style To My Current CC Library button at the bottom of the panel. To use this style in another document, apply it from the CC Library. It is then automatically added to the document's Paragraph Styles panel.

Styles are available in the document in which you create them. However, it's easy to share styles between InDesign documents by loading (importing) styles from other InDesign documents. In this exercise, you'll import a paragraph style from the finished document 09_End.indd and apply the style to the first body paragraph on page 2.

1 Double-click page 2 in the Pages panel, and then choose View > Fit Page In Window.

2 If it's not already visible, choose Type > Paragraph Styles to view the Paragraph Styles panel.

3 Choose Load All Text Styles from the Paragraph Styles panel menu.

4 In the Open A File dialog box, double-click 09_End.indd, in the Lesson09 folder. The Load Styles dialog box appears.

5 Click Uncheck All; you do not need to import all the styles because most already exist in this document.

6 Select the paragraph style Drop Cap Body. Scroll down to the Drop Cap and Italic character styles and make sure they are selected as well.

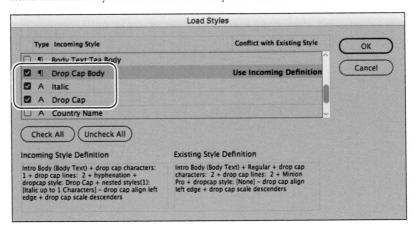

Because the selected paragraph style uses the Drop Caps And Nested Style feature to automatically apply the Drop Cap character style, this style is also selected.

7 Click OK to import the three styles.

8 Using the Type tool (**T.**), place an insertion point in the second body paragraph, which starts with "We carry."

9 Click the new Drop Cap Body style in the Paragraph Styles panel.

The initial "W" in "We" should become a khaki drop cap in Myriad Pro Italic.

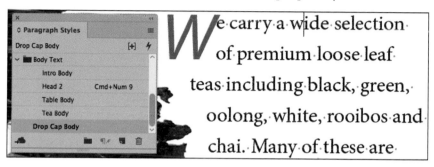

10 Choose Edit > Deselect All, and then choose File > Save.

Finishing up

As a final step, you'll preview the document in its finished state.

1 At the bottom of the Tools panel, select Preview.

2 Choose View > Fit Page In Window.

3 Press Tab to hide all of the panels and review the results of your work.

Congratulations! You have now completed this lesson.

Exploring on your own

When you're creating a long document or a template to use as the basis for other documents, you want to take full advantage of all features related to styles. To fine-tune the styles further, try the following:

- Rearrange styles in the Paragraph Styles panel. For example, drag the new Drop Cap Body style into the Body Text group.

- Experiment with modifying the formatting of styles, including object, table, character, and paragraph styles. For example, change the font in a paragraph style or change the background color of a table style.

- Create additional character styles that change only one attribute of formatting—such as creating a character style that applies only a different color.

- Add more keyboard shortcuts to the existing styles.

Review questions

1 How can using object styles speed up your workflow?

2 What must you create before you can create a nested style?

3 What are the two ways to globally update a style you've applied in an InDesign document?

4 How would you import styles from another InDesign document?

Review answers

1 Object styles save time by allowing you to group formatting attributes and quickly apply them to frames and lines. If you need to update the formatting, you don't have to change each object formatted with the style individually. Instead, you can simply modify the object style to automatically update all the objects to which it is applied.

2 The two prerequisites for creating a nested style are (1) that you have first created a character style and (2) that you have built a paragraph style in which to nest it.

3 InDesign offers two ways to update styles. The first is to edit the style itself by making changes to the formatting options. The other is to use local formatting to change an instance and then redefine the style based on that instance.

4 From any Styles panel (Paragraph, Object, Cell, etc.), choose Load Styles from the panel menu. Locate the InDesign document from which you want to load the styles. The styles are then loaded into the respective panels and are immediately available for use in your document.

10 IMPORTING AND MODIFYING GRAPHICS

Lesson Overview

In this lesson, you'll learn how to do the following:

- Distinguish between vector and bitmap graphics.

- Manage imported graphic files using the Links panel.

- Import Adobe Photoshop and Adobe Illustrator graphics.

- Adjust the display quality of graphics.

- Work with different types of dropped backgrounds.

- Adjust the appearance of graphics by manipulating paths and alpha channels.

- Create an anchored graphics frame that flows with text.

- Create and use libraries of objects.

- Import graphics using Adobe Bridge.

 This lesson will take about 75 minutes to complete.

Please log in to your account on peachpit.com to download the lesson files for this chapter, or go to the "Getting Started" section at the beginning of this book and follow the instructions under "Accessing the Lesson Files and Web Edition." Store the files on your computer in a convenient location.

InDesign makes it easy to enhance your document with photographs and artwork imported from Adobe Photoshop, Adobe Illustrator, and other graphics applications. If these imported graphics change, InDesign can notify you that a newer version of a graphic is available. You can update or replace imported graphics at any time.

Getting started

In this lesson, you'll work on a two-fold, three-panel brochure for a CD by importing, manipulating, and managing graphics from Adobe Photoshop and Adobe Illustrator. The insert is designed so that after printing and trimming, it fits into a CD case.

This lesson includes steps that you can perform using Adobe Photoshop if you have it installed on your computer.

● **Note:** If you have not already downloaded the project files for this lesson to your computer from your Account page, make sure to do so now. See "Getting Started" at the beginning of the book.

1 To ensure that the preferences and default settings of your Adobe InDesign program match those used in this lesson, move the InDesign Defaults file to a different folder following the procedure in "Saving and restoring the InDesign Defaults file" on pages 4–5.

2 Start Adobe InDesign. To ensure that the panels and menu commands match those used in this lesson, choose Window > Workspace > [Advanced], and then choose Window > Workspace > Reset Advanced.

3 Choose File > Open, and open the 10_Start.indd file in the Lesson10 folder, located inside the Lessons folder within the InDesignCIB folder on your hard drive. A message appears saying that the document contains links to sources that have been modified.

4 Click Don't Update Links. You will fix the modified links later in the lesson. (If the Missing Fonts dialog box displays, click Sync Fonts, and then click Close after the fonts have successfully synced from Typekit.)

5 If necessary, close the Links panel so it doesn't obscure your view of the document. The Links panel opens automatically whenever you open an InDesign document that contains missing or modified links.

6 To see what the finished document looks like, open the 10_End.indd file in the same folder. If you prefer, you can leave the document open as you work to act as a guide. If you leave it open, choose 10_Start.indd from the Window menu or click the 10_Start.indd document tab to return to that document.

7 Choose File > Save As, rename the file **10_cdinsert.indd**, and save it in the Lesson10 folder.

● **Note:** As you work through the lesson, move panels around or change the magnification to a level that works best for you. For more information, see "Changing the magnification of a document" In Lesson 1, "Introducing the Workspace."

Adding graphics from other programs

InDesign supports many common graphic file formats. While this means that you can use graphics that were created using a wide range of applications, InDesign works best with other Adobe professional graphics applications, such as Photoshop, Illustrator, and Acrobat.

By default, imported graphics are linked to an InDesign document, which means that InDesign displays a preview of the graphic file in your layout without actually copying the entire graphic file into the document file.

There are three major advantages to linking graphic files. First, it reduces the size of InDesign files because they don't need to include embedded image data. Second, it saves disk space, and third, you can edit a linked graphic in the application you used to create it and then simply update the link in the InDesign Links panel. Updating a linked file that has been modified maintains the current location and settings for the graphic file and replaces the preview image in InDesign with the updated graphic.

All linked graphics and text files are listed in the Links panel (Window > Links), which provides buttons and commands for managing links. When you print an InDesign document or export a document as an Adobe Portable Document Format (PDF) file, InDesign uses the links to produce the highest level of quality available from the original, externally stored versions of the placed graphics.

Comparing vector and bitmap graphics

The drawing tools of Adobe InDesign and Adobe Illustrator create vector graphics, which are made up of shapes based on mathematical expressions, like plotting points on a graph. Vector graphics consist of smooth lines that retain their clarity when resized. They are appropriate for illustrations, type, and graphics such as logos, all of which are typically scaled to different sizes. Vector graphics can be scaled to any size with no loss of quality.

Bitmap images, or raster graphics, are made up of a grid of pixels and are typically created with digital cameras and scanners and then modified using an image-editing application, such as Adobe Photoshop. In working with bitmap images, you edit pixels rather than objects or shapes. Raster graphics are appropriate for continuous-tone images, such as photographs and artwork created in painting applications. A disadvantage of raster graphics is that they lose definition and appear "jagged" when enlarged. Additionally, bitmap images are typically larger in file size than a similar vector graphic. Raster graphics *do* lose quality when enlarged.

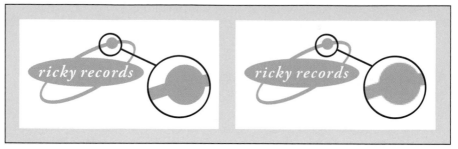

Logo drawn as vector art (left) and rasterized as 300 dpi bitmap art (right).

In general, use vector-drawing tools to create art or type with clean lines that look good at any size, such as a logo used on a business card and also on a poster. You can create vector artwork using the InDesign drawing tools, or you might prefer to take advantage of the wider range of vector-drawing tools available in Illustrator. Use Photoshop to create bitmap images that have the soft edges of painted or photographic art, retouch or alter photographs, and to apply special effects to artwork.

Managing links to imported files

When you opened the lesson file, you saw an alert message about problems with the linked files. You'll resolve those issues using the Links panel, which provides complete information about the status of all linked text and graphic files in a document.

● **Note:** By default, InDesign does not create links to imported text files and spreadsheet files. You can change this behavior in the File Handling section of the Preferences dialog box by selecting Create Links When Placing Text And Spreadsheet Files.

You can use the Links panel to manage placed graphics and text files in many other ways. For example, you can update graphics and text files that have been modified since they were placed, and you can replace graphic and text files with different files.

Identifying imported images

To identify some of the graphics that have already been imported into the document, you'll use two different techniques involving the Links panel. Later in this lesson, you'll also use the Links panel to edit and update imported graphics.

1 Center page 4 in the document window by choosing it from the Page Number box at the lower-left corner of the document window.

2 If the Links panel is not visible, choose Window > Links.

3 Using the Selection tool (▶), select the Orchard of Kings logo type on page 4, which is the rightmost page of the first spread. (Click outside the content grabber in the center of the frame so you select the frame and not the graphic.) Notice that the graphic's filename, 10_i.ai, becomes selected in the Links panel when you select the graphic in the layout.

A. Filename column

B. Status column

C. Page column

D. Show/Hide Link Information button

E. Relink From CC Libraries button

F. Relink button

G. Go To Link button

H. Edit Original button

I. Select Next Link In The List button

J. Select Previous Link In The List button

K. Update Link button

Now you'll use the Links panel to locate another graphic in the layout.

4 In the Links panel, select 10_g.psd, and then click the Go To Link button (⊿). The graphic becomes selected and centered on the screen. This is a quick way to find a graphic in a document when you know its filename.

These techniques for identifying and locating linked graphics are useful throughout this lesson and whenever you work with a large number of imported files.

▶ **Tip:** You can click the page number to the right of a filename in the Links panel to go to the link and center it in the document window.

Viewing information about linked files

The Links panel makes it easy to work with linked graphics and text files and to display additional information about linked files.

1 Make sure that the graphic named 10_g.psd is selected in the Links panel. If you cannot see the names of all the linked files without scrolling, drag the horizontal divider bar in the Links panel downward to enlarge the top half of the panel so that all the links are visible. The Link Info section at the bottom half of the panel displays information about the selected link.

2 In the Links panel, click the Select Next Link In The List triangle (›) to view information about the following file in the Links panel list, 10_f.pdf. You can quickly examine all the links in the list this way. Currently, every link displays an alert icon (⚠) in the Status column. This icon indicates a linking problem, which you'll address later. After you've examined the link information for various images, choose Edit > Deselect All, and then click the Show/Hide Link Information button (⌄) above Link Info to hide the Link Info section.

▶ **Tip:** You can detach the Links panel from its group of panels by dragging its tab. Once you've detached the panel, you can resize it by dragging an edge or lower corner.

By default, files are sorted in the Links panel by page number, with files used multiple times in a document listed at the top. You can sort the file list in different ways.

3 Another and faster way to view link information is to customize the information displayed in the Links panel columns. Click the flyout menu in the Links panel and choose Panel Options. Click on Color Space, Actual PPI, Effective PPI, and Transparency, under Show Column. Click OK. (The important information in your workflow may vary from this example.)

4 Pull out the panel to the left to see the new columns. The Links panel now shows this information in additional columns. This customized view is a fast way to see important information about imported graphics, such as whether something has been scaled up so much that it will look bad (jagged edges, blurry, or pixelated) when printed.

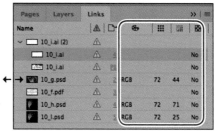

Options turned on under Show Column in the Panel Options will display in additional columns in the Links panel. (Note that the images used for the exercise are low resolution, which you can now see quickly.)

Showing files in Explorer (Windows) or Finder (macOS)

● **Note:** The Reveal In Explorer (Windows) or Reveal In Finder (macOS) command is not available for missing links.

Although the Links panel gives you information about the attributes and location of a specific imported graphic file, it does not let you make changes to the file or change the name of the file. You can access the original file of an imported graphic file by using the Reveal In Explorer (Windows) or Reveal In Finder (macOS) option.

▶ **Tip:** You can also choose Reveal In Bridge from the Links panel menu to locate an imported graphics file and rename it.

1 Select 10_g.psd. From the Links panel flyout menu, choose Reveal In Explorer (Windows) or Reveal In Finder (macOS) to open the folder where the linked file is currently stored on your computer, and select the file. This feature is useful for locating files on your hard drive and renaming them, if necessary.

2 Close the window and return to InDesign.

Updating revised graphics

Even after you place text or graphic files in your InDesign document, you can still use other applications to modify those files. The Links panel indicates which files have been modified outside of InDesign and gives you the choice of updating your document with the latest versions of those files.

In the Links panel, the file 10_i.ai has an alert icon (⚠), indicating that the original file has been modified. This is one of the files that caused the alert message to appear when you first opened this document. You'll update the link for this file so that the InDesign document uses the current version.

1 If necessary, click the disclosure triangle (›) in the Links panel to the left of the file 10_i.ai to reveal two instances of the imported file. Select the instance of the 10_i.ai file that's on page 4, and click the Go To Link button (⬚) to view the graphic in magnified view. You don't have to do this step, but it's a quick way to double-check which imported file you are about to update and see the results.

▶ Tip: You can update multiple instances of a graphic at the same time by updating when the disclosure triangle is closed.

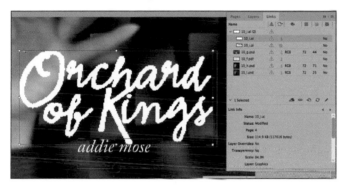

2 Click the Update Link button (↻). The appearance of the image in the document changes to represent its newer version, the Modified alert icon is no longer displayed in the Links panel, and the Link Badge near the upper-left corner of the graphics frame changes from Modified (⚠) to OK (∞).

▶ Tip: You can also double-click the Modified Alert in the Links panel or click the Modified Alert displayed in the upper-left corner of the graphics frame to update the link.

3 To update the rest of the modified graphic files, choose Update All Links from the Links panel flyout menu.

Now you'll replace the image of the hands on the first spread (pages 2–4) with a modified image. You'll use the Relink button to reassign the link to another graphic.

4 Go to pages 2–4 (the first spread), and choose View > Fit Spread In Window.

5 Use the Selection tool (▶) to select the 10_h.psd image on page 4. It's the photograph of the interlocked hands. (If you click within the content grabber, you'll select the graphic rather than the frame, but for this task, you can select either.) You can tell when you've selected the right image because the filename becomes selected in the Links panel.

6 Click the Relink button (∞) in the Links panel.

7 Browse to find the 10_j.psd file in the Lesson10 folder, and then click Open. The new version of the image (which has a different background) replaces the original image, and the Links panel is updated accordingly.

8 Click a blank area of the pasteboard to deselect all the objects on the spread.

9 Choose File > Save to save your work.

Link status icons in the Links panel

A linked file can appear in the Links panel in any of the following ways:

- An up-to-date graphic displays only the filename and the page on which it's used.

- A modified file displays a yellow triangle with an exclamation point (⚠). This icon means that the version of the file on disk is more recent than the version in your document. For example, this icon appears if you place a Photoshop graphic into InDesign, and then you or someone else edits and saves the original graphic in Photoshop. A slightly different version of the Modified icon appears when a graphic is modified, and one or more instances are updated while others are not. To update a modified graphic, select it in the Links panel, and then choose Update Link from the panel menu or click the Update Link button (↻).

- A missing file displays a red hexagon with a question mark (❓). This icon means the graphic is no longer in the location from which it was placed, although it may still exist somewhere. Missing links can happen if someone deletes the original file or moves it to a different folder or server after it's been placed in the document. You can't know whether a missing file is up to date until its original is located. If you print or export a document when this icon is displayed, the file will not print or export at full resolution. To fix a missing graphic, select it in the Links panel, and then choose Relink from the panel menu. Use the Relink dialog box to locate the correct graphic file, and then click Open.

- A graphic that has been embedded in the InDesign document (by selecting the filename in the Links panel and choosing Embed Link from the panel menu) displays an embedded icon (▣). Embedding the contents of a linked file suspends management operations for that link. Unembedding the file restores management operations to the link.

Display performance and GPUs

InDesign CC 2018 provides support for computers with video cards that include a graphics processing unit (GPU). If your computer has a compatible GPU card, InDesign automatically displays documents using the GPU and sets the default Display Performance to High Quality. If your computer does not have a compatible GPU card, the default Display Performance setting is Typical. This book presumes that readers are using computers without a GPU. If your computer has a compatible GPU, you can ignore steps that ask you to switch to High Quality display. For more information about GPU support in InDesign CC, go to https://helpx.adobe.com/indesign/using/gpu_performance.html. If you have a compatible GPU card, you can change GPU settings in the GPU Performance section of the Preferences dialog box. Choose Edit > Preferences > GPU Performance (Windows) or InDesign CC > Preferences > GPU Performance (macOS) to open the Preferences dialog box.

Adjusting display quality

Now that you've resolved all of the links, you're ready to start adding more graphics. First, however, you will adjust the view quality of the Illustrator file (10_i.ai) that you updated earlier in this lesson.

When you place an image in a document, InDesign automatically creates a low-resolution (proxy) view of it, corresponding to the current settings in the Display Performance section of the Preferences dialog box. The images in this document are currently low-resolution proxies, which is why they appear to have jagged edges. Reducing the onscreen quality of placed graphics displays pages faster and doesn't affect the quality of the final output. You can control the degree of detail InDesign uses to display placed graphics.

1 In the Links panel, select the 10_i.ai file you updated in the previous exercise (the instance on page 4). Click the Go To Link button (⏎) to view the graphic in magnified view.

2 Right-click (Windows) or Control-click (macOS) the Orchard of Kings graphic, and then choose Display Performance > High Quality Display from the context menu. The image appears at full resolution. You can use this process to confirm the clarity, appearance, and position of a placed graphic in your InDesign layout.

Onscreen display using Typical Display.

High Quality Display.

3 Choose View > Display Performance > High Quality Display. This setting changes the display performance for the entire document. All graphics are displayed at the highest quality.

On older computers and for designs with many imported graphics, this setting can sometimes result in slower screen redraw. In many cases, it is advisable to set your Display Performance to Typical Display and then change the display quality of individual graphics as needed.

Working with dropped backgrounds

There are two basic types of images with white, or "dropped," backgrounds, both of which are widely used. The difference is whether the edge between the foreground and background is a crisp, sharp edge or a soft, blending edge. The type of edge used depends on what is appropriate for the image content.

▶ **Tip:** A mask is a shape that's used to contain and crop an image. The portion of the image within the mask shape is visible; any areas outside the mask shape are not visible.

Images with sharp edges between the foreground and background can use a vector path to separate the foreground from the background. This is called a *clipping path*.

- If you draw a path in Photoshop and save it with the image, you can choose this path in InDesign, and you can choose different paths from within the same image.

- If the image has a relatively light or white background (or a relatively dark background if the subject matter is light), InDesign can automatically detect the edge between the subject and the background and create a clipping path. However, this technique works best for simple shapes or for creating a path to use for Text Wrap, as we saw in Lesson 4.

- If you create an *alpha channel* in Photoshop and save it with the image, InDesign can create a clipping path from it. Alpha channels store selections you've made as grayscale images, and can include transparent and opaque areas.

Images with a soft, blending edge between the foreground and background need transparency and soft brushes to delete the background in Photoshop.

Working with clipping paths from Photoshop in InDesign

1 Navigate to page 7 of the document by double-clicking page 7 in the Pages panel, and choose View > Fit Page In Window.

2 In the Layers panel, make sure that the Photos layer is selected so that the imported image is placed on that layer. Choose File > Place, and double-click the file Pears.psd in the Lesson10 folder.

▶ **Tip:** If you accidentally click within the existing frame, choose Edit > Undo Place and try again.

3 Position the loaded raster graphics icon (⌷) outside the blue square in the center of page 7—to the left and slightly below the top edge (make sure you are

not placing the pointer in the square itself)—and click to place an image of two pears. If you need to reposition the graphics frame to match the following image, do so now.

This is what a vector path looks like in Photoshop.

4 Choose Object > Clipping Path > Options. Move the Clipping Path dialog box, if necessary, so that you can see the pear image.

5 Choose Photoshop Path from the Type menu. Choose the path named "Two Pears." If Preview is not selected, select it now. The background is now hidden by the path.

6 Click OK.

7 Switch to the Selection tool (▶) and click the lower-right corner handle. Press Shift+Ctrl (Windows) or Shift+Command (macOS) and drag up and to the left. This will scale both the frame and its contents. Make the pears fit inside the purple box as shown. Then choose Object > Fitting > Fit Frame To Content and use the Selection tool to move the pears toward the bottom of the purple box.

8 Press Alt (Windows) or Option (macOS) and drag up and to the right. This creates a copy of the image. Choose Object > Clipping Path > Options, and choose Photoshop Path from the Type menu. This time choose the path named "Right Pear" and click OK. Switch back to the Selection tool (▶) and choose Object > Fitting > Fit Frame To Content. Use the same technique to scale this pear to about 60% of the original size. Then move the pointer outside the bounding box until it changes to the Rotate Pointer (↻). Rotate the photo to the right about −28° and move it down a little.

9 Press Alt (Windows) or Option (macOS) and drag down and to the left to create a copy of the single pear. Choose Object > Clipping Path > Options and choose Photoshop Path from the Type menu. This time choose the path named "Left Pear" and click OK. Switch back to the Selection tool (▶) and choose Object > Fitting > Fit Frame To Content. Move the pointer outside the bounding box until it changes to the Rotate Pointer (↻). Rotate the photo to the left about 22° and move it down a little.

10 Notice how the clipping path allows the image to overlap multiple other objects. You can also move images in front of or behind other objects. Take a few moments to experiment.

11 Choose File > Save to save the file.

Working with transparent backgrounds from Photoshop in InDesign

1 Navigate to page 6 of the document by sliding page 7 to the right. Do this by holding down the spacebar. The hand icon (🖐) appears. Keep the spacebar pressed and drag until page 6 is centered in your window.

2 Select the Rectangle Frame tool (⊠) in the Tools panel and draw a frame in the lower area as shown. Then choose Object > Fitting > Frame Fitting Options. Choose Fit Content Proportionally and then choose the top center point in the Align From area. Click OK.

This is what a transparent background looks like in Photoshop.

3 Choose File > Place and double-click the Tulips.psd file in the Lesson10 folder. InDesign fits the image proportionally to the frame as specified. Choose Edit > Deselect All.

4 Now we want to scale the picture without scaling the frame. Switch to the Selection tool, and notice that when you move the pointer over the picture, the frame of the text lights up. This is because the Text layer is above the Graphics layer. Open the Layers panel and lock the Text layer so that you can easily work with the photo. Click the photo, and you'll see the circle of the content grabber and the handles of the bounding box of the photo (not the frame) will be active. Set the Reference Point in the Control Panel to the upper center (🔲) position and scale to 70%. Most of the image will be cropped out, with just the tops of flowers and leaves showing.

Notice how different the edges of this image to the background are compared to the pears image. Here, the edges blend softly into the background. This is the purpose of using transparency in Photoshop to remove a background: to create a soft edge by painting away the background with a soft-edge brush.

Working with alpha channels

● **Note:** If you place a Photoshop (.psd) file that consists of an image with a transparent background, InDesign keeps the transparency without relying on clipping paths or alpha channels. However, even if a graphic has an alpha channel with a feathered edge, InDesign will create a hard-edged clipping path when using the clipping path options and will not maintain the soft edge.

When an image has a background that isn't solid white or black, you can use the advanced background-removal tools in Photoshop to specify transparent areas using paths or alpha channels and then let InDesign make a clipping path from the path or alpha channel.

Importing a Photoshop file with alpha channels

InDesign can use Photoshop paths and alpha channels directly—you don't need to save the Photoshop file in a different file format. You imported the previous image using the Place command. This time, you will use an alternate method: dragging a Photoshop image directly onto an InDesign spread.

1 In the Layers panel, make sure that the Photos layer is selected so that the image is placed on that layer.

2 Navigate to page 2 of your document, and choose View > Fit Page In Window.

3 Switch to File Explorer (Windows) or the Finder (macOS), and open the Lesson10 folder, which contains the 10_d.psd file.

 Resize and arrange your File Explorer window (Windows) or Finder window (macOS) and your InDesign window, as needed, so that you can simultaneously see the list of files in the Lesson10 folder and the InDesign document window. Make sure that the lower-left quarter of page 2 in your document is visible.

● **Note:** When you place the file in step 4, be careful to drop it on the pasteboard area to the left of page 2. If you drop it on a preexisting frame, it is placed inside the frame. If this happens, choose Edit > Undo, and try again.

4 Drag the 10_d.psd file to the pasteboard area to the left of page 2 in the InDesign document and release the mouse. On Windows, click the pasteboard to place the image at full size and return to InDesign; or, on macOS, click the pasteboard to return to InDesign, and then click the pasteboard again to place the image at full size.

5 Use the Selection tool (⬙) to reposition the graphic so that the lower-left corner of the frame aligns with the lower-left corner of the page.

Examining Photoshop paths and alpha channels

In the Photoshop image that you just dragged into InDesign, the hand and the background share many of the same lightness values. You'll set up InDesign to use an alpha channel from the Photoshop image. First, you'll use the Links panel to open the image directly in Photoshop to see what paths and alpha channels it already includes.

The procedure in this exercise requires that you have Photoshop installed on your system and is easier if you have enough RAM available to leave both InDesign and Photoshop open as you work. If your configuration doesn't include these two conditions, you can still read these steps to help you understand what Photoshop alpha channels look like and do, and you can resume your work in the next section of this lesson.

1 Using the Selection tool (▶), select the 10_d.psd image you imported in the previous task.

2 If the Links panel is not already open, choose Window > Links. The image filename appears selected in the Links panel.

3 In the Links panel, click the Edit Original button (✏). This opens the image in an application that can view or edit it. This image was saved from Photoshop, so if Photoshop is installed on your computer, InDesign starts Photoshop and opens the selected file.

4 In Photoshop, choose Window > Channels to display the Channels panel, or click the Channels panel icon. Click the tab at the top of the Channels panel and drag the panel to the document window.

5 Lengthen the Channels panel, if necessary, to view the three alpha channels (Alpha 1, Alpha 2, and Alpha 3) in addition to the standard RGB channels. These channels were drawn using the masking and painting tools in Photoshop.

Photoshop file saved with three alpha channels.

● **Note:** Adobe Photoshop CC is an image-editing application available to Creative Cloud users and must be installed separately. You can install Photoshop using the Creative Cloud desktop application in the task bar (Windows) or menu bar (macOS).

▶ **Tip:** In addition to using the Edit Original button in the Links panel to edit the selected graphic, you can choose Edit With from the Links panel menu, and then choose the application you want to use to edit the graphic.

● **Note:** The Edit Original button may open an image in an application other than Photoshop or the application in which it was created. When you install software, some installer utilities change your operating system's settings that associate file types with applications. The Edit Original command uses these settings for associating files with applications. To change these settings, see the documentation for your operating system.

6 In the Channels panel in Photoshop, click Alpha 1 to see how it looks, and then click Alpha 2 and Alpha 3 to compare them.

7 Click the RGB channel.

8 In Photoshop, choose Window > Paths to open the Paths panel, or click the Paths panel icon.

The Paths panel contains two named paths: Shapes and Circle. These were drawn using the Pen tool (✐,) and other path tools in Photoshop, although they could also be drawn in Illustrator and pasted into Photoshop.

9 In the Photoshop Paths panel, click Shapes to view that path, and then click Circle.

Because you've made no changes, there's no need to save the file.

10 Quit Photoshop. You've finished using it for this lesson.

Using Photoshop paths and alpha channels in InDesign

▶ **Tip:** You can fine-tune the clipping path that InDesign creates from an alpha channel by adjusting the Threshold and Tolerance options. For alpha channels, start with a low Threshold value, such as 1.

Now you'll return to InDesign and see how you can create different clipping paths from the Photoshop paths and alpha channels.

1 Switch to InDesign. Make sure that the 10_d.psd file is still selected on the page; if necessary, select it using the Selection tool (▶).

2 With the hand image still selected, choose Object > Clipping Path > Options to open the Clipping Path dialog box. If necessary, move the Clipping Path dialog box so that you can see the image as you work.

3 Make sure that Preview is selected, and then choose Alpha Channel from the Type menu. The Alpha menu becomes available, listing the three alpha channels you saw in Photoshop.

4 In the Alpha menu, the first of the alpha channels (Alpha 1) is selected. InDesign creates a clipping path from the alpha channel. Choose Alpha 2 from the same menu, and compare the results.

5 Choose Alpha 3 from the Alpha menu, and then select the Include Inside Edges option. Notice the changes in the image.

Selecting the Include Inside Edges option makes InDesign recognize a butterfly-shaped hole painted in the Alpha 3 channel and adds it to the clipping path.

▶ **Tip:** You can see how the butterfly-shaped hole looks in Photoshop by displaying the Alpha 3 channel in the original Photoshop file.

6 Choose Photoshop Path from the Type menu. The first of the paths (Shapes) is automatically selected. InDesign reshapes the frame of the image to match the Photoshop path.

7 Choose Circle from the Path menu. Click OK.

8 Choose File > Save to save the file.

Importing native Adobe graphic files

InDesign allows you to import files saved from Adobe applications, such as Photoshop (.psd), Illustrator (.ai), and Acrobat (.pdf), in unique ways and provides options for controlling how the files are displayed. For example, you can adjust the visibility of Photoshop layers in InDesign, as well as view different layer comps. Similarly, if you import a layered Illustrator file into an InDesign layout, you can vary the illustration by adjusting layer visibility.

Importing a Photoshop file with layers and layer comps

In the previous exercise, you worked with a Photoshop file with saved paths and alpha channels; however, the file had only a single background layer. When you work with a layered Photoshop file, you can adjust the visibility of the individual layers. Additionally, you can view different layer comps.

▶ **Tip:** Created in Photoshop and saved as part of the file, layer comps are often used to make multiple compositions of an image to compare different styles or artwork. When the file is placed in InDesign, you can preview the different layer comps in relation to your entire layout. You'll view some layer comps now.

1 In the Links panel, click the link for 10_j.psd, and click the Go To Link button (⊕) to select the file and center it in your document window. This file, which you relinked in a previous exercise, has four layers and three layer comps.

2 Choose Object > Object Layer Options to open the Object Layer Options dialog box. This dialog box allows you to show and hide layers and to switch among layer comps.

3 Move the Object Layer Options dialog box so that you can see as much as possible of the selected image. Select the Preview option to view changes while keeping the dialog box open.

4 In the Object Layer Options dialog box, click the eye icon (👁) to the left of the Hands layer. This turns off the Hands layer, leaving only the Simple Background layer visible. Click the square next to the Hands layer to turn visibility back on.

5 Choose Green Glow from the Layer Comp menu. This layer comp has a different background. Now choose Purple Opacity from the Layer Comp menu. This layer comp has another different background, and the Hands layer is partially transparent. Click OK.

Layer comps are not merely an arrangement of different layers. They can also include Photoshop layer effects, visibility, and position values. When the visibility of a layered file is modified, InDesign informs you in the Link Info section of the Links panel.

6 In the Links panel, select the 10_j.psd graphic. If necessary, click the Show/Hide Link Information button (▶) to display the Link Info section at the bottom of the panel. Locate the Layer Overrides listing. "Yes (2)" is displayed for Layer Overrides to let you know that two layers are overridden. "No" is displayed when there are no layer overrides.

7 Choose File > Save to save your work so far.

Creating an anchored graphics frame

An anchored graphics frame moves with the text to which it's anchored if editing causes the text to reflow. In this exercise, you'll anchor the album logo to a text frame on page 6.

1 In the Pages panel, double-click the second spread, and choose View > Fit Spread In Window. Open the Layers panel and unlock the Text layer. Scroll down if necessary. At the bottom of the pasteboard is the Orchard of Kings logo. You'll insert this graphic into a paragraph on the page.

▶ **Tip:** If the Anchored Object Control square is not visible when selecting the logo, choose View > Extras > Show Anchored Object Control.

2 Using the Selection tool (▶), click the logo. (Be careful to click outside the content grabber so you select the frame and not the graphic within.) Notice the small solid green square near the upper-right corner of the frame. You can drag this square into a text frame to anchor an object to text.

3 Press and hold Z to temporarily access the Zoom tool, or select the Zoom tool (🔍) and click so that you can see the logo and the text frame above it.

4 Choose Type > Show Hidden Characters to view the spaces and paragraph returns in the text. This helps you locate where you want to anchor the frame.

● **Note:** Showing hidden characters is not a necessary step when placing anchored graphics; it is used here to help identify the structure of the text.

5 Select the Type tool (T,) and click in front of the word "Addie" at the beginning of the second paragraph. Press Enter (Windows) or Return (macOS) so that the anchored graphic will be in a paragraph by itself.

6 Use the Selection tool and click the logo again. Hold down the Shift key and drag the green square near the upper-right to the beginning of the second paragraph. Holding the Shift key creates an inline graphic that flows with the text (as opposed to floating outside the text frame). You'll see a bold cursor indicating the point where the graphic anchor will be inserted. After the graphic is anchored, the green square on the graphic frame changes to an anchor symbol. Notice that the text after the graphic reflows when the image is placed. Now if the

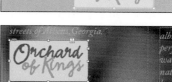

text in the paragraph above is edited, the graphic will stay where you positioned between the two paragraphs without you having to adjust its position.

Now you'll create space between the graphic and the surrounding text with the Space Before option. Once a graphic is anchored, you can select it with the Type tool and apply text attributes that affect its position.

7 Select the Type tool (T,) and then click to the right of the inline graphic to establish the insertion point in that paragraph.

8 Click the Paragraph Formatting Controls button (¶) in the Control panel. In the Space Before option (⁺≣), click the up arrow button to the right of the icon to change the value to 0p4. As you increase the value, the anchored graphics frame and the text below it shift downward slightly.

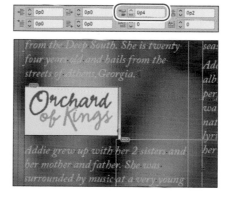

9 To see how the anchored graphic flows when text is edited, click to the right of the period that ends the first paragraph, then press Enter or Return twice. Notice how the graphic moves down each time you press the key. Press Backspace twice to remove the extra paragraph returns.

10 Choose File > Save to save your work so far.

Adding text wrap to an anchored graphics frame

You can easily add text wrap to an anchored graphics frame. Text wrap allows you to experiment with different layouts and see the results immediately.

1 Using the Selection tool (▶), select the graphics frame with the Orchard of Kings logo you placed in the previous exercise.

2 Press Shift+Ctrl (Windows) or Shift+Command (macOS), and drag the upper-right handle of the frame up and to the right until you've scaled the graphic roughly 25% across the second column. The key combination lets you proportionally scale the graphic and resize the frame simultaneously.

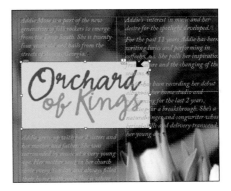

3 Choose Window > Text Wrap to access the Text Wrap panel. Even though the graphic is anchored to the text, it is placed beneath the existing text.

4 In the Text Wrap panel, select Wrap Around Object Shape (▦) to add text wrap to the graphic.

5 To increase space around the bounding box of the graphic, click the up arrow button in the Top Offset option (⊤) and change the value to **1p**.

Text can also wrap around a graphic's shape rather than the rectangular bounding box.

6 To see this more clearly, click the gray pasteboard to deselect all objects, and then click the Orchard of Kings logo. In the Swatches panel, make sure that Select Fill color (▨), not stroke (▨), is active, and press the Forward Slash key (/) on the keyboard to apply no fill color.

7 In the Text Wrap panel under Contour Options, choose Detect Edges from the Type menu. Because this image is a vector graphic, the text wrap is determined by the shape formed by the letters.

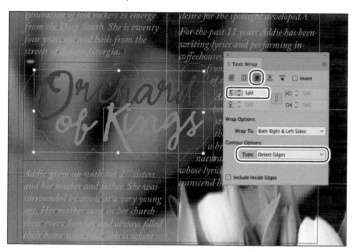

8 To view the document clearly, click the pasteboard to deselect the graphic, and choose Type > Hide Hidden Characters to hide the paragraph returns and spaces.

9 Using the Selection tool (▶), select the graphics frame with the Orchard of Kings logo again.

10 In the Text Wrap panel, choose these options from the Wrap To menu in turn:

- Right Side. The type moves to the right side of the image, avoiding the area just below the image, even though there is space for it to display beneath the text wrap boundary.

- Both Right & Left Sides. The type moves into all available areas around the image. You'll notice that a small break in the type appears where the text wrap boundary drops into the type area.

- Largest Area. The text moves into the largest area to one side of the text wrap boundary. Keep this as your final choice.

11 Optionally, select the Direct Selection tool (▷), and then click the graphic to view the anchor points used for the text wrap. When using the Detect Edges contour option, you can manually adjust the anchor points that define the text wrap by clicking the anchor points and dragging them to a new position.

12 Close the Text Wrap panel.

13 Choose File > Save.

Importing an Illustrator file

▶ **Tip:** When you use high-quality screen display, vector graphics and type appear with smooth edges at any size or magnification.

InDesign takes full advantage of the smooth edges of vector graphics, such as those from Adobe Illustrator. Most vector graphics don't require a clipping path because most applications save them with transparent backgrounds. In this section, you'll place an Illustrator graphic into your InDesign document.

1 In the Layers panel, select the Graphics layer. Choose Edit > Deselect All to make sure nothing is selected in your document.

2 Choose View > Fit Spread In Window to see the entire spread.

3 Choose File > Place, and select the Illustrator file 10_e.ai from the Lesson10 folder. Make sure that Show Import Options is not selected. Click Open.

● **Note:** If an illustrator file imports with a white background, delete it and import again, but turn on Show Import Options and turn on Transparent Background.

4 Click in the upper-left corner of page 5 with the loaded vector graphics icon (⌖) to add the Illustrator file to the page. Use the Selection tool (▶) to position it as shown here. Graphics created in Illustrator have transparent backgrounds by default.

5 Choose File > Save to save your work.

Importing an Illustrator file with layers

You can import native Illustrator files with layers into an InDesign layout and control the visibility of the layers and reposition the graphic. However, you cannot edit the paths, objects, or text.

1 Deselect all objects by clicking in the pasteboard of the document window.

2 Choose File > Place. In the lower-left corner of the Place dialog box, select Show Import Options. Select the file 10_n.ai, and click Open. The Place PDF dialog box appears when Show Import Options is selected (because Illustrator files are written in PDF file format).

3 In the Place PDF dialog box, make sure that Show Preview is selected. In the General section, choose Bounding Box (All Layers) from the Crop To menu and make sure that Transparent Background is selected.

4 Click the Layers tab to view the layers. This file has three layers: a background image of trees (Layer 3), a layer of text in English (English Title), and a layer of text in Spanish (Spanish Title).

Although you can designate now which layers you would like to display in the imported graphic, the small Preview area makes it difficult to see the results.

5 Click OK. You'll select the layers to display in the layout itself.

6 With the loaded vector graphics icon (⌐⅄), position the cursor to the left of the large blue box on page 5. Do not position the loaded graphics icon within the blue box, because doing so inserts the graphic into that frame. Click once to place the graphic, and then use the Selection tool (▶) to position the graphic so that it is visually centered over the blue box.

7 Use the Zoom tool (🔍) to zoom in on the graphic.

8 With the graphic still selected, choose Object > Object Layer Options. Move the dialog box if necessary so that you can see the graphic in the document.

9 Select Preview, and then click the eye icon (👁) next to the English Title layer to turn it off.

10 Click the empty box next to Spanish Title to turn on that layer. Click OK, and then deselect the graphic by clicking the gray pasteboard.

Using layered Illustrator files allows you to repurpose illustrations without having to create separate files for each variation.

11 Choose File > Save to save your work.

Using an InDesign library to manage objects

▶ **Tip:** You might use a library to store a photo of each writer who contributes to a publication, boilerplate text, or frequently used page elements, such as an image with a caption.

Object libraries let you store and organize graphics, text, and design elements that you use frequently. InDesign libraries are stored as files on your hard drive or a shared device. You can also add ruler guides, grids, drawn shapes, and grouped images to a library. Each library appears as a separate panel that you can group with other panels any way you like. You can create as many libraries as you need—for example, different libraries for each of your projects or clients. In this section, you'll import a graphic currently stored in a library, and then you'll create your own library.

1 If you're not already on page 5, type **5** into the Page Number box at the bottom of the document window, and then press Enter or Return to go to that page.

2 Choose View > Fit Page In Window to see the entire page.

● **Note:** When you open it, the 10_k library may be grouped with the default Sample Buttons And Forms library.

3 Choose File > Open, select the file 10_k.indl in the Lesson10 folder, and then click Open to open the library file. Drag the lower-right corner of the 10_k Library panel to reveal all of the items it contains.

4 In the 10_k Library panel, select the Show Library Subset button (🔍). In the last box for the Parameters option, type **tree**, and click OK. This searches the library for all objects that have the word "tree" in their name. Two objects are found.

● **Note:** After you drag the tree image onto the page, the Links panel may display a missing link icon (●) or a modified link icon (⚠) because you copied the Tree.psd file from its original location to your hard drive. To remove the warning, click the Update Link button in the Links panel or click the Relink button in the Links panel and navigate to the Lesson10 folder to find Tree.psd.

5 In the Layers panel, make sure the Graphics layer is selected. Open the Links panel.

6 Of the two objects visible in the 10_k Library panel, drag Tree.psd anywhere on page 5. The file is added to the page. Notice that the filename appears in the Links panel.

7 Using the Selection tool (▷), position the Tree.psd image so that the top and right edges of the frame align with the top and right edges of the purple background frame.

8 Choose File > Save to save your work.

Creating and using CC Libraries

Creative Cloud Libraries make your favorite assets available to you anywhere. You can use CC Libraries to create and share colors, character and paragraph styles, graphics, Adobe Stock assets, and more using your favorite Creative Cloud desktop and mobile apps and then access them across other Creative Cloud apps whenever you need them. You can also share libraries with anyone who has a Creative Cloud account, so it's easy to collaborate, keep designs consistent, and even create style guides to use across projects.

CC Libraries work much like the Indesign libraries you use in this lesson. To create a new CC Library, follow these steps:

1 Choose Window > CC Libraries to display the CC Libraries panel, or click the CC Libraries panel icon(⊚).

2 Click the Library panel menu, and choose Create New Library.

3 Enter **CD Elements** in the Create New Library field, and then click Create.

4 Use the Type tool to select all of the text in the address at the bottom of page 3, click the plus sign at the bottom of the CC Library panel, and then click the Add button. Both the text and the paragraph style will be added to the library. New with Creative Cloud 2018 is the ability to add both formatted and unformatted text to a library. Move the pointer over the new element in the panel to display information about the formatting of the paragraph style.

▶ **Tip:** The CC Libraries menu includes several commands that let you create and manage CC Libraries and control how library elements are displayed in the panel.

5 Use the Selection tool (▷) to select the "Orchard of Kings" graphic on page 4, and then drag it into the library window. Double-click on the name "Artwork 1" and type to change the name to "**Orchard of Kings Logo**."

After you've saved assets to a CC Library, you can use them in other InDesign documents, as well as in other Adobe CC applications, such as Photoshop and Illustrator.

6 Choose File > New > Document to open a new InDesign document. Click Create to use the default settings.

7 Use the Type tool (T) to create a text frame, and then enter a line of text. Select the text, and then click the "Address" asset in the CC Library. (The Address paragraph style uses Paper as the fill color, so you'll need to add a fill color to the text frame to see the white text.) The Address paragraph style is also added to the list of styles in the Paragraph Styles panel.

▶ **Tip:** When you add an asset to a CC Library, it's assigned a default name. If you want to change the name of an asset, double-click its name, and then enter a new one.

8 Drag the "Orchard of Kings" asset from the CC Library to the page, and then click with the loaded graphics icon to place the graphic.

9 Close the document without saving changes and return to the document you were working on.

You can also share CC Libraries with team members and other colleagues. For more information, see the "Exploring on your own" section at the end of this lesson.

Creating an InDesign library

Now you'll create your own library and add text and a graphic to it. When you add a graphic to an InDesign library, the original graphic file is not copied into the library; instead, InDesign maintains a link to the original source file. Graphics stored in a library still require the original, high-resolution file for high-resolution display and printing.

1 Choose File > New > Library. (If the CC Libraries alert displays asking whether you want to try out CC libraries now, click No.) Type **CD Projects** as the library file name, navigate to the Lesson10 folder, and click Save.

2 Navigate to page 3. Using the Selection tool (▷), drag the Ricky Records logo to the library you just created. The logo is now saved in the library for use in other InDesign documents.

▶ **Tip:** If you Alt-drag (Windows) or Option-drag (macOS) an object into a library, the Item Information dialog box appears, and you can assign a name to the object.

3 In the CD Projects library, double-click the Ricky Records logo. For Item Name, type **Ricky Records Logo**, and click OK.

4 Using the Selection tool, drag the address text block to the CD Projects library.

5 In the CD Projects library, double-click the address text block. For Item Name, type **Ricky Records Address**, and click OK. Click the panel flyout menu and choose Large Thumbnail View so that it's easier to see the items.

Now your library contains both text and graphics. As soon as you make changes to the library, InDesign saves the changes.

6 Close both libraries by clicking the close button at the top of the library panel group.

Using Adobe Bridge to import graphics

Adobe Bridge is a separate application available to Creative Cloud users with an All Apps subscription. Adobe Bridge is a cross-platform application that lets you browse your local and networked computers for graphics and then place them into an InDesign layout. (You can also use Bridge to import text files.) This is just one of many features the application provides. (If you don't have a copy of Bridge installed, you can complete this section using the Place command in the File menu.)

1 Choose File > Browse In Bridge to launch Adobe Bridge. Click the folder icons in the Favorites panel or double-click in the Folder panel to navigate to the Lesson10 folder.

● **Note:** If you do not already have Bridge installed, Creative Cloud will install it when you choose Browse In Bridge.

Adobe Bridge lets you view the thumbnails of all your images. Use the slider in the lower right to make the previews larger or smaller.

2 Adobe Bridge provides an easy way to locate and rename files. Because you see a preview, you can locate graphics visually without knowing the exact name. Click the graphic named maple-leaf-.psd once, and then click the filename to select the filename box. Rename the file **maple-leaf-yellow,** and press Enter or Return to commit the change.

3 Make the Bridge window smaller by dragging the lower-right corner, and position it so that you can see page 4 of the InDesign document. Drag the maple-leaf-orange.psd file into your InDesign document and onto an open area of the pasteboard. Click the pasteboard to place the image at full size and return to InDesign (Windows); or click the pasteboard to return to InDesign, and then click the pasteboard again to place the image at full size (macOS).

▶ **Tip:** To learn more about what you can do with Bridge, start at the Bridge page on the Adobe website: https://helpx.adobe.com /support/bridge.html.

4 Use the Selection tool (▶) to position the leaf graphic in the upper-left corner of page 4, on top of the empty purple frame. Press Shift+Ctrl (Windows) or Shift+Command (macOS) and drag a corner of the frame to make it smaller. Using this key combination will scale both the frame and its contents. Scale the frame and the picture at the same time to about the size of the empty purple frame. Align the top and right edges of the graphic frame with the top and right edges of the purple frame.

5 Open the Layers panel. The graphic is placed on the Text layer because that's the last layer you worked on. Drag the small colored square on the right side of the panel from the Text layer to the Photos layer.

A very useful feature of dragging photos from Bridge is that you can quickly change pictures in a frame, while seeing the new image in Bridge and the result in InDesign. This is very useful in projects where the layout repeats but you need to import different pictures. You'll try this now.

6 With the orange maple leaf still selected, bring the Bridge window to the front again (if needed) and choose the file maple-leaf-red.psd. Drag and drop it right over the orange maple leaf. InDesign retains the scaling, and now you've switched out the images with the new one in position in just a few seconds. Try it again with maple-leaf-yellow.psd. Now rotate the image within the frame a bit to the left, to about 6°. Drag and drop the red leaf again. Both the scaling and rotation are retained, but the image is switched.

Congratulations! You've created a three-panel brochure for a CD by importing, updating, and managing graphics from several different graphic file formats.

Using snippets

A snippet is a file that holds objects and describes their location relative to one another on a page or page spread. Use snippets to conveniently reuse and position page objects. You create a snippet by exporting objects in a snippet file, which has the .idms extension. (Earlier InDesign versions use the .inds extension.) When you place a snippet file in InDesign, you can determine whether the objects are placed in their original positions or where you click. You can store snippets in an object library and Adobe Bridge as well as on your hard disk. Artwork added to CC Libraries from InDesign is also stored as a snippet.

When a snippet contains resource definitions and these definitions are also present in the document to which it is copied, the snippet uses the resource definitions in the document.

To create a snippet, do one of the following:

- Using a selection tool, select one or more objects, and then choose File > Export. From the Save As Type (Windows) or Format (macOS) menu, choose InDesign Snippet. Type a name for the file, and click Save.

- Using a selection tool, select one or more objects, and then drag the selection to your desktop. A snippet file is created. Rename the file.

- Drag an item from the Structure panel (View > Structure > Show Structure) to your desktop.

To add a snippet to a document, follow these steps:

1 Choose File > Place.

2 Select one or more snippet (.IDMS or .INDS) files, and then click Open.

3 Click the loaded snippet cursor where you want the upper-left corner of the snippet file to be.

 If you placed the insertion point in a text frame, the snippet is placed in the text as an anchored object.

 All objects remain selected after you place the snippet. By dragging, you can adjust the position of all objects.

4 If you loaded more than one snippet, change the snippet loaded in the cursor by pressing the arrow keys, and click the loaded snippet cursor to place the currently selected snippet.

> **Tip:** Pressing Alt (Windows) or Option (macOS) when you click with the loaded snippet cursor allows you to override the current Snippet Import settings.

Rather than place snippet objects according to where you click on a page, you can place them in their original locations. For example, a text frame that appeared in the middle of a page when it was made part of a snippet can appear in the same location when you place it as a snippet. To place snippets in their original location:

Open the File Handling section of the Preferences dialog box. Within the Snippet Import area, choose Original Position (macOS) or Original Location (Windows).

The default is Position At: Cursor Location, which places the object based on where you click on a page.

Exploring on your own

Now that you've had some practice working with imported graphics, here are some exercises to try on your own:

1 Place different file formats with Show Import Options selected in the Place dialog box, and see what options appear for each format. You can use any of the sample graphics files for this lesson or any other lessons or any other available graphics. For a full description of all the options available for each format, see InDesign Help.

2 Place a multiple-page PDF file or an Adobe Illustrator (.ai) file with multiple artboards with Show Import Options selected in the Place dialog box, and import different pages from the PDF or different artboards from the Illustrator file.

3 Create libraries of text and graphics for your work.

4 During this lesson, you created a CC Library named "CD Elements." In addition to being able to access assets in CC Libraries using several Adobe graphics applications, you can share these libraries with team members and other colleagues to ensure that everyone is using the latest iterations.

 Choose Window > CC Libraries to open the CC Libraries panel, and then select CD Elements from the Libraries menu at the top of the panel. Choose Collaborate from the panel menu. In the Invite Collaborators window that opens in your browser, enter the email addresses of the colleagues with whom you want to share your library. Choose Can Edit or Can View from the menu to specify whether recipients can view and edit elements (Can Edit) or view only (Can View). Click Invite. The recipients will receive an email invitation to collaborate on the library.

5 Another way to import Illustrator graphics into InDesign is to copy the vector shapes from Illustrator and switch over to InDesign and paste. The Illustrator vector objects are converted into InDesign vector objects. You can use these objects as if you had drawn them in InDesign. If you have Illustrator, try this yourself. After you paste the objects into InDesign, change the color with the colors from your InDesign Swatches panel. Then use the Pen tool to select points and change the vector shape.

 If you do not have Illustrator, you can use the vector art of a butterfly that is in the pasteboard of the Start.indd file, to the left of page 2.

Review questions

1 How can you determine the filename of an imported graphic in your document?

2 What is the difference between dropping a background with a clipping path versus with transparency?

3 What is the difference between updating a graphic file's link and relinking the file?

4 When an updated version of a graphic becomes available, how do you make sure that it's up to date in your InDesign document?

5 How do you scale an imported graphic and its frame at the same time?

Review answers

1 Select the graphic, and then choose Window > Links to see if the graphic's filename is highlighted in the Links panel. The graphic appears in the Links panel if it was imported by choosing File > Place or dragged into the layout from Explorer (Windows), Finder (macOS), or Bridge.

2 Clipping paths are vector drawn paths that create a crisp, sharp edge. Photoshop images that use transparency to remove the background create a soft, blended edge using soft-edge brushes to paint away the background.

3 Updating a file's link simply uses the Links panel to update the onscreen representation of a graphic so that it represents the most recent version of the original. Relinking a selected graphic uses the Place command to allow you to insert a different graphic in place of the selected graphic. You might do this, for example, to replace a .png graphic with an identical graphic in the .jpg fomat.

4 In the Links panel, make sure that no alert icon is displayed for the file. If an alert icon is displayed, you can simply select the link and click the Update Link button. If the file has been moved, you must locate it again using the Relink button.

5 Press Shift+Ctrl (Windows) or Shift+Command (macOS) and drag to scale either larger or smaller.

11 CREATING TABLES

Lesson Overview

In this lesson, you'll learn how to do the following:

- Convert text to a table, import tables from other applications, and create tables from scratch.

- Change the number of rows and columns in a table.

- Rearrange rows and columns.

- Adjust row and column sizes.

- Format tables with strokes and fills.

- Specify repeating header and footer rows for long tables.

- Place graphics in table cells.

- Create and apply table and cell styles.

This lesson will take approximately 45 minutes to complete.

Please log in to your account on peachpit.com to download the lesson files for this chapter, or go to the "Getting Started" section at the beginning of this book and follow the instructions under "Accessing the Lesson Files and Web Edition." Store the files on your computer in a convenient location.

GREENTOWN
Community
COLLEGE **Summer Schedule**

ENRICHMENT COURSES

Department	No.	Course Name	Credits	
Art 🐟	102	Street Photography	3	
Art	205	Fundraising for the Arts	2	
Baking 🐟	101	Pies and Cakes	2	
English	112	Creative Writing	3	
Fashion	101	Design and Sewing	2	
Math	125	Math for Liberal Arts	3	
Recreation	101	Planning Summer Camp	3	

🐟 Indicates off-site course.

1

With InDesign, you can easily create tables, convert text to tables, and import tables from other applications. Rich formatting options—including headers, footers, and alternating row and column patterns—can be saved as table and cell styles.

Getting started

In this lesson, you'll work on a fictional college flyer designed to be attractive, easy to use, and easy to revise. You'll convert text to a table, and then format the table using options in the Table menu, Control panel, and Table panel. The table will include header rows that repeat when the table flows across multiple pages. Finally, you will create a table style and a cell style so the formatting can be quickly and consistently applied to other tables.

● **Note:** If you have not already downloaded the project files for this lesson to your computer from your Account page, make sure to do so now. See "Getting Started" at the beginning of the book.

1 To ensure that the preferences and default settings of your Adobe InDesign program match those used in this lesson, move the InDesign Defaults file to a different folder following the procedure in "Saving and restoring the InDesign Defaults file" on pages 4–5.

2 Start Adobe InDesign.

3 The InDesign Start Screen displays. Click Open at left. (If the Start Screen does not display, choose File > Open from the InDesign menu bar.)

4 Open the 11_Start.indd file in the Lesson11 folder, located inside the Lessons folder within the InDesignCIB folder on your hard disk.

5 If the Missing Fonts dialog box displays, click Sync Fonts to access any missing fonts through Adobe Typekit. Click Close when font syncing is complete.

● **Note:** For higher contrast in the printed manual, the screen captures in this book show the Medium Light interface. Interface elements such as panels and dialog boxes may be darker on your screen.

6 To ensure that the panels and menu commands match those used in this lesson, choose Window > Workspace > [Advanced], and then choose Window > Workspace > Reset Advanced.

7 To display the document at a higher resolution, choose View > Display Performance > High Quality Display (if it's not already enabled).

8 Choose File > Save As, rename the file **11_Tables.indd**, and save it in the Lesson11 folder.

9 If you want to see what the finished document looks like, open the 11_End.indd file in the same folder. You can leave this document open to act as a guide as you work.

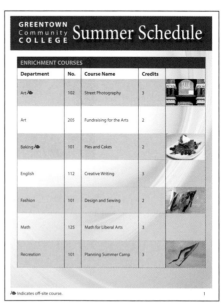

Creating a table

Tables are grids of individual cells set in vertical columns and horizontal rows. In InDesign, a table is always contained within a text frame. To create a table, you can convert existing text into a table, insert a new table at a text insertion point in a text frame (which adds the table to the text flow), or create a new freestanding table. Here, you will experiment with creating a new table. You will then delete that table because the table you will use in this exercise is created by converting text into a table.

1 With page 1 of the 11_Tables.indd document centered in the document window, choose Table > Create Table.

▶ **Tip:** If you click the table creation pointer between column guides, the new table will span the width of the column.

2 In the Create Table dialog box, leave the default settings for Body Rows and Columns as is. Click OK.

3 Drag the table creation pointer (⊞) anywhere on the page. When you release the mouse button, InDesign creates a table that matches the dimensions of the rectangle you draw.

4 Using the Selection tool (▶), select the text frame containing the new table you just created.

5 Choose Edit > Clear to delete the new text frame and table.

6 Choose File > Save.

Converting text to a table

Often, the text for a table already exists in the form of "tab-delimited text," in which the columns of information are separated by tab characters and the rows of information are separated by paragraph returns. In this case, the catalog text was received in an email from the college and then pasted into the document. You will select this text and convert it to a table.

▶ **Tip:** You use the Type tool to edit and format tables.

1 Using the Type tool (T), click in the text frame starting with the words "ENRICHMENT COURSES."

2 Choose Edit > Select All.

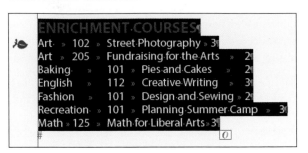

3 Choose Table > Convert Text To Table.

In the Convert Text To Table dialog box, you will indicate how the selected text is currently separated. Because Hidden Characters (Type menu) is selected, you can see that the columns of information are separated by tabs (>>) and that the rows are separated by paragraph returns (¶).

4 From the Column Separator menu, choose Tab. From the Row Separator menu, choose Paragraph.

5 Confirm that Table Style is set to [No Table Style], and then click OK.

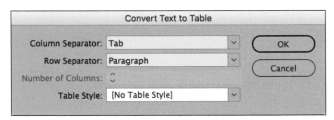

The new table is automatically anchored in the frame that contained the text.

ENRICHMENT. COURSES#	#	#	#
Art#	102#	Street·Photography#	3#
Art#	205#	Fundraising·for·the·Arts#	2#
Baking#	101#	Pies·and·Cakes#	2#
English#	112#	Creative·Writing#	3#
Fashion#	101#	Design·and·Sewing#	2#
Recreation·#	101#	Planning·Summer·Camp#	3#
Math#	125#	Math·for·Liberal·Arts#	3#
#	#	#	#

6 Choose File > Save.

Importing tables

InDesign can import tables from other applications, including Microsoft Word and Microsoft Excel. When you place a table, you can create a link to the external file. Then, if you update the Word or Excel file, you can easily update that information in the InDesign document.

To import a table, follow these steps:

1 Using the Type tool (T), click to place an insertion point in a text frame.

2 Choose File > Place.

3 In the Place dialog box, select Show Import Options.

4 Select a Word file (.doc or .docx) that contains a table, or select an Excel file (.xls or .xlsx).

5 Click Open.

6 Use the Import Options dialog box to specify how to handle the formatting in Word tables. For Excel files, you can specify what worksheet and cell range to import along with how to handle the formatting.

To link to tables when they are imported, you would follow these steps:

1 Choose Edit > Preferences > File Handling (Windows) or InDesign CC > Preferences > File Handling (macOS).

2 In the Links section, select Create Links When Placing Text And Spreadsheet Files, and then click OK.

3 If the data in the source file changes, use the Links panel to update the table in the InDesign document.

Note that for tables to retain their InDesign-applied formatting when the Excel file is updated, all cells in the InDesign table must be formatted with table and cell styles. Header and footer rows must be reapplied when updating a link.

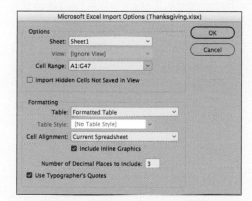

The Import Options dialog box for specifying the spreadsheet, cells, and formatting to import.

Changing rows and columns

When you start with source data from a client, you will often need to add a few rows, rearrange text, and more in a table during a document's design and review cycle. Once a table is created, you can easily add rows and columns, delete rows and columns, merge cells, rearrange rows, adjust row height and column width, and specify text inset for cells. In this section, you will complete the shell of the table so you know its size before you start formatting it.

Adding and deleting rows

Tip: Throughout this lesson, you will experiment with different options for selecting table elements and modifying tables. These include using the Table menu, Table panel, and Control panel. Once you become accustomed to working with tables, you can use the options that work best for you.

You can add rows above or below a selected row. The controls for adding and deleting columns work the same as for adding and deleting rows. Here, you will add a row to the top of the table to contain the column descriptions.

1 Using the Type tool (**T**), click in the first row of the table, which starts with "ENRICHMENT," to activate a cell. You can click in any cell.

2 Choose Table > Insert > Row.

3 In the Insert Row(s) dialog box, type **1** in the Number box, and click Below. Click OK to add the row.

4 Click in the first new cell, and type **Department**. To add column heads to the remaining cells, click with the Type tool in each empty cell, or press the Tab key to navigate from cell to cell. Type the following text in each cell, as shown:

• Second cell: **No.**

• Third cell: **Course Name**

• Fourth cell: **Credits**

ENRICHMENT·COURSES#	#	#	#
Department#	No.#	Course·Name#	Credits#
Art #	102#	Street·Photography#	3#
Art#	205#	Fundraising·for·the·Arts#	2#
Baking #	101#	Pies·and·Cakes#	2#
English#	112#	Creative·Writing#	3#
Fashion#	101#	Design·and·Sewing#	2#
Recreation #	101#	Planning·Summer·Camp#	3#
Math#	125#	Math·for·Liberal·Arts#	3#

5 Using the Type tool, click in the first cell of the second row, and then drag to the right to select all cells in the row with the new column headings.

6 Choose Type > Paragraph Styles.

7 Click Table Column Heads in the Paragraph Styles panel.

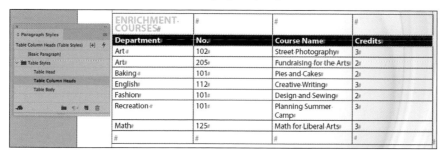

8 Click in the cell containing the word "Credits" to activate the cell.

You will insert a column to the right of this column to contain images.

9 Choose Table > Insert > Column.

10 In the Insert Column(s) dialog box, type **1** in the Number box, and click Right. Click OK to add the column.

The table is now wider than the frame and the page; you will resolve that later.

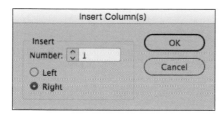

11 Choose File > Save.

Deleting rows

Tip: To activate a row or column, click in it. To select multiple rows to delete, position the Type tool on the left edge of the table until the arrow displays; then drag to select the rows. To select multiple columns to delete, position the Type tool on the top edge of the table until the arrow displays; then drag to select the columns.

You can delete selected rows and columns. Here, you will delete the blank row at the bottom of the table.

1 Using the Type tool (T), click the left edge of the last row of the table, which is blank.

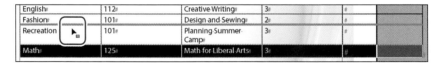

2 Choose Table > Delete > Row.

3 Choose File > Save.

Rearranging rows and columns

Tip: To drag and drop rows or columns, you must select the entire row or column. To drag a copy of a row or column to a new position, press Alt (Windows) or Option (macOS) while dragging.

While working on a table, you may find that information works better in a different order, or you may discover a mistake. In that case, you can select and drag rows or columns to a new location. This table is in alphabetical order by department, but the "Math" row is in the wrong location.

1 Locate the last row of the table, which starts with "Math".

2 Using the Type tool (T), move the pointer over the left edge of the "Math" row until it appears as a horizontal arrow (➜). Click to select the row.

3 Click and hold on the selected row, and then drag the "Math" row up and drop it just under the "Fashion" row. A bold blue line indicates where the row will be inserted.

English#	112#	Creative·Writing#	3#	#
Fashion#	101#	Design·and·Sewing#	2#	#
Recreation#	101#	Planning·Summer·Camp#	3#	#
Math#	125#	Math·for·Liberal·Arts#	3#	#

4 Choose File > Save.

Adjusting column widths, row heights, and text placement

Columns and rows, and the way text fits within them, often need fine-tuning according to the content and the design. By default, table cells expand vertically to fit their content—so if you keep typing within a cell, it gets taller. You can, however, specify a fixed row height or have InDesign create columns or rows of equal size within the table. If you want columns of the same width, rows of the same height, or both, choose Table > Distribute Columns Evenly or Table > Distribute Rows Evenly.

In this exercise, you will manually adjust the column widths, and then you will modify how the text fits within the cells.

1 Using the Type tool (**T**), point at a vertical stroke between two columns. When the double-arrow icon (↔) displays, drag to the left or right to resize the column.

2 Choose Edit > Undo. Experiment with resizing columns a few more times to get a feel for the tool. Choose Edit > Undo after each move. As you drag, keep an eye on the horizontal ruler at the top of the document window.

3 Place the final columns by dragging the right edge of each column, using the horizontal ruler at the top of the window as a guide.

- Department column: 2.5"
- No. column: 3.125"
- Course Name column: 5.25"
- Credits column: 6.25"
- Blank image column: 7.75"

▶ **Tip:** Dragging the cell boundary between two columns changes the size of the column and moves the remainder of the columns out or in (depending on whether you increase or decrease the column size). To retain the overall table width when dragging cell boundaries, press Shift and then drag the boundary. The columns adjoining the boundary are now increased or decreased in size while the table dimensions remain the same.

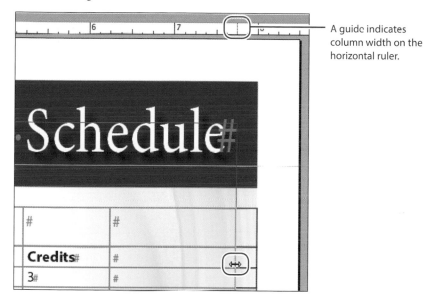

A guide indicates column width on the horizontal ruler.

ENRICHMENT COURSES#	#	#		#	#
Department#	**No.#**	**Course Name#**		**Credits#**	#
Art #	102#	Street Photography#		3#	#
Art#	205#	Fundraising for the Arts#		2#	#
Baking #	101#	Pies and Cakes#		2#	#
English#	112#	Creative Writing#		3#	#
Fashion#	101#	Design and Sewing#		2#	#
Math#	125#	Math for Liberal Arts#		3#	#
Recreation #	101#	Planning Summer Camp#		3#	#

Now that the columns widths better fit the text, you will add a little space around the text in the cells. In this case, you will change the entire table, but you can modify selected cells only.

4 Choose Window > Type & Tables > Table to open the Table panel.

5 Click anywhere in the table, and choose Table > Select > Table.

6 Type **.125 in** in the Top Cell Inset field (▤), and press Enter or Return. If necessary, click Make All Settings The Same (▤) to increase the inset on all four edges of each cell.

7 With the table still selected, click Align Center (≡) in the Table panel.

This centers the text vertically within each cell.

8 Click anywhere in the table to deselect the cells.

9 Choose File > Save.

Merging cells

You can merge adjacent selected cells to produce a single cell. Here, you will merge the cells in the top row so the header "ENRICHMENT COURSES" spans the table.

1 Using the Type tool (T,), click in the first cell of the first row, and then drag to select all the cells in the row.

▶ **Tip:** The Control panel has a Merge Cells icon for easy access.

2 Choose Table > Merge Cells.

3 Choose File > Save.

ENRICHMENT·COURSES#				
Department⋕	**No.**⋕	**Course Name**⋕	**Credits**⋕	#

Formatting a table

The border of a table is a stroke that lies outside the entire table. Cell strokes are lines within the table that set the individual cells apart from each other. InDesign includes many easy-to-use formatting options for tables. You can use these to make tables attractive and help them convey information to readers. In this section, you will specify fills and strokes for the table.

Adding a fill pattern

To achieve effects such as shading every other row, InDesign provides fill patterns for both rows and columns. You can specify where the pattern starts, which allows you to exclude any header rows. As you add, delete, and move rows and columns, the pattern updates automatically. You will add a fill to every other row in this table.

1 Using the Type tool (T), click anywhere in the table to activate it.

2 Choose Table > Table Options > Table Setup. In the Table Options dialog box, click the Fills tab at the top.

3 From the Alternating Pattern menu, choose Every Other Row. Leave the default settings for the remaining options.

4 Click OK. Every other row now has a gray background.

ENRICHMENT·COURSES#				
Department#	**No.**#	**Course·Name**#	**Credits**#	#
Art#	102#	Street·Photography#	3#	#
Art#	205#	Fundraising·for·the·Arts#	2#	#
Baking#	101#	Pies·and·Cakes#	2#	#
English#	112#	Creative·Writing#	3#	#

5 Choose File > Save.

Applying a fill color to cells

An entire table can have a fill color, and each cell can have its own fill color. Using the Type tool, you can drag to select any contiguous cells to apply a fill color. In this section, you will apply a fill color to the header row so the gray text is easier to read.

1 Using the Type tool (**T.**), move the pointer over the left edge of the "ENRICHMENT" row until it appears as a horizontal arrow (→). Click to select the row.

2 Choose Window > Color > Swatches.

▶ **Tip:** You can use the Fill box on the Control panel to apply color to cells as well.

3 Select the Fill box () in the Swatches panel, and then click the Dark Green swatch.

4 Drag the Tint slider all the way to the right to 100%.

5 Choose Edit > Deselect All to view the color. Choose File > Save.

Editing cell strokes

Cell strokes are the lines around individual cells. You can remove or change the stroke for selected cells or for the entire table. In this section, you will remove the stroke width from all the horizontal strokes, as the alternating pattern provides enough delineation.

1 Using the Type tool (**T.**), click anywhere in the table, and then choose Table > Select > Table.

2 Locate the proxy preview () in the center of the Control panel.

Each horizontal and vertical line represents a row stroke, column stroke, or border stroke. You can click the lines to toggle the selection on or off. Clicking a line on selects that particular stroke for formatting.

3 Click all three horizontal lines in the proxy to select them. Ensure that all horizontal lines (and no vertical lines) are selected (toggled on) on the proxy.

4 Type **0** in the Control panel's Stroke field. Press Enter (Windows) or Return (macOS).

ENRICHMENT COURSES#				
Department#	**No.**#	**Course·Name**#	**Credits**#	#
Art·#	102#	Street·Photography#	3#	#
Art#	205#	Fundraising·for·the·Arts#	2#	#
Baking·#	101#	Pies·and·Cakes#	2#	#
English#	112#	Creative·Writing#	3#	#
Fashion#	101#	Design·and·Sewing#	2#	#
Math#	125#	Math·for·Liberal·Arts#	3#	#
Recreation·#	101#	Planning·Summer·Camp#	3#	#

5 Choose Edit > Deselect All to see the results.

6 Choose File > Save.

Adding table borders

A table border is a stroke around the entire table. As with other strokes, you can customize the border's width, style, color, and more. In this section, you will apply a border to the table.

1 Using the Type tool (**T**), click anywhere in the table.

2 Choose Table > Select > Table.

3 Choose Table > Table Options > Table Setup to open the Table Options dialog box. Select Preview in the lower-left corner.

4 In the Table Setup tab, in the Table Border section, choose 0.5 pt from the Weight menu.

5 Click OK, and then choose Edit > Deselect All.

6 Choose View > Screen Mode > Preview to see the results of your formatting.

7 Choose View > Screen Mode > Normal, and then choose File > Save.

Adding graphics to table cells

▶ **Tip:** In addition to converting a cell to a graphic cell, you can anchor objects and images within the text of a table cell.

You can use InDesign to create effective tables that combine text, photographs, and illustrations. By default, table cells are essentially small text frames, but you can convert a text cell to a graphic cell. At that point, the cell essentially functions as a graphics frame whose dimensions are governed by the table. In this exercise, you will add photos to some of the course descriptions.

Converting cells to graphic cells

First, you will convert a selected cell to a graphic cell using the Table menu and the Table panel. Later, you will see how to automatically convert a cell to a graphic cell by placing an image.

1 Using the Type tool (T), click inside the far-right cell of the table's first body row (the row describing Art 102: Street Photography).

2 Chose Table > Select > Cell to select the cell.

3 With the cell selected, choose Table > Convert Cell To Graphic Cell.

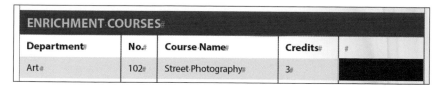

4 With the converted cell still selected, choose Table > Cell Options > Graphic to see the options for positioning a graphic within a cell.

▶ **Tip:** You can convert a text cell to a graphics cell simply by placing an image in it. However, if you are creating a template that indicates where images should be placed, you can do this by converting the cells to graphics cells.

5 After viewing the options in the Graphic tab of the Cell Options dialog box, click Cancel.

6 Click inside the far-right cell in the third body row (the row describing Baking 101: Pies and Cakes). Drag to the right to select the cell.

7 If necessary, choose Window > Type & Tables > Table to display the Table panel.

8 Choose Convert Cell To Graphic Cell from the Table panel menu.

▶ **Tip:** To edit Cell Options or convert a graphic cell to a text cell, you must first select the cell. To select a graphic cell with the Type tool, drag across the graphic cell.

Placing images in graphic cells

Now, you will place images in the two cells converted to graphic cells. You will then automatically convert two text cells to graphic cells as you place images.

1 Using the Selection tool (▶), click inside the new graphic cell in the Art 102: Street Photography row.

2 Choose File > Place. In the Place dialog box, select the StreetArt.jpg file in the Lesson11 folder.

3 Select Replace Selected Item, and then click Open.

● **Note:** If necessary, deselect Show Import Options in the Place dialog box.

4 To fit the cell to the image, choose Object > Fitting > Fit Frame To Content.

ENRICHMENT COURSES#				#
Department#	**No.**#	**Course Name**#	**Credits**#	#
Art#	102#	Street Photography#	3#	

5 Click inside the new graphic cell in the Baking 101: Pies and Cakes row.

6 Choose File > Place. In the Place dialog box, select the Bake.jpg file in the Lesson11 folder, and click Open.

7 To fit the cell to the image, use the keyboard shortcut for Fit Frame To Content: Ctrl+Alt+C (Windows) or Command+Option+C (macOS).

8 Double-click the far-right cell in the Fashion 101: Design and Sewing row.

9 Choose File > Place. In the Place dialog box, select the Fashion.jpg file. Then, Ctrl-click (Windows) or Command-click (macOS) the Kite.jpg file to load the pointer with both the Fashion.jpg and Kite.jpg files. Click Open.

10 Click the loaded graphics icon (▤) in the last cell of the Fashion 101: Design and Sewing row.

11 Click the loaded graphics icon in the last cell of the Recreation 101: Planning Summer Camp row.

12 Using the Selection tool, click the image of scarves and fit the cell to the image using the keyboard shortcut or the Object > Fitting > Fit Frame To Content command.

13 Using the Selection tool, click the kite image. Click the Fit Content Proportionately icon (▤) on the Control panel.

14 Choose File > Save.

Adjusting the row heights

The images are 1" in height, so you will now make all the table body rows 1" high.

1 If necessary, choose Window > Type & Tables > Table to open the Table panel.

2 Using the Type tool (T), move the pointer over the left edge of the first body row until it appears as a horizontal arrow (➜).

3 Drag from the first table body row, starting with "Art," to the last table row, ending with "Recreation."

4 With the table body rows selected, choose Exactly from the Row Height menu. Then, type **1 in** in the Row Height field to the right of the menu. Press Enter (Windows) or Return (macOS).

5 Choose Edit > Deselect All to see the results.

6 Choose File > Save.

ENRICHMENT COURSES				
Department	**No.**	**Course Name**	**Credits**	
Art	102	Street Photography	3	
Art	205	Fundraising for the Arts	2	
Baking	101	Pies and Cakes	2	
English	112	Creative Writing	3	
Fashion	101	Design and Sewing	2	
Math	125	Math for Liberal Arts	3	
Recreation	101	Planning Summer Camp	3	

Anchoring graphics in table cells

You can have both text and graphics in a cell by anchoring images in the text. In this exercise, you will place a leaf icon next to the classes that are held off-campus.

1 Choose View > Fit Page In Window to center page 1 in the document window.

2 Using the Selection tool (), select the leaf icon immediately to the left of the header row.

3 Choose Edit > Cut.

4 Select the Type tool (T), or double-click inside the table to automatically switch to the Type tool.

5 In the first body row of the table, click immediately after "Art."

6 Choose Edit > Paste.

7 Click the Type tool after "Baking" and choose Edit > Paste.

8 Choose File > Save.

Creating a header row

▶ **Tip:** When you edit text in a header row, the text is automatically updated in other instances of the header row. You can edit the text in the original header only; the other instances of the header are locked.

A table's name and the column headings are often formatted to stand out from the rest of the table. To do this, you can select and format the cells that contain the header information. This header information needs to repeat if the table flows across multiple pages. With InDesign, you can specify header and footer rows that repeat when a table continues to the next column, frame, or page. Here, you will format the first two rows of the table—which often contain the table name and the column headings—and specify them as header rows that repeat.

1 Using the Type tool (T), move the pointer over the left edge of the first row until it appears as a horizontal arrow (➔).

2 Click to select the entire first row, and then drag to include the second row. You will have selected "ENRICHMENT" through "Credits."

3 With the two rows still selected, choose Table > Convert Rows > To Header.

4 Click the Type tool in the last row of the table.

5 Choose Table > Insert > Row.

6 In the Insert Row(s) dialog box, type **4** in the Number box, and click Below. Click OK to add the rows.

7 Choose Layout > Next Page to view the table on page 2. Notice that the continuation of the table has the same header rows.

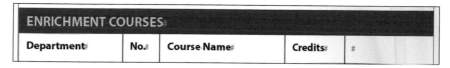

8 Choose Layout > Previous Page to return to page 1, and then choose File > Save.

Creating and applying table and cell styles

To quickly and consistently apply formatting to tables, you can create table styles and cell styles. A table style applies to the entire table, whereas cell styles can be applied to selected cells, rows, and columns. Here, you will create a table style and a cell style so the formatting can be quickly applied in other tables.

Creating table and cell styles

In this exercise, you will create a table style for the basic table formatting and a cell style for the header rows. Rather than specify formatting in the styles, you will simply create styles based on the formatting of the table.

1 Using the Type tool (**T**), click anywhere in the table.

2 Choose Window > Styles > Table Styles, and then choose New Table Style from the panel menu.

> **Tip:** The Table panel is grouped with the Table Styles and Cell Styles panels by default.

3 Name the style **Catalog Table** in the Style Name box.

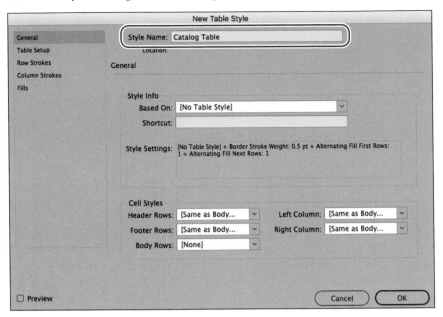

4 Click OK. The new style appears in the Table Styles panel.

5 Using the Type tool, click in the first row of the table, which says "ENRICHMENT COURSES."

6 Choose Window > Styles > Cell Styles, and then click Create New Style at the bottom of the panel. Double-click the new Cell Style 1 to open the Cell Style Options dialog box.

7 Name the style **Table Header** in the Style Name box.

You will now specify a different paragraph style for the text in cells with the Header Rows style applied.

8 From the Paragraph Style menu, select Table Head. This is the paragraph style already applied to the text in the header rows.

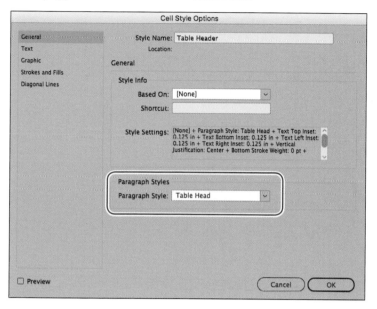

9 Click OK.

10 Choose File > Save.

Applying table and cell styles

Now, you will apply the styles to the table. To make global changes to table formatting later, you can simply edit the table or cell styles.

1 Using the Type tool (**T**), click anywhere in the table.

2 Click the Catalog Table style in the Table Styles panel.

3 Using the Type tool, click in the first header row of the table. Choose Table > Select > Row to select the row.

4 Click the Table Header style in the Cell Styles panel. To see the difference, click [None] in the Cell Styles panel. Then click Table Header again.

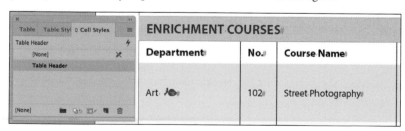

5 Deselect all, choose View > Fit Page In Window, and choose File > Save.

> ▶ **Tip:** To automate formatting, you can specify a paragraph style for header rows within a table style.

As a final step, you'll preview the flyer in its current state. If you were going to complete this flyer, you might enter data into the table cells in the blank rows on page 2 and add more rows as necessary.

6 On the Application bar, select Preview from the Screen Mode menu to view the final table.

Congratulations! You have now completed this lesson.

Exploring on your own

Now that you're skilled in the basics of working with tables in InDesign, you can experiment with other techniques for building tables.

1 First, create a new document. The page size and other specifications do not matter.

2 Choose Table > Create Table, and enter the number of rows and columns you want. Click OK. Click and drag to create a table of any size.

3 Using the Type tool (T), click the insertion point in the first cell and then type. Use the arrow keys on the keyboard to navigate among the cells.

4 To add a new column by dragging, position the Type tool over the right edge of one of the columns in your table so that the pointer becomes a double-arrow icon (↔) and begin dragging to the right. Hold down Alt (Windows) or Option (macOS) and drag a short distance to the right, perhaps half an inch or so. When you release the mouse button, a new column appears. (The column has the same width as the distance you dragged.)

5 To rotate text within a cell, click with the Type tool to place an insertion point in a cell. Choose Window > Type & Tables > Table. In the Table panel, select the Rotate Text 270° (⊷) option. Then type the text you want in this cell. Increase the height of the cell as necessary to see the text.

6 To convert the table to text, choose Table > Convert Table To Text. Tabs can separate what were previously columns, and paragraph breaks can separate rows. You can also modify these options. Similarly, you can convert tabbed text to a table by selecting the text and choosing Table > Convert Text To Table.

Review questions

1 What are the advantages of using tables rather than just typing text and using tabs to separate the columns?

2 How can you ensure that a table's title and column headings repeat if a table continues on multiple pages?

3 What tool is used most frequently when you work with tables?

Review answers

1 Tables give you much more flexibility and are far easier to format. In a table, text can wrap within a cell, so you don't have to add extra lines to accommodate cells that contain a lot of text. Also, you can assign styles to selected cells, rows, and columns—including character styles and even paragraph styles—because each cell functions like a separate text frame.

2 Select the heading rows you want to repeat and then select Table > Convert Rows > To Header. You can also repeat footer rows using Table > Convert Rows > To Footer.

3 The Type tool must be selected to work with a table. You can use other tools to work with the graphics within table cells, but to work with the table itself, such as selecting rows or columns, inserting text or graphics, adjusting table dimensions, and so forth, you use the Type tool.

12 WORKING WITH TRANSPARENCY

Lesson Overview

In this lesson, you'll learn how to do the following:

- Colorize an imported grayscale image.

- Change the opacity of objects drawn in InDesign.

- Apply transparency settings to imported graphics.

- Apply transparency settings to text.

- Apply blending modes to overlapping objects.

- Apply feathering effects to objects.

- Add a drop shadow to text.

- Apply multiple effects to an object.

- Edit and remove effects.

This lesson will take about 75 minutes to complete.

Please log in to your account on peachpit.com to download the lesson files for this chapter, or go to the "Getting Started" section at the beginning of this book and follow the instructions under "Accessing the Lesson Files and Web Edition." Store the files on your computer in a convenient location.

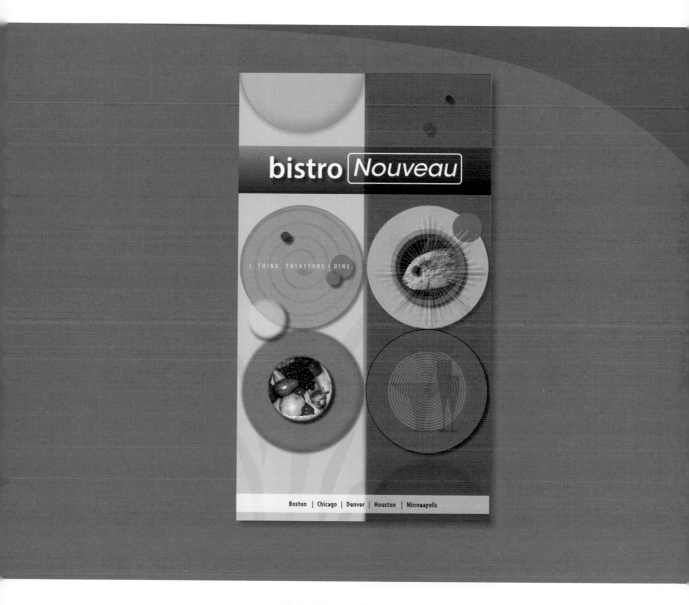

Adobe InDesign offers an array of transparency features to feed your imagination and creativity. These include controls over opacity, special effects, and color blends. You can also import graphic files that use transparency and apply additional transparency effects.

Getting started

The project for this lesson is the cover of a menu for a fictional restaurant, Bistro Nouveau. By applying transparency effects and using multiple layers, you'll create a visually rich design.

● **Note:** If you have not already downloaded the project files for this lesson to your computer from your Account page, make sure to do so now. See "Getting Started" at the beginning of the book.

1 To ensure that the preferences and default settings of your Adobe InDesign program match those used in this lesson, move the InDesign Defaults file to a different folder following the procedure in "Saving and restoring the InDesign Defaults file" on pages 4–5.

2 Start Adobe InDesign. To ensure that the panels and menu commands match those used in this lesson, choose Window > Workspace > [Advanced], and then choose Window > Workspace > Reset Advanced. To begin working, you'll open an InDesign document that is already partially completed.

3 Choose File > Open, and open the 12_Start.indd file in the Lesson12 folder, which is located within the Lessons folder in the InDesignCIB folder on your hard drive. (If the Missing Fonts dialog box displays, click Sync Fonts, and then click Close after the fonts have successfully synced from Typekit.)

4 Choose File > Save As, name the file **12_Menu.indd**, and save it in the Lesson12 folder.

The menu appears as a long, blank page because all the layers that contain objects are currently hidden. You'll reveal these layers one by one as you need them, so it will be easy to focus on the specific objects and tasks in this lesson.

5 To see what the finished project looks like, open the 12_End.indd file in the Lesson12 folder.

6 When you are ready to start working, either close the 12_End.indd file or leave it open for your reference. Then return to your lesson document by choosing 12_Menu.indd from the Window menu or clicking the 12_Menu.indd tab in the upper-left corner of the document window.

Importing and colorizing a grayscale image

You'll begin by working with the Background layer for the restaurant menu. This layer serves as a textured background visible through the objects above it that have transparency effects. By applying transparency effects, you can create see-through objects that reveal any objects underneath.

Because nothing is below the Background layer in the layer stack, you won't apply any transparency effects to objects on this layer.

1 Choose Window > Layers to display the Layers panel.

2 In the Layers panel, select the layer labeled Background, scrolling as necessary to find it at the bottom of the layer stack. You'll place the image you import on this layer.

3 Make sure that the two boxes to the left of the layer name show that the layer is visible (the eye icon [👁] appears) and unlocked (the layer lock icon [🔒] does not appear). The pen icon (✏) to the right of the layer name indicates that this is the layer on which the imported objects will be placed and new frames will be created.

4 Choose View > Grids & Guides > Show Guides. You'll use the guides on the page to align the background image that you import.

5 Choose File > Place, and then open the 12_Background.tif file in your Lesson12 folder. This file is a grayscale TIFF.

▶ **Tip:** TIFF stands for Tagged Image File Format, a common bitmap graphic format often used for print publishing. TIFF files use the .tif file extension.

6 Move the loaded raster graphics icon () slightly outside the upper-left corner of the page; then click the corner where the red bleed guides meet so that the placed image fills the entire page, including the margins and bleed area. Keep the graphics frame selected.

7 Choose Window > Color > Swatches. You'll use the Swatches panel to colorize the graphics frame and the image.

▶ **Tip:** InDesign offers many convenient ways to apply colors. You can also select the Fill box at the bottom of the Tools panel, and you can choose a fill color from the Fill menu in the Control panel.

8 In the Swatches panel, select Fill color (⬚). Scroll down the list of swatches to find the Light Green swatch and select it. Click the Tint menu at the top of the panel and drag the slider to 76%.

The white background of the graphics frame is now a 76% tint of the green color, but the gray areas of the graphic remain unchanged.

9 Using the Selection tool (▶), move the pointer within the content grabber at the center of the frame. When the hand pointer (✋) appears, click to select the graphic instead of the frame, and then select Light Green in the Swatches panel. Light Green replaces gray in the image, leaving the Light Green 76% fill color for the frame unchanged.

After applying a fill color and tint to the frame.

After applying color to the graphic.

InDesign lets you apply color to grayscale or bitmap images saved in PSD, TIFF, BMP, or JPEG format. When you select the graphic within a graphics frame and then apply a fill color, the color is applied to the gray portions of the image rather than to the background of the frame, as it was in step 8, when the frame was selected.

10 In the Layers panel, click the empty box to the left of the Background layer name to lock the layer. Leave the Background layer visible so that you can see the results of the transparent objects you will be placing above this layer.

11 Choose File > Save to save your work.

You've just learned a quick method for colorizing a grayscale image. While this method works well for creating composites, you may find the color controls available in Adobe Photoshop more effective for creating your final artwork.

Applying transparency settings

InDesign has extensive transparency controls. For example, by lowering the opacity of objects, text, and even imported graphics, you can reveal underlying objects that would otherwise not be visible. Additional transparency features, such as blending modes, drop shadows, feathered and glowing edges, and bevel and emboss effects, provide a wide range of options for creating special visual effects. You'll learn about these additional features later in the lesson.

In this part of the project, you'll practice using a variety of transparency features on several objects placed on the various layers in the menu.

▶ **Tip:** Applying a blending mode lets you vary the ways in which the colors of overlapping objects blend with each other.

About the Effects panel

You use the Effects panel (Window > Effects) to specify the opacity and blending mode of objects and groups, isolate blending to a particular group, knock out objects in a group, and apply a transparency effect.

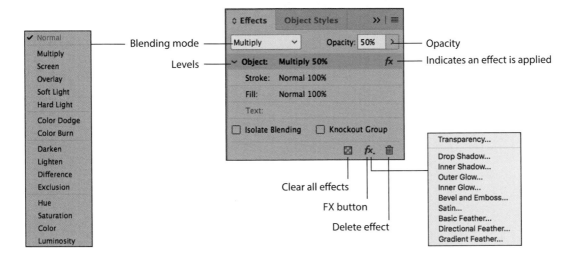

Effects panel overview

Blending mode—Specifies how colors in transparent objects interact with the objects behind them.

Opacity—Determines the opacity of an object, stroke, fill, or text, from 100% (completely opaque) to 0% (completely transparent). As you lower the opacity value of an object, the object becomes increasingly translucent and underlying objects become increasingly visible.

Levels—Tells you the Object, Stroke, Fill, and Text opacity settings of the object, as well as whether transparency effects have been applied. Click the triangle to the left of the word Object (or Group or Graphic) to hide or display these level settings. The FX icon appears on a level after you apply transparency settings there, and you can double-click the FX icon to edit the settings.

Clear effects—Clears effects (object, stroke, fill, or text) from an object, sets the blend mode to Normal, and changes the Opacity setting to 100% throughout the object—that is, remove all transparency.

FX button—Displays a list of transparency effects.

Delete—Removes effects, but not a blending mode or opacity, from an object.

Isolate Blending—Applies a blending mode to a selected group of objects.

Knockout Group—Makes the opacity and blending attributes of every object in a group knock out, or block out, underlying objects in the group.

— Adapted from InDesign Help

Changing the opacity of solid-color objects

With the background graphic complete, you can start applying transparency effects to objects on layers stacked above it. You'll start with a series of simple shapes that were drawn using InDesign.

1 In the Layers panel, select the Art1 layer so that it becomes the active layer, and click the lock icon (🔒) to the left of the layer name to unlock the layer. Click the empty box on the far left of the Art1 layer name so that the eye icon (👁) appears, indicating that the layer is now visible.

2 Using the Selection tool (▶), click the full circle filled with the Yellow/Green swatch on the right side of the page. This ellipse frame with a solid fill was drawn in InDesign.

3 Choose Window > Effects to display the panel.

4 In the Effects panel, click the arrow on the right side of the Opacity percentage. An Opacity slider adjustment appears. Drag the slider to 70%. Alternatively, enter **70%** in the Opacity box and press Enter or Return.

● **Note:** The shapes mentioned are named by the color swatch applied to the fill of the object. If the Swatches panel is not open, choose Window > Color > Swatches to open it.

After you change the opacity of the Yellow/Green circle, it becomes translucent, and the resulting color is a combination of the Yellow/Green fill of the circle and the Light Purple rectangle below it that covers the right half of the page.

5 Select the Light Green–filled semicircle in the upper-left corner of the page, and then go to the Effects panel and set the Opacity value to 50%. The semicircle now appears as a subtle variation in color against the background.

Before applying 50% Opacity.

After applying 50% Opacity.

6 Repeat step 5 for the following three circles on the Art1 layer, using the following settings to change the opacity of each circle:

- Left side, middle circle filled with the Medium Green swatch, Opacity = 60%.

- Left side, bottom circle filled with the Light Purple swatch, Opacity = 70%.

- Right side, bottom semicircle filled with the Light Green swatch, Opacity = 50%.

7 Choose File > Save to save your work.

Applying a blending mode

Changing an object's opacity creates a color that combines the color applied to an object with the colors applied to objects below it. Using blending modes is another way to create color interactions between stacked objects.

In this procedure, you'll apply a blending mode to three objects on the page.

1 Using the Selection tool (▶), select the Yellow/Green–filled circle on the right side of the page.

2 In the Effects panel, choose Overlay from the Blending Mode menu. Notice how the appearance of the colors changes.

70% opacity, Normal
blending mode.

Same opacity and Overlay
blending mode.

3 Select the Light Green–filled semicircle in the lower-right corner of the page, and then hold down the Shift key and select the Light Green–filled semicircle in the upper-left corner of the page.

4 In the Effects panel, choose Multiply from the Blending Mode menu.

5 Choose File > Save.

For more information on the different blending modes, see "Specify how colors blend" in InDesign Help.

Adding transparency effects to imported vector and bitmap graphics

So far in this lesson, you have applied various transparency settings to objects drawn using InDesign. You can also apply opacity values and blending modes to imported graphics created with other applications, such as Adobe Illustrator and Adobe Photoshop.

Applying transparency to a vector graphic

1 In the Layers panel, select the Art2 layer. Unlock this layer and make it visible.

2 In the Tools panel, make sure that the Selection tool (▶) is selected.

3 On the left side of the page, select the graphics frame that contains the black spiral image by clicking within the frame when the arrow pointer (▶.) is displayed. (Don't click within the content grabber when the hand pointer [🖑] is displayed or you'll select the graphic rather than the frame.) This frame is in front of a Medium Green–colored circle.

4 With the black spiral frame still selected, hold down the Shift key and click to select the graphics frame that contains a black spiral on the right side of the page. This frame is in front of and within a Light Purple–colored circle. Again, make sure you select the graphics frame and not the graphic within. Both of the graphics frames with spirals should now be selected.

5 In the Effects panel, choose Color Dodge from the Blending Mode menu and set the Opacity value to 30%.

Selected frames before applying blending mode and opacity.

After applying blending mode and opacity.

Next you will apply a blending mode to the stroke on the fish image.

6 With the Selection tool (▶), select the circular graphics frame with the fish image on the right side of the page. Make sure the arrow pointer (▶) and not the hand pointer (✋) is displayed when you click.

7 In the Effects panel, click the Stroke level beneath Object to select it. Selecting the Stroke level applies any blending mode or opacity changes you make to only the stroke of the selected object.

A level indicates the Object, Stroke, Fill, and Text opacity settings of the selected object and the applied blending mode, as well as whether transparency effects have been applied. This means you can apply different transparency effects to the stroke or fill or text of the same object. You can hide or display these level settings by clicking the triangle to the left of the word Object (or Group or Graphic, depending on the selection).

8 From the Blending Mode drop-down menu, choose Hard Light.

9 Choose Edit > Deselect All, and then choose File > Save to save your work.

Applying transparency to a bitmap graphic

Next you'll apply transparency effects to an imported bitmap graphic. Although this example uses a monochromatic image, you can also apply transparency settings to multicolor photographs. The process is the same as applying transparency effects to any other InDesign object.

1 In the Layers panel, select the Art3 layer. Unlock this layer and make it visible. You can hide or lock either the Art1 layer or the Art2 layer to make it easier to work. Be sure to keep at least one underlying layer visible so that you can see the results of the transparency interactions.

2 Using the Selection tool (▶), select the graphics frame with the black starburst image on the right side of the page. Because it's on the Art3 layer, the frame edge is displayed in blue, the color of the layer.

3 In the Effects panel, enter **70%** as the Opacity value and press Enter or Return.

4 Move the pointer within the content grabber in the middle of the starburst image so that it changes to a hand (✋), and then click once to select the graphic within the frame.

5 In the Swatches panel, select Fill color (▨), and then select the Red color swatch so that red replaces the black areas of the image.

 If other layers are visible below the Art3 layer, you can see the starburst as a muted orange color. If no other layers are visible, the starburst is red.

6 If the starburst image is not still selected, reselect it by clicking within the content grabber.

7 In the Effects panel, choose Screen from the Blending Mode menu and leave the Opacity value at 100%. The starburst changes colors based on the layers visible beneath it. Notice how the result is different when the starburst is over different backgrounds, such as the pink circle compared to the gray circle.

Note: If you hid any layers in step 1, your screen may look slightly different than the example here.

8 Choose Edit > Deselect All, and then choose File > Save to save your work.

Importing and adjusting Illustrator files that use transparency

When you import Adobe Illustrator (.ai) files into an InDesign layout, InDesign recognizes and preserves any transparency settings that were applied in Illustrator. You can also adjust opacity, add a blending mode, and apply additional transparency effects in InDesign.

Now you will place an image of some drinking glasses, and then adjust its transparency.

1 Choose View > Fit Page In Window.

2 In the Layers panel, make sure that the Art3 layer is the active layer and that the Art3, Art2, Art1, and Background layers are visible (👁).

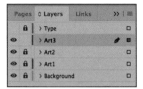

3 Lock the Art2, Art1, and Background layers to prevent them from being modified.

4 Select the Selection tool (▶) in the Tools panel, and then choose Edit > Deselect All to ensure that the image you import is not placed into a selected frame.

▶ **Tip:** To enable Show Import Options without selecting the option in the Place dialog box, select the graphic to import; then press the Shift key and click Open.

5 Choose File > Place. Select Show Import Options at the bottom of the Place dialog box. (You might have to click the Options button to see this choice.)

6 Locate the 12_Glasses.ai file in your Lesson12 folder, and double-click or click Open.

7 In the Place PDF dialog box, choose Bounding Box (All Layers) from the Crop To menu, and make sure that Transparent Background is selected.

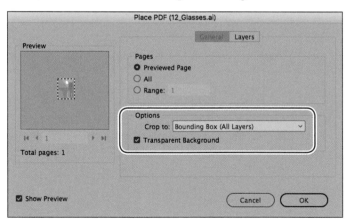

8 Click OK. The dialog box closes, and the pointer becomes a loaded vector graphics icon (⌐Ⅼ) with a preview of the file.

9 Position the loaded vector graphics icon (📐) within the Light Purple–colored circle on the right side of the page, and then click to place the graphic at full size. Drag the graphics frame to center it visually within the purple circle. Smart Guides are displayed when the frame is centered.

▶ **Tip:** When repositioning the image, Smart Guides can help you center the image perfectly within the purple circle.

10 In the Layers panel, click to hide the Art2, Art1, and Background layers so that only the Art3 layer is visible, and you can view the placed image on its own and see the transparent color interactions within the Illustrator image.

▶ **Tip:** To show only the Art3 layer and hide all other layers, Alt-click (Windows) or Option-click (macOS) the Toggle Visibility icon for the Art3 layer in the Layers panel.

11 Click to redisplay the Art2, Art1, and Background layers. Notice that the white "olive" shape is completely opaque, whereas the other shapes of the drinking glasses are partly transparent.

12 With the glasses image still selected, change the Opacity setting in the Effects panel to **60%**. Keep the image selected.

13 In the Effects panel, choose Color Burn from the Blending Mode menu. Now the colors and interactions of the image take on a completely different appearance.

14 Choose Edit > Deselect All, and then choose File > Save.

Applying transparency settings to text

Changing the opacity of text is as easy as applying transparency settings to graphic objects in your layout. You'll try the technique now as you change the color of text.

1 In the Layers panel, lock the Art3 layer, and then unlock the Type layer and make it visible.

2 In the Tools panel, select the Selection tool (▶) and then click the text frame "I THINK, THEREFORE I DINE." If necessary, zoom in so that you can read the text easily.

To apply transparency settings to text or to a text frame and its contents, you must select the frame with the Selection tool. You cannot specify transparency settings when text is selected with the Type tool.

3 In the Effects panel, select the Text level so that any opacity and blending mode changes you make will apply to the text only.

4 Choose Overlay from the Blending Mode menu and change the Opacity to **70%**.

5 Double-click the Hand tool to fit the page in the window, and then choose Edit > Deselect All.

Now you'll change the opacity of a text frame's fill.

6 Using the Selection tool (▶), click the text frame at the bottom of the page that contains "Boston | Chicago | Denver | Houston | Minneapolis." If necessary, zoom in so that you can read the text easily.

7 Select the Fill level in the Effects panel and change Opacity to **70%**. Notice that this changes the white background while the text remains black.

8 Try the same effect with the Object level selected, and notice how this time the text turns gray as well, which is not what we want. This demonstrates the advantage of the ability to apply effects to different parts of the same object. Choose Edit > Undo Set Transparency Parameters.

9 Choose Edit > Deselect All, and then choose File > Save.

Working with effects

So far in this lesson, you've learned how to apply transparency by changing the blending mode and the opacity of objects drawn in InDesign, imported graphics, and text. Another way to apply transparency is by using the nine transparency effects in InDesign. Many of the settings and options for creating these effects are similar.

Transparency effects

Drop Shadow—Adds a shadow that falls behind the object, stroke, fill, or text.

Inner Shadow—Adds a shadow that falls just inside the edges of the object, stroke, fill, or text, giving it a recessed appearance.

Outer Glow and **Inner Glow**—Add glows that emanate from the outside or inside edges of the object, stroke, fill, or text.

Bevel and Emboss—Adds various combinations of highlights and shadows to give text and images a three-dimensional appearance.

Satin—Adds interior shading that makes a satiny finish.

Basic Feather, **Directional Feather**, and **Gradient Feather**—Soften the edges of an object by fading them to transparent.

—From InDesign Help

```
Transparency...

Drop Shadow...
Inner Shadow...
Outer Glow...
Inner Glow...
Bevel and Emboss...
Satin...
Basic Feather...
Directional Feather...
Gradient Feather...
```

You'll try some of these effects now, as you fine-tune the menu's artwork.

Applying a basic feather to the edges of an image

Feathering is another way to apply transparency to an object. Feathering creates a subtle transition from opaque to transparent around the edge of an object so that any underlying object or the page background is visible through the feathered area. InDesign features three types of feathering:

- **Basic Feather** softens or fades the edges of an object over a distance that you specify.

- **Directional Feather** softens the edges of an object by fading the edges to transparent from directions that you specify.

- **Gradient Feather** softens the areas of an object by fading them to transparent.

First, you'll apply Basic Feather, and then you'll move on to Gradient Feather.

1 In the Layers panel, unlock the Art1 layer if it's locked.

2 If necessary, choose View > Fit Page In Window to see the entire page.

3 Select the Selection tool (▶), and then select the Light Purple–filled circle on the left side of the page.

4 Choose Object > Effects > Basic Feather. The Effects dialog box appears, displaying a list of the transparency effects on the left and an accompanying set of controls on the right.

5 In the Options section of the Effects dialog box, set these options:

- In the Feather Width box, type **0.375 in**.

- Change both the Choke value and Noise value to **10%**.

- Leave the Corners option set at Diffused.

6 Make sure that Preview is selected and, if necessary, move the dialog box to view the effects of your changes. Notice how the edges of the purple circle are now blurred.

7 Click OK to apply the settings, and close the Effects dialog box.

8 Choose File > Save.

Applying a gradient feather

● **Note:** In addition to applying transparency effects by choosing Object > Effects and then choosing an option from the submenu, you can add effects from the Effects panel menu, or you can click the FX button at the bottom of the Effects panel and then choose an option from the submenu.

You can use the Gradient Feather effect to fade an object from opaque to transparent.

1 Using the Selection tool (▶), click the Light Purple–filled vertical rectangle that covers the right half of the page.

2 At the bottom of the Effects panel, click the FX button (*fx.*) and choose Gradient Feather from the menu.

The Effects dialog box appears, displaying Gradient Feather options.

3 In the Gradient Stops section of the Effects dialog box, click the Reverse
Gradient button (⬚) to reverse the solid and transparent colors.

4 Click OK. The purple rectangle should fade to transparent from right to left.

Now you will use the Gradient Feather tool to adjust the direction of the fade.

5 In the Tools panel, select the Gradient Feather tool (⬚). (Be careful not to
choose the Gradient Swatch tool.) Hold down the Shift key, and drag the pointer
from the bottom to the top of the Light Purple rectangle to change the gradient
direction. The Shift key constrains the direction to exactly vertical.

6 Choose Edit > Deselect All, and then choose File > Save.

Next, you will apply multiple effects to a single object and then edit them.

Adding a drop shadow to text

● **Note:** The Effects dialog box allows you to apply multiple effects to a single object and shows you which effects are applied to a selected object (indicated by a check mark on the left side of the dialog box).

When you add a drop shadow to an object, the result is a 3D effect that makes the object appear to float above the page and cast a shadow on the page and objects below. You can add a drop shadow to any object, and you have the option to assign a shadow independently to an object's stroke or fill or to the text within a text frame.

Now you'll try this technique by adding a drop shadow to the "bistro" text. It's important to note that effects can only be applied to a whole text frame, not to some of the words within a frame.

1 Using the Selection tool (▶), select the text frame that contains the word "bistro." Hold down the Z key to temporarily access the Zoom tool, or select the Zoom tool (🔍) and magnify the frame so that you can see the text clearly.

2 At the bottom of the Effects panel, click the FX button (*fx.*), and choose Drop Shadow from the menu.

3 In the Options section of the Effects dialog box, enter **0.125 in** for Size and **20%** for Spread. Make sure that Preview is selected so that you can see the effects on your page.

You can also adjust the size and angle of a drop shadow with the settings in the Position area, either by typing numbers in the settings or by dragging the line in the angle circle to a new position.

4 Click OK to apply the drop shadow to the text.

5 Choose File > Save to save your work.

Applying multiple effects to an object

You can apply several different types of transparency effects to an object. For example, you can create the impression that an object is embossed and that it has a glow around it by applying two transparency effects.

In this exercise, you'll apply an embossed effect and an outer glow effect to the two semicircles on the page.

1 Choose View > Fit Page In Window.

2 Using the Selection tool (▶), select the Light Green–filled semicircle in the upper-left corner of the page.

3 At the bottom of the Effects panel, click the FX button (*fx.*), and choose Bevel And Emboss from the menu.

4 In the Effects dialog box, make sure that Preview is selected so that you can view the effects on the page. Then specify the following settings in the Structure section:

- Size: **0.3125 in**

- Soften: **0.3125 in**

- Depth: **30%**

5 Leave the rest of the settings as they are, and keep the Effects dialog box open.

6 On the left side of the dialog box, click the check box to the left of Outer Glow to add an outer glow effect to the semicircle.

7 Click the words Outer Glow to edit the effect, and specify these settings:

- Mode: **Multiply**

- Opacity: **80%**

- Size: **0.25 in**

- Spread: **10%**

8 Click the Set Glow Color box to the right of the Mode menu. In the Effect Color dialog box, make sure that Swatches is selected in the Color menu, choose Black from the list of colors, and then click OK.

9 Click OK to apply the settings for the multiple effects.

Next, you will apply the same effects to the other semicircle on the page, simply by dragging the FX icon from the Effects panel to the semicircle.

Copying effects between objects

1 Double-click the Hand tool (🖐) to fit the page in the window.

2 Using the Selection tool (▶), select the green semicircle in the upper-left corner of the page, if necessary.

3 With the Effects panel open, drag the FX icon (*fx.*) on the right side of the Object level to the page and directly on top of the green semicircle in the lower-right corner.

▶ **Tip:** You can also open the Effects dialog box by double-clicking the FX icon to the right of the Object level in the Effects panel.

Dragging the FX icon onto the semicircle (left and center) yields the result seen here (right).

Now you will apply the same effects to the small gray circle on the page.

4 In the Layers panel, click the eye icon (👁) to turn off the visibility for the Art3 layer, and then unlock the Art2 layer.

5 Make sure the green semicircle in the upper-left corner of the page is still selected. Drag the FX icon (*fx.*) from the Effects panel onto the small gray circle above and to the right of the fish image.

6 Choose File > Save.

Transparency settings and options

Many transparency effect settings and options are the same across different effects. Common transparency settings and options include the following:

Angle and Altitude—Determines the lighting angle at which a lighting effect is applied. A setting of 0 is equivalent to ground level; 90 is directly above the object. Click the angle radius or enter a degree measurement. Select Use Global Light if you want a uniform lighting angle for all objects. Used by the Drop Shadow, Inner Shadow, Bevel and Emboss, Satin, and Feather effects.

Blending Mode—Specifies how colors in transparent objects interact with the objects behind them. Used by the Drop Shadow, Inner Shadow, Outer Glow, Inner Glow, and Satin effects.

Choke—Along with the Size setting, determines how much of the shadow or glow is opaque and how much is transparent; large settings increase opacity and small settings increase transparency. Used by the Inner Shadow, Inner Glow, and Feather effects.

Distance—Specifies the offset distance for the Drop Shadow, Inner Shadow, or Satin effect.

Noise—Specifies the amount of random elements in the opacity of a glow or shadow as you enter a value or drag the slider. Used by the Drop Shadow, Inner Shadow, Outer Glow, Inner Glow, and Feather effects.

Opacity—Determines the opacity of an effect; drag the slider or enter a percentage measurement. (See Set the opacity of an object.) Used by the Drop Shadow, Inner Shadow, Outer Glow, Inner Glow, Gradient Feather, Bevel and Emboss, and Satin effects.

Size—Specifies the amount of shadow or glow. Used by the Drop Shadow, Inner Shadow, Outer Glow, Inner Glow, and Satin effects.

Spread—Determines the transparency of the blur within the shadow or glow effect as established by the Size setting. A higher percentage makes the blur more opaque. Used by the Drop Shadow and Outer Glow effects.

Technique—These settings determine how the edge of a transparency effect interacts with background colors. Softer and Precise are available for the Outer Glow and Inner Glow effects:

> **Softer**—Applies a blur to the edge of the effect. At larger sizes, doesn't preserve detailed features.

> **Precise**—Preserves the edge of the effect, including its corners and other sharp details. Preserves features better than the Softer technique.

Use Global Light—Applies the global light setting to the shadow. Used by the Drop Shadow, Bevel and Emboss, and Inner Shadow effects.

X Offset and Y Offset—Offsets the shadow on the x- or y-axis by the amount you specify. Used by the Drop Shadow and Inner Shadow effects.

—From InDesign Help

You can also use this same technique to apply effects to objects in other documents.

1 Go to File > Open and open the file 12_Start.indd again.

2 Go to Window > Arrange > Tile so that you can see both files side by side.

3 In the file 12_Start.indd, navigate to page 2 and then make sure that the Background layer is active (since it is already unlocked).

4 Draw a shape, such as a rectangle or ellipse frame, with one of the drawing tools, and choose a color for the fill from the Swatches panel.

5 Click back on the 12_Menu.indd file and select the Light Green–filled semicircle in the upper-left corner of the page, which now has multiple effects applied.

6 Use the same technique as in step 3 of the previous procedure: With the Effects panel open, drag the FX icon (*fx.*) on the right side of the Object level, and drop it directly on top of the shape you just drew.

7 Close the 12_Start.indd file without saving.

Another way to apply effects to other objects is to create an object style, as you learned in Lesson 9.

Editing and removing effects

Applied effects can easily be edited or removed. You can also quickly check whether any effects have been applied to an object.

First you'll edit the gradient fill behind the restaurant title, and then you'll remove the effects applied to one of the circles.

▶ **Tip:** To quickly see which pages in your document contain transparency, choose Panel Options from the Pages panel menu, and then select Transparency. A small icon (▦) is displayed next to any pages containing transparency.

1 In the Layers panel, make sure that the Art1 layer is unlocked and that it is visible.

2 Using the Selection tool (▶), click the frame with the gradient fill that's behind the text "bistro Nouveau."

3 With the Effects panel open, click the FX button (*fx.*) at the bottom of the panel. In the menu that appears, the Gradient Feather effect has a check mark next to it, which indicates that it is already applied to the selected object. Choose the Gradient Feather option from the menu.

When not to use transparency

Transparency vs. Tints: Transparency effects are great creative tools, but they do result in a more complex file. They should be used purposefully, and not used when the visual style can be accomplished more simply.

The most common place this happens is when you want to make the color of a frame lighter and that frame has nothing behind it that needs to show through, such as on a white background. In those cases you should use a tint of the color, not an Opacity setting. Use the slider in the Color panel or the Swatches panel, or use a tint swatch. See Lesson 8 for more details on tints.

Tip: If you like to use the sliding function of the Opacity slider to see a color change before making a choice, note that you can also use the same slider functionality in the Color panel to create a tint. The only difference is that you must release the mouse as you move along the slider to see the change.

100% of a color.

Tint of that color on a white background.

Opacity setting applied to that color on a white background.

4 In the Effects dialog box, under Gradient Stops, click the color stop (the small white square) at the right end of the gradient ramp. Change the Opacity to **30%**, and change the Angle to **90°**.

5 Click OK to update the Gradient Feather effect.

Now you will remove all of the effects applied to an object.

6 In the Layers panel, turn on visibility for all layers and unlock all layers.

7 Select the Selection tool (▶). While holding down the Ctrl key (Windows) or Command key (macOS), click the small gray circle to the right and above the fish image on the right side of the page. Your first click will select the rectangular frame above the circle. Click again within the small circle to select it.

Tip: When you hold down the Ctrl key (Windows) or Command key (macOS) and click overlapping objects, the first click selects the topmost object, and each successive click selects the next object below in the stacking order.

Note: The Clear Effects button also removes blending mode and opacity setting changes from the object.

8 At the bottom of the Effects panel, click the Clear Effects button () to remove the Drop Shadow effect applied to the circle.

9 Choose File > Save.

Congratulations! You have completed the lesson.

Exploring on your own

Try some of the following ways of working with InDesign transparency options:

1 Scroll to a blank area of the pasteboard and create some shapes (by using the drawing tools or by importing new copies of some of the image files used in this lesson) on a new layer. Apply fill colors to any shapes that don't have content, and position your shapes so that they overlap each other, at least partially. Then:

 • Select the uppermost object in your arrangement of shapes. Using the controls in the Effects panel, experiment with other blending modes, such as Luminosity, Hard Light, and Difference. Then select a different object and choose the same blending modes in the Effects panel to compare the results. When you have a sense of what the various modes do, select all of your objects, and choose Normal as the blending mode.

 • In the Effects panel, change the Opacity value of some of the objects but not others. Then select different objects in your arrangement and use the Object > Arrange > Send Backward and Object > Arrange > Bring Forward commands to observe different results.

 • Experiment with combinations of different opacities and different blending modes applied to an object. Do the same with other objects that partially overlap the first object to explore the variety of effects you can create.

2 In the Pages panel, double-click page 1 to center it in the document window. Open the Layers panel and then click the eye icon for the different Art layers one at a time to see the differences this creates in the overall effect of the layout.

3 In the Layers panel, make sure that all the layers are unlocked. In the layout, click the image of the glasses to select it. Use the Effects panel to apply a drop shadow.

Review questions

1 How do you change the color of the white areas of a grayscale image? How do you change the gray areas?

2 If you've applied transparency effects to an object, what is the easiest way to apply the same effects to a different object?

3 What is the importance of the stacking order of layers and of objects within layers when you work with transparency?

4 What's the quickest and easiest way to remove transparency effects from an object to which multiple effects are applied?

Review answers

1 To change the white areas, select the graphics frame with the Selection tool, click the Fill box in the Tools panel or Swatches panel, and then select a color in the Swatches panel. To change the gray areas, select the content within the frame by clicking the content grabber, and then select a color from the Swatches panel.

2 Select the object to which you've applied transparency effects, and then drag the FX icon displayed on the right side of the Effects panel to another object.

3 The transparency of an object affects the view of objects below (behind) it in the stacking order. For example, objects below a semitransparent object can be seen behind it—like objects behind a colored plastic film. An opaque object blocks the view of the area behind it in the stacking order, regardless of whether the objects behind it have reduced opacity values, feathering, blending modes, or other effects.

4 Select the object, and then click the Clear Effects button at the bottom of the Effects panel.

13 PRINTING AND EXPORTING

Lesson Overview

In this lesson, you'll learn how to do the following:

- Check a document for potential printing issues.

- Manage the colors used in a document.

- Confirm that an InDesign file and all of its elements are ready for printing.

- Preview a document onscreen before printing.

- Create different Adobe PDFs for proofing and for press.

- Create an Adobe PDF preset for Press-Ready PDFs.

- Print a proof of a document.

- Create a print preset to automate the printing process.

- Assemble all necessary files for printing or delivery to a service provider or commercial printer.

This lesson will take approximately 45 minutes to complete.

Please log in to your account on peachpit.com to download the lesson files for this chapter, or go to the "Getting Started" section at the beginning of this book and follow the instructions under "Accessing the Lesson Files and Web Edition." Store the files on your computer in a convenient location.

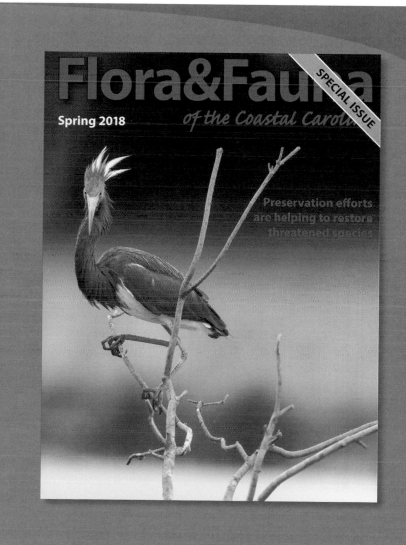

Adobe InDesign CC provides advanced print-preparation and printing controls to help you manage the printing process, regardless of the output device. You can easily output your work to a laser or inkjet printer, a Press-Ready PDF, high-resolution film, or a computer-to-plate imaging device.

Getting started

In this lesson, you'll do some print-preparation work on a magazine cover that contains a full-color image and also uses a spot color. The document will be printed on a color inkjet or laser printer for proofing and also on a high-resolution imaging device, such as a platesetter used in offset printing. Prior to printing, you will export the document to a PDF file that can be used in a review process.

Note: If you have not already downloaded the project files for this lesson to your computer from your Account page, make sure to do so now. See "Getting Started" at the beginning of the book.

1 To ensure that the preferences and default settings of your Adobe InDesign program match those used in this lesson, move the InDesign Defaults file to a different folder following the procedure in "Saving and restoring the InDesign Defaults file" on pages 4–5.

2 Start Adobe InDesign. To ensure that the panels and menu commands match those used in this lesson, choose Window > Workspace > [Advanced], and then choose Window > Workspace > Reset Advanced.

3 Choose File > Open and open the 13_Start.indd file in the Lesson13 folder, located inside the Lessons folder within the InDesignCIB folder on your hard drive.

4 An alert message informs you that the document contains missing and modified links. Click Don't Update Links. You will correct these problems later in this lesson. (If the Missing Fonts dialog box displays, click Sync Fonts, and then click Close after the fonts have successfully synced from Typekit.)

Tip: A preferences option in InDesign lets you control whether an alert is displayed when you open a document with missing or modified links. To disable the alert, deselect Check Links Before Opening Document in the File Handling section of the Preferences dialog box.

When you print an InDesign document or export a PDF file for printing, InDesign must access the original artwork that was placed in the layout. If imported artwork has been moved, graphic filenames have changed, or the original files are no longer available, InDesign alerts you that the original artwork cannot be located or has been modified. This alert appears when a document is opened, printed, exported, or checked for printing using the Preflight panel. InDesign shows the status of all files necessary for printing in the Links panel.

5 Choose File > Save As, rename the file **13_Press.indd**, and save it in the Lesson13 folder.

6 To see what the finished project looks like, open the 13_End.indd file in the Lesson13 folder. For this lesson, the difference between the Start and End files is not visible in a preview; instead, you'll need to examine the Links and Color Swatches panels to see the differences.

7 When you are ready to start working, either close the 13_End.indd file or leave it open for your reference. Then return to your lesson document by choosing 13_Press.indd from the Window menu or clicking the 13_Press.indd tab in the upper-left corner of the document window.

Preflighting files

InDesign provides controls for performing a quality check on a document prior to printing, handing off the document to a print service provider, or publishing to a digital format. *Preflight* is the standard industry term for this process. In "Preflighting as you work," in Lesson 2, you learned how you can take advantage of the live preflight capabilities in InDesign. This lets you monitor a document as you create it to prevent potential printing problems.

You can use the Preflight panel to confirm that all graphics and fonts used in the file are available for printing and exporting and that there are no instances of overset text. Here, you'll use the Preflight panel to identify a pair of missing graphics in the sample layout.

1 Choose Window > Output > Preflight.

2 In the Preflight panel, make sure that On is selected and confirm that [Basic] (working) is selected in the Profile menu. Notice that one type of error is listed (LINKS). The 2 in parentheses indicates two link-related errors.

 Notice that no text errors appear in the Error section, which confirms that the document has no missing fonts and no overset text.

3 Click the triangle to the left of Links; then click the triangle to the left of Missing Link to display the name of the missing graphic file. Double-click the Tagline.ai link name; this centers the graphic in the document window and selects the graphics frame.

▶ **Tip:** You can also access the Preflight panel by double-clicking "2 errors" at the bottom of the document window or by selecting Preflight Panel from the menu to the right of "2 errors."

4 At the bottom of the Preflight panel, click the triangle to the left of Info to display information about the missing file. The fix is to use the Links panel to find the file, as shown when you display the information under Info. If you look carefully at the frame that contains the magazine title, you'll notice a red-circled question mark in the upper-left corner, which indicates that the original graphic file is missing. Also notice that the color of the tagline is different than the title.

A typical problem in production might be that the decision was made to change the color for this issue, but the InDesign file is still linked to the tagline with the previous color. You will link to this new version of the tagline.

● **Note:** Modified or missing graphics are displayed in low resolution regardless of the current Display Performance setting.

5 If the Links panel isn't open, click the Links panel icon or choose Window > Links to open it. Make sure that the Tagline.ai file is selected in the Links panel. Notice that it shows the red-circled question mark (❓) here as well, and then choose Relink from the panel menu. Browse to the Links folder inside the Lesson13 folder. Double-click the Tagline-periwinkle.ai file. The new file is now linked, replacing the original file.

Notice that after you relink the Tagline-periwinkle.ai graphic, the magazine tagline ("of the Coastal Carolinas") is a different color and is displayed at low resolution, the default setting for imported vector graphics, such as Adobe Illustrator files. Also notice that the red-circled question mark in the upper-left corner has changed to a link symbol (⇔), meaning that the graphic is linked to the InDesign file and is not missing or modified.

▶ **Tip:** The Display Performance section of the Preferences dialog box lets you change default settings for the display of raster images, vector graphics, and objects to which transparency is applied. Choose Edit > Preferences > Display Performance (Windows) or InDesign CC > Preferences > Display Performance (macOS) to open the Preferences dialog box.

6 To display the document at high resolution, choose View > Display Performance > High Quality Display.

Missing graphic before relinking. After relinking.

7 Click the Status icon (⚠) at the top of the Links panel. This sorts the links by status rather than name or page. Status includes whether a link is missing, modified, or embedded. The graphics that might be a problem sort to the top of the list. You'll see that the graphic named sea-oats-small.jpg displays the modified graphic alert (⚠). Click the page number to the right of the filename, and InDesign navigates to the page where the modified graphic is, selects it, and centers it on your screen.

8 Notice that the modified graphic alert (⚠) is also displayed in the upper-left corner of the graphic frame. You can click this alert button or double-click the one in the Links panel to update this graphic. Click one of those now. Another typical scenario in production is that the photographer did some color correction to this photo and sent a new version to layout. The file was replaced in the Links folder but was never updated in the InDesign file.

Notice that after you relink the sea-oats-small.jpg graphic, the color has changed. Also notice that the modified graphic alert in the upper-left corner has changed to a link symbol, meaning that the graphic is linked to the InDesign file and is not missing or modified.

Modified graphic before updating. After updating.

9 Choose File > Save to save the changes you've made to the document and close the Preflight panel.

● **Note:** If any links remain modified at this point, open the Links panel flyout menu and choose Update All Links.

Previewing separations

If your documents need to be prepared for commercial printing, you can use the Separations Preview panel to check whether the colors are set up properly for the particular printing process that will be used for this particular document. For example, will the document be printed with process CMYK inks or with spot-color inks? The answer determines what you need to check for and fix. You'll try out this feature now.

1 Navigate to page 1 and choose Window > Output > Separations Preview.

2 Select Separations from the View menu in the Separations Preview panel. Move the panel so that you can see the page, and adjust the panel's height so that all of the listed colors are visible. If necessary, choose View > Fit Page In Window.

3 Click the eye icon (●) next to CMYK to hide all page elements that use CMYK colors and show only elements to which spot (PANTONE) colors are applied.

► Tip: If you choose Ink Limit from the View menu in the Separations Preview panel, InDesign displays in red any areas that exceed the specified maximum ink percentage. (The default Ink Limit value is 300%.)

► Tip: Sometimes special effects are achieved in printing with spot color inks where the same ink is printed twice. This is called a second hit and must be set up in the file like an additional color.

You may have noticed that two of the PANTONE colors used in the layout share the same number (PANTONE 647). These are the same ink. The difference represents what this ink looks like when printed on different kinds of paper: Coated (C) and Uncoated (U). In the vast majority of projects printed with spot

color inks, there is only one plate for each ink. So if this file were to print using Pantone 647, you would need to make sure that only one 647 printing plate would be produced. You'll correct this problem later using the Ink Manager.

4 Click the eye icon next to PANTONE 647 C. The title disappears. This means that the title is using the ink you turned off. Click the eye icon again to turn this ink back on.

5 Click the eye icon next to PANTONE 647 U. Now the text on the right disappears, meaning it's using this other version of the same ink. If this project is indeed printing with CMYK plus PANTONE 647, you need to correct the file so that both of these items print on the same 647 plate.

6 Click the eye icon next to CMYK and navigate to page 2. Click the eye icon next to Black. Notice that the headline disappears, but the body text is still visible. This means that the body text will print on several plates when it should be black only.

7 To investigate why and fix this, turn Black back on. Slide the page to the left so that you can see part of the body text from page 3. They are supposed to be the same, but something is wrong. Open the Paragraph Styles panel and click in the body text from page 3. The style "Body copy-no indent" is highlighted. Now click in the body copy on page 2. No paragraph style is highlighted. Now select some text at the end of the first paragraph and the beginning of the second paragraph and click the "Body copy-no indent" paragraph style to apply it to both paragraphs.

8 Turn off Black again in the Separations Preview panel. Now all of the text that you expect to be black disappears. This is because the Character Color is part of the Paragraph Style, and that color is Black. You can see how using Paragraph Styles can prevent many errors, including text in the wrong color.

9 Choose Off from the View menu in the Separations Preview panel to enable viewing of all colors, and then close the panel.

10 Choose File > Save.

Creating a preflight profile

When the live preflight feature is enabled (that is, when On is selected in the Preflight panel), the default working profile, called [Basic], is used to preflight your InDesign documents. This profile checks for basic output conditions, such as missing or modified graphic files, unresolved caption variables, inaccessible URL links, overset text, and missing fonts.

You can also create your own custom preflight profiles or load profiles from your print service provider or another source. When you create a custom preflight profile, you specify the conditions you want to detect. Here's how to create a profile that alerts you when non-CMYK colors are used in a layout:

1 If the Preflight panel is not open, choose Window > Output > Preflight, and then choose Define Profiles from the Preflight panel flyout menu.

2 Click the New Preflight Profile button (+) on the lower-left side of the Preflight Profiles dialog box to create a new preflight profile. In the Profile Name box, enter **CMYK Colors Only**.

3 Click the triangle to the left of Color to display color-related options, and select Color Spaces And Modes Not Allowed.

4 Click the triangle to the left of Color Spaces And Modes Not Allowed, and then select all of the available options except CMYK and Gray (RGB, Lab, and Spot Color). Gray works with CMYK because it prints on the black plate only. Deselect Cyan, Magenta or Yellow Plates Not Allowed. (This would be perfect for a spot color preflight profile.)

5 Leave existing preflight criteria for Links, Images And Objects, Text, and Document as is. Click Save, and then click OK.

6 Choose CMYK Colors Only from the Profile menu in the Preflight panel. Notice the additional errors listed in the Error section of the panel.

7 Click the triangle next to Color to expand the display, and then click the triangle next to Color Space Not Allowed to see a list of objects that do not use the CMYK color model. Click various objects to view information about the problem and how to fix it. (Make sure the Info section of the Preflight panel is visible. If not, click the triangle to the left of Info to display it.)

8 When you're done viewing information, choose [Basic] (working) from the Profile menu to return to the default profile used for this lesson.

Managing colors

One of the best practices when making sure a file is ready for commercial printing is to make sure that only the colors actually used appear in the Swatches panel, and that all colors used are shown.

▶ **Tip:** Notice the color called TRUMATCH 35-b3. Trumatch is a library of color swatches built into InDesign that is specific to the CMYK printing process.

1 To quickly find all unused swatches, choose Select All Unused from the Swatches panel flyout menu. Notice that several versions of the blue color are used in the file, including an RGB version. This commonly happens in the creative process, but it should be the same blue throughout, so this must be fixed. Choose Delete Swatch from the panel menu to remove the unused swatches.

2 Choose Add Unnamed Colors from the Swatches panel flyout menu. Two colors appear that were not there before. (This happens when you create colors in the Color panel and use them but don't take the step of adding them to the Swatches panel.) What we are concerned with here is whether these colors are using inks that will work with this file. These are CMYK colors, so they are not a problem.

Select All Unused Colors.

Add Unnamed Colors.

Choose the right swatch library

Swatch libraries are a way to have a large array of colors ready to choose from when creating a design. But be aware that some swatch libraries consist of custom inks and if your project is not actually printing with those inks, you may not get the result you expect. The most popular custom ink swatch library is the Pantone Solid Coated library. Pantone inks (and all spot colors) are like custom-mixed paint. They are not created with CMYK ink mixes. Some can be matched with CMYK ink mixes, but many cannot. You should know the printing process that will be used to produce your document and use a swatch library that corresponds to that process.

Using the Ink Manager

The Ink Manager provides control over the inks used at output time. Changes you make using the Ink Manager affect the output, not how the colors are defined in the document.

The Ink Manager options are especially useful to clean up how inks will print without having to go back and change imported graphics. For example, if a publication will be printed with CMYK process inks but it uses a spot color, the Ink Manager provides the option of changing the spot color to the equivalent CMYK process color. If a document contains two similar spot colors when only one is required, or if the same spot color has two different names, the Ink Manager lets you map the variations to a single spot color.

Next, you'll learn how to use the Ink Manager to convert a spot color to a CMYK color, and you'll create an ink alias so that the desired number of separations is created when the document is output as color separations.

1 Click the Swatches panel icon or choose Window > Color > Swatches to open the Swatches panel, and then choose Ink Manager from the Swatches panel menu.

2 In the Ink Manager dialog box, click the spot icon (◨) to the left of the PANTONE 647 C color swatch. It changes to a CMYK icon (◪). The color will now print as a combination of CMYK colors instead of printing on its own, separate color plate. Click OK and close the Ink Manager.

3 Now open the Separations Preview again, and see that PANTONE 647 C is no longer there. PANTONE 647 U still shows as a separate ink. We'll deal with that next.

● **Note:** You can also open the Ink Manager by choosing Ink Manager from the Separations Preview panel menu (Window > Output > Separations Preview).

The All Spots To Process option at the bottom of the Ink Manager dialog box lets you convert all spot colors to process colors. This is a good solution if you want to limit the printing to four-color process without having to change the spot colors in the source files of the imported graphics. However, if the spot color graphics use transparency, the results from Ink Manager are not reliable. In those cases, you must open the graphic and change the spot colors to process in the original

application. In fact, Adobe Illustrator displays the following warning when you save a file in which transparency effects have been applied to spot color objects.

Tip: If the file will in fact print with spot inks, you can use transparency effects without a problem, as long as you are careful that the effect uses the same inks as the rest of the file.

4 Now we'll combine the two versions of the same spot color so that only one spot ink separation will be produced. This is what you would do if the job were printing with CMYK plus PANTONE 647. Open the Ink Manager again and click the CMYK icon (▣) to the left of the PANTONE 647 C color swatch to change it back to a spot ink. Then click PANTONE 647 U. Click the Ink Alias drop-down menu and choose PANTONE 647 C. This remaps all 647 U objects to print on the same plate as 647 C. Click OK.

Previewing transparency effects

Documents that contain objects to which transparency effects have been applied, such as drop shadows, opacity, and blending modes, used to need to undergo a process called *flattening* when they were printed or exported. Flattening divides transparent artwork into vector-based areas and rasterized areas. This was needed before image processors at commercial printing companies and office laser printers understood transparency.

Modern image processors *do* understand transparency. You will get the best results by *not* flattening, and instead using Live Transparency. The Flattener Preview panel in InDesign can help you see which objects in the file are using transparency effects so that you can make sure that you've used them purposefully and not by accident.

Some of the objects in this magazine use transparency effects. Next, you'll use the Flattener Preview panel to determine the objects to which transparency effects have been applied and the areas on the page that are affected by transparency.

1 Navigate to page 1 and choose View > Fit Spread In Window.

2 Choose Window > Output > Flattener Preview, and then position the Flattener Preview panel so that you can see the entire page.

3 In the Flattener Preview panel, choose Transparent Objects from the Highlight menu. The entire page is displayed with a dimmed grayscale preview, except for the areas with transparency effects.

4 If it's not already selected, choose [High Resolution] from the Preset menu.

Notice how two of the objects at the top of the page are displayed with a red highlight. These are objects to which transparency effects, such as a blending mode, opacity, drop shadow, or any of nine additional special effects, are applied. You can use this highlight to help identify areas of your layout that may be unintentionally affected by transparency so that you can adjust either your layout or your transparency settings accordingly.

▶ **Tip:** Transparency can be applied in Photoshop, in Illustrator, or directly in an InDesign layout. The Flattener Preview panel identifies transparent objects, regardless of whether the transparency was created using InDesign or imported from another application.

5 Scroll or click through to the next spread. Now nothing is highlighted in red, and the spread looks the same as when the Flattener preview is off. That's because there are no objects with transparency on this spread. Scroll or click through to the last page. Once again, the page is displayed with a dimmed grayscale preview, except for the areas with transparency effects.

6 Choose None from the Highlight menu to disable the Flattener preview, and then close the panel.

Previewing the page

Now that you've previewed the color separations and areas of transparency in the layout, you'll preview the page to get an idea of how the magazine will look when printed.

1 If you need to change the display magnification, Choose View > Fit Spread In Window.

2 At the bottom of the Tools panel, click and hold down the Screen Mode button (▦), and then choose Preview from the menu. All guides, frame edges, invisible characters, pasteboard, and other nonprinting items are hidden. This is the best onscreen view of how the document will look when it is printed and trimmed.

▶ **Tip:** You can also toggle between the different screen modes by choosing a mode from the Screen Mode control in the Application bar.

3 Click and hold down the Screen Mode button, and then choose Bleed. Additional space outside the perimeter of the final document size is displayed. This confirms that the color background extends beyond the edge of the document, ensuring complete coverage in the printed piece. After the job is printed, this excess area is trimmed to the final printed size.

4 Scroll the entire document and look over everything before printing or exporting. In Bleed mode, you can see whether items at the edge are extended far enough into the pasteboard, in addition to looking at everything you can see in Preview mode.

5 Choose Normal from the Screen Mode menu.

After confirming that the file looks acceptable, you are ready to print it.

Creating an Adobe PDF proof

If your documents need to be reviewed by others, you can easily create Adobe PDF (Portable Document Format) files to transfer and share. There are several benefits to this convenient format: Files are compressed to a smaller size, all fonts and graphic links are self-contained in a single composite file, and files are displayed onscreen and print the same whether opened on a PC or a Mac. InDesign exports directly to Adobe PDF.

Saving a composite of your publication as an Adobe PDF document also has many advantages for printing. You can create a compact, reliable file that you or your service provider can view, edit, organize, and proof. Your service provider can either output the Adobe PDF file directly or process it using tools from various sources for such post-processing tasks as preflight checks, trapping, imposition, and color separation.

You will now create an Adobe PDF file suitable for review and proofing purposes.

1 Choose File > Export.

▶ **Tip:** The presets available in the Adobe PDF Preset menu are used for creating a range of Adobe PDF files, from small files suitable for onscreen viewing to Press-Ready files suitable for high-resolution output.

2 Choose Adobe PDF (Print) from the Save As Type (Windows) or Format (macOS) menu. For the filename, type **13_Press_Proof.pdf**. If necessary, navigate to the Lesson13 folder, and then click Save. The Export Adobe PDF dialog box opens.

3 In the Adobe PDF Preset menu, choose [High Quality Print]. This setting creates PDF files suitable for output on desktop printers and proofers and for onscreen proofing, without creating a file that is too large to easily share or with too low resolution to be able to proof any raster graphics.

Note: Adobe PDF (Print) export in InDesign is performed in the background, which enables you to continue working while an Adobe PDF is being created. If you try to close your document before the background process is completed, InDesign will display a warning message.

Select View PDF After Exporting. Automatically viewing the PDF file after exporting is an efficient way of checking the results of the file export process.

The Export Layers menu lets you choose the layers to be exported when creating the PDF. For this exercise, use the default option: Visible & Printable Layers.

4 Click Export. An Adobe PDF file is generated and displays on your monitor in Adobe Acrobat Pro DC or Adobe Acrobat Reader DC.

5 Review the Adobe PDF, and then return to InDesign. This type of PDF is appropriate to share with colleagues or customers for review purposes, or to print to an office printer for review.

Tip: You can view the PDF export progress by opening the Background Tasks panel (Window > Utilities > Background Tasks).

Creating a Press-Ready PDF and saving a PDF preset

InDesign files are submitted to commercial printers either as native files (which we'll learn about later in this chapter) or as Press-Ready PDFs. Press-Ready PDFs are high resolution and include the bleed area. You will now learn about creating an Adobe PDF file suitable for commercial printing.

InDesign includes a PDF export preset called [Press Quality]. However, it does not work for documents that include any objects that bleed. You will start with that preset and modify it so that you have a Press-Ready preset that includes the bleed.

1 Choose File > Adobe PDF Presets > Define. Scroll down to [Press Quality], select it, and click New. This enables creating a new preset based on the options already set up in the default Press Quality preset.

2 In the top field, change the name to **Press Quality with Bleed**.

3 Click the Marks And Bleeds settings. Make the following changes: Turn on Crop Marks. Make the Crop Mark Offset **0p9**. Make the bleed **0p9**. Click the Same Settings icon (⬚) to set the same bleed settings on all sides.

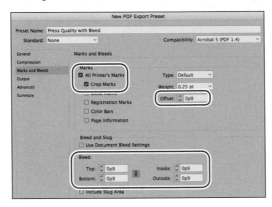

4 Click OK and then Done. This preset will now be available whenever you export to PDF.

5 Choose File > Adobe PDF Presets > Press Quality with Bleed. Name the file **13_Press_HighRes.pdf**, then click save, and then Export. When the PDF opens in Acrobat, notice how the cover photo extends past the crop marks. The crop marks indicate where the blade will cut through the paper to trim the magazine to the final size. In this case, it will cut through the printed image and produce a clean edge with no paper showing at the edge.

The most important settings in creating a PDF for commercial printing are:

* High resolution for raster graphics

* Including the bleed

* PDF compatibility of at least Acrobat 5 so that transparency effects are not flattened

The preset you have made does all of these things. However, you may want to edit it. For example, you may want to increase the version of Acrobat compatibility because you know that everyone in your production workflow is up to date and there is no reason to be compatible back to Acrobat 5.

6 To confirm whether the PDF will have live transparency or will be flattened, choose File > Adobe PDF Presets > Define > Press Quality with Bleed. Choose Edit. Click Advanced from the column on the left to see those settings. Notice

that the Transparency Flattener settings are dimmed and not available. Now change the Compatibility setting to Acrobat 4. The Transparency Flattener settings are now available because exporting to Acrobat 4 means exporting to a file format that does not understand transparency, and therefore you must compensate for that by flattening these effects. Click Cancel and then Done.

Printing a proof and saving a print preset

InDesign makes it easy to print documents to a variety of output devices. In this part of the lesson, you'll create a print preset to save settings—and save time in the future—without having to individually set each option for the same device. The process is very similar to saving a PDF preset. This preset will be for proofing on your office printer, assuming the printer has only Letter or A4 paper.

1 Choose File > Print.

2 From the Printer menu in the Print dialog box, choose your inkjet or laser printer.

 The options you see throughout this lesson will be different depending on the device selected. Follow the steps with your printer's options as best as you can.

3 On the left side of the Print dialog box, click the Setup category, and then choose the following options:

 • Paper Size: US Letter (or A4)

 • Orientation: Portrait

 • Scale To Fit

4 On the left side of the Print dialog box, click the Marks And Bleed category, and then choose these options:

 • Crop Marks

 • Page Information

 • Use Document Bleed Settings

Tip: If you need to create a flattened Press-Ready PDF, use the [High Resolution] flattener preset in the Advanced panel of the Export Adobe PDF dialog box.

Note: If you do not have access to a printer, you can choose PostScript File from the Printer menu. If you do, you can choose an Adobe PDF PPD (if available) and complete all of the steps in the remainder of the lesson. If no other PPDs are available, you can choose the Device Independent PPD; however, some of the controls covered in the remainder of the lesson are not available if you choose Device Independent.

Tip: The preview pane in the lower-left corner of the Print dialog box shows how the page area, marks, and bleed area will print.

5 In the Offset box, enter a value of **0p9**.

The crop marks print outside of the page area and provide guides showing where the final document is trimmed after printing, just as we saw in the Press-Ready PDF. The page information automatically adds the document name and the page number, along with the date and time it was printed, to the bottom of the printout. Because the crop marks and page information are printed outside the page edges, it's necessary to choose Scale To Fit to fit everything onto a Letter or A4 piece of paper.

Selecting Use Document Bleed Settings causes InDesign to print objects that extend outside the edge of the page area. This option eliminates the need for entering the amount of extra area that should be imaged, because that value is set up in the Document Setup. If no bleed was set up there, it would be necessary to enter values here.

● **Note:** You can have InDesign maintain the existing colors used in a job by choosing Composite Leave Unchanged in the Color Management section of the Print dialog box. Certain printers, such as an RGB proofer, may not let you choose Composite CMYK.

▶ **Tip:** If your document contains transparency that is flattened during the printing process, select Simulate Overprint in the Output section of the Print dialog box when printing for the best print result.

6 On the left side of the Print dialog box, click the Output category. Choose Composite CMYK from the Color menu. (If you are printing to a black-and-white printer, choose Composite Gray.)

Choosing Composite CMYK causes any RGB colors, including those in RGB graphics, to be converted to CMYK at the time of printing. This setting changes neither the original, placed graphic files nor any colors applied to objects.

7 On the left side of the Print dialog box, click the Graphics category. Choose Optimized Subsampling from the Send Data menu.

When Optimized Subsampling is selected, InDesign sends only the image data necessary for the printer selected in the Print dialog box. This can reduce the time it takes to send the file to print. To have the complete high-resolution graphic information sent to the printer, which may take longer to image, select All from the Send Data menu.

● **Note:** The Optimized Subsampling option cannot be selected if you are using the Device Independent PPD, because this generic driver can't determine what information a selected printer may need later.

8 Choose Subset from the Fonts Download menu. This causes only the fonts and characters that are actually used in the document to be sent to the output device and can reduce the time it takes to print single-page documents and short documents without much text.

The Color Management category enables you to set options that provide control over how colors are printed across different devices. You'll use the default settings for this lesson.

9 On the left side of the Print dialog box, click the Advanced category and choose [Medium Resolution] from the Transparency Flattener Preset menu.

10 Click Save Preset at the bottom of the Print dialog box, name the preset **Proof fit to page**, and click OK.

▶ **Tip:** To quickly print using a preset, choose File > Print Presets and select the device preset. Holding down the Shift key while doing this will print using the settings in the selected preset without opening the Print dialog box.

11 Click Print.

Creating a print preset saves Print dialog box settings so you don't need to individually set every option each time you print to the same device. You can create multiple presets to meet various quality needs of individual printers you may use and your various project needs. When you want to use these settings in the future, you can choose them from the Print Preset menu at the top of the Print dialog box.

Print Booklet

A very useful way to proof documents that will be stitched into a booklet, as opposed to a flat postcard, is to use the Print Booklet feature. This enables you to make a proof on paper that will be constructed similarly to the commercially printed booklet. When you print a document this way, you can fold the stack of pages in half, staple them on the spine, and page through the proof to review.

1 Choose File > Print Booklet.

2 Click Print Settings and change the Setup > Orientation to Landscape or Horizontal. Click OK. Leave the Booklet Type set to 2-up Saddle Stitch.

3 Click Preview. Notice how the last page is next to the cover. This is called a printer's spread—in this case, the outside covers.

4 Click Cancel (or print the document if you choose). Open the file named 13_SixteenPager.indd. Choose File > Print Booklet and follow the same steps as in steps 2 and 3 above. Click through the spreads using the arrows and slider at the bottom of the preview window. This file has large page numbers on it so that you can easily see how the pages fit together in printer spreads. Click Cancel (or Print the document if you choose), and then close the 13_SixteenPager.indd file.

Packaging files

The Package command assembles a copy of your InDesign document and all linked items, including graphics, into a single, convenient folder. InDesign also copies the fonts needed for printing when you package a document. Now you'll package the files for the magazine in preparation for sending them to your print provider. Packaging ensures that all project components required for output are provided. This process, along with a Press-Ready PDF, are the two industry-standard ways of providing an InDesign project to a commercial printer.

● **Note:** Typekit Desktop fonts available as part of your Creative Cloud membership are not included when you use the Package command.

1 Choose File > Package. The Summary section of the Package dialog box notifies you of one more printing-related issue.

Because the document contains RGB images, InDesign alerts you to their presence. This alert is standard because some printers want you to convert all images to CMYK before submitting the file. But others want to do the conversion from RGB to CMYK using standards for their presses, so notice this alert, but don't change anything. A best practice is to talk to your print provider and ask what they prefer.

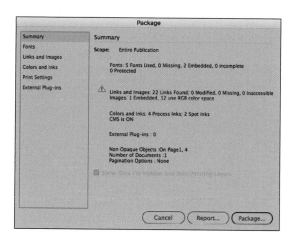

2. Click Package. If asked to save the document, click Save.

3. In the Printing Instructions dialog box, type a filename for the file that accompanies the InDesign document (for example, "Info for Printer") in the Filename box, and also include your contact information. Click Continue.

 InDesign uses this information to create a text file of instructions that will accompany the InDesign file, links, and fonts in the package folder. The recipient of the package can use the instructions file to better understand what you want done and how to contact you if there are questions.

4. In the Create Package Folder dialog box, browse to locate the Lesson13 folder. Notice that the folder that will be created for the package is named 13_Press Folder. InDesign automatically names the folder based on the document name, which you assigned at the beginning of this lesson, but you can change this name as you wish.

5. Confirm that the following options are selected:

 • Copy Fonts (Except CJK and Typekit)

 • Copy Linked Graphics

 • Update Graphic Links In Package

 • Include IDML (so that others can open the file in a previous version of InDesign if necessary)

 • Include PDF(Print) (so that you can't forget to send a PDF proof along with the native files)

> **Tip:** When Copy Fonts (Except CJK and Typekit) is selected in the Create Package Folder dialog box, InDesign generates a folder called "Document fonts" in the package folder. If you open an InDesign file located in the same folder with the Document fonts folder, InDesign will activate these fonts for you and make them available only for that document while it's open.

> **Note:** IDML stands for InDesign Markup Language. IDML files can be opened in an earlier version of InDesign, while native InDesign files can only be opened in the same version in which they were last saved or a later version.

- ☑ Copy Fonts (Except CJK and Typekit)
- ☑ Copy Linked Graphics
- ☑ Update Graphic Links In Package
- ☐ Use Document Hyphenation Exceptions Only
- ☐ Include Fonts and Links From Hidden and Non-Printing Content

- ☑ Include IDML
- ☑ Include PDF(Print) Select PDF Preset: [High Quality Print]

6 Choose [High Quality Print] for the Select PDF Preset.

7 Click Package.

8 Read the warning message that informs you about the licensing restrictions that may affect your ability to include the fonts when you send the file, and then click OK.

9 Switch to Explorer (Windows) or Finder (macOS), and then navigate to the 13_Press Folder in the Lesson13 folder (located inside the Lessons folder within the InDesignCIB folder on your hard drive). Open the folder.

Notice that InDesign created a duplicate version of your document and also copied all fonts, graphics, and other linked files necessary for high-resolution printing. Because you selected Update Graphic Links In Package, the duplicate InDesign file now links to the copied graphic files located in the package folder instead of to the original linked files. This makes the document easier for a printer or service provider to manage and also makes the package file ideal for archiving.

10 When you have finished viewing its contents, close 13_Press Folder and return to InDesign. Typically, this folder is zipped and uploaded to the service provider with the included PDF serving as the proof for them to check their work.

Congratulations! You've completed this lesson.

Exploring on your own

1 Create new print presets by choosing File > Print Presets > Define. Define presets to use for oversized formats or for printing to various color or black-and-white output devices you may use. For example, if you have a printer that uses tabloid paper, create a preset that allows you to print letter size pages at full size with bleed.

2 Practice using the Press Quality with Bleed preset you saved with other documents, such as those from other lessons in this book or your own files.

3 Practice using the Package function with other documents, such as those from other lessons in this book or your own files. Examine the contents of the resulting folder to become familiar with what is needed when sending your file to a service provider such as a commercial printer.

4 Learn how to open imported graphics that need to be fixed for printing. Click a graphic from the Links panel. Choose Edit With from the Links panel flyout menu. Choose Photoshop to open raster images and Illustrator to open vector graphics. Make changes to the imported art, and save close the file. Go back to InDesign and update the links.

Review questions

1 What problems does InDesign look for when using the [Basic] (working) profile in the Preflight panel?

2 What elements does InDesign gather when it packages a file?

3 What are the three most important characteristics of a Press-Ready PDF file?

4 What functions does the Ink Manager provide?

5 What are the two industry-standard ways of sending files to a service provider such as a commercial printer?

Review answers

1 You can confirm that all items necessary for high-resolution printing are available by choosing Window > Output > Preflight. By default, the Preflight panel confirms that all fonts used in the document or inside placed graphics are available. InDesign also looks for linked graphic files and linked text files to confirm that they have not been modified since they were initially imported and also warns you of missing graphic files, unresolved caption variables, inaccessible URL links, missing fonts, and overset text frames.

2 InDesign gathers a copy of the InDesign document along with copies of all the fonts and graphics used in the original document. The original files remain untouched. If you select Include IDML, InDesign creates an .idml version of the document that can be opened in previous versions of InDesign. If you select Include PDF(Print), InDesign creates an Adobe PDF (Print) version of the document. If you choose to include a PDF, you can also choose a PDF preset.

3 High resolution, including the bleed, and using a later version of Acrobat as the file format so that transparency effects remain live and are not flattened.

4 The Ink Manager provides control over inks at output time, including the ability to convert spot colors to process colors and to map individual ink colors to different colors.

5 A Press-Ready PDF with bleed or an InDesign Package folder.

14 CREATING ADOBE PDF FILES WITH FORM FIELDS

Lesson Overview

In this lesson, you'll learn to do the following:

- Set up a workspace for forms.

- Add and configure different types of form fields.

- Learn the differences between different types of form fields.

- Use prebuilt form elements.

- Set the tab order of form fields.

- Add a Submit button to a form.

- Export an Adobe PDF (Interactive) file with form fields.

- Test your form in Adobe Acrobat Reader.

 This lesson will take approximately 45 minutes to complete.

Please log in to your account on peachpit.com to download the lesson files for this chapter, or go to the "Getting Started" section at the beginning of this book and follow the instructions under "Accessing the Lesson Files and Web Edition." Store the files on your computer in a convenient location.

We're looking for some help

Are You Interested in Volunteering?

If you share our love of animals, you can spread the love by volunteering. Can you offer a home to an orphaned cat or dog? Donate a few hours a month to a local shelter? Make a financial contribution to any of the numerous area non-profits dedicated to improving the lives of our friends in the animal kingdom? If so, please fill out and submit the form below.

First Name:

Last Name:

Address:

City:

State:

ZIP:

E-mail Address:

Click to submit your information

Submit

In what way are you best able to help?

- Adopt a pet
- Volunteer time
- Financial donation

Yes, I would like to receive your quarterly newsletter.

Please send me your newsletter in the following format:

Profile of a Recent Rescue ...

This month's featured pet is Mister Tea, a three-year-old tabby who before birth seemed destined for the feral life of his mother in the back alleys of Albuquerque, N.M. Fortunately, Mister Tea's mother was rescued shortly before he and his three siblings arrived. Mister Tea and his brother, Obiwan, were adopted by a Colorado woman and now live a life of comfortable domesticity with 24/7 outdoor access. Mister Tea remains a free spirit, but is quick to show fondess for those he trusts. He loves corned beef and hiding under a pile of crumpled up newspaper pages.

Adobe InDesign CC provides all the tools you need to create simple PDF forms, and you have the option of using Adobe Acrobat Pro DC to add features and functionality that aren't available in InDesign.

Getting started

In this lesson, you'll add several different types of form fields to a volunteer registration form, export an Adobe PDF (Interactive) file, and then open the exported file in Adobe Acrobat Reader and test the fields you created.

● **Note:** If you have not already downloaded the project files for this lesson to your computer from your Account page, make sure to do so now. See "Getting Started" at the beginning of the book.

● **Note:** If an alert informs you that the document contains links to sources that have been modified, click Update Links.

1 To ensure that the preferences and default settings of your Adobe InDesign program match those used in this lesson, move the InDesign Defaults file to a different folder following the procedure in "Saving and restoring the InDesign Defaults file" on pages 4–5.

2 Start Adobe InDesign. To ensure that the panels and menu commands match those used in this lesson, choose Window > Workspace > [Interactive For PDF], and then choose Window > Workspace > Reset Interactive For PDF. To begin working, you'll open an InDesign document that is already partially completed.

3 Choose File > Open, and open the 14_Start.indd file in the Lesson14 folder, located inside the Lessons folder within the InDesignCIB folder on your hard drive. This one-page document is a registration form. (If the Missing Fonts dialog box displays, click Sync Fonts, and then click Close after the fonts have successfully synced from Typekit.)

4 To see what the finished document looks like, open the 14_End.indd file in the Lesson14 folder.

5 Close the 14_End.indd file after you have finished examining it, or you can leave this document open for reference.

Start file.

Completed document.

PDF form.

6 Open the 14_Start.indd file and choose File > Save As, rename the document **14_PDF_Form.indd**, and save it in the Lesson14 folder.

Set up a workspace for forms

When creating a fillable form with InDesign, you'll start with a page that has already been designed. The step of taking a designed form and turning it into a form that can be filled out in a PDF uses specific tools. The Interactive For PDF workspace has many of the tools you'll need readily available. But if you customize the workspace a little, you will be that much more efficient.

1 First, drag panels off the panel dock that are not needed for forms: Page Transitions, Hyperlinks, Bookmarks, Media, and SWF Preview. Click each panel and drag it to the left over the pasteboard. These are useful for other types of interactive PDFs but are not needed for forms. Also drag the Links, Color, and Gradient panels to the pasteboard, as they won't be used for forms. It doesn't matter if some of them dock together as you drag them.

2 Close each of the panels you just dragged dragged to the pasteboard.

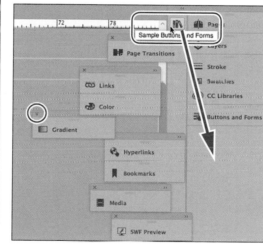

3 Drag the Sample Buttons And Forms panel under the Buttons And Forms panel. This InDesign library includes pre-built buttons for check boxes, radio buttons, buttons that can be used to submit or print a form, and some form fields.

4 Save this workspace so you can use it again. Choose Window > Workspace > New Workspace. Use a name like **Forms-Basic** or whatever makes sense to you. (For more complicated and long forms, you will want additional tools in the dock, including the Paragraph Styles, Character Styles, and Object Styles panels, as well as the Articles panel.)

Adding form fields

Some setup work on the form fields has already been done. You'll complete the form by adding some more fields and then modifying some of them.

Adding text fields

In a PDF form, a text field is a container into which the person who fills out the form can enter text. All but two of the frames have already been converted into text fields. You'll add two new frames and convert them into text fields.

● **Note:** You can simplify the display of the page by hiding Layer 1 in the Layers panel. Only the objects in the form area are displayed when you hide Layer 1.

1 Open the Layers panel. Notice that the file is set up with a separate layer, Form Elements, for the objects that are part of the form. Lock the other layer, Layer 1, so that you can work with the form objects without accidentally moving anything else.

2 Use the Zoom tool (🔍) to zoom in on the area in the top half of the page that contains the form objects. This is where all of your work in this lesson will be done.

3 Select the Selection tool (▶), and move the pointer over the text field below "First Name." Notice that a red dotted line is displayed around the object, and a small graphic of a text field is displayed at the lower right. The dotted line indicates that the object is a PDF form element; the icon of the text frame indicates that the element is a text field. Click in the text field to select the object.

● **Note:** When adjusting the appearance of a combo box, list box, text field, or signature field, keep in mind that only a solid stroke and fill are retained when you export as Adobe PDF. These attributes are visible in an exported PDF file when Highlight Existing Fields is not selected in Adobe Acrobat Reader DC or Adobe Acrobat Pro DC when the form is opened.

4 Click the Buttons And Forms panel icon (🗐) to display the Buttons And Forms panel. Notice the settings for the text field. Text Field is selected in the Type menu, and the Name of the element is First Name. Text entered in the Description field is displayed when the pointer rolls over a field to provide additional guidance to viewers who fill out a form. The Description for this field is also First Name. Printable is checked to enable printing of this form, and the Font Size is 10 because the default of 12 is just too big in many cases.

Different types of form fields have different icons in the lower-right corner. This is a text field icon.

5 Select the frame of the "First Name" form field and Alt - (Windows) or Option - (macOS) drag a copy of it to below "Last Name." Resize it to make it longer, ending in alignment with the fields below, by dragging the center right handle to the left. The Smart Guides will appear when the pointer is aligned.

6 In the Buttons And Forms panel, notice that the name of this field is First Name 1. This is an InDesign behavior to be aware of when creating forms: No fields can have the same name. InDesign enforces this rule by adding sequential numbers to the name of duplicated fields. To make this a unique field with the correct information, change both the Name and Description fields to **Last Name**.

7 To create a field from scratch, choose the Rectangle tool (▢) in the Tools panel and draw a frame under the text frame under "E-mail Address." Align the right edge with the City frame above and the top edge with the bottom of the "E-mail Address" text frame. You can convert any kind of frame—text, graphics, or unassigned—into a PDF form field. A text field does not have to be made from a text frame.

8 Now we will assign the same fill and stroke as the other text fields. An object style for the text field boxes has already been created for this lesson. Choose Window > Styles > Object Styles to open the Object Styles panel. Choose the Selection tool (▶), and click the box you just drew if it's not still selected. Click the object style called Text Field Box. Now the same fill and stroke have been applied to the new frame. Next, make the text field the same height as the other fields by changing the reference point in the Control panel to the upper left (▦) and clicking the up arrow on **H:** to **1p10**. Close the Object Styles panel.

9 In the Buttons And Forms panel, choose Text Field from the Type menu, and assign it the Name and Description **E-mail Address**. Make the Font Size **10** point and make sure that Printable and Scrollable are selected. Scrollable means that if the user types more characters than will fit in the box, the field will allow them to keep typing, but not all of the text will be visible in the field. This option is appropriate for email addresses since they can be very long.

10 Choose File > Save.

Adding either/or choices: radio buttons

Radio buttons present the person filling out the form with two or more choices, but only one choice can be selected at a time. A group of radio buttons is considered one field, with a unique value for each button. Check boxes can look like a similar list, but each check box in the list can be on or off.

Radio buttons are often simple circles; however, you can design your own, more elaborate buttons or choose from several sample buttons included with InDesign. In this lesson, you'll use one of the sample radio buttons. The prebuilt buttons in this library are simply vector shapes with various attributes for fill, stroke, and effects.

Note: Use a radio button for Either/Or choices, such as whether someone must specify a status that can have only one answer—for example, whether they are a member, non-member, or student member of an organization.

Note: Use a check box when a question can be followed by "check as many as apply." For example, a training school might ask, "Which programs are you interested in?" Then list several, such as InDesign, Photoshop, Illustrator, and Acrobat. The person filling out the form could be interested in more than one.

1 Choose View > Fit Page In Window, and then use the Zoom tool (🔍) to magnify the "In what way are you best able to help?" portion of the form.

2 Choose the Sample Buttons And Forms panel (📇) that you dragged below the Buttons And Forms panel (🗏) in the dock to display the Sample Buttons And Forms panel.

3 Drag the radio button named "018" from the Sample Buttons And Forms panel and position it below the text frame with the text "In what way are you best able to help?" Close the panel by clicking the double arrows (») at the upper right of the panel. Align the top of the topmost radio button with the top of the line of text to the right. Refer to the screen capture below for the correct position.

4 In the Control panel, make sure that the upper-left reference point is selected in the reference point locator (⊞), enter **40%** in either of the Scale Percentage boxes, make sure that the link for the Same Settings button (🔗) is selected, and then press Enter or Return. If necessary, move the buttons to match the figure below.

Radio buttons before being scaled. After being scaled 40%.

5 With all three buttons still selected, in the Buttons And Forms panel, enter **Form of Assistance** in the Name and Description boxes, and then press Enter or Return. Notice that the Type is already set to Radio Button.

6 Choose Edit > Deselect All or click an empty area of the page or pasteboard.

7 Use the Selection tool (▶) to select the first radio button (to the left of "Adopt a pet").

8 In the Buttons And Forms panel, enter **Adopt a pet** in the Button Value field at the bottom of the panel, and then press Enter or Return. Under Appearance, click [Normal Off]. This means that when the user first opens the form, the button will be unselected.

9 Repeat steps 7 and 8 to change the Button Value of the middle button **Volunteer time** and the bottom button **Financial donation**. Notice that the name of the field is the same for all three buttons; only the Button Value changes.

10 Choose File > Save.

Adding yes or no choices: check boxes

A check box presents a yes-or-no choice for an individual item. A viewer of the form can click the empty check box (the default setting in the exported PDF) to add a check mark or leave it unchecked. Next, you'll add a check box.

1 Use the Selection tool (▶) to drag the check box named "001" from the Sample Buttons And Forms panel, and place it so that the top of the check mark that extends above the box aligns with the top of the text frame that contains "Yes, I would like to receive your quarterly newsletter."

2 Press Shift+Ctrl (Windows) or Shift+Command (macOS) and scale the check box graphic so that it is the same height as the text frame to the right.

3 In the Buttons And Forms panel, enter **Receive Newsletter** in the Name field, and then press Enter or Return. Notice that the Type is already set to Check Box and that the icon for the field is a check mark. In the Description field, enter **Check here if you'd like to receive our newsletter**.

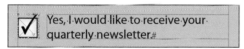

Check box after being scaled.

4 The check box and radio buttons that you dragged from the Sample Buttons And Forms panel should have red highlights because they should be on the Form Elements layer. Items that you drag from the library should be added to the active layer. As you work, it's a good practice to check that elements are on the layer where they belong. This helps keep your work organized and will be especially important when you work on complicated forms. Select all the buttons you dragged from the library with the Selection tool (▶) and open the Layers panel. If the new items are not on the Form Elements layer, correct this by dragging the square in the Layers panel to the Form Elements layer.

5 Choose File > Save.

Adding a list of choices: combo box

A combo box is a menu that lists multiple predefined choices. A viewer of the form can select only one of the choices. Next, you'll create a combo box that offers three choices.

Note: List boxes are similar to combo boxes in that you add list items; however, combo boxes allow you to select only one item from a list in the PDF form. If you select Multiple Selection for a list box, a viewer of the PDF can select more than one choice.

1 Use the Selection tool (▶) to select the text frame below the heading "Please send me your newsletter in the following format:."

2 In the Buttons And Forms panel, choose Combo Box from the Type menu, and then enter **Newsletter Format** in the Name field. In the Description field, enter **Choose which way you'd like to receive our newsletter**. Change the Font Size to **10**. To provide the viewer of the PDF form with different choices, you'll add three list items.

3 In the lower half of the Buttons And Forms panel, in the List Items box, enter **Print Publication: Standard Mail**, and then click the plus sign to the right of the box. Notice that the text you entered is now displayed in the list below the box.

4 Repeat the previous step to add **Adobe PDF: E-mail Attachment** and **ePUB: E-mail Attachment** to the list.

▶ **Tip:** To sort list items alphabetically, select Sort Items in the Buttons And Forms panel. You can also modify the order of list items by dragging them up or down in the list.

▶ **Tip:** To display a combo box without a default selection, make sure that none of the list items is selected. When a list item is selected, it becomes the default selection when the PDF is opened.

5 Click Print Publication: Standard Mail in the list of items to make it the default selection. When a viewer opens the exported PDF file, Print Publication: Standard Mail will already be selected.

6 Choose File > Save.

Setting the tab order of the fields

The tab order you establish for a PDF form determines the order in which fields are selected as a user of the form presses the Tab key. These must be in a logical order to make the form user-friendly. Next, you'll set the tab order for the fields on the page.

1 From the Object menu, choose Interactive > Set Tab Order.

2 In the Tab Order dialog box, click Last Name (the name of the text field you created that holds the surname of the person filling out the form), and then click Move Up until it appears below First Name near the top of the list. Use the Move Up and Move Down buttons or drag field names up or down to rearrange them so that they match the order on the page. Click OK to close the dialog box.

Tab order before being rearranged.

You can drag more than one field at a time.

After being rearranged.

3 Choose File > Save.

Adding a button to submit the form

If you distribute a PDF form, you'll want to include a way for anybody who fills out the form to return it to you electronically. To accomplish this, you'll create a button that sends the filled-out PDF form to your email address.

1 Use the Selection tool (▶) to select the rounded-corner text frame with a blue fill and the text "Submit."

2 In the Buttons And Forms panel, choose Button from the Type menu, enter **Submit Form** in the Name field, and then press Enter or Return. Enter **Send the completed form via email** for the Description.

3 Click the Add New Action For Selected Event (**+**) button, and then choose Submit Form from the drop-down menu.

4 In the URL field, enter **mailto:**. Make sure you enter a colon after "mailto". Do not enter a space or a period before or after the colon.

5 Enter your email address (for example, pat_smith@domain.com) after mailto:. This will return the completed form to you.

To cause the button's appearance to change when a user of the PDF form moves the pointer over the Submit button, you'll add a Rollover appearance.

6 Click [Rollover] in the Buttons And Forms panel. Open the Swatches panel, enter **50** in the Tint field, press Enter or Return, and then close the panel.

7 Return to the Buttons And Forms panel. Notice that the [Rollover] appearance is now lighter than the [Normal] appearance, reflecting the tint change you just made. Click [Normal] to display the default appearance.

Tip: Any object or group can be converted into a button. For example, a text frame with a fill color and the text "Submit" could become a Submit button. To convert a selected object or group into a button, choose Button from the Type menu in the Buttons And Forms panel.

Tip: A button's appearance can have three different states. The state that's displayed depends on the user's interaction. The Normal state is the default display when no interaction occurs; the Rollover state displays when the mouse pointer is over the button; and the Click state displays when the mouse button is clicked.

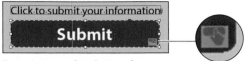

Zoom in to see that the icon for
the button is a finger pointing to a
rounded-corner rectangle.

8 Open the Layers panel (Windows > Layers) and make sure all layers are visible
(in case you hid Layer 1 earlier in the lesson).

9 Choose File > Save.

Exporting an interactive Adobe PDF file

Now that you've finished work on the form fields, you're ready to export an interactive Adobe PDF file and then test the exported file.

1 Choose File > Export.

2 In the Export dialog box, choose Adobe PDF (Interactive) from the Save As Type
menu (Windows) or Format menu (macOS). Name the file **14_PDF_Form.pdf**
and save it to the Lesson14 folder, located inside the Lessons folder within the
InDesignCIB folder on your hard drive. Click Save.

3 In the General tab, in the Options section of the Export To Interactive PDF dialog
box, make sure that Include All is selected for Forms And Media. This most
important setting makes the
form fields work in the PDF.

4 Choose Fit Page from the
View menu in the Export To
Interactive PDF dialog box to
display the entire page when
the exported PDF is opened.
Leave all other settings
unchanged. Click Export,
and then click OK to close
the alert about document
color conversion.

Form field types

 Button: The most versatile interactive element. A button can trigger many actions.

 Check box: For yes or no choices, a check box is either checked or not checked. Use check boxes for "Check all that apply" questions.

 Combo box: The user can choose only one answer from a list.

 List box: Similar to a combo Box except that the user can choose more than one answer.

 Radio button: For either/or choices, the user can choose only one answer.

 Signature field: Enables the user to sign a form with a digital signature.

 Text field: For the user to type text information.

Testing your form in Adobe Acrobat Reader

You should always test your forms in Adobe Acrobat Reader because the end-user is most likely to use that when filling out the form. (Most people do not have Adobe Acrobat Pro.) If you do not have Adobe Acrobat Reader, install it now. The current version is called Adobe Acrobat Reader DC. It's a free download at https://get.adobe.com/reader/.

1 Open Adobe Acrobat Reader and open the PDF you just exported. First, click in the First Name field and press the Tab key. Continue to tab through all the fields to make sure that the tab order is correct.

2 Next, click the radio buttons under "In what way are you best able to help?" and notice that you can only turn on one choice at a time.

3 Then click the check box for "Yes, I would like to receive your quarterly newsletter" to see that it turns on. Then choose one of the newsletter formats from the drop-down menu below.

4 Move the pointer across each field, pausing for a moment, and notice the tips that pop up. These are the Descriptions that you entered in the Buttons And Forms panel for each field.

 If you find any errors, go back to the InDesign file and fix them. Then export and test again.

5 When you're done, click the button that emails the filled-out form to you. (A security warning dialog box may display when Acrobat creates an email message with the completed form as an attachment.) Click Allow and then click Continue in the next dialog box to submit the form information, or click Cancel. Return to InDesign.

6 Look at the email you received and notice the subject line: Form Returned: 14_PDF_Form.pdf. This is a default function of the Submit Form action within the Submit button. Therefore it's important to consider the name of the PDF when you create forms to be emailed.

Congratulations! You've created a PDF form and tested it.

Exploring on your own

Now that you've created a simple PDF form, you can explore a little further by creating other kinds of fields and by creating your own custom-designed buttons.

1 Open a new document, create a text frame, and then use the Buttons And Forms panel to convert it to a signature field. A signature field in a PDF form lets the user apply a digital signature to the PDF file. Assign the field a name, and then export an Adobe PDF (Interactive) file. Open Adobe Acrobat Pro DC or Adobe Acrobat Reader DC to test the signature field by clicking it and then following the onscreen instructions to create a digital signature. Click Cancel if you get a dialog box about Trusted Certificates. That is part of a system of securely identifying signatures, which is not needed for creating a signature.

2 Use the Ellipse tool (⬭) to create a small circular frame. Use the Gradient panel to fill the circle with a radial gradient. If you want, use the Swatches panel to change the colors of the gradient. Use the Buttons And Forms panel to convert the frame into a button. Assign the button the Go To URL action and enter a complete URL in the URL field (for example, http://www.adobe.com). To test this button, export an Adobe PDF (Interactive) file and click the button.

3 Experiment with one of the other prebuilt form fields in the Sample Buttons And Forms panel. Drag one onto the page, and then view its properties in the Buttons And Forms panel. Try different modifications to its appearance, change some of its properties, or both. Export and test the result.

Review questions

1 What panel lets you convert an object into a PDF form field and specify settings for form fields?

2 What is the difference between a radio button and a check box?

3 What action can you assign to a button that enables a viewer of the exported PDF form to send a copy of the filled-out form to an email address?

4 What programs can be used to open and fill out an Adobe PDF form?

5 What are the two most important things to do when exporting your InDesign file to create a fillable form PDF?

Review answers

1 The Buttons And Forms panel (Window > Interactive > Buttons And Forms) lets you convert objects into PDF form fields and specify settings for them.

2 Radio buttons are for questions that have an either/or answer; the user of the form can choose only one. Check boxes are either checked or not checked individually. So a question for which the user can choose more than one answer, or whose answer is a simple yes if the box is checked, needs a check box, not a radio button.

3 To enable the viewer of a PDF form to return a filled-out form, use the Buttons And Forms panel to assign the Submit Form action to the button. After you assign the Submit Form action, enter **mailto:** followed by an email address (for example, mailto:pat_smith@domain.com) in the URL field.

4 You can open and fill out PDF forms using Adobe Acrobat Pro DC or Adobe Acrobat Reader DC.

5 First, in the Export dialog box, choose Adobe PDF (Interactive) from the Save As Type menu (Windows) or Format menu (macOS). Then in the Options section of the General tab, make sure that Include All is selected for Forms And Media.

15 CREATING A FIXED-LAYOUT EPUB

Lesson Overview

In this lesson, you'll learn how to do the following:

- Create a new document for mobile delivery.

- Create animations using a motion preset and a motion path.

- Configure the timing of multiple animations.

- Create buttons that trigger various actions.

- Preview animations and interactivity within InDesign.

- Add a movie, a sound, a slideshow, buttons, and a hyperlink.

- Export a fixed-layout EPUB and preview it in a viewing app.

This lesson will take approximately 60 minutes to complete.

Please log in to your account on peachpit.com to download the lesson files for this chapter, or go to the "Getting Started" section at the beginning of this book and follow the instructions under "Accessing the Lesson Files and Web Edition." Store the files on your computer in a convenient location.

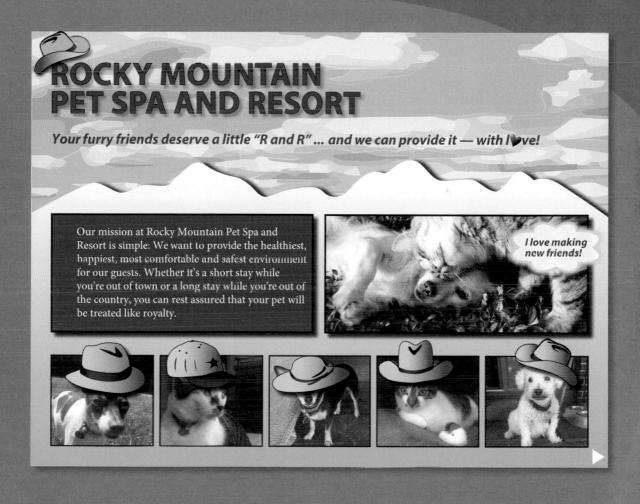

The fixed-layout EPUB capabilities of InDesign let you create media-rich publications with animations, movies, slideshows, sounds, and hyperlinks, and you can include buttons that enable viewers to perform a variety of actions, from clicking through a slideshow to playing a sound file.

Getting started

● **Note:** If you have not already downloaded the project files for this lesson to your computer from your Account page, make sure to do so now. See "Getting Started" at the beginning of the book.

In this lesson, you'll begin by creating a new InDesign document using settings appropriate for a fixed-layout EPUB. After you've set up the new document, you'll open a partially completed version of the publication, add several multimedia and interactive elements, and then save and preview a fixed-layout EPUB that can be viewed on a variety of EPUB readers.

1 To ensure that the preferences and default settings of your Adobe InDesign program match those used in this lesson, move the InDesign Defaults file to a different folder following the procedure in "Saving and restoring the InDesign Defaults file" on pages 4–5.

2 Start Adobe InDesign. To ensure that the panels and menu commands match those used in this lesson, choose Window > Workspace > [Digital Publishing], and then choose Window > Workspace > Reset Digital Publishing. This optimizes the panel arrangement for the work you'll do in this lesson and provides quick access to several of the controls you'll use.

3 To see what the finished document looks like, open the 15_End.indd file in the Lesson15 folder. (If the Missing Fonts dialog box displays, click Sync Fonts, and then click Close after the fonts have successfully synced from Typekit.) If an alert informs you that the document contains links to sources that have been modified, click Update Links.

4 Navigate through the finished document to view the cover page and the page that follows.

In all previous lessons that use sample print documents, the completed InDesign layouts look the same onscreen and in print; however, because the exported publication in this lesson is intended for display on an EPUB reader, what you seen onscreen when you open the sample files in InDesign doesn't exactly match the appearance of the exported EPUB. The following images show what the completed lesson file looks like when displayed in an ereader.

Page 1.

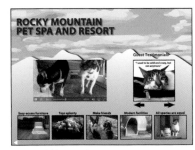

Page 2.

5 Close the 15_End.indd file after you have finished examining it, or you can leave this document open for reference.

Creating a new document for fixed-layout export

Because exported EPUBs are viewed onscreen (on mobile devices such as tablets or on desktop computers, for example) and can include elements such as buttons, animations, and video that can't be included in print documents, creating a document that's intended for export in the EPUB format differs in some ways from creating a print document. That said, all the typographic and page-layout features covered in this book are available and work the same when creating digital publications. To begin, you'll create a new mobile document.

1 Choose File > New > Document.

2 In the New Document dialog box, choose the Mobile tab and then iPad from the Page Size menu. Also specify the following:

In the Number of Pages box, type **2,** and deselect Primary Text Frame. Leave all other settings unchanged, and click Create.

<div style="float:right; width:20%;">

Note: Setting a new document's Intent to Mobile (or Web) deselects the Facing Pages option, sets the default page orientation to Landscape, and changes the unit of measurement to pixels. It also sets the Transparency Blend Space (Edit > Transparency Blend Space) to RGB and the default color swatches in the Swatches panel to Process RGB for the new document.

</div>

3 Choose File > Save As, name the file **15_Setup.indd**, navigate to the Lesson15 folder, and click Save.

Rather than creating the remainder of the document from scratch, you'll continue this lesson by opening a partially completed document that already contains most of the required objects. You can keep the 15_Setup.indd document open or close it and continue.

EPUB: reflowable versus fixed-layout

An EPUB is a document created for viewing on a device such as a tablet, rather than for printing on paper. This allows for capabilities such as adding many kinds of multimedia elements and interactive features, or reflowing text for the particular device.

The biggest difference between a fixed-layout EPUB and a reflowable EPUB, which is the other option for exporting EPUBs, is that a fixed-layout EPUB retains the design of the InDesign document (like a PDF) regardless of the device on which

it's displayed. In contrast, a reflowable EPUB displays content in a continuous thread and reflows the content based on the size of the ereader screen and the zoom level. Readers of reflowable EPUBs can change the font and font size to suit their preference.

The fixed-layout format lets you include buttons, animations, video, and audio in your publications, and viewers of fixed-layout EPUBs can view the pages and interact with the buttons and multimedia elements. This format is better suited for more design-intensive publications, such as children's books, textbooks, and comic books—anything for which the visual layout is critical to the experience for the reader. The reflowable format is the preferred choice for text-intensive publications such as fiction and non-fiction books where the visual layout is not as important.

Adding animation

Animation effects let you add movement and other visual effects to InDesign objects and groups. For example, you can animate a graphics frame by making it fly into place from outside the page, or you can fade in a text frame so that it turns from invisible to opaque. InDesign includes several *motion presets*, which are preset animations that you can quickly apply to objects. You can also use any object as a motion path for another object or group.

Next, you'll examine a group that has already been assigned animation settings that cause it to automatically "fly" onto the page when a viewer opens the exported EPUB file. You'll preview this animation within InDesign, and then you'll create some animations of your own that automatically play when the page is displayed. To complete this section, you'll adjust the timing of the animations so that they play in the desired sequence.

Using a motion preset to create animation

The quickest and easiest way to animate an object or group is to apply any of more than 40 built-in motion presets. After you apply a preset, you have several options for controlling how the animation is played, including the event that triggers the animation and the duration.

1 Choose File > Open, and then open the 15_FixedLayout_Partial file in the Lesson15 folder.

2 Choose File > Save As, name the file **15_FixedLayout.indd**, and save it in the Lesson15 folder.

Before you create an animation, you'll take a look at a group that's already had animation effects applied to it.

3 Use the Zoom tool to zoom in on the text frame in the top half of page 1 beneath the main heading that begins "and we can provide it …" and then use the Selection tool (▶) to click the text frame. A dotted-line border indicates that you've selected a group, which includes the text frame and the red, heart-shaped object.

Notice the small icon in the lower-right corner of this group of objects. This indicates that an animation has been applied to the group. Notice, too, that a green line extends from the pasteboard to the center of the group. The circle at the right end of the green line indicates the starting point of the path; the arrowhead at the left end is the end point of the path.

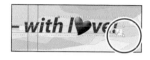 The icon in the lower-right corner indicates that the group has been animated.

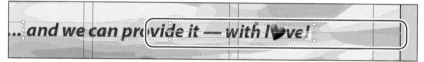

The green line indicates the path along which the group will move.

4 Choose Window > Interactive > Animation, or click the Animation icon (•᎓) to open the Animation panel. Notice that the group has a name (Animated Group), and Custom (Fly In From Right) is selected from the Preset menu. (The word "Custom" at the beginning of the preset name indicates that the default settings for this preset have been modified. You'll modify other presets later in this lesson.) On Page Load is selected in the Event(s) menu, which means the animation will start playing automatically as the page is displayed.

Clicking the triangle next to Properties in the Animation panel expands the panel and provides access to several additional animation controls.

5 To preview the animation, click the Preview Spread button () at the bottom left of the Animation panel. The EPUB Interactivity Preview panel opens. Drag the lower-right or -left corner of the panel to make it large enough to view the publication. Click the Play Preview button, which is the farthest left along the bottom control panel, and the animated headline flies in from the right side of the page. See the sidebar on the next page for a full explanation of the EPUB Interactivity Preview panel.

6 Drag the EPUB Interactivity Preview panel to the bottom of the dock, as you'll use it throughout this lesson. The panel icon (▣) displays in the dock.

Next, you'll add a preset to another group and then to a text frame, and you'll customize the settings of both animations.

1 Choose View > Fit Page In Window.

2 With the Selection tool (▶), click any of the dog or cat graphics at the bottom of the page except the one on the far left, which you will work with separately later in the lesson. Clicking any of the graphics selects the group of four graphics.

▶ **Tip:** When you choose a motion preset, a proxy preview of the animation is displayed at the top of the Animation panel. Move the pointer within the proxy window to repeat the preview of the selected preset.

3 Open the Animation panel (•ʲ) and choose Fly In From Bottom from the Preset menu. Notice how the proxy preview shows you what the preset does using a pink butterfly image. Try several presets and then return to Fly In From Bottom. Ensure that On Page Load is selected in the Event(s) menu.

4 Select the red text frame with white text. In the Animation panel, ensure that On Page Load is selected in the Event(s) menu. Apply the Fade In preset and set the Duration to 2 seconds.

5 Click the Play Preview button in the lower-left corner of the EPUB Interactivity Preview panel to view the animations. Notice that the group at the top of the page appears first, followed shortly by the group of graphics at the bottom of the page, and finally the red text frame. The sequence is a result of the order in which the animations were created. Next, you'll modify the order in which these animations play.

The EPUB Interactivity Preview panel

The EPUB Interactivity Preview panel lets you preview an InDesign document that includes multimedia, animation, and interactivity without having to switch to a separate program. You can display the panel by choosing Window > Interactive > EPUB Interactivity Preview or by clicking the Preview Spread button in the lower-left corner of the Animation, Timing, Media, Object States, or Buttons And Forms panels.

You can perform the following functions in the EPUB Interactivity Preview panel:

- Play Preview (▶): Click to play a preview of the document. Alt-click (Windows) or Option-click (macOS) to replay the preview.

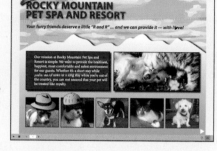

- Clear Preview (■): Click to clear the preview.

- Navigate between previous page (◀) and next page (▶): Click the left or right arrows to navigate between previous and next pages. Preview Document Mode must be enabled to navigate to the previous or next page. Click Play to enable the previous page and next page buttons.

- Set Preview Spread Mode (▢): Click to set the mode to preview spread mode. This is the default mode and is especially useful for testing interactive elements on the current page.

- Set Preview Document Mode (▢): Click to set the mode to preview document mode. This mode allows you to run through each page of the document and test the interactive elements.

- Collapse/Expand panel (◊): Click to expand/collapse the EPUB Interactivity Preview panel.

Adjusting the timing of animations

The Timing panel lists the animations on a page or spread and lets you change the order in which animations are played, play animations simultaneously, or delay animations. You'll use the Timing panel to change the order in which the three animations on page 1 are played and to play two of the animations simultaneously.

1 Choose Window > Interactive > Timing or click the Timing icon (⏱)to open the Timing panel from the dock. Ensure that On Page Load is selected in the Event menu. The three animations you worked with in the previous section are listed, along with others you'll work with later in this lesson.

2 Click Animated Group in the list of animations. Because it was created first, it's at the top of the list and will play first.

3 Drag Animated Group to the bottom of the list so that it plays last.

4 Select the Dog/Cat Group, and then Shift-click the animation named "Our mission ..." to select it as well.

5 Click the Play Together button (▻⊙) at the bottom of the Timing panel.

6 Select only the Dog/Cat Group and specify a delay of 1.5 seconds. This will delay the display of this animation when the page opens. After the delay, the Dog/Cat Group will fly in, and the red text frame will simultaneously fade in.

7 Click the Preview Spread button at the bottom of the Timing panel to open the EPUB Interactivity Preview panel, and then click Play Preview to preview the page.

8 Choose File > Save to save your work.

Buttons

● **Note:** A good way to keep organized and to make sure the buttons are on top of other content is to put the buttons on their own layer. This has already been done in the file you're using for this lesson.

Buttons are one of the most versatile tools for adding multimedia features to a publication. A button can trigger many actions. Next, you'll configure buttons to play animations and add two buttons using two different possible actions.

Using buttons to play animations

The animations you worked with in the previous section are configured to play automatically when the page in the exported EPUB is displayed. You can also create animations that play when you perform other actions, such as moving the pointer over an animated object or clicking an object or group that's been configured to work as a button.

In this section, you'll first examine an object that's already been animated and converted into a button that plays an animation. Then you'll create a new button that animates an already-animated object.

1 Use the scroll bar on the right side of the document window to scroll down slightly. You'll see a hat on the dog's head, illustration below the dog on the far left. Use the Selection tool (▶) to position the hat, matching the screen capture below, and then choose View > Fit Page In Window.

Notice the two icons in the lower-right corner of the group's bounding box: The icon on the right indicates that the group is animated; the icon on the left indicates that the group is also a button.

2 The hat illustration is made up of several paths created with the Pen tool, and the paths have been grouped together (Object > Group). With the hat group selected, open the Animation panel. Its name is HatGroup1.

Notice that the Spin preset has been applied, and Release is selected in the Event(s) menu. This means that a button will trigger the animation. The Duration and Play values show that the animation will take one second to play and will play two times.

3 Close the Animation panel and open the Buttons And Forms panel (📑), which is located in the dock on the right when you use the [Digital Publishing] workspace. Or choose Window > Interactive > Buttons And Forms. Notice that the group has been configured to work as a button that plays the HatGroup1 animation.

Buttons and Forms	» ≡
Type:	Button
Name:	HatGroup1
Event:	On Release or Tap
Actions:	+ −
☑ Animation (HatGroup1)	
Animation:	HatGroup1
Options:	Play

● **Note:** Throughout this lesson, if you have trouble with the interactivity functioning in the EPUB Interactivity Preview panel, press the Clear Preview button (■) and then press the Play button (▶) again.

4 Click the Preview Spread button (🗋) at the bottom of the Buttons And Forms panel to open the EPUB Interactivity Preview panel. After the opening animations are displayed, click the hat group to play the animation and then close the panel.

Next, you'll configure a button that animates a different object.

1 Select the hat illustration in the lower-right corner of the page.

The icon in the lower-right corner indicates that this group is animated; however, you may have noticed that when you preview the page, the group is not visible. That's because although the group is configured to fly in from above the page, there's no way to play the animation. To address this, you'll convert the accompanying pet graphic into a button.

2 Select the Rectangle Frame tool (⊠) in the Tools panel and draw a frame over the photo with the white dog in the lower-right corner of the page. You should still be on the Buttons layer, but if not, open the Layers panel and move this frame up to the Buttons layer. Make sure the frame is set to None for both Fill and Stroke. This makes an object you can use as a button that appears to be one of the visual elements on the page but is actually a separate object on the Buttons layer above, making sure you don't disturb the artwork.

The size of the frame becomes the tappable or clickable area in the EPUB, so you can use a frame with no fill and no stroke to make a button with a larger tappable area than a small graphic would have.

3 In the Buttons And Forms panel, click the + sign next to Actions: (+) and choose Animation from the drop-down menu. Then choose HatGroup5 from the Animation menu, which shows the animations in the current file.

4 Name the button **AddHat**. Always name your buttons; otherwise things will get very confusing because InDesign will automatically name them Button 1, Button 2, and so on. Make sure On Release Or Tap is selected in the Event(s) menu.

You don't need to choose a Type first because when you add an action the object is automatically turned into a button. Notice the list of possible actions, but note that the bottom group is only for PDFs. In the Buttons And Forms panel, click the triangle next to PDF Options at the bottom of the panel to close that area. You won't need those while working on an EPUB.

5 Click the Preview Spread button at the bottom of the Buttons And Forms panel to open the EPUB Interactivity Preview panel. After the opening animations are displayed, move the pointer over the photo of the white dog and click to play the new animation, and then close the panel. Notice that the pointer becomes a pointing finger when you hover over something such as this button that the reader can click to activate.

6 Choose File > Save to save your work.

Using a button to trigger custom motion paths for animations

Many of the motion presets in InDesign cause an object to move along a path. In addition to using this type of preset to animate an object, you can use any InDesign object as the path for animating another object by converting it to a motion path. Next you'll configure a button to play an animation that already has a custom path; then you'll create a custom path of your own and use it as a motion path.

1 Use the scroll bar on the right side of the document window to scroll up slightly. You'll see a hat illustration above the fourth column. Use the Selection tool (▶) to select the graphic.

As you've seen with the animations you worked on earlier, the green motion path indicates how the hat will move when the animation is played. This custom path was created in InDesign using the Pen tool.

Next, you'll convert the graphics frame at the bottom of the column into a button that plays the already-configured hat animation. Then, you'll create your own custom path for a different hat and configure a button to play it.

2 Choose View > Fit Page In Window. Select the Rectangle Frame tool (⊠) and draw a frame over the photo with the cat at the bottom of the fourth column, making sure that it has no stroke and no fill and that it is on the Buttons layer.

3 In the Buttons And Forms panel, click the + sign next to Actions: (+) and choose Animation from the drop-down menu. Then choose HatGroup4 from the Animation menu.

4 Name the button **FloatingHat1**. Make sure On Release Or Tap is selected in the Event(s) menu.

5 Click the Preview Spread button at the bottom of the Buttons And Forms panel to open the EPUB Interactivity Preview panel. After the opening animations

are displayed, move the mouse over the photo with the cat at the bottom of the fourth column. Notice that the pointer changes to a pointing hand because it is sensing the button you just created. Click to play the new animation, and then close the panel.

Now that you know how a custom motion path works, you'll create your own custom animation path and then configure a button to play it.

6 Use the scroll bar on the right side of the document window to scroll up slightly. You'll see a hat illustration above the third column.

7 Use the Pen tool (✐) to draw a zigzag path that begins near the middle of the hat and ends slightly above the middle of the dog's head in the third column. To create straight path segments rather than curved segments, make sure you click and release the mouse each time you create a point. (If you're comfortable, you can use the Pen or Pencil tool to draw a more complex path.)

8 Use the Selection tool to select both the hat group above the third column and the line you just created, and then click Convert To Motion Path (✐→) at the bottom of the Animation panel. On Page Load is selected in the Event(s) menu. Deselect it by choosing On Page Load again and set the Duration to 2 seconds.

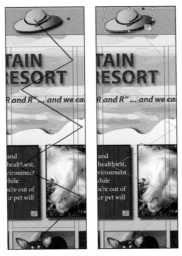

Left: Create path with Pen tool.
Right: After converting to motion path.

9 Select the Rectangle Frame tool (⊠) and draw a frame over the photo of the dog at the bottom of the third column, making sure that it has no stroke and no fill and that it is on the Buttons layer.

10 Click the + sign next to Actions in the Buttons And Forms panel (+) and choose Animation from the drop-down menu. Then choose HatGroup3 from the Animation menu. Name the button **FloatingHat2**.

11 Click the Preview Spread button at the bottom of the Buttons And Forms panel to open the EPUB Interactivity Preview panel. After the opening animations are displayed, click the dog photo in the third column (which is the button you just configured to play the new animation), and then close the panel.

If you need to modify the position of the endpoint of the motion path so that the hat is placed accurately at the end of the animation, use the Selection tool (▶) to select the hat group; then switch to the Direct Selection tool (▷) and use it to move the endpoint of the path or, optionally, to modify other points or segments of the path.

12 One pet remains without a hat. Use the scroll bar to display the pasteboard below page 1 and the remaining hat. Use any of the animation techniques you've learned so far or experiment with other techniques to position the hat on the pet above it. (Note: The 15_End file uses the Fly In From Bottom preset.)

13 Choose File > Save to save your work.

Creating a navigation button

The next button you'll create will be a navigation button for the reader to move through the pages. This is one of the most common uses for buttons.

1 Select the Rectangle Frame tool (⊠) and draw a frame over the white triangle in the lower right corner of the page, making sure that it has no stroke and no fill and that it is on the Buttons layer. Make it larger than the triangle so that the reader does not have to click it exactly.

2 Open the Buttons and Forms panel (🥄) and click the + sign next to Actions: (+). Choose Go To Next Page. Name this button **Next Page**.

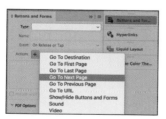

3 Open the EPUB Interactivity Preview panel, and this time choose the Preview Document Mode button (🗔) so that you can preview more than the current page. If you have trouble with the interactivity functioning, press the Clear Preview button (■), double check that you have chosen the Preview Document Mode button, and press Play (▶) again.

4 After the opening animations are displayed, click the white navigation button you just created, and the next page will display. You will see other animations on page 2 that you'll work with later in this lesson.

5 Click the white triangle in the lower left to navigate back to the first page.

▶ **Tip:** Many apps for viewing EPUBs include navigation buttons, but each app will perform navigation differently. Adding your own buttons ensures that the reader will easily see the navigation buttons.

▶ **Tip:** In a long document, create the navigation buttons on the master page. If there are several master pages, use the parent master so that you can create the buttons once and ensure that they are consistent on all pages.

Creating a pop-up caption

Pop-up captions are frequently used in EPUBs. There are many ways to create them. Using InDesign's ability to hide and show objects is one of the simplest methods. You'll learn that next.

1 Select the paw graphic on top of the large photo of the dog and cat. First you'll add some animation so that the reader is prompted to click it.

2 Open the Animation panel (). Name the animation **Paw Caption Trigger**. Choose the Fade In preset, Duration **1.5** seconds, and Play **4** times.

3 Open the Buttons And Forms panel (), click the + sign next to Actions: (+), and choose Show/Hide Buttons And Forms. Name the button **Caption Trigger**.

4 Select the caption above that says "I love making new friends." This is a group of InDesign text and path objects with effects applied. Click the + sign next to Actions: (+), and again choose Show/Hide Buttons And Forms in the Buttons And Forms panel (), and name this button **Caption**.

▶ **Tip:** The Visibility list available to the Show/Hide action lists all of the buttons on the current page or spread. You can't use this action to work with buttons elsewhere in a document.

5 In the Visibility section, leave everything on Ignore (✘) except Caption and Caption Trigger. Click the Ignore (✘) symbol next to Caption and click again to cycle through the options until it is set to Hide (). Do the same with Caption Trigger until it is set to Show (). Also select Hidden Until Triggered below the Appearance area.

6 Select the paw object that you converted to a button in step 3. In the Buttons And Forms panel () (which will still be open), change the Visibility of Caption to Show () and Caption Trigger to Hide ().

Settings for the caption object.

Settings for the trigger object.

As a result, the trigger object will be visible when the reader opens the page, and the caption object will be hidden. When the trigger object is clicked or tapped, it will disappear, and the caption object will appear. When the caption object is clicked or tapped, it will disappear and the trigger object will reappear.

7 Open the EPUB Interactivity Preview panel and test this by clicking the paw trigger object and then the caption.

8 Choose File > Save to save your work.

Adding multimedia and interactive elements

The ability to add movies and sounds to an InDesign document that will be exported as a fixed-layout EPUB means that you can create media-rich, interactive publications that aren't possible with print publishing.

In many ways, imported movies and sounds are like other InDesign objects. For example, you can copy, paste, move, and delete movies and sounds just like other objects—but they also have unique properties that you can adjust within InDesign.

Adding a movie

Adding a movie to a fixed-layout EPUB InDesign document is similar to adding a photo or illustration to a print document. Next, you'll import a movie into the document, scale it, and use the Media panel to choose a poster image that's displayed when the movie isn't playing.

Note: You can import video files in H.264-encoded MP4 format and audio files as MP3 format. You can use the Adobe Media Encoder application that is part of a Creative Cloud membership to convert other video or audio formats to MP4 or MP3.

1 Navigate to page 2. Choose File > Place. Select the CuteClips.mp4 video file in the Links folder in the Lesson15 folder, and then click Open.

2 Click the loaded video icon (⬛) where the horizontal ruler guide below the mountain peaks intersects with the vertical ruler guide in the middle of the leftmost column. Clicking the loaded video icon places the video at full size, which is too large for the layout, so you need to make it smaller.

3 Make sure that the top-left reference point is selected at the left end of the Control panel (⬛). Enter **43** in the Scale X Percentage or Scale Y Percentage box in the Control panel and press Return or Enter. The movie now fits within the predrawn guides.

Note: A static poster image is displayed in an ereader before the video plays.

4 Choose Window > Interactive > Media to open the Media panel, or click the Media icon (▦) to open it from the dock. If you want, use the controls below the movie image to preview the movie.

Instead of displaying the first frame of the movie when the movie is not playing, you'll choose a poster image to display instead.

5 Drag the slider below the preview window almost all the way to the right. The final seconds of the movie show a catchphrase. You'll specify the selected frame as the default poster image. From the Poster menu in the Media panel, choose From Current Frame. Click the Click To Use Current Frame As Poster button (↻) to select the frame and display it in the movie frame.

Note: Each ereader app will have different video player controls. After you export your EPUB, test the video player in different ereaders.

6 Click the Preview Spread button at the bottom of the Media panel to view the page. In the EPUB Interactivity Preview panel, click the Play preview button to preview the page, and then click the Play/Pause button in the movie controller to play and pause the movie. There is a separate control to adjust the sound volume.

7 Close the EPUB Interactivity Preview panel.

8 Choose File > Save.

Adding a sound

Adding a sound to a page is the same as adding a movie, but the options for controlling how sounds are displayed and played are a little different from those for modifying movies because movies and sounds are different types of media.

Next, you'll add a sound to the cover page, and then you'll convert one of the objects on the page into a button that plays the sound when clicked. You'll also hide the sound object so that it's not visible on the page.

1 Navigate to page 1. Choose File > Place, select the BckgMusic.mp3 sound file in the Links folder in the Lesson15 folder, and then click Open.

2 Click the pasteboard outside the upper-left corner of the page. Don't worry about placing the sound precisely because you'll hide this object later.

3 Open the Media panel (▤), and notice the options available for a sound file. If you want, use the Play and Pause buttons to preview the sound. Leave the default settings unchanged.

This is all you need to do to add a sound, but for this lesson, instead of displaying sound controls in the ereader, as would happen if you left the object where it is, you'll make it smaller, hide it, and then configure a button to play it.

4 In the Control panel, change the Width and Height of the sound frame to **30** (pixels).

● **Note:** By default, a controller is displayed for a sound file. The Media panel doesn't include an option that enables you to turn off display of the controller for a sound file.

5 Use the Selection tool to position the sound frame on top of the hat illustration.

6 Choose Object > Arrange > Send To Back.

7 Use the Selection tool to select the hat illustration that's now in front of the sound frame.

8 Open the Buttons And Forms panel. Choose Button from the Type menu in the Buttons And Forms panel, and enter **Play Music** in the Name field.

9 Make sure On Release Or Tap is selected in the Event menu. Click the + sign next to Actions: (**+**) and choose Sound. Because the page has only one sound, it is automatically selected in the Sound menu. Ensure that Play is selected in the Options menu.

10 Click the Preview Spread button. Click the Play Preview button in the EPUB Interactivity Preview panel, and then click within the hat illustration to play the sound. The audio clip (approximately 30 seconds in length) will play once and stop.

11 Close the EPUB Interactivity Preview panel.

12 Choose File > Save.

Creating a slideshow

A slideshow is a sequence of stacked images displayed one at a time as a viewer taps Previous and Next buttons. The sample document for this lesson already includes the graphics you need to create an interactive slideshow. You'll arrange these graphics in a stack, convert them into a multi-state object, and then configure buttons that enable a viewer to navigate through the slides.

1 Navigate to page 2 of the document.

2 Using the Selection tool (▶), select the top image of the dog, the frontmost of the five overlapping graphics frames, to the right of the movie frame.

3 Press Shift, and then select each of the other four overlapping graphics frames in succession from front to back. Release the Shift key after you've selected all five frames.

4 Choose Window > Object & Layout > Align. In the Align panel, choose Align To Selection (⊞) from the Align To menu if it's not already selected. Click the Align Left Edges button (▙), and then click the Align Bottom Edges button (▟).

5 With the graphics frames still selected, choose Window > Interactive > Object States to display the Object States panel, or click the Object States icon (🔲) to open it from the dock, and then click the Convert Selection To Multi-State Object button (▼) at the bottom of the panel. If necessary, lengthen the panel to display the names of all objects. (The panel looks empty until you do the conversion.)

6 In the Object States panel, enter **Guest Quotes** in the Object Name box, and then press Enter or Return.

▶ **Tip:** Each state in a multi-state object can be named. The stack is like a layer stack and the order of the objects can be changed by dragging them up or down.

Graphics frames combined into a multi-state object. Each image appears as a separate state in the Object States panel.

Now that you've created a multi-state object, you'll provide a way to let viewers scroll through the images.

1 Use the Selection tool to select the red arrow below the lower-left corner of the multi-state object and open the Buttons And Forms panel (🖳). This will be the button to scroll backwards through the slides.

2 In the Buttons And Forms panel, click Convert To Button (⊙) at the bottom of the panel, and enter **Previous** in the Name box.

3 Click the + sign next to Actions: (+.) and choose Go To Previous State from the menu. (The "Guest Quotes" multi-state object is automatically added to the list of actions.)

4 Select Stop At First State. This prevents the button from selecting the last state when it's clicked and the first state is selected.

5 Select the right-pointing red arrow and repeat steps 2–5 to configure a button named **Next**. To make a button that scrolls forward through the slides, when you click Add New Action For Selected Event, choose Go To Next State from the Actions menu, and then select Stop At Last State.

▶ **Tip:** When there are multiple multi-state objects on a page, you may need to choose the correct multi-state object from the Object menu in the Buttons And Forms panel. In this file, InDesign automatically selects the Guest Quotes multi-state object because it's the only one on the page.

6 Open the EPUB Interactivity Preview panel, click the Play Preview button, and then click the Previous and Next buttons you created to view the slideshow.

7 Close the EPUB Interactivity Preview panel.

8 Choose File > Save.

Creating a hyperlink

Hyperlinks let viewers jump to other locations in a document, as well as to other documents or to websites. A hyperlink includes a source element (text, a text frame, or a graphics frame) and a destination, which is the URL, email address, page, or text anchor to which the hyperlink jumps. Next, you'll create a hyperlink to a website using a graphics frame.

1 Use the Selection tool to select the graphics frame in the lower-right corner of page 2. An animation icon is displayed in the lower-right corner because the graphics frame—along with the other graphics frames along the bottom of the page—is configured to fly in when the page loads.

2 Choose Window > Interactive > Hyperlinks to display the Hyperlinks panel, or click the Hyperlinks icon (🔗) to open it from the dock.

3 Choose New Hyperlink from the Hyperlinks panel flyout menu.

4 Select URL from the Link To menu, and type a URL in the URL box (the sample document uses http://www.humanesociety.org). Deselect Shared Hyperlink Destination.

5 Open the EPUB Interactivity Preview panel, click the Play Preview button, and then click the text frame to which you added the hyperlink. The Humane Society of the United States home page is displayed in your browser.

6 Return to InDesign, and display the first page of the document.

7 Close the EPUB Interactivity Preview panel.

8 Choose File > Save.

Exporting an EPUB file

Much as the settings in the Print dialog box control the appearance of printed pages, the settings you use when you export an InDesign document as an EPUB control the appearance of the EPUB.

1 Choose File > Export.

2 In the Export dialog box, choose EPUB (Fixed Layout) from the Save As Type menu (Windows) or the Format menu (macOS).

3 In the File Name box (Windows) or the Save As box (macOS), name the file **15_FixedLayout.epub** and save the file in the Lesson15 folder, located inside the Lessons folder within the InDesignCIB folder on your hard drive. Click Save.

● **Note:** Rasterize First Page creates an image that will be used as an icon for the publication in the ebook reader app and on an ebook storefront.

4 In the General section of the EPUB – Fixed Layout Export Options dialog box, notice that EPUB 3.0 is automatically displayed for Version. This is the only EPUB version available for fixed-layout EPUBs. Make sure the following options are selected:

• Export Range: All Pages

• Cover: Rasterize First Page

• Navigation TOC: None

• Spread Control: Disable Spreads

5 Click Metadata in the list on the left of the EPUB – Fixed Layout Export Options dialog box. Enter **Multimedia Brochure** in the Title field and your name in the Creator field.

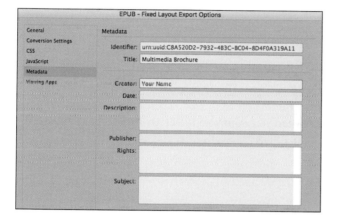

▶ **Tip:** If your EPUB will be formally published, the information in the Metadata dialog box is very important. Ebook sites require that this information be provided. Download the metadata specifications from the publisher.

6 Click Conversion Settings in the list on the left of the EPUB – Fixed Layout Export Options dialog box. Choose PNG from the Format menu to ensure that the graphics in grouped objects are displayed correctly in the exported EPUB.

7 Click Viewing Apps in the list on the left of the EPUB – Fixed Layout Export Options dialog box.

The System Default in the Viewing Apps section will vary depending on your operating system. For this lesson, we'll use Adobe Digital Editions as the viewing application (ebook reader). If you've installed Adobe Digital Editions and it's not listed as an application, click Add Application and select it from the Program folder (Windows) or Applications folder (macOS) on your computer, and then select it as the preferred viewing application. Alternatively, select another

program that reads EPUBs. When the EPUB is exported, it is automatically opened in the selected program. The Adobe Digital Editions software is available as a free download from www.adobe.com and is available on Creative Cloud.

8 Click OK to export a fixed-layout EPUB. If an alert is displayed warning that certain objects might not appear as expected after export, click OK to continue and view the EPUB.

If Adobe Digital Editions is installed on your computer, the EPUB file will open automatically, and you can navigate through it to view the content and work with the multimedia and interactive elements you created. You can also open the EPUB file on any device that supports the EPUB format. If you selected both iBooks.app and Adobe Digital Editions, the EPUB opens in both programs.

Notice the differences in the interface between different ebook readers. Part of the process of creating a digital publication such as a fixed-layout EPUB is to test the functionality on the various devices the target audience might use.

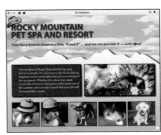

Opened in Adobe Digital Editions.

Opened in iBooks.

9 Return to InDesign.

10 Choose File > Save.

Congratulations! You've created a fixed-layout EPUB with multimedia and inter-activity that will have the same layout across all viewing devices.

InDesign CC Publish Online

The Publish Online feature in InDesign CC allows you to distribute digital versions of your InDesign documents on the Internet. Documents you publish online can be viewed on any desktop or mobile device and easily shared on Facebook and Twitter. You can easily provide hyperlinks to these documents in emails or embed the hyperlinks in web pages.

The InDesign documents you publish online are visually identical to the original layouts, and all interactive features are supported.

1 To publish the currently displayed document online, click Publish Online in the Application bar or choose File > Publish Online.

2 In the General section of the Publish Your Document Online dialog box, use the default name or enter a new one in the Name field and, optionally, add a Description.

3 The Advanced section of the Publish Your Document Online dialog box lets you choose a cover page and specify image export settings. Make any changes you want in this dialog box, and then click Publish.

▶ **Tip:** You can also select Publish Online After Printing in the General section of the Print dialog box (File > Print) to distribute a document online when you print it.

▶ **Tip:** If you don't intend to distribute your documents online, you can hide all Publish Online commands and controls by selecting Disable Publish Online in the Publish Online section of the Preferences dialog box.

A window displays as the document uploads and provides a preview of the first page, the name of the document, the description (if any), a status bar showing the progress of the upload, and the opportunity to cancel the upload.

4 When the upload is complete, click View Document to display the document in a web browser and click Copy to copy the URL to the Clipboard. You

can also click the Facebook, Twitter, or email buttons to share the link on social networks. Test the interactive features in your browser. Note that it may take a few minutes for both pages to be loaded and working. Also notice that the interface looks different from the ebook readers and will vary between browsers.

5 After viewing your file online, return to InDesign and
 click Close to close the Publish Online window and return to
 your document.

After you publish documents online, you can easily access the five most recently
published documents from within InDesign by choosing File > Recently Published.
(The Recently Publish menu does not appear until after your have published your first
document.) Choose a name from the list to open the document in your web browser.

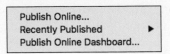

The Publish Online Dashboard lets you view, share, and delete all published docu-
ments. If you want to remove a document that you've published online, choose File >
Publish Online Dashboard. A web page opens in your default browser and displays
in chronological order a list of the documents you've uploaded with the most recent
at the top. To delete a published document, point at it in the list, and then click the
trash can icon on the right.

Exploring on your own

For additional practice, try some of the following exercises. You can continue work-
ing on the sample document and save your changes, or you can choose File > Save
As and save a new document with a new name to the Lesson15 folder.

Timing animations

In this lesson, you used the Timing panel to configure the timing of three animated
objects on page 1 that play automatically when the page opens. The controls in the
Timing panel also let you play the animations sequentially in any order you want,
and you can even create combinations of simultaneous and sequential timing.

1 With page 2 displayed in the document window, make sure nothing is selected,
 and then open the Timing panel.

2 The five animations are listed in the order in
 which they were created. Use the Selection
 tool (▶) to select the first animation, then
 Shift-click the last animation to select all
 animations. Click the Play Together button (▶⊃)
 at the bottom of the panel.

3 Click the Preview Spread button at the
 bottom of the panel to preview the page to see
 what happens.

4 Select all of the animations again, and then click Play Separately () at the
 bottom of the Timing panel.

5 Continue to adjust the settings in the Timing panel. The Delay field lets you add
 pauses between animations. Experiment with this field by selecting individual
 animations and specifying a Delay value. Preview the page each time you
 make a change.

6 Continue to experiment by creating different combinations of sequential and
 simultaneous animations. For example, configure two of the animations to play
 together first, and configure the remaining animations to play together after a
 short delay.

Adding sound control buttons

You also can add controls to a sound file in the Media panel. After you imported a
sound file in this lesson, you configured a button to play the sound. You also hid the
sound object, which also hides the sound controller in the exported file. See what
happens if you choose to display the sound.

1 Place the same BckgMusic.mp3 sound file in the Links folder in the Lesson15
 folder onto the pasteboard, and then drag it onto one of the pages.

2 Enter **300** in the Scale X Percentage or Scale Y Percentage box in the Control
 panel and press Enter or Return. (Enlarging the object makes the sound controls
 in the exported EPUB more visible and easier to operate.)

3 In the Media panel, choose Standard from the Poster menu. This displays a
 sound icon within the frame on the InDesign page, as well as in an exported
 interactive PDF file.

4 Preview the page in the EPUB Interactivity Preview panel. Use the controls on
 the sound controller to play and pause and to mute and unmute the sound.
 Optionally, export a fixed-layout EPUB and see how the sound controls are
 displayed and function in the selected viewing app(s).

Viewing your EPUB on a tablet

It's important to test the experience that readers of your epub will have when using
an ebook reader on devices such as a tablet. First, install one or more ebook readers
on the device, such as Adobe Digital Editions. The easiest way to view your EPUB on
an iPad or Android tablet is to email it to yourself as an attachment. On the tablet,
open the email and tap the attachment to download it and choose the ebook reader
on your device to open it, such as Adobe Digital Editions or iBooks. (The exact steps

will vary with different email apps on different devices.) Test the interactive features in the ebook reader.

Once you know the audience for your publication, it's a best practice to test the publication in the ebook readers they are most likely to use and make adjustments if necessary.

Examine a slide-in caption

Another type of caption effect is the slide-in caption. It's complex to create, so instead you'll examine the finished effect to see how it works.

A step-by-step guide to creating this caption effect is available with the lesson download.

1 Open the file 15_FixedLayout-Alternate. The box with the mission statement has been changed to a slide-in caption.

2 Open the EPUB Interactivity Preview panel and click the red triangle above the words "Our Mission" on the far left of the picture of the dog's head with a white background. A text box containing the mission statement slides in from the left, over the picture of the dog.

3 Click the red triangle again and the mission statement slides back off the photo and the button returns to the start position. Close the EPUB Interactivity Preview panel.

 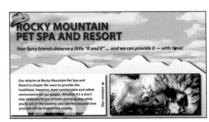

4 This effect is created using three duplicate object states with different button actions, animation, and timing settings. Click the object and open the Object States panel to start exploring the structure.

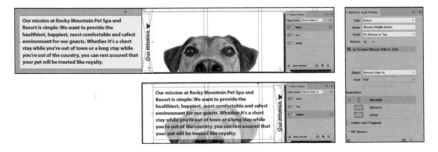

Review questions

1 What's the primary difference between a reflowable EPUB and a fixed-layout EPUB?

2 InDesign provides two methods for animating objects. What are they, and how do they differ?

3 By default, animations play in the order in which they were created. How can you change the order in which animations are played, and how can you play multiple animations simultaneously?

4 How can you preview multimedia and interactive elements within InDesign?

5 How do you create a slideshow?

Review answers

1 The reflowable EPUB format allows the EPUB reader to optimize the content depending on the display device. For example, the viewer of a reflowable EPUB can adjust the display size of the text, which affects the amount of text on a given page and the flow of text from page to page. In fixed-layout EPUBs, the dimensions of the original InDesign pages are maintained, as is the fidelity to the original layout.

2 You can animate objects in groups by choosing a motion preset in the Animation panel, or you can create a motion path. A motion path consists of two elements: the animated object or group and a motion path along which the animated object moves.

3 The controls in the Timing panel let you control when animations are played. All animations associated with the selected Event (such as On Page Load) are displayed. You can drag the names within the list to change the order in which they're played. To play them simultaneously, you can select multiple animations and click the Play Together button (▶∞).

4 The EPUB Interactivity Preview panel lets you preview and test multimedia and interactive elements. The Animation, Timing, Media, Object States, and Buttons And Forms panels all include a Preview Spread button, and you can also display the panel by choosing Window > Interactive > EPUB Interactivity Preview.

5 To create a slideshow, first create a stack of objects, and then use the Object States panel to create a multi-state object. Next, create and configure two buttons: one that displays the previous state of the multi-state object, and one that displays the next state.

INDEX

SYMBOLS

() (parentheses), displaying, 76

A

abbreviations, formatting, 154

acronyms, formatting, 154

addition, positioning and sizing, 104

Adobe Acrobat Reader, testing forms, 377–378

Adobe Bridge, importing graphics, 289–290

Adobe Capture CC app, 228

Adobe PDF proof, creating, 356–357

Adobe Typekit fonts, 171

aligning

objects, 95, 116–117

text, 167–168

alpha channels

clipping paths, 278

defined, 272

importing Photoshop files, 276

and Photoshop paths, 277–278

Alt key. *See* keyboard shortcuts

anchored graphics frame, 280–283

Angle and Altitude setting, 339

Animated Zoom, 25–26

animations

playing using buttons, 388–395

timing, 404–405

Apple menu, system shortcuts, 26

Application bar

commands, 37

identifying, 9

using, 14–15

Arrange Documents, 16

arrowheads, modifying, 120–121

audio, adding to EPUBs, 396–398, 405

Auto-Size feature, using with text frames, 130

B

background layer, moving items to, 90–91. *See also* layers

backgrounds

dropping, 272–275

transparency, 275

baseline grid. *See also* grid of frames

aligning text, 167–168

choosing, 170

viewing, 168–169

Bevel and Emboss effect, 333

bitmap images

applying transparency, 329

file formats, 323

and vector graphics, 265–266

bleed guides, 78–80

Bleed mode, 37

blending modes

applying, 323, 326–327

explained, 324

removing, 342

and transparency, 339

booklet, starting, 128. *See also* text

break characters, using with flowing text, 143

breaking lines. *See* line breaks

Bridge, importing graphics, 289–290

brochure, starting, 264–265

bulleted lists, 193

bullets, inserting, 243

buttons. *See also* tools

 displaying on pages, 394

 using on forms, 375–377

 using to play animations, 388–395

C

captions

 adding to graphics frames, 104–105

 creating for EPUBs, 394–395

Capture CC app, 228

catalog. *See* styles

CC (Creative Cloud), using, 277

CC Libraries. *See also* libraries

 color themes, 227–228

 creating and using, 287

CC Publish Online feature, 403–404

cell strokes, editing, 306–307

cell styles

 applying, 315–316

 creating, 250–253, 313–315

cells. *See also* tables

 applying colors, 306

 converting to graphic cells, 308–309

 fill color, 306

 merging, 304

centimeters, 57

changes, tracking, 161–162

character formats, 40. *See also* hidden characters; special characters

character styles

 applying, 238–239

 creating, 237–238

creating and applying, 44–46

 nesting, 240–241

 using, 42

characters, replacing with glyphs, 174–175

check boxes, using on forms, 371, 373, 377

Choke setting, 339

circle, creating, 12

clear effects, explained, 324

clipping paths, 272–274, 278

clipping paths from Photoshop, 272–274

CMYK

 color swatch, 210–212

 composite, 360

 files, 362

collaborating on documents, 162

college flyer. *See* tables

color groups, 224–225

color management, 201–204

color mode, converting for swatch, 207

color settings, 203

color swatches

 CMYK, 210–211

 PANTONE, 208–209, 211

Color Theme tool, 208

color themes

 adding to CC Library, 227–228

 adding to Swatches panel, 226–227

 creating, 225

 managing, 228

 viewing, 226

colorizing grayscale images, 321–323

colors. *See also* tint swatches

 applying, 213–218, 322

 applying to cells, 306

 applying to strokes, 215–216

 applying to text, 216–218

 creating, 207–211

 gradients, 220–223

 maintaining in print jobs, 360

 managing, 352–354

E

editing
- cell strokes, 306–307
- and formatting tables, 297
- and removing effects, 340–342
- text, 129

editorial tasks
- dragging and dropping, 159–160
- entering text, 151
- finding and changing formatting, 154–155
- finding and changing text, 153–154
- importing text, 151–152
- missing fonts, 149–150
- starting, 148–149
- Story Editor, 160–161
- style guides, 162
- tracking changes, 161–162

effects. *See also* special effects
- adding to objects, 336–338
- copying between objects, 338, 340
- editing and removing, 340–342

Effects dialog box, opening, 338

Effects panel, 324

Ellipse Frame tool, 12

em space, 64

EPUB files. *See also* fixed-layout EPUB
- exporting, 400–402
- Interactivity Preview panel, 387
- reflowable versus fixed-layout, 383–384

ereader apps, 396

exporting
- EPUB files, 400–402
- interactive PDF files, 376

F

feather effects, applying, 333–334

file formats, bitmap images, 323

files
- packaging, 362–364
- preflighting, 347–349

fill colors, 213–215, 306

fill pattern, adding to table, 305

Find/Change feature, 154–155, 238

fitting commands, accessing, 102

fixed-layout EPUB. *See also* EPUB files
- animation, 384–387
- buttons, 388–395
- ereader apps, 396
- hyperlinks, 399–400
- movies, 395–396
- multi-state objects, 398–399
- navigation button, 393
- pop-up caption, 394–395
- reordering objects, 398
- slide-in caption, 406
- slideshows, 398–399
- sound, 396–398
- sound control buttons, 405
- timing animations, 387–388, 404–405
- viewing on tablets, 405–406

fixed-layout export, creating document for, 383

flattening, 354

floating panels, 18, 20–21

flowing text
- adding pages while, 139
- automatically, 138–139
- break characters, 143
- creating text frames while, 134–135
- into frames, 129–131
- manually, 132–133

flyer. *See* colors

Grids & Guides, viewing, 37

grouped objects, selecting and modifying, 119–120. *See also* objects

grouping, panels, 18

guides. *See also* Smart Guides

 adding to master pages, 60–61

 deleting, 63

 dragging from rulers, 61–62

 pasting, 63

 stepping and repeating, 63

 viewing, 37

gutter, defined, 61

H

Hand tool, 11–12, 28

hanging indent, 192–193

header, defined, 61–62

header row, creating in table, 312–313

hidden characters, viewing, 37, 96, 282–283. *See also* character formats

hiding

 layers, 331

 panels, 80

hyperlinks, creating for EPUBs, 399–400

hyphenation settings, 188

I

IDML (InDesign Markup Language), 363

Illustrator files

 importing, 284–285

 transparency adjustments, 330–331

images

 displaying at full resolution, 202

 moving in frames, 101–103

 placing in graphic cells, 309–310

 rotating in frames, 116

imported files, managing links, 266–268

importing

 Adobe graphic files, 279–285

 and colorizing grayscale image, 321–323

 graphics using Adobe Bridge, 289–290

 Illustrator files, 284–285

 Illustrator files using transparency, 330–331

 Photoshop files, 279–280

 tables, 299

 video files for EPUBs, 395–396

importing text into frames, 129, 132

inch marks, 57

indentation, adjusting, 192

Ink Manager, 353–354

Inner Glow effect, 333

Inner Shadow effect, 333

Intent Mobile setting, 383

interactive PDF files, exporting, 376

Isolate Blending, 324

J

jump line page number, 143–144. *See also* page numbering

Justification settings, 186

K

kerning and tracking, 185

key object, assigning, 117. *See also* objects

keyboard shortcuts

 character styles, 239

 Go To Page, 28

 magnification, 24

 paragraph styles, 236

 search direction, 153

 sizing images, 102

 switching between documents, 60

 text formatting, inconsistency, 233

 Undo, 10

Knockout Group, 324